W9-AZE-008

Dynamic Manufacturing

DYNAMIC MANUFACTURING

Creating the Learning Organization

Robert H. Hayes
Steven C. Wheelwright
Kim B. Clark

THE FREE PRESS
A Division of Macmillan, Inc.
NEW YORK

Collier Macmillan Publishers
LONDON

Copyright © 1988 by The Free Press
A Division of Macmillan, Inc.

All rights reserved. No part of this book may be reproduced
or transmitted in any form or by any means, electronic or
mechanical, including photocopying, recording, or by any
information storage and retrieval system, without permission
in writing from the Publisher.

The Free Press
A Division of Macmillan, Inc.
866 Third Avenue, New York, N.Y. 10022

Collier Macmillan Canada, Inc.

Printed in the United States of America

printing number

1 2 3 4 5 6 7 8 9 10

Library of Congress Cataloging-in-Publication Data

Hayes, Robert H.
  Dynamic manufacturing

  Bibliography: p.
  Includes index.
  1. United States—Manufacturers—Management.
I. Wheelwright, Steven C.   II. Clark, Kim B.
III. Title.
HD9725.H38 1988   658.5   88–367
ISBN 0–02–914211–3

Contents

Preface

Why have American manufacturing companies been responding so hesitantly and half-heartedly to the onslaught of foreign competition? Why have they been so reluctant to learn from the example of their most effective competitors? Can companies that have for many years, possibly even decades, regarded manufacturing excellence as a secondary contributor to competitive success—as an uncertain liability rather than a powerful asset—transform their manufacturing function into a source of competitive advantage? And how can they go about doing so? These are some of the questions that led us to write this book.

America's manufacturing competitiveness has been in serious decline for well over a dozen years, and we have been writing, collectively and individually, about this problem for much of that period. Our voices, together with a few others, initially were drowned out by a chorus of confident assertions that no problem existed or, if it did, that it was minor and transitory. Now, however, there appears to be wide agreement that the problem is major and enduring. A torrent of books and articles has appeared in the past few years describing the manufacturing philosophies and techniques used by world class companies, and why they have proven to be so effective. A number of highly visible companies have applied many of these approaches in their own factories and have experienced astounding improvements in their manufacturing competitiveness. Management experts, academics and practitioners alike, for once are almost united in their assessment of the deep-seated nature of the competitive problems American companies are facing and in their recommendations: quality improvement and inventory reduction programs, employee involvement, closer interfunctional linkages, flatter organizational hierarchies, and more rapid adoption of new manufacturing technologies. CEOs of companies in industries ranging from steel to semiconductors declaim the need for a "cultural revolution" in management.

Yet despite this outpouring of diagnoses, prescriptions, and virtuous resolutions, not enough has changed. A number of companies have taken the first steps to address the problems that have been accumulating over many years, and some have made considerable progress. However, too few have fully grasped and implemented the kind of fundamental changes that the new industrial competition requires, changes that usually begin in the manufacturing function but may extend to encompass the entire organization. As a result, journalists looking for rays of optimism in the American industrial landscape return again and again to the same handful of companies for inspiration. Even within many of these companies the new approaches spread with difficulty.

As the U.S. dollar plummets against other major currencies, and foreign manufacturers move in to acquire or build factories in North America, American companies retain their foreign suppliers and are puzzlingly reluctant to shift production back from their offshore facilities. Even high-tech companies that find themselves losing position to foreign competitors—often from countries that have traditionally been viewed as followers and copiers rather than technological innovators—appear to be reluctant to invest in new manufacturing technologies and proprietary processes. Why haven't such firms responded more aggressively to the erosion of their world markets? How *should* they respond? In the pages that follow we try to provide an answer.

Our perspective throughout this book is that the responsibility, both for these problems and their solution, rests firmly on the shoulders of management. But it is not just the management of the manufacturing function that has to change. Building a manufacturing advantage must begin there, but those changes must be augmented by reinforcing changes in other functions; consequently, this book is directed at managers throughout the company. Sustained progress can only occur if a significant proportion of them modify their attitudes, expand their understanding of the nature of changes required, and make a direct commitment to leading those changes. Many companies have the inherent capability to become manufacturing powerhouses, but they must choose to do so before it is too late. We hope this book will prove useful in that effort.

This book could not have been written without the cooperation and contribution of many others, including both fellow researchers and the literally hundreds of business managers who have shared their experience and insight with us. We are also grateful for the institutional support provided by the Harvard and the Stanford Business Schools and their respective Deans, John McArthur and Robert Jaedicke. A complete listing of those who have assisted us in understanding the various facets of the subject we have tackled would be impossible, but we would be remiss if we did not acknowledge the role that a few key individuals played in our intellectual growth.

For example, our discussion of the historical development of American manufacturing in Chapter 2 was deeply influenced by the writings of and personal interchanges with Professors Alfred Chandler, Jr., and Nathan Rosenberg. In this, as well as other chapters, we also drew upon the perspectives of our former colleagues, Professors Wickham Skinner and the late William Abernathy. Similarly, part of Chapter 3 is drawn from a *Harvard Business Review* article, "Managing as if tomorrow mattered," that one of us co-authored with Professor David Garvin, and a portion of Chapter 4 is based on another *Harvard Business Review* article, "How should you organize manufacturing?," co-authored with Professor Roger Schmenner. In like fashion, our analysis of the impact of cost accounting systems on manufacturing behavior benefitted from the writings of Professor Robert Kaplan and our many discussions with him.

The research reported on in Chapter 6 was conducted with the assistance of Paul Adler, Bruce Chew, and Russell Radford when they were doctoral students or postdoctoral associates at Harvard. We are delighted that they, as faculty members at prestigious universities, are still carrying on aspects of this research and continue to contribute to our understanding of the impact of managerial practice on productivity growth. Our discussions of process control and organizational learning in Chapters 8 and 9 also benefitted greatly from our association with Professors Roger Bohn, Ramchandran Jaikumar, and Richard Walton. Many of the ideas reported on in Chapter 10 originated in work that we did in conjunction with our colleague, Professor Earl Sasser. Similarly, our doctoral student, Takahiro Fujimoto, and our colleagues, Professors Paul Adler and Hank Riggs, collaborated with us in exploring and developing some of the ideas about managing product development projects that are reported on in Chapter 11.

At this point in most prefaces, there is a statement thanking the authors' families for their support and for providing islands of stability during the hectic process of writing a book. Our experience suggests that nothing could be further from the truth. In this enterprise we were the ones who provided the only discernible source of stability in our personal environments. Our families always knew where we were and what we were doing—dull and esoteric though it might have been. We seldom could say the same. But again and again their energy and enthusiasm lifted our spirits after a hard day's work. Without their constant activity and creativity—their very instability, in a sense—we would have found it difficult to keep plugging away.

As in our previous books, the assistance of Sally Markham, Romayne Ponleithner, and Ruth Band was invaluable. Wiser by a couple of years, and now equipped with the latest in word-processing technology, their productivity growth has far outstripped ours. More important, they kept our offices running smoothly despite our preoccupations with this book. Perhaps we should assign the writing of the next book to them as well.

Boston, MA.   Robert H. Hayes
Stanford, CA.   Steven C. Wheelwright
Boston, MA.   Kim B. Clark

Dynamic Manufacturing

Rebuilding a Manufacturing Advantage

Introduction: The Decline of American Industry's Competitiveness

The storm that flickered on the horizon for American industry during the 1970s came ashore with a rush in the 1980s. Torrents of imported products flooded our markets and eroded the profitability of domestic suppliers. The U.S. balance of trade in manufactured products went negative for the first time this century in 1971, recovered briefly in the late 1970s, and then plunged into increasing deficits after 1981. In 1986 America's imports of manufactured goods exceeded exports by almost $140 billion. The trade deficit for non-manufactured goods, such as agricultural and petroleum-based products, pushed the total deficit to $170 billion, or 3 percent of GNP. West Germany displaced the United States as the world's mightiest exporting nation.

In 1985, as a result, a country that had been the world's largest creditor nation (its international investment position had peaked at about $150 billion in 1982) became the world's largest debtor nation—with a deficit greater than the next two largest debtors combined. By late 1987, the United States net international investment position was approaching $400 billion in the red.

A deterioration in corporate profits reduced the real (adjusted for inflation) pretax rate of return on manufacturing assets in the United States below the prime interest rate, discouraging investment in the new equipment and products required to improve competitiveness. Over the same period, and partly as a result, the U.S. standard of living sagged. By 1986 both the hourly earnings of the average worker and the weekly earnings of the average family—adjusted for inflation and taxes—had fallen at least 5 percent from their peaks in the mid-1970s and were about where they had been in the mid-1960s. The GDP (gross domestic product) per employee in the United States was no longer the highest of the developed countries, and most of America's major competitor nations were expected to surpass it by 1990 if current trends continued. Reflecting this decline in relative wealth, only one of the world's ten largest banks (and none of the five largest) in terms of deposits was American. Six, on the other hand, were in Japan—the home of more than half the top twenty-five banks versus America's two.

This faltering competitive position would not have been so disturbing if it had been restricted largely to a few nonessential industries. It was possible to rationalize the loss of the U.S. domestic shoe industry as the natural working of David Ricardo's famous law of comparative advantage: that such an ancient and labor-intensive item should rightly be produced in countries whose workers had simple manual skills and low wage rates, while the United States should concentrate its attention on newer, higher technology and capital-intensive products like airplanes and electronics. The same logic softened the loss of much of the textile and apparel industries (despite the fact that they were major employers) but became troubling when applied to such "strategic" industries as machine tools, shipbuilding, and steel. Most Americans comforted themselves, however, with the thought that despite the temporary inconvenience and dislocations associated with the decline of a few industries, the laws of economics were working properly as long as the overall U.S. trade deficit in the older, declining, low-technology products was offset by a surplus in the newer, growing, high-technology products.

Indeed, these two groups were in rough balance until about 1980, at which point a high-tech surplus of almost $30 billion largely offset the low-tech deficit of almost $50 billion. But then a deluge of both kinds of imports pushed the low-tech deficit to over $130 billion in 1986, and the surplus in high-tech products went negative for the first time. Of the ten major industry classifications (out of twenty-six in total) that were classified by the Department of Commerce as high tech—on the basis that they spent at least 3 percent of their sales revenues on R & D—seven lost world market share between 1965 and 1986. By 1983 America's trade deficit with Japan in electronics products was $15 billion, bigger than its bilateral deficit in autos.

By the mid-1980s imports had taken about 25 percent of the U.S. domestic market in autos, steel, and textiles—and would probably have taken considerably more were it not for a variety of bilateral and multilateral protectionist barriers engineered by the U.S. government: "voluntary" restrictions on Japanese imports in the case of autos and steel, and the "multifiber arrangement" (whose roots were planted as early as 1957) in textiles. The world's largest auto company, G.M., flirted with unprofitability even in an expanding market, as did the U.S. steel industry. LTV, the steel industry's second largest company, declared bankruptcy in 1986, while rumors of a similar action swirled around Bethlehem Steel, the third largest. U.S. Steel, once the symbol for American industrial might, having lost its position as the largest steel company in the world in the early 1970s, found steel production increasingly less attractive than opportunities in oil and chemicals. By 1985 steel production accounted for less than half its revenues, and it even removed the word "Steel" from its new name: USX.

The situation was just as bad in semiconductors, one of America's flagship high-tech industries. Even though Americans had invented the semiconductor and the integrated circuit (IC)—as well as almost every one of its major derivative products, such as random access memories and microprocessors—and almost totally dominated world production through the mid-1970s, by 1984 foreign producers had taken almost 25 percent of the American domestic market. The major U.S. merchant houses were hemorrhaging cash and seeking assistance. In mid-1986 the U.S. government, under strong pressure from its semiconductor industry, was forced to negotiate a trade agreement with Japan that resulted in sharply higher prices for imported ICs.

A similar situation prevailed in the machine tool industry—perhaps less glamorous than semiconductors, but almost as critical in its impact on American industry's long-term ability to compete. Although U.S. producers had been in the forefront of developing computer-controlled machine tools and multipurpose machining centers, between 1977 and 1986 imports rose from less than 10 percent to over 50 percent of domestic consumption. The prospect of irreversible damage to America's industrial and military infrastructure forced its government to negotiate trade pacts with both Japan and Taiwan in late 1986, restricting their exports (and, by inference, those of several European companies) to the United States to the levels prevailing in 1981.

There was no clause in the law of comparative advantage that suggested that the United States should want to import such products as high-performance autos, sophisticated videotape recorders and electronic cameras, state-of-the-art integrated circuits and fiber optics, or computerized robots and machine tools. Even the American food products industry, long dominated by U.S. producers because of their size and market power as well as their closeness to low cost sources of materials, experienced a growing trade deficit (beginning in 1984) and increasing competition from the U.S. plants owned by foreign producers. Either the laws of economics were no longer working as we had thought they worked, or America had lost its comparative advantage almost everywhere.

The Underlying Causes: Cost, Quality, and Innovativeness

Every industry is different, and a careful explanation of its success or failure in the world marketplace must be tailored to the specifics of each situation. But the kind of broad-based competitive decline just described must have some common roots. The obvious ones are the three primary bases for competitive differentiation in manufactured products: relative cost, relative quality, and relative innovativeness.

Cost

The difference in the cost of two similar products produced by two companies in different countries is due both to the difference in the companies' productivity (their effectiveness in translating such resources as labor, materials, and capital into products) and to the exchange rate between the currencies of the two countries.

For several years the apparent inability of U.S. companies to compete effectively with foreign producers in industry after industry was blamed primarily on the overvalued dollar. The high value of the dollar, it was argued, both effectively priced American products out of world markets and made imported products more attractive. Although there is little doubt that an overvalued dollar had a significant impact on U.S. industrial competitiveness, it was not at all clear that it was the most important factor. In fact, examining the behavior of the measures of competitiveness that we have been describing over the past twenty years shows quite clearly that the problem developed long before the dollar began to surge in late 1979.

Moreover, within two and a half years after reaching its peak in early 1985 the dollar had been pushed down over 40 percent against

a weighted average of the currencies of the major developed countries with which the U.S. competed (and over 50 percent against both
the Japanese yen and the German mark). Yet, although it led to a
resurgence in some industries, including steel and semiconductors,
this tremendous relative price change had little impact on America's
overall trade deficit in manufactured products; in late-1987 it continued at a record level. The competitive positions of a number of
prominent companies, including once mighty GM and Caterpillar,
continued to deteriorate. A variety of explanations were offered:
that the inevitable corrective action was simply experiencing a somewhat longer-than-usual delay; that the fall of the dollar had thus far
had little effect on America's trading relationships with countries
like Taiwan, Korea, and Singapore, whose currencies were roughly
tied to the dollar; and—most ominous of all—that U.S. consumers
had simply gotten used to the high quality and good service associated with many imported products and were willing to pay more for
them rather than switch to lower-cost domestically produced products. As one business writer phrased it, "The good news we're waiting for may never come."[1]

The evidence with regard to productivity was more conclusive.
The rate of increase in the productivity of American manufacturing
workers (the value of their output, adjusted for inflation, divided by
the labor hours required to produce it) fell by 50 percent over the
15-year period extending from the mid-1960s to the late 1970s: from
an average of over 3 percent a year between 1948 and 1965 to about
1.5 percent a year between 1973 and 1979. The decline in the growth
rate of total factor productivity, which includes both labor productivity and capital productivity, followed a similar path.

Between 1979 and 1986, however, manufacturing labor productivity increased once again at over 3 percent per year. This resurgence
in productivity was heartening to many, particularly when contrasted
with the continuing stagnation of nonmanufacturing productivity
(which grew by less than 1 percent through 1986). But while it indicated that American industry had gotten back on track, in a sense,
it did not necessarily mean that American industry was becoming
more competitive. In fact, while U.S. manufacturing productivity
was growing at almost 4 percent per year during the first half of the
1980s, Japan's was growing at over 5 percent. More encouraging was
its performance versus its major European competitors during this
period. Total factor productivity comparisons were similar.

This point is worth stressing: America's cost position relative to foreign firms is not determined by how quickly the productivity of a given industry or company is improving relative to its past rate of improvement, but by how quickly it is improving relative to its competitors' rates. To put this into perspective, between 1970 and 1984 the total number of people employed in manufacturing in the United States remained essentially the same, as it did in Japan. By the end of that period, however, real production of manufactured products had more than doubled in Japan but only increased by about 50 percent in the United States.

With this in mind, there is growing concern about the behavior of capital investment, one of the major drivers of productivity growth, because there is abundant evidence that productivity grows most rapidly in companies and countries where investment in new plant and equipment is highest. Whereas gross capital investment in the U.S. economy as a whole, whether expressed in terms of its growth rate or as a percent of GNP or sales, exhibited a relatively consistent pattern between 1955 and 1986, problems revealed themselves as one made corrections for the effect of inflation, for the amount of investment in residential construction and company automobiles (which would not be expected to have much impact on business productivity), and for the increase in the rate of depreciation that occurred over this period. After removing the effect of inflation, for example, the dollar investment (after depreciation allowances) in nonresidential structures and equipment during the first half of the 1980s was about the same as it was during the last half of the 1960s—even though the inflation-adjusted GNP grew by 50 percent during this interval. As a result, the real (adjusted for inflation and depreciation) rate of increase in business investment dropped from about 7 percent per year during the 1960s to less than 1 percent per year between 1982 and 1987. As a result, America's plant and equipment was both older and aging more rapidly than its major competitors'.

The bulk of this slowdown occurred in the service sector of the economy, however. The manufacturing sector fought against the trend, and its real investment per worker grew at about 3 percent per year—maintaining its long-term rate. Unfortunately, simply maintaining that previous trend was unlikely to lead to productivity parity because the major countries with which the United States was competing were increasing their capital investment per worker at an even faster rate. In Japan, for example, the growth in real investment per manufacturing worker was about twice the U.S. level.

Just as ominously, the productivity of this capital investment (output divided by the capital required to produce it) appeared to be declining in the United States. After growing at about 0.6 percent per year between 1948 and 1965, manufacturing capital productivity fell at a rate of almost 2 percent per year between 1973 and 1979, and by 0.3 percent per year between 1979 and 1985. As a result, the growth rate of the combined productivity of both labor and capital in U.S. manufacturing fell below its long-term growth rate to roughly half that of Japan's.

A closer examination of the causes of American industry's productivity resurgence in the 1980s suggested that it was due primarily to three factors: market expansion, corporate restructuring (downsizing), and manufacturing rationalization. Companies could not depend on these forces alone for their future productivity growth, however. Sustained improvement in international competitiveness would require ongoing changes in such areas as capital investment, R & D spending, and management behavior.

Quality

In virtually every industry in which American manufacturers lost market share over the past decade, there was evidence that their products were perceived by consumers as offering poorer quality than equivalently priced foreign products. The day of reckoning for the U.S. semiconductor industry, for example, came on March 25, 1980, when Richard W. Anderson, general manager of Hewlett-Packard's Data Systems Division, reported on H-P's results from testing 300,000 similar memory chips (16K DRAMs) from six different producers, three American and three Japanese. The incoming inspection failure rate of the American products was at least twenty times greater than that of the Japanese products, and their field failure rate ranged from three to twenty-five times greater.[2] Similar differences in the defect rates of room air conditioners were reported in 1983,[3] and a variety of studies in other industries (including *Consumer Reports'* annual survey of a large number of consumer products) all pointed in the same direction: American manufactured products generally were perceived as offering poorer performance, and were more likely to experience operating problems, than Japanese or European products.

As a result of these studies, quality-improvement efforts were stepped up in company after company. A 1986 survey of manufacturing managers in the United States, Europe, and Japan—across a broad cross section of industries—showed that quality had become

American managers' chief concern. But it was also the chief concern of Japanese and European managers.[4] Hence, American producers were chasing a moving target, and there was considerable evidence that by the mid-1980s they still had not eliminated the gap between the perceived quality of their products and that of their foreign competitors. For example, a 1986 study of new-car buyers in the United States showed that purchasers of American-built cars experienced an average of over 1.7 problems per car in the first ninety days of ownership (down dramatically from 2.5 in 1985), whereas Japanese-car owners reported an average of less than 1.3 problems per car.[5]

Innovation

The huge lead in technology that the United States built up during and after World War II was also crumbling, as reflected by a variety of measures. First, American firms lost position in a number of specific high-technology industries, such as semiconductors, telecommunications, scientific instruments, and various types of advanced capital equipment—in fact, as mentioned earlier, in seven of the ten industries classified by the Department of Commerce as high technology. As a result, the U.S. balance of payments for these seven industries went negative (by about $2 billion) for the first time in 1986. The picture was especially bleak in high-technology capital goods. One economist estimated that by late 1984 over 80 percent of U.S. firms' expenditures on high-tech capital equipment were absorbed by imported products.[6]

Second, in industry after industry U.S. companies were effectively withdrawing from specific high-tech segments because of their inability to keep up with the innovativeness of foreign products. As of late 1987, no U.S. firm had developed or produced a video tape recorder, a camcorder (electronic camera plus recorder), or a compact-disc player. All but two American merchant semiconductor firms had withdrawn from the production of DRAM memory chips.

Third, several rankings of relative capabilities in a variety of specific technologies placed the United States behind countries that it had previously dominated. A study group sponsored by the National Research Council, for example, concluded in early 1986 that Japan led the United States in seven major areas that were key to future developments in electronics and optics.[7] That same year the European Management Forum (a Swiss-based research group) rated Japan and Germany, among others, as being ahead of the United States in terms of total industry technological effort.[8]

A number of different measures of technological vitality were pointed to as the causes of this deterioration. The percentage of U.S. GNP devoted to R & D, for example, fell from almost 3 percent in 1965 to about 2.2 percent in 1977 before rebounding to nearly 2.7 percent (slightly ahead of Japan's) in the mid-1980s. Moreover, over half this total was spent by the American government, and almost three-quarters of that went to defense and space-related projects that were much less likely to have significant commercial application. Only about 1 percent of the U.S. government's research budget went to promoting industrial growth, while the West German government invested 14 percent of its research budget in such activities, and Japan 13 percent.

Just as alarming, less than 6 percent of American industry's total investment in R & D went to basic research—the kind that leads to entirely new products, markets, and industries. Even when combined with government spending on basic research, basic research accounted for less than 10 percent of the United States' total R & D spending. Other countries were spending proportionally more both on basic research and on industrial research, and during the mid-1970s the United States began experiencing a "balance of patents" deficit to go along with its balance of payments deficit: more West Germans and Japanese filed patents in the United States than U.S. inventors filed in Japan or Germany. In fact, almost 45 percent of the patents granted in the United States in 1985 were given to foreign applicants. Other measures of the rate of innovation in various American industries, such as their increasing propensity to source high-technology components from foreign rather than domestic suppliers, showed similar declines.

This was coupled with a decline in the attractiveness of scientific professions in the United States. The number of Americans graduating with engineering degrees each year was less than in Japan, which had half America's population; as a result, by 1986 there were more electrical engineers in Japan than in the United States. Leading American technical universities, such as MIT, began expressing concern about the nature and adequacy of the education they were providing their graduates and initiated curriculum reviews.

Finally, just as in the case of capital investment, there was troubling evidence that the productivity of R & D investment in the United States was decreasing. Not only was the country spending less—less than it had in the past, less than was required in specific areas of R & D, and less (proportionally) than some of its major competitors—America was getting less "bang for the buck" than it used to.

The Causes Behind the "Causes"

Declining productivity growth, insufficient capital spending, inadequate quality, and sluggish technological innovation are obvious reasons why a nation's competitiveness might be expected to decline. But these explanations raise more questions than they answer, because one then has to explain why these "causes" have arisen in a country whose workers, for at least thirty years, have been the most productive in the world, whose products have set the standards for high quality, and whose technological virtuosity has dominated world industry. In the national debate that arose around these causal issues, at least three widely differing explanations surfaced.

One school of thought argued that there was no real problem— that the difficulties being experienced by American industry were simply the normal response of an economic system to a series of external shocks (such as the dislocations caused by world energy shortages and price rises during the 1970s), the maturation of certain older "sunset" industries (which, as in the past, had caused them to move offshore), or the symptoms of an accelerating transition to a "post industrial" service-dominated society. Although this view became increasingly difficult to defend as industry after industry crumbled under the pressure of foreign competitors, it continued to be espoused by powerful adherents—including the Reagan administration and the bulk of the economics profession.

A second school held that a serious problem did exist, but that it was due primarily to macroeconomic policies and events: a mushrooming federal debt that had led to comparatively high interest rates (and therefore contributed to an overvalued dollar); a tax system that warped investment decisions in certain ways, implicitly favoring consumption and borrowing over saving and investing, and residential construction over industrial modernization; and a maze of inconsistent trade and industrial policies that thwarted a coherent response to attacks from countries that targeted specific industries for development and foreign expansion. This school included those who placed much of the blame for America's noncompetitiveness on the structure and operation of American capital markets, on the grounds that the increasing incidence of hostile takeovers, financed by "junk bonds" and encouraged by investment banks that stood to gain whatever the outcome, forced a short-term perspective on corporate managers and encouraged the formation of a "casino society" mentality in the United States.

The adherents of this point of view included a number of influential Democratic senators and representatives, most economists who did not belong to the first school, and a broadly dispersed group that believed in the necessity of establishing a coordinated industrial policy for the United States.

A third school also believed that the problem was serious and would not go away of its own accord, but that simply correcting some of the obvious inconsistencies and imbalances in macroeconomic and industrial policy would not be sufficient to restore the nation's competitiveness. The real problem, this school argued, lay in human behavior—especially American managers' attitudes, capabilities, and strategies—particularly in the areas of manufacturing and technological development.[9]

There were relatively few adherents to this position when it was initially expressed, and not surprisingly they came under severe criticism, particularly by some influential corporate managers. The chairman of General Motors, for example, asserted in late 1986 that "it was not declines in the competitiveness of American firms' management and technology that were responsible for the deterioration of the U.S. trade position, but rather . . . the business climate of the United States,"[10] and shortly thereafter he engineered the removal of H. Ross Perot, a man who strongly disagreed with that position, from his own board of directors.

But this school began attracting converts as the situation worsened in the mid-1980s, despite the fact that corrective actions at the macroeconomic level had taken place. Even some members of the Reagan administration, which had long been publicly united in its adherence to the first school, began to espouse it. Richard Darman, deputy secretary of the treasury and one of the architects of the administration's tax and financial policies, fired the first salvo in late 1986 when he criticized big corporations for being "bloated, risk-averse, inefficient, and unimaginative" and for not spending enough on R & D. Corporate executives were being paid too much for doing too little, he suggested.[11] And at about the same time, the president of Harvard University began speaking out about the need for the American educational system to take action to improve the nation's ability to meet the economic challenge from abroad, lest it follow Great Britain into economic decline.

Where We Stand
The authors of this book stand firmly in this third camp. Even though we agree that better management of fiscal, monetary, and trade policies at the national level might provide some assistance to American industry, we feel that its flagging competitiveness is in large measure the result of human factors—and specifically management factors—at least as much as it is due to unfair competition or an unsupportive economic climate. The evidence for our position falls into four categories:

Simple Logic. Although high interest rates might be expected to dampen capital investment, and an overvalued dollar to burden American products with comparatively high costs, it is highly unlikely that macroeconomic policies would cause companies to produce products whose quality and reliability are inferior to those of foreign producers. Nor can they explain why some foreign companies were able to produce similar products with less than a quarter of the work-in-process inventory required by their American counterparts or half the floor space and capital investment. Finally, although a decline in technological literacy might explain part of the loss of America's technological leadership in automobiles, consumer electronics, integrated circuits, and computer peripherals, it could not explain why some foreign producers of these same products were able to cut the design-to-introduction time almost in half and thereby introduce new products at a faster rate than their competitors.

Turnarounds. Despite the supposedly debilitating economic climate that American firms had to struggle against, there were numerous examples of companies that had been able to make tremendous improvements in their competitive posture in a relatively short period of time. Chrysler, for example, was able to improve its productivity (as measured by cars per worker per year) from the worst to the best of the Big Three over a period of five years. Xerox was able to blunt and then reverse the inroads made by foreign competitors in its copier markets. And a number of other lesser known companies in a variety of industries responded to severe competitive pressure by making astonishing improvements in their labor productivity—on the order of 100 percent or more—by cutting their work-in-process inventories by 60 percent, or by reducing their defect levels by a factor of 100, to parts-per-million levels. Similar evidence was provided by the widely publicized success of a number of leveraged buy-outs (LBOs)—companies on the brink of bankruptcy that, after being taken private, were able within a few years to achieve dramatic improvements in their profitability and market position.

In most cases such improvements were not achieved through exotic—or even unfamiliar—management approaches. Instead they followed the familiar "turnaround management" recipe: cutting out unnecessary people and getting back to basics. As if in affirmation of Darman's charge that American companies had become bloated, hundreds of large corporations began reducing the size of, and the number of levels in, their management hierarchies. Various observers estimated that between 1981 and the end of 1986 at least 10 percent of the middle management positions in American industry were eliminated. Even as GM's chairman was responding angrily to Darman's attack, his company was preparing to announce plans to reduce its salaried ranks within three years by more than thirty-five thousand people—one-fourth of its total—following the example set by IBM, Kodak, AT&T, Du Pont, G.E., Exxon, Xerox, and many of the other flagship American companies.

Longitudinal Comparisons. A turnaround provides one means for doing a longitudinal analysis: looking at the performance of a single organization over a period of time and trying to determine the causes of the changes that occur. This can be done either at the company or the country level. As an example of the latter, consider the assertion (long popular in American business circles) that powerful unions and a top-heavy government bureaucracy were major causes of America's competitive decline. Yet union power, as measured by the percentage of the work force that belongs to unions, by their ability to influence legislation in Congress, or by a variety of other indicators, has been on a steady decline since the end of World War II. And the government has been reducing the number of its nondefense employees since about 1970—when our competitive decline was just beginning to become visible.

Individual companies or factories can be similarly analyzed, as we do in Chapter 6. All these analyses suggest that the major causes of performance changes are due to management actions, not macroeconomic factors.

Cross-sectional Analyses. Similarly, one can assess the impact of various external factors by comparing the behavior of two or more organizations that confront the same or very similar macroeconomic conditions. Again, such comparisons can be made either at the company or the country level.

At the country level, for example, it is possible to test the effect of oil price increases, strong labor unions, high tax rates, and a massive influx of unskilled workers into a labor force by comparing the performance of U.S. industry during the 1970s with that of West Germany's manufacturing sector during the same period. West German manufacturers had to deal with oil-crisis dislocations that were at least as severe as those experienced in the United States (since Germany almost totally lacked internal sources of crude oil), confronted much more powerful labor unions (which forced a reduction of the standard German workweek to 38.5 hours in 1984, against the united opposition of the German business community), endured higher taxes (both on average and in terms of marginal rates) than in the United States, and had to assimilate a proportionally larger number of unskilled "guest workers" from a variety of southern European and northern African countries (most of whom arrived not only without industrial training but unable to read or speak the German language). Yet the productivity growth rate of German manufacturing actually increased during the 1970s, while that of U.S. industry fell by 50 percent.

At the company level, on the other hand, one study of over 200 American business units over periods of eight or more years found that on average they only achieved about 40 percent of their potential, and only 12 percent exceeded that potential.[12] Indeed, in most U.S. industries it was possible to find some companies that did very well, even though the rest of the industry was succumbing to foreign competition. Even in the steel industry, such companies as Chaparral, Nucor, Allegheny Ludlum, and Worthington were prospering as bigger companies retreated. And within the same company it was not unusual to find that different factories—all residing in the same country, all producing the same or very similar products, and all using similar manufacturing equipment—had widely differing levels of performance.

For example, in the studies we summarize in Chapter 6, the variation between one company's best and poorest plants—whether performance was measured in terms of labor or total factor productivity, defect rates, number of days worth of inventory, or effectiveness in assimilating new capital equipment—was often over 80 percent. This variation in between-plant performance was far greater than could be explained by differences in the size, age, or location of the plants. In fact, we found that it was possible to ascribe the great bulk of it to specific management activities that were taking place within each factory.

Another type of cross-sectional analysis can be based on comparing the performance of U.S.-owned factories in the United States with that of factories owned by foreign companies in the same industry. Since both are subject to almost the same economic climate, one would expect to see similar behavior if macroeconomic variables were the primary drivers of performance differences. But whether one is looking at new factories (such as Sony's television plant in San Diego, California, or Honda's automobile assembly plant in Marysville, Ohio) or old ones (such as the Quasar facility in Chicago that Matsushita purchased from Motorola or the Toyota-GM joint venture in Fremont, California), the performance of the foreign-owned facilities is often strikingly superior to that of its indigenous American counterparts.

What Went Wrong?

If the problems faced by American industry are largely the product of inadequate management, it follows that their solution requires a different approach to management. Specifically, it requires a different mind-set toward manufacturing and technology. As we argue in the next chapter, American industry entered the 1960s with an enormous capital base, a skilled and inherently enthusiastic work force, an experienced and aggressive management group, and acknowledged leadership in most of the world's important process and product technologies. Yet, for reasons we will later explore, many companies began to treat those resources as if they were constraints. Lulled by sluggish competitors and an inflation psychology that allowed them to pass along cost increases to their customers, they began to look upon their factories—all that brick and mortar, all those complicated machines, all those people—as though they were impediments, obstacles to their flexibility and creativity. Their attitude was summed up by one business manager a few years ago: "How's business?" we asked. "Oh, business would be fine," he answered, "if only we didn't have to make the stuff."

Making the stuff was the dirty part; it involved the grubby details of coaxing products out of recalcitrant machines and uncaring workers. Manufacturing managers spent most of their time "fighting fires," scrambling every minute to try to repeal, or at least find loopholes in, Murphy's Law (If anything can go wrong it will go wrong—and usually at the worst possible time). It was the last hurdle—more often the last roadblock—to bringing all their beautiful product designs, all their careful marketing plans, all their precise financial calculations, to fruition. As a result, they tended to treat those manufacturing resources as liabilities, not as assets—which is, after all, the way they are entered on a company's balance sheet.

When one looks upon something as a liability, not as an asset, it tends to change the way one manages it. One manages *around* it, not *through* it. It gets a low place in the pecking order when the time comes to allocate corporate resources, with predictable consequences. Equipment runs down. Buildings get old and dirty. Workforce relations get ever more strained. In an effort to regain control over a deteriorating situation, management installs more sophisticated measurement and control systems, which tend both to increase overhead costs and to stifle innovation. Power and expertise increasingly migrate from the line to the staff, from the factory floor to the corporate counting room. The prime motivator becomes the fear of punishment.

A downward spiral of performance, then confidence, and finally investment takes place: lower performance creates doubt about a plant's ability to use additional investment effectively, so money is channeled elsewhere. Workers and managers see this, assume that nobody else is interested in them, and so start looking out for themselves. People look elsewhere for opportunities, and some of them—usually the best ones—leave. Performance and morale suffer further, and the cycle repeats itself, at an ever lower level.

We have been in many factories around America that exhibited the results of this kind of spiral: old, worn-out equipment, dispirited workers looking to unions for support and protection, and cynical, tired managers. Suddenly somebody at corporate headquarters does an analysis and says, "Let's close this place down and go somewhere else." So the company builds a new plant in a new location—far away from those tired managers and hostile workers. But unless it changes its attitudes and practices, the same downward spiral begins all over again. After twenty-five years or so, it will find itself again with twenty-five-year-old equipment, and workers and managers locked into the same old endgame.

In such an environment, American managers became preoccupied with simply getting goods through the process. Meeting production schedules—in the face of machines that were always breaking down, uncooperative workers, middle managers who were continually fighting fires when they weren't protecting their turf, and worse, suppliers that were just like oneself—became the overriding objective. Quality was relegated to secondary status and dealt with through such conceits as an "acceptable quality level," which implied that there *was* an acceptable level of bad quality. It wasn't called bad quality, of course; it was called "off spec product." And it was dealt with by setting up repair facilities—as profit centers—and selling service warranties.

To guarantee production in such an environment required lots of buffer inventories, rework stations, and expediting. Because all those expediters tended to get in each other's way, companies tried to maintain order by hiring coordinators. They piled staff on staff (a phenomenon that has been called "staff infection") until they had three or four overhead personnel for every production worker, and top management became increasingly removed—both physically and psychologically—from the production line. One of the authors has in his files the written summary reaction of participants to a course on manufacturing management that he taught to high-level general managers of American companies in the mid-1970s: "[You] did very well with a subject that unfortunately has limited appeal."

Many business schools became trapped into the same kind of thinking. Their faculties and students focused their attention primarily on how to develop techniques and systems for managing the flow of products through processes that were loaded with uncertainties and constraints, on how to manage the inventories that appeared to be so indispensable in such processes, and on how to expedite orders in such a way that as few as possible of them were indefinitely delayed. Such topics, needless to say, were not the most exciting that business school students were exposed to; therefore not many were encouraged to go to work in factories. Manufacturing people were like the infantry in our industrial army: minus the glory and usually without air support.

Fighting within the company and against the U.S. government's attempts to impose its will (as Will Rogers put it, "We don't get half the government we pay for, thank God!''), both in the attempt to wrestle materials through the process and to avoid blame when they didn't get through, became such a way of life in that kind of environment that one tended to forget who the real enemy was. It was, as it always has been, people who want what you have. But this time the enemy, foreign competitors, were playing by different rules. They were working together—workers and managers, suppliers and customers, engineering and marketing *and* manufacturing—exploiting new technology, and stressing output quality above quantity. They were using their manufacturing resources as assets, as opportunities, and they were gaining a competitive edge by competing *through* manufacturing.

American managers eventually learned that all that infighting and pointing of fingers was a luxury they couldn't afford. Fortunately, they now had the opportunity to study what their competitors were doing and learn from them. For a long while Americans didn't think they could learn much from others, but that has changed. The bad news is that it will take time to put those ideas—and some of the ones Americans have developed themselves—into practice. The good news is that it can be done.

One of the reasons a resurgence is going to be more difficult than it might have been is that too many companies became infatuated with the notion of ''leverage'' during the past couple of decades. When applied to financial management, that means adding other people's money to one's own: if one can get a lot of other people's money, one doesn't need to commit as much of one's own. But one can apply the same approach to other kinds of resources. For example, one can develop less of one's own new technology—new product ideas and new processing techniques—and borrow or buy it from the companies that do develop new technology. One can also rely on other companies to design and build one's manufacturing equipment and hire more and more of one's skilled workers out of other companies' training programs.

This other kind of leverage isn't like financial leverage, however, and it doesn't work for long. If one uses too much of it, one will never again be able to be a technological leader. One's manufacturing equipment will be the same as that available to all one's competitors, and one's workers will be less skilled than those in companies who train them internally. In short, this kind of leverage may allow a company to augment its profitability in the near term, but it will eventually find itself at a disadvantage vis-à-vis those of its competitors who try to be leaders. Forging manufacturing excellence therefore means making investments and taking risks that many companies once thought they could avoid; indeed, they could—as long as none of their competitors were making those investments and taking those risks.

A number of American companies are coming to grips with this realization. The challenge is clear: they have to try to be the best in the world in selected aspects of their business. They have to learn how to grow their own technology and their own skilled people, not simply scavenge the leavings of others. They have to make their factories run right again. Workers and managers have to stop fighting each other and work together to turn back their common enemies. They must guard against the onset of that downward spiral that begins with complacency and selfishness and ends with vacant plants and wasted human resources. Rather than accept the limitations imposed by unreliable workers, machinery, and suppliers, companies must set about developing new relationships with workers and learn to design, make, and operate equipment and systems that can produce perfect products and run without interruption. Then they must push the same philosophy and commitment back down into their suppliers.

This will not be easy. Nor will it happen by itself. The organizations they have created, with all their checks and balances, are intensely resistant to change. Breaking down old barriers, creating new values, and encouraging new ways of thinking demand strong leaders: people who look at their situation and say, "This can't go on like this"; business statesmen who can create a new vision and persuade others to turn it into reality. This book is about this task, and is directed toward such men and women.

Becoming a World-class Manufacturer

As we described in an earlier book,[13] the ultimate purpose of strategic management is to focus an organization's resources, capabilities, and energies on building a sustainable advantage over its competitors along one or more dimension of performance. Such an advantage may derive, for example, from lower cost, from higher product performance, from more innovative products, or from superior service. This does not mean that your competitors will not occasionally match or better your competitive position for a short period of time by, for example, acquiring a new technology, establishing production in a low-cost location, or moving rapidly to exploit a narrow window of market opportunity. But if one's goal is to develop a *sustainable* competitive advantage, one's efforts must be directed not toward opportunistic deal making but rather toward the development of specific organizational competences and relationships that are difficult for competitors to match over the long term.

Many companies around the world have become household names because of their success in doing this: Rolls-Royce has become synonymous with luxurious, Ferrari with high performance, and Toyota with dependable automobiles. Depending on the competitive advantage they are seeking, different corporate functions are emphasized. For example, Hewlett-Packard has historically competed on the basis of innovative products and has therefore placed particular emphasis on R & D. IBM, although its products sometimes were not as technologically advanced as its competitors', won business from them by offering superior customer service; and Caterpillar's enduring reputation for dependability has been based both on product design and on the logistics system it has established to service its independent dealers.

Unfortunately, during the past two decades relatively few companies in the United States have sought to build a competitive advantage around their manufacturing ability. Yet the organizational and technological skills required to produce products better than one's competitors are extraordinarily difficult to duplicate, and therefore constitute one of the soundest bases for achieving a sustainable advantage. Many companies have recently begun to appreciate this. They have discovered that the "secret weapon" of their fiercest competitors is often based not on better product design, greater marketing ingenuity, or superior financial strength but on the ability to make relatively standard products more efficiently, more reliably, and with higher precision. As they seek to marshal their own organizations to respond to this new threat, many of them have been forced to confront the fact that they have systematically neglected their manufacturing function over a rather long period of time. Like an unused muscle, their manufacturing capabilities have been allowed to atrophy.

Their problem is not that they cannot "make the stuff." They can, but so can their competitors. Their problem is that they are not *world-class* manufacturers but are facing competitors who are. Another title for this book could have been "Building a World-

Class Manufacturing Organization,'' for that is what we shall be discussing in the chapters ahead. But before we begin, we should describe what is implied by the term "world-class manufacturing." Basically, this means being better than almost every other company in your industry in at least one important aspect of manufacturing.

Once it has been decided what kind of competitive advantage the organization is going to seek (or, going further, once priorities have been established among various performance criteria, such as cost, quality, dependability, flexibility, or innovativeness), it has to configure itself in such a way that it can achieve, and continually enhance, that competitive advantage. This requires making a series of coordinated decisions of both a structural and an infrastructural nature. The former refers to such "bricks and mortar" decisions as

1. The amount of total production capacity to provide;
2. How this capacity should be broken up into specific production facilities (how they should be specialized and where they should be located);
3. What kind of production equipment and systems to provide those facilities with; and
4. Which materials, systems, and services should be produced internally and which should be sourced from outside the organization (and what kind of relationships should be established with outside suppliers).

By infrastructure, on the other hand, we refer to the management policies and systems that determine how the bricks and mortar are managed:

5. Human resource policies and practices, including management selection and training policies;
6. Quality assurance and control systems;
7. Production planning and inventory control systems;
8. New product development processes;
9. Performance measurement and reward systems, including capital allocation systems; and
10. Organizational structure and design.

Because of their influence on an organization's behavior and effectiveness, such policies are analogous to the "software" that guides a computer's "hardware." And just as when designing an effective computer system, not only must the software fit the hardware, but the hardware and software design choices must be consistent with organizational objectives.

Our earlier book focused most of its attention on manufacturing structural decisions, but over the years we have become increasingly impressed by the importance of infrastructural elements. We have seen a number of companies that were able to build a powerful competitive advantage around their internal capabilities and teamwork, even though their plants and equipment were not exceptional; but we have never seen one that was able to build a sustainable advantage around superior hardware alone. For this reason, as we shall later argue, it is almost impossible for a company to "spend" its way out of a competitive difficulty.

In its closing chapter that earlier book described the four stages of manufacturing competitiveness. Stage I companies consider their manufacturing organization to be *internally neutral*, in that its role is simply to "make the stuff," without any surprises. Such companies believe that their product designs are so unusual or their marketing organizations so powerful that if the product can simply be delivered to customers, as advertised, the company will be successful.

Although often naive, such a philosophy is sometimes successful, particularly if a company is able to find a niche in its market that protects it from immediate competitors. But as such companies grow, one of two things typically happens. Either they outgrow their niche and come up against competitors in adjoining niches, or the niche itself grows to the point where it becomes attractive to other companies. At this point simply making the stuff is not enough; one must also meet the cost, quality, and delivery standards achieved by one's competitors. Therefore, Stage II companies look outward and ask their manufacturing organizations to be *externally neutral*, that is, able to meet the standards imposed by their major competitors. Such companies tend to adhere to industry practice and industry standards. They buy their parts, materials, and production equipment from the same suppliers that their competitors use, follow similar approaches to quality and inventory control, establish similar relationships with their work force, and regard technicians and managers as interchangeable parts—hiring both, as needed, from other companies in the industry.

Some companies eventually reach a point, however, where this kind of copycat behavior no longer seems appropriate. If their competitive strategy is different from that of most of their competitors, why should they follow industry practice as regards manufacturing?

In seeking to develop a coordinated set of manufacturing structural and infrastructural decisions tailored to their specific competitive strategy, such companies evolve to Stage III: a manufacturing organization that is *internally supportive* of other parts of the company.

But for a few companies even this is not enough. It is clear that a regional airline that is competing on the basis of flexibility will probably want to choose airplanes that are different from those adopted by its large competitors; but this does not mean that it will prevail over other small airlines that have chosen similar equipment. Success will depend on its ability to use its equipment more effectively than its competitors use theirs, and to exploit better the capabilities of that equipment in other parts of the organization. Stage IV companies regard their manufacturing organizations as *externally supportive*, that is, playing a key role in helping the whole company achieve an edge over its competitors. Such companies are not content simply to copy their competitors, or even to be the "toughest kid on the block" in their own neighborhood. They seek to be as good as anybody in the world at the things they have chosen to be good at—that is, world-class.

How does one know when one is world-class? The obvious way is by observing how one's products fare in the marketplace and by checking one's cashbox. World-class (Stage IV) companies tend to grow faster and be more profitable than their competitors. But there are a number of other more subtle indicators:

1. Having workers and managers who are so skilled and effective that other companies are continually seeking to attract them away from one's organization;
2. Being so expert in the design and manufacture of production equipment that equipment suppliers are continually seeking one's advice about possible modifications to their equipment, one's suggestions for new equipment, and one's agreement to be a test site for one of their pilot models;
3. Being more nimble than one's competitors in responding to market shifts or pricing changes, and in getting new products out into the market faster than they can;
4. Intertwining the design of a new product so closely with the design of its manufacturing process that when competitors "reverse engineer" the product they find that they cannot produce a comparable one in their own factories without major retooling and redesign expenses; and

5. Continually improving facilities, support systems, and skills that were considered to be "optimal" or "state of the art" when first introduced, so that they increasingly surpass their initial capabilities.

This kind of behavior does not "just happen" by itself. In fact, in many ways it is very unnatural behavior in companies whose organizational structure, staffing policies, and performance measurement and control systems are predicated on the assumption that an organization should be composed of a collection of specialists who operate within fairly narrow job descriptions. Such companies (Stages I or II, described earlier) typically operate under a "command and control" mentality: senior management is expected to make the major resource allocation decisions (with the help of staff and external experts whenever necessary), and the role of line management is simply to operate the resulting configuration of facilities, systems, and personnel in such a way that the performance expected from them is attained.

This command and control mentality values specialists, assumes that whatever capabilities are lacking in an organization can be purchased from the outside, and considers management's primary task to be the orderly assimilation, exploitation, and coordination of separate sources of expertise. Factory location decisions are made by real estate experts and outside consultants, equipment decisions by engineers (the equipment itself is designed and built by independent equipment suppliers), the selection of production scheduling and inventory control systems by computer specialists, quality systems by outside consultants, and personnel decisions by human resource specialists. Whenever a particular set of worker (or manager) skills is desired, the outside world is combed for them. Finally, these organizations are inherently hierarchical, in the sense that the primary relationships between people are *vertical*: decisions (and rewards or punishments) flow down and information flows back up.

World-class Stage IV companies dislike being dependent on outside organizations for expertise. They want to grow their own people, equipment, and systems, but they also respect the capabilities of others. Therefore they continually scour the outside world—and particularly their best competitors—to ensure that they are on top of all the newest ideas and approaches. They strive to build strong *horizontal* relationships throughout the company, so that product design decisions are closely coupled with manufacturing process decisions, vendor management with production scheduling and quality management, and personnel with everything. Finally, they place great emphasis on R & D, experimentation, training, and the building of general organizational capabilities. They continually push at the margins of their expertise, trying on every front to be a bit better than before. Standards, to them, are ephemeral—milestones on the road to perfection. They strive to be *dynamic*, learning companies.

This emphasis on continual improvement is the ultimate test of a world-class organization. Any well-run and adventurous company may seize a temporary advantage over its competitors by adopting a particularly innovative product or process design, or by investing (usually at great expense) in a state-of-the-art production facility. It may appear to the outside world—the company may delude itself, in fact—that it has achieved parity with those other companies that truly compete through their manufacturing capability. But if this new design or facility comes to be regarded as a goal in and of itself, if the organization does not immediately begin experimenting and tinkering with it, pushing it to do things for which it wasn't intended (but which it might eventually accommodate), the advantage is soon lost. Their energy spent, they watch in frustration and helplessness as their world class competitors relentlessly march past them.

Although this book's focus is ostensibly on manufacturing, our concern extends to the larger problem of creating and managing this kind of learning organization. We have found that companies that are quick both to learn new things and to perfect familiar things, that adapt imaginatively and effectively to change, and that are looked up to by their competitors because of their ability to lead the way into new fields, tend to have certain attributes in common. Moreover, companies with these attributes tend to be excellent throughout. Reforging manufacturing into a competitive weapon lays the foundation, therefore, for building a company that is world-class in everything it does.

An Outline of This Book

Our studies of a number of companies have convinced us that history matters. Unless one understands how an organization got where it is, it is difficult to determine the appropriate steps to take next. If not properly understood, the forces that drive it in a certain direction will continue to operate, despite whatever well-intentioned decisions are imposed upon it. It is for this reason that we conclude the first part of this book with an historical perspective.

We start in Chapter 2 by examining the basic beliefs, concepts, and approaches to manufacturing management that have developed—largely in the United States—over the past 100 years, and that continue to shape the attitudes of many managers today. We pay particular attention to two topics: the development of "scientific management" and the subsequent development of a more holistic and humanistic approach to manufacturing management that flowered in the United States during the 1940s and 1950s, when its production expertise turned the tide in World War II and won the admiration of the rest of the world. Today much of the expertise, and most of the philosophy, that underlay that approach to manufacturing have been lost in the United States. They live on, unfortunately for us, in the foreign competitors that studied us carefully back then and transplanted our approaches to their own soil.

The basic beliefs, assumptions, and approaches that have developed over time still color the way we think about the role of production management. They are clearly reflected, for example, in the contrasting responsibilities assigned to line versus staff organizations, to shop-floor-level workers versus managers, and to manufacturing infrastructure (systems and policies) versus structure (facilities and equipment) that we see throughout American industry. As we explore changes in each of these areas later in this book, we must be aware how deeply they are rooted in management philosophy and historical practice.

In the book's second part we turn our full attention to these infrastructure issues: the management policies, systems, and procedures that establish the organizational context within which manufacturing (in fact, any functional organization) must operate. In Chapter 3 we look at the modern capital budgeting paradigm and how it affects—either positively or negatively—the creation of a competitive advantage in manufacturing. We describe three contrasting but representative investment proposals and point out the pitfalls that companies can encounter when trying to evaluate them using traditional capital-budgeting approaches. Not only does the investment decision-making process help shape top management's thinking regarding specific projects, it colors their overall view of the nature of manufacturing competitiveness. We close the chapter by outlining a more comprehensive framework for guiding capital-investment decisions.

In Chapter 4 we look at the organization of the manufacturing function, which profoundly influences how various manufacturing resources (people, systems, capital, and technology) are marshalled, coordinated, and enhanced. We describe some of the different approaches that a company may select in organizing its manufacturing function, and the major implications of each choice. We also examine the contrasting roles of staff and line organizations, and how each can mesh with and complement the other in pursuing the business unit's desired competitive advantage. Finally, we look at the impact of growth on a manufacturing organization and explain why many companies find it so hard to adapt to the changes it brings.

In Chapter 5, the end of the second part, we address issues associated with measuring manufacturing performance. We describe why we are uneasy both with the aspects of performance that companies typically choose to measure and with the measurement techniques they employ. The methods an organization employs for measuring, evaluating, and rewarding performance not only influence people's behavior but constitute an integral component of any management "control" system. After identifying several of the dysfunctional aspects of current practices, which are largely based on the traditional cost-accounting model, we briefly describe an alternative approach (known as total factor productivity) for measuring how rapidly an organization is improving its effectiveness in utilizing all the major resources available to it. We conclude by outlining an approach for comparing a company's performance against an external reference system: the performance of its best competitors.

In the third part we focus specifically on manufacturing management at the factory level. We begin, in Chapter 6, by describing some of the recent research that we have done in trying to understand why, within the same company, some factories are more productive than others. After analyzing the data we have collected, we summarize some of the basic approaches to managing improvement—as reflected in the growth of total factor productivity—that appear to be particularly effective. We place particular emphasis on the impact that factory complexity and confusion, as well as organizational learning, have on productivity growth. Because the factory is such an important nursery for growing manufacturing capabilities, we emphasize that general managers, as well as those in manufacturing, need to understand the underlying concepts and principles of outstanding factory performance.

Building on these fundamental concepts and principles, in Chapter 7 we examine the competitive leverage that can come from effective management of the flow of both physical materials and information in the factory environment. We present two contrasting manufacturing "architectures" for managing these flows and show how each interacts with a factory's capital and human assets to influence both its current performance and its potential for continued improvement.

In Chapter 8 we explore the relationships between the concepts of control, knowledge creation, and manufacturing capability by describing four levels of control: reactive, preventive, progressive, and dynamic. The types of knowledge required for each level of control, and the organizational capabilities that are required to implement it, are outlined. We also describe how the requisite layers of knowledge can be developed within the factory environment, through problem solving and controlled experimentation. We conclude by outlining an approach for starting an organization along a path of steadily increasing improvement.

Chapter 9 concludes the third part by focusing on human resource management, and the role that people play in extracting the full potential from equipment, processes, and systems. Although most economists and government leaders argue that technology, particularly as embodied in modern equipment, is the primary solution for declining manufacturing competitiveness, we explain why we think people—the way they are trained, organized, and managed—are at least as important. We end by describing some of the basic principles that we feel should guide the management of human resources in a manufacturing organization.

The last part is devoted to issues associated with the management of technology, from the perspective of both new product and new process development. Our view is that both types of technological development provide rich opportunities to capitalize on and enhance manufacturing capabilities, thereby strengthening a firm's competitive position. Chapter 10 describes how general managers can assess their organization's readiness for product or process development projects, and some of the steps that can be taken to increase the likelihood of a project's success. Product and process development projects can provide an important vehicle both for altering the way functional groups interact, coordinate, and communicate and for strengthening an organization's competitive position. Unfortunately, this potential is too seldom exploited, because general managers hesitate to involve themselves directly in such projects.

In Chapter 11 we explore the characteristics of superior project management. We have observed a number of organizations whose development projects take half the time and half the resources of their industrial competitors, yet result in superior products and processes that are not easily imitated by others. We describe a number of the approaches such companies follow, and how those approaches enable them to continuously improve the effectiveness of their product and process development efforts.

In the last chapter we attempt to weave together the various threads of the tapestry that we have been assembling and provide advice about how a company can get started on the road to manufacturing excellence. We describe how it can objectively assess its manufacturing capabilities, and the steps it has to take if it is to restructure itself so that manufacturing becomes a source of competitive advantage. Then we examine why the changes required are so difficult for most companies to implement, and describe the leadership role that top management has to play if these changes are to occur.

A Final Note

Throughout this book we adopt a point of view that may be puzzling to some readers and is therefore important to understand from the onset. Much of modern management theory is based on rationalist principles: that events, behavior patterns, and specific decisions reflect logical processes; that complex activities can be decomposed into underlying variables and the relationships between them; and that the key to understanding (or predicting) the outcome of the complicated interplay between people, organizations, and their environment is through ascertaining these causal relationships. Although the authors were all trained in these rationalist principles and conduct the bulk of their research under its dictates, we have become increasingly convinced that certain important human phenomena are not yet sufficiently understood to be satisfactorily modeled in this fashion. Even though modern medicine may understand quite clearly what causes a certain disease and how to treat it, it still does not fully understand how the psychological condition of a specific patient, and the relationship between that patient and the attending physician, affect the prognosis. Briefly, we believe in modern medicine, but we also believe in the importance of the physician's bedside manner.

Hence, in the pages that follow we often emphasize the importance of human qualities that are as yet too poorly understood to predict or even measure properly: qualities like trust, confidence, commitment, integrity, vision, and leadership. Such human traits often combine with other phenomena that are equally obscure to produce behavior patterns in organizations that defy conventional analysis. To use our previous terminology, there is an overlay of human software that often overwhelms the hardware of precise relationships and rational thinking that we like to think drives managerial behavior. The interaction of such hardware and software, of clear structure and obscure infrastructure, produces what we refer to as "organic" or "holistic" behavior in organizations. We focus considerable attention on this kind of behavior because it is key to understanding why some organizations are able to achieve superior performance even though they appear, on the surface at least, to be behaving irrationally.

In fact, it is often important in business *not* to be too rational. People who are totally rational do not start up new businesses, attack the largest company in an industry, or try to overtake, with limited resources, the leading industrial power of the time. When business becomes too analytical, too concerned with the calculus of costs versus benefits and risks versus returns, it becomes prey to those who seek market share, the dynamics of growth, and a place in the sun. As John Maynard Keynes wrote fifty years ago,

> A large proportion of our positive activities depend on spontaneous optimism rather than on [mathematical logic]. . . . Our decisions to do something positive, the full consequences of which will be drawn out over many days to come, can only be taken as a result of animal spirits—of a spontaneous urge to action rather than inaction, and not as the outcome of a weighted average of quantitative benefits multiplied by quantitative probabilities. . . . If the animal spirits are dimmed and the spontaneous optimism falters, leaving us to depend on nothing but [logic], enterprise will fade and die.[14]

A business acquaintance phrased it slightly differently: "The easiest competitor to drive out of a business is the most rational one. All you have to do is convince him you're not."

| 2 |

America's Manufacturing Heritage

Introduction

The middle of this century capped the golden age of American manufacturing, the high-water mark of its power and influence throughout the world. The "American way" of manufacturing, after more than a century of perfecting itself, had achieved feats of production and innovation during World War II that galvanized its allies and demoralized its enemies. After the war legions of American managers and consultants roamed the world, training foreign managers and assisting them in rebuilding their industries. American multinationals expanded their factories into these countries as well, soon becoming so powerful that by the mid-1960s foreign observers were bewailing the threat posed by the "American challenge." European and Japanese managers and engineers flocked to the United States to visit its factories and try to understand what made them so effective.

Today they come again, not to learn but to teach—and to set up their own factories on American soil. It is American managers' turn to go abroad to study the latest technologies, the newest approaches to materials and supplier management, the secrets of defect-free production. "Can their approaches work here?" they are asked on their return. The response of most is that they can. Not only that, *they have*: they are largely approaches that American managers developed, taught the rest of the world, and then, their attention directed elsewhere, forgot.

This is not the first time, of course, that investigators have visited some emerging industrial power to see firsthand the companies that have begun to challenge once dominant domestic firms, and to ascertain whether that nation's success is due to low wages, to new technology, or to a supportive government or national culture. Such investigators' findings, however, are usually disappointingly pedestrian; their reports tend to be dominated by observations about clean, well run factories and skilled, intelligent workers who eagerly assist in the adoption of new technologies and management approaches. Although such reports have been received with some surprise by many American managers in the 1980s, similar reports were written over 100 years ago by British observers. And they were about American, not Japanese, factories.[1]

Knowing that U.S. manufacturing companies were once the object of tremendous interest and admiration, that they were renowned for their intense competitiveness and their ability to develop and exploit new technologies, may seem barely relevant to the companies who today are struggling to meet the challenge of ferocious international competition. But for managers intent on rebuilding their companies into Stage IV competitors—true world-class manufacturers—this historical perspective is useful for two reasons. First, an understanding of history provides a sort of mirror from which a mature firm can learn much about itself. But it can also act like a powerful lens, bringing into sharp focus the bases for its original growth and prosperity.

We are not suggesting that the key to success in today's world lies in imitating the past, but rather that there are recurring patterns in the ebb and flow of enterprise that, if discerned and understood, can teach much about what is fundamental and enduring in industrial success. In this chapter, we examine the historical development of some of the most influential managerial approaches, assumptions, and philosophies that shaped American manufacturing into the powerhouse it became in the mid-1900s. After tracing the development of both factory and technology management, we interpret the patterns that we find and suggest some of the lessons that can be learned from them.

The Early Evolution of Manufacturing Management

In the last half of the nineteenth and the first half of the twentieth centuries, in a variety of industries, American manufacturers carved out leading positions around the world. Their ability to compete effectively against larger, more experienced, and entrenched foreign competitors was regarded as astonishing at the time—hence the study teams (referred to at the beginning of this chapter) sent out by such countries as Great Britain, the industrial colossus of the nineteenth century. This success, they found, was not due to cheap labor, military power, the invention of interchangeable parts, or any other technological advantage. Skilled labor was scarce, America's military posture was primarily defensive in nature (relying largely on the protection afforded by the Atlantic Ocean), and U.S. technology (including the notion of interchangeable parts) was largely borrowed. Instead it was due to something quite unique: the application of some profoundly new concepts relating to production processes, organization, and technology.

Much of what was new involved the application of science to production and production management. But the real power of this new American approach to manufacturing came from the blending of science and scientific management with the value system and skill base of the old-world craftsman. This combination of old-world traditions and new-world approaches that took root in the United States transformed the very notion of manufacturing and had a lasting influence throughout the world. The nature of that powerful combination of the old and the new—and the problems that later emerged when it came unglued—is illustrated by the story of the Mesta Machine Company, once one of America's premier manufacturers.[2]

The Mesta Machine Company

In 1902 Lorenz Iversen, a Danish immigrant, joined the Mesta Machine Company in the drafting department. Mesta was a bustling, growing four-year-old company at the time, and it is unlikely that anyone treated Iversen's arrival as anything special. But over the next sixty-one years no one had more influence in shaping and guiding the company. Iversen came to Mesta with the skills of a machinist acquired as an apprentice in Denmark. But he also brought with him the knowledge and discipline acquired from a degree in the new field of engineering. Even more important, he loved building and using machines, and he was full of ideas.

It was a perfect match. Mesta was a small company with big ambitions, and its growing list of customers wanted new and different kinds of machines. Unencumbered by bureaucracy and surrounded by skilled and supportive colleagues, Iversen thrived. He designed machinery, invented and patented a variety of devices, and eventually became chief engineer. The company prospered as well. In the years before World War I Mesta grew to three thousand employees and its products ranged from giant turbines for power plants to rolling mills for the steel industry.

By the time Iversen became president in 1930, the company had established itself as one of the nation's premier suppliers of industrial machinery, particularly to the steel industry. It had a reputation for innovation, for excellent engineering, and for customer service. Iversen's influence was felt everywhere, from the top of the company to the shop floor. He was not a distant administrator; his was a hands-on, walk around, face to face style of leadership. He was at home with the most sophisticated machinery design problems and the most complex machining tasks, and he was a perfectionist who demanded precision, discipline, and excellence. Yet he also knew how to create a sense of purpose in his people. One long time employee recalled that Iversen "really knew how to instill pride. We had then what the Japanese are bragging about now."

The capabilities and skills in engineering and production that Mesta had developed by the 1930s were tested to the fullest during World War II. Mesta took on the design and production of naval guns, ship propeller shafts, mortars, and cannons. Working under intense pressure to meet the needs of the U.S. armed forces, Mesta's people performed extraordinary feats. At the end of the war, it was honored by the Army-Navy Production Board as one of the top suppliers in the country.

In the two decades following World War II, Mesta did not rest on its laurels. In fact, the late 1940s and 1950s were something of a heyday. The United States had become the leader of the industrial world, and Mesta machines played a central role in a number of critical industries, ranging from steel to aerospace. When Iversen retired in 1963 at the age of eighty-seven, the company's equipment was operating in more than 500 plants around the world. As one customer noted, "If you had the nerve to ask them to do something, they could find a way to do it."

In retrospect Iversen's retirement marked not only the end of his career but also the end of an era for Mesta. The world of technology and competition changed dramatically over the next twenty years, and the new generation of leadership at Mesta was not equal to the challenge. New international competitors and new customer demands called for changes in selling practices and more attention to production methods. These were too slow in coming, and the company suffered.

More important, the company lost its technological drive, and its long established competitive advantage in engineering eroded. Throughout its history Mesta had built its business on doing what others could not do, and that meant pushing the state of the art, creating and then capitalizing on new opportunities. Yet in the late 1960s and early 1970s the company failed to develop expertise in what was probably that era's most important process development as far as the steel industry was concerned: continuous casting transformed the semifinished stage of steel production and spawned many other developments in related equipment. By the mid-1980s, a company that was not a supplier of continuous-casting equipment (and Mesta was not) was simply not a serious player in steel mill equipment.

Much of what happened to Mesta as its reputation slipped and its ability to compete diminished can be traced to a new generation of managers who assumed power following Iversen's retirement. Largely brought in from outside the company, most were professional managers with a financial background. Lacking in engineering experience, and therefore unfamiliar with the core of the business, they responded to the competitive challenge by adding new layers of corporate staff, introducing committees for decision-making, and installing new, more stringent accounting and capital budgeting systems. They rarely appeared in the shops or in the engineering centers, and the direct communication that was Iversen's hallmark was lost. Together with a failure to keep pace with technology, the growing distance and distrust between Mesta's work force and managers, fostered by their remote-control approach to management, proved to be the company's undoing. Crippled by strikes and lost orders, Mesta lost over $60 million between 1979 and 1982 and filed for bankruptcy in early 1983.

The story of the Mesta Machine Company's inspiring success and slow demise is not unique. In industry after industry similar problems have befallen once strong and effective firms. Their success in the hundred years up to 1970 makes these recent problems all the more intriguing. Did U.S. industry appear to be so impressive only because it had little competition, or did American manufacturers lose touch with something that was powerful and effective?

Art and Science in American Manufacturing
Much of what gave American companies like Mesta Machine their distinctive advantages had its roots in the workshops of the master

craftsmen of medieval Europe. The factory that developed during the industrial revolution was a very different institution, of course; making things in factories created new kinds of jobs and new relationships. Yet in some industries, particularly those associated with precision machinery, the guiding values and practices of the artisan workshop continued to shape factory management through the turn of the century. Some of the more distinctive characteristics of the craftsman tradition in production management are presented in Table 2-1.

The artisan mode of production relied heavily on individual skills and attitudes. In solving problems, controlling quality, or making improvements, workers relied primarily on the technical skill they acquired through long apprenticeships. This strong belief in the value of experience, constant practice, and an understanding of the realities of the shop floor carried over to the work of directing the activities of others. Just as the work itself was based on direct contact, so management was also a matter of exercising personal leadership in a hands-on fashion. "Management-by-walking around" was the order of the day in the artisan workshop. So too was "product mindedness": a deep understanding of the product, and a strong interest in how it was used.

Workshops operating in the artisan mode succeeded or failed according to their entrepreneurialism, their technical ingenuity, the

Table 2-1 The Artisan Mode of Production

Management Activities/Philosophy	Key Characteristics
Problem solving	Experience reveals problems; solved through trial and error
Creation of knowledge	Learning by doing; long apprenticeship to master craftsmen
Control	Hands on, personal leadership, based on the know-how of the master
Source of improvement	The ingenuity and creativity of the individual; learning from each other
Orientation/priorities	Product/customer orientation; technical excellence in the practical arts
View of the world	Holistic and organic; an understanding of customer relationships and competitor dynamics based on tradition and long experience

quality of their execution, and their ability to meet their customers' specific needs. Commercial success was achieved by becoming expert at what the Germans call *Technik:* the art of manufacturing. *Technik* requires mastery of the whole complex interplay of processes, production design, and related activities. In contrast, what the modern world regards as good management practice—planning, analysis, specialization and delegation, control systems, clever marketing, adroit financing—these were all of little import. What was critical, and thus highly valued, was the ability to create (that is, design, craft, and assemble) the product the customer desired in a way that met the craftsman's own standards of excellence. His name went on the product, and his future financial security depended on his customers returning to seek his services again and again.

The principles of the artisan mode of management imply obvious strengths; individual responsibility, technical excellence, attention to detail, loyalty, personalized customer service, and continual improvement. But this management style also has its weaknesses. It can be rigid and resistant to change; while tradition and experience are good teachers, they can also be strong anchors. As the scale of an operation grows and the need to produce higher volumes at ever lower costs encourages more and more division of labor, close personal direction and control become more difficult.

If workers and their supervisors no longer understand or internalize these norms—of high personal standards, customer orientation, and leadership through technical competence—production becomes rudderless. It can be governed by personal whim, by obsolete tradition, by superstition, or by empty imitation. Worse, when confidence diminishes in the workers' ability to regulate themselves based on their internal standards of behavior and quality, they can become increasingly guided by fear: fear of losing their jobs if they work too slowly (or even, because of peer resentment, too rapidly), as well as fear of undermining the value of their skill if they teach the tricks of their particular trade to others. Thus, what Frederick Taylor called "systematic soldiering"—the conscious withholding of effort—can become a problem. This elicited a method of supervision that relied heavily on verbal harangue, threats, and physical abuse.

These weaknesses in the traditional artisan mode of factory management were especially apparent to the generation that entered the business world in the latter part of the nineteenth century. For the first time, many of these new managers had been trained as engineers. For people trained in the sciences yet also imbued with the practical arts of the workshop, the need for a systematic approach to the management of large-scale factory production that would retain some of the strengths of the artisan mode was obvious. By applying scientific thinking to shop-floor management, these new *industrial* engineers hoped to create a new and superior mode of production experience. In this sense the rise of a more systematic, scientific approach to factory management inevitably followed the first application of science and the scientific method to industrial products and processes.

Science on the Shop Floor: The Ideas and Concepts of Scientific Management

Of the engineers who grew to influence the course of U.S. business in the late nineteenth and early twentieth centuries, few had the impact or earned the renown of Frederick Taylor. Although there were many who attempted to apply scientific principles to production before him, and although many who came after him contributed additional ideas, Taylor's concepts remain central to understanding the rethinking about the management of manufacturing that took place around the turn of this century. In the popular mind Taylor is associated with the extreme division of labor and with using time and motion studies to turn people into mindless automatons. Although it contains some truth, this view shortchanges and seriously misrepresents Taylor's philosophy.

There are four basic principles of "scientific management" that reflect Taylor's beliefs about the nature of work, the nature of production knowledge and its creation, and the motivation of workers:

Find the "One Best Way." For Taylor, work was governed by scientific laws. Discovery of these laws (using scientific methods) allowed one to define the best—most efficient—way to do a job. Finding this "one best way" was thus the first step to efficient production.

Match People to Tasks. Taylor believed that people were different; each one was suited for some things and not for others. Thus, the second principle: pick the right people (using scientific methods), and train them (again, scientifically). In Taylor's scheme, specialization applied to every phase of the enterprise. Workers could make suggestions, but the ideas of the workers were just that, suggestions. Management (i.e., those best suited for making decisions) would be the judge of their fitness for use.

Supervise, Reward, and Punish. Taylor offered the following justification for the third principle: "You may scientifically select and train workmen just as much as you please, but . . . we are all of us so constituted that about three-fourths of the time . . . we will do our work . . . just as we see fit, unless some one is there to see that we do it in accordance with the principles of the science."[3]

Supervision was essential to see that the "one best way" was followed. But Taylor also believed that if the workers understood the logic behind this way, and if they had proper incentives, they would follow that logic out of self-interest. His incentive scheme rewarded workers for producing above the standard (or expected level of output, as determined scientifically by management) and penalized them for producing below it. Finally:

Use Staff to Plan and Control. Taylor advocated the creation of staff groups to develop the processes, to establish procedures and routines, and in general, to control the work. Workers were to focus on the work itself, and receive their instructions, procedures, and assignments from people who specialized in these support activities. Although Taylor sometimes referred to the fourth principle as "intimate, friendly cooperation between the management and the men," it is clear that he envisioned a kind of cooperation that was tightly circumscribed, with managers and staff responsible for planning and control, and workers for carrying out their directions—somewhat like masters and apprentices in the craftsman tradition. Unlike the artisan masters, however, he believed that factory management should also be conducted by specialists whose work was governed by scientific principles.

During his life, Taylor's concept of scientific management—with its staff groups, its piece-rate system, its reliance on time and motion studies, and its scientific selection and training of people—attracted widespread attention. Complete applications of the system were quite rare, but its ideas were powerful. Thousands of American managers refined and developed Taylor's concepts and adapted them to the realities of twentieth-century manufacturing.

Gradually this evolving notion of scientific management demonstrated its power and value. It replaced an older, less effective approach to management that was too often based on guesswork, rules of thumb, imitation, and tradition. Scientific management, in contrast, was based on understanding the forces governing the enterprise, on careful planning and control, and on the creation of an effective factory organization.

In the first forty years of this century, bright, well-trained, dedicated people focused their attention on new ways to manage production, and their efforts resulted in such concepts as statistical process control, and in more precise methods of planning and managing material flows. Yet like the artisan mode of management it sought to replace, the new scientific approach had certain weaknesses. These weaknesses lay primarily in its separation of managers (with their staffs) from workers, and in its focus on static efficiency (a "one best way" that was seldom revised) and the consequent lack of attention to continual improvement in worker skills and organizational capabilities. The strengths were obvious when contrasted with the shortcomings of the artisan mode; the weaknesses became obvious only much later.

Applying Science to Business: The Management of Technology

Science has had such a profound influence on every aspect of modern life that most people today regard scientific research as the wellspring for all new technology. Indeed, there are hundreds of examples in which the application of scientific knowledge resulted in inventions that led to new products, even whole new industries. But this is an incomplete picture of how scientific exploration and manufacturing technology interact. It does not properly explain, for example, the growth in the application of science to industry in the late nineteenth and early twentieth centuries.

In contrast to the current popular conception of science as being the "driver" behind technological development, in the late nineteenth century science was largely "pulled" into American factories by engineers and managers to help them solve specific problems. Their difficulties in meeting increasingly stringent customer and production needs led them to search for a more systematic understanding of products, manufacturing processes, and materials. This harnessing and application of science occurred first in the food and materials-processing industries, where chemistry and physics were applied to achieve more accurate measurements, better tests, and more accurate identification of product properties. The use of science to develop new and improved products and processes came only much later.

Led by the large firms in the chemical and electrical industries, such as G.E., Du Pont, AT&T, Eastman Kodak, and Westinghouse, many American firms began to conduct industrial research and development in the early part of this century. Technological developments were no longer regarded as spontaneous, fortuitous events that occurred through the genius of the lone inventor. Like Taylor on the shop floor, the engineer-managers that guided these companies believed that systematic investigation and the focused application of knowledge could result in better products and processes. Just like production, technological development could be—and needed to be—managed.

Themes in Technology Management
The approach to the management of science and technology that emerged in leading U.S. companies exhibited several common themes. Four of them (summarized in Table 2-2) were particularly important:

Continual Improvement in Small Steps. The work of the laboratories and engineering departments in the late nineteenth and early twentieth centuries was grounded in the assumption that progress

Table 2-2   Themes in the Management of Technology in Early Twentieth-Century American Enterprise

Theme	Factors Influencing its Development
Technological development is evolutionary; progress occurs in small steps.	Industrial labs regarded as an aid to practical problem solving; dependent on the training and experience of supervisors and middle managers
A close and intimate interaction between laboratory work and commercial problems (in plant or market) is essential.	Commercial needs determine the research agenda; orientation of R & D personnel to practical affairs
Product and process innovation are intimately related; internal development of equipment is imperative for success.	Origins in chemical and electrical industries; existing equipment considered always improvable
Progress occurs through organized effort; teamwork and collaboration across functional boundaries are critical.	Complexity of products; systemic and integrative nature of innovation

in technology occurred primarily through continual improvement, through small steps forward achieved with painstaking effort. George Eastman based the research at Eastman Kodak on that principle:

> I have come to think that the maintenance of a lead in the apparatus trade will depend greatly upon a rapid succession of changes and improvements, and with that aim in view, I propose to organize the Experimental Department in the Camera Works and raise it to a high degree of efficiency. If we can get out improved goods every year nobody will be able to get out original goods the same as we do.[4]

This emphasis on continual improvement contrasts sharply with a research approach that is based on the expectation of infrequent major breakthroughs.[5]

Commercial Needs Establish the Agenda. Part of the explanation for this belief in the power of continual innovation in small steps lay in that era's second principle of technology management: the close connection between science and practice. Science was brought into business by people who understood its potential, but whose orientation was commercial and whose motive was the desire to solve practical problems. The idea was to harness science, to bring it under control for practical ends. Moreover, success was not a once-and-for-all condition; active competition required ongoing improvements.

Rooting industrial R & D firmly in the problems of factories and customers had a profound influence on its management, even after central research laboratories were established. Both general managers and managers of research shared a strong desire to turn science into practical products and processes, to make it useful and commercially valuable. This was evident in America's very first industrial research laboratory, established by Thomas Edison.[6] By temperament and background, Edison was at home in the world of commerce, and from the beginning his laboratory's purpose was to create inventions with commercial appeal. Although Edison has gone down in folklore as the inventor-genius (in his new laboratory's first major effort, electric lighting, he did indeed develop patentable inventions), he was also intensely practical. He conducted very careful studies of potential demand, and guided the scientific work with specific commercial targets (e.g., the price of electric light had to be equivalent to the price of gas light).

Close Linkage between Product and Process Innovation. In those industries where research initially took root and flourished—such as in the food products, chemical, and electrical equipment industries—products and processes were tightly linked: product advances depended on parallel advances in production processes. Internal development of equipment was often essential, in fact, because it was not available from outside suppliers. Moreover, the entrepreneurs who exploited opportunities in these new businesses saw the advantages available to those who developed their own equipment. Thus, Armco Steel developed the first continuous hot-rolling process for steel sheet, and Thomas Edison not only developed the electric light but also set up a company to make the equipment (which he, of course, had invented) for generating electric power, and other companies to distribute that power.

Teamwork and Cross-functional Collaboration. Innovation in these same industries was based on a level of scientific knowledge that was quite unlike anything achieved before. New products, such as electric lighting and the telephone, had consequences that extended far beyond the confines of a company's laboratory or factory. Interactions across functional boundaries were both essential and extensive. The task of integration was carried out by a new group—the research and development department—whose role was not only to supervise the R & D work but also to provide critical links both with the other functional areas of the business and with outside organizations that were pursuing related work.

These four themes characterize an approach to linking science with business that seems to have been tremendously effective. Comparing the development of American industry with that in Great Britain and France shows that it was not simply the technology itself but the way in which it was managed and applied that determined commercial success. By the 1920s and 1930s, leading U.S. firms had enlisted large numbers of scientifically trained people, whose work significantly increased the technical sophistication of their products and processes. The forces that would separate R & D activity from the rest of the business and downplay the importance of continual improvement and cumulative progress, that would enshrine technological breakthroughs as the primary objective and state-of-the-art science as the way to get there—these were present in the 1920s and 1930s but their impact was only dimly felt. For most of the years from 1900 up to 1940, industrial research activity was firmly grounded in practical realities and managed according to the principles and themes outlined here.

Production and Technology in Action: The Experience of World War II

The growing might of American industry in the first half of this century confirmed the potency of the marriage of the artisan and scientific mentalities: when the skills and value system, the patience and discipline, the emphasis on quality and direct experience, and the long-term perspective of the old-world craftsman were combined with the power of science and the scientific method, the insight and willingness to change established procedures that spring from careful analysis, and the new approaches for organizing and controlling large numbers of people, something more effective than either was created. The industrial entrepreneurs who founded, or directed the early growth of, many of America's premier manufacturing companies at the juncture of the nineteenth and twentieth centuries were, in one sense, uniquely qualified to effect this marriage. Many, like Mesta's Lorenz Iversen and William Knudsen (who became president of General Motors), were immigrants whose training included both apprenticeships in European workshops and formal education in engineering. Others, such as Henry Ford, had assimilated the craftsman mentality through parents or mentors who had been raised in artisan traditions.

By thinking creatively and systematically about factory work—within the context of a coherent and unswerving philosophy of business behavior, however—they were able to create organizations whose capabilities far outstripped those that preceded them. Consider Henry Ford's account of the process flow governing the production of his Model T:

> Our system consists of planning the methods of doing the work as well as the work. . . . Our aim is always to arrange the material and machinery and to simplify the operation so that practically no orders are necessary. . . . Our finished inventory is all in transit. So is most of our raw material inventory. . . . Our production cycle is about eighty-one hours from the mine to the finished machine in

the freight car, or three days and nine hours instead of the fourteen days which we used to think was record breaking. . . . Let us say one of our ore boats docks at Fordson at 8:00 a.m. on Monday. . . . minutes after the boat is docked, its cargo will be moving toward the High Line and become part of the charge for the blast furnace. By noon Tuesday, the ore has been reduced to iron, mixed with other iron in the foundry cupolas, and cast. Thereupon follow fifty-eight operations which are performed in fifty-five minutes. By 3 o'clock in the afternoon the motor has been finished and tested and started off in a freight car to a branch for assembly into a finished car. Say that it reaches the branch plant so that it may be put into the assembly line at 8 o'clock Wednesday morning. By noon the car will be on the road in the possession of its owner.[7]

In this light, it is no wonder that Taiichi Ohno, architect of Toyota's famed "just-in-time" production system, once remarked that "if [the young] Henry Ford were alive today, I am positive that he would have done what we did."[8]

There are numerous other examples of the manufacturing and technological capabilities that this marriage of old and new created, but there is no better example, and there was no better test of those capabilities, than their application in World War II. When the world went to war in 1939, there was no doubt that U.S. manufacturers were capable of producing fairly standardized products in high volume; firms like Ford, Singer, Du Pont, and AT&T had become masters of mass production. But under wartime conditions the production systems in the United States were called on to produce high volumes of products that were simultaneously undergoing rapid technological change. To add to the challenge, firms faced severe limits on resources and had to operate under tight schedules.

In short, war production pushed the American production system to its limits. The war revealed that the evolution of a management approach that combined scientific management with artisan values and skills was capable of performance that spelled the difference between victory and defeat. It was the epitome of world-class manufacturing. The production of guns and aircraft provides excellent illustrations.

The Production of Guns: From Handcraft to High-volume Manufacturing
When the U.S. auto industry shifted to wartime production, many of its plants and firms focused on familiar products such as trucks

and jeeps, and related products such as tanks. It was not surprising that the world's largest auto industry could turn out large numbers of such items. What was remarkable was the impact of putting the auto industry's skills to work on products that previously had been manufactured in very small volumes, such as guns. It was in such activities that the strengths of the American production system, and the principles on which it was based, were most evident. Consider the following examples:[9]

- Saginaw Steering Gear (a GM subsidiary) took on the task of making machine guns for the army. The original contract called for the following schedule:

Date	Amount
Dec. 1941	1
Jan. 1942	40
Feb. 1942	80
Mar. 1942	160
Total	281

  The site for the new plant was not chosen until November of 1940, and the building's masonry was not finished until early 1941. The first gun came off the line in March of 1941; by March of 1942, Saginaw had produced not 281, but 28,728 machine guns.

- The Swiss-designed Oerlikon gun, the best antiaircraft gun in the world in 1940, was licensed by the British and brought to the United States for production. Engineers at Pontiac not only developed a process capable of producing the gun in high volume; they also introduced several design changes to make the gun easier to produce and use. Changes in design continued throughout the time the gun was in production. Some were introduced to reduce cost and simplify processing, but some of the changes added new features and increased the gun's effectiveness:
  - Cocking the gun was initially done by three people pulling on a rope attached to the barrel. The American engineers designed a new hand-cocking device that allowed one operator to cock the gun much faster and with less risk of accident.
  - As originally designed the Oerlikon gun used a very elegant

but complex mechanism to cushion the barrel of the gun against recoil after firing. This mechanism required 290 separate machining and finishing operations to manufacture. The Pontiac engineers developed a new mechanism that not only cut out 150 of those operations but also made the remaining operations easier to do.

- The Springfield Arsenal needed vast numbers of rifles and called on Hank Krueger, founder of the Ex-Cell-O Corporation and a well known Detroit machine toolmaker, for assistance. One of Krueger's most famous projects was the automatic chambering machine. The standard method for machining the cartridge chambers in rifle barrels involved many tedious operations; output for a skilled machinist averaged about four to five per hour. After spending time in the plant watching the machinists work and discussing the problem with them, Krueger returned to his plant and went to work. Working with several skilled engineers and machinists, he took the project from rough sketches to detailed drawings to wooden models and finally to the Krueger Vertical Automatic Chambering Machine in just four months. On the day it was finished the chief of Army Ordnance arrived at Krueger's shop with a load of rifle barrels; the first ten pieces (a full load) went through the machine without a problem and came out perfect. The effect was to increase output per operator by a factor of 10.

In each of these examples the power of modern tools of analysis and modern production concepts is evident. Standardization and simplification of design, the use of detailed drawings, breaking complex processes down into more manageable ones, organizing straight-line flows of materials, careful analysis of methods—these approaches allowed for dramatic improvements in output and productivity. The new concepts in statistical process control, in combination with better engineering methods, produced significant advances in reliability and quality.

Yet by themselves, these modern analytical approaches cannot account for everything that happened. These powerful tools were employed and directed by people who brought a personal philosophy and experience rooted in the artisan mode of production. Perhaps no one better illustrates what could happen when the old and the new were combined than Ex-Cell-O's Hank Krueger. Although steeped in the practices and precepts of modern high-volume production, and valuing modern tools of analysis, Krueger was above all else a crafts-man. He looked at designs for new machines from the vantage point of the shop floor, and he drew upon the experience of the people there. Moreover, he brought to his work an old-world commitment to excellence in *Technik*, and particularly in design, that was a hall-mark of the artisan mode of production.

The most striking thing about these examples is probably the vast increases in production volume that were achieved. But it is impor-tant to note that product designs were also undergoing constant change. Moreover, what was seen at Saginaw and Pontiac was not a strikingly new approach but the application of skills, procedures, concepts, and capabilities that had been built up over many years. The mastery of production displayed under wartime pressure was what made the U.S. auto industry, and its associated tool builders and machinery makers, preeminent in the world: systematic manage-ment, individual creativity, sophisticated engineering analysis, and the relentless pursuit of improvement.

The Challenge of Aircraft Production

Success in the production of armaments was a triumph of proven methods of engineering and management, within the context of con-tinual refinement of rather stable designs. The triumph in aircraft design and production, on the other hand, required that science be employed to achieve significant and rapid advances in product tech-nology and high volume production at the same time.[10] It is useful to keep in mind that in 1940 the U.S. aircraft industry was a fledg-ling. When President Roosevelt stated before Congress that the country would produce 50,000 airplanes in two years (this in May 1940), the industry was stunned. Total production of all types of aircraft had amounted to 5,851 during 1939. What Roosevelt de-manded was a fivefold expansion of capacity in an industry at the leading edge of technology.

From its earliest beginnings the aircraft business had been science based and R & D intensive—dominated by people like David Doug-las, William Boeing, Jack Northrop, and others who combined prac-tical experience with a fairly high level of formal scientific and engi-neering training. Douglas was trained at MIT, while Phil Johnson and Clairmont Egtvedt, trained at the University of Washington's engineering school, were the pioneering technical brains behind Boeing's success.

Advances in the aircraft industry rested on the application of the latest scientific developments in aerodynamics, in engine and control systems design, and in new materials. Improvements in airplane performance were dependent on improvements in manufacturing processes; Northrop's heliarc welding process for stainless steel and magnesium is but one example. World War II greatly accelerated and expanded the demands placed upon America's aircraft manufacturers. Consider, for example, the following problems that had to be dealt with—under continual pressure for output:

1. Solving the puzzle of compressibility (the behavior of air, which, at a certain speed, alternates between suction and pressure);
2. Creating synthetic rubber that would not freeze in the stratosphere;
3. Heating and pressurizing the fuel lines, pumps, etc., so that they would operate as at sea level;
4. Developing alloys that could handle white-hot exhaust gases while operating in freezing temperatures; and
5. Learning how to arm and protect a plane, yet get it high enough and fast enough to fight.

In meeting these challenges, the industry demonstrated not only the quality of its technical skills but also the effectiveness of its technology management. No example better illustrates the importance of evolutionary development, the close links between science and practice, the connections between process and product innovation, and the necessity for collaboration across discipline boundaries than the design and production of the Mustang fighter.

In 1940 the British were desperate for a new fighter plane and asked North American Aviation to supply them with an existing American plane. The company declined because the design of that fighter was already obsolete (well behind, for example, the famous Japanese Zero fighter plane that was just being introduced) but said it would design and build a new plane. The British agreed but asked for delivery of the new design in four months. North American went to work. In spite of the time pressure they used a new "laminar flow" concept in the design of the wing, and mathematical techniques to develop streamlined contours. Everyone worked overtime; bureaucracy went by the boards—things were informal and loosely structured. The result was a new plane, the Mustang, that was ready to fly in 100 days. (This was a prototype; the production version took another few weeks.) Similarly, a squadron of Grumman Hellcats, which changed air combat in the Pacific virtually overnight in 1943, was delivered to the U.S.S. *Essex* only seven months after the initial flight of the first prototype.

As the conditions of the war changed, planes like the Mustang were modified to meet new needs. Some planes were transformed to meet objectives and missions that had not been previously envisioned. Others maintained their original mission but went through evolutionary changes to improve performance, or to incorporate new equipment. In the case of the Mustang, innovation continued throughout the life of the plane. Through several generations of changes in fuselage, engine, cockpit, and controls, the plane improved until at the end of the war it was judged to be "probably the best all-around single-seat piston-engined fighter to be employed by any of the combatants."[11]

The production of aircraft during the war confronted managers with a classic dilemma: how to produce high performance products based on innovative designs at high volumes in a short period of time. The test was to design not only new kinds of aircraft but a new kind of production system as well—a system so powerful that housewives, blind men, grandparents, and teenagers who had never entered a factory or touched an airplane were able to build better planes, faster than they had ever been built before. Convair's experience with the B-24 illustrates some of the methods used and suggests the wealth of production and technical expertise on which the manufacturers could draw:

1. Production engineering used techniques to reduce the number of parts, so as to simplify assembly by novices.
2. Production control developed systems for timing the arrival of over 500,000 parts, subsystems, and systems for final assembly—without computers.
3. Engineers continued to improve the design of tools, machinery, jigs, fixtures, and so forth; deburring machines were developed that smoothed 982 rivet holes in five seconds—a huge saving in time and people.
4. Manufacturing people used suggestion systems for workers and supervisors to get ideas for saving time and effort; they devised kitting systems and myriad methods improvements (simple fixtures like a wiring board that made assembly and soldering of complex wire harnesses a simple task).

In 1943 it took 40,000 labor-hours to build a B-24; in 1945, after all these improvements and changes, it took 8,000. And this in the face of myriad design changes introduced to improve the plane's performance.

These problems were not solved by old-world skill and ingenuity alone—although there was plenty of that around—but also by the cooperative efforts of thousands of people. Sophisticated mathematics, aeronautics, materials science, physics, and so forth, in combination with mechanical, aeronautical, and electrical engineering, were organized and managed using procedures and systems of control that ensured high precision in an atmosphere that fostered creativity. In a real sense, production of thousands of increasingly sophisticated aircraft in a few short years during World War II put to the test the technological and manufacturing capabilities that had been created in the United States during the first forty years of this century. They passed with flying colors.

Manufacturing in the Postwar Era

At the end of World War II, U.S. manufacturing was preeminent in the world, not only because of the destruction in Japan and Europe but also because of the power of the management systems and capabilities it had developed. Acknowledgment of that preeminence came in many forms, but in retrospect the most telling was the reception that U.S. managers and engineers received in Japan shortly after the war ended. American know-how in manufacturing and technology management was the subject of intensive study by a whole generation of Japanese managers.

In programs organized by the U.S. occupation authorities, American engineers taught courses on production management, statistical quality control, and industrial engineering. What these instructors tried to do was teach what was then regarded as "best practice" in manufacturing management. There was, as we would expect, a healthy dose of modern methods and tools of analysis: statistics, cost systems, work standards, scheduling, planning, and so forth. But as we might also expect, given the marriage of artisan values and scientific management that characterized U.S. manufacturing up to this time, there was strong emphasis on the need for consistency and personal leadership, as well as on the importance of fostering ingenuity and continual improvement.[12]

Americans today often comment, with a mixture of amusement and envy, on the extent to which Japanese companies rally around a central, compelling vision or corporate philosophy, often one extolling the importance of high quality. The unifying power of such constancy of purpose is regarded as admirable—but very non-American. Yet these early seminars spent considerable time emphasizing the value of such enduring statements of purpose, using as one example that of the founder of Newport News Shipyard:

> We shall build good ships here.
>> At a profit, if we can,
>> At a loss, if we must,
>>> But always good ships.

The lesson drawn from this was that "the primary objective of the company is to put the quality of the product ahead of every other consideration. A profit or loss notwithstanding, the emphasis will always be on quality."[13] About 15 percent of the content of the flagship eight-week "CCS" course, in fact, dealt with quality control.

Years later, M. Matsushita, by then Chairman of Matsushita Electric, recalled proudly that when the course's American teachers asked if any of the Japanese companies represented had this kind of formal company philosophy, his was the only one that did. Many of the others immediately set out to copy and exploit this "very non-American" idea.

The basic approach advocated by the instructors in the Japanese courses is illustrated in one of the textbooks they used. In his 1946 book, *Fundamentals of Successful Manufacturing*, George Hyde emphasized classic industrial engineering disciplines, including job descriptions, job analysis, procedures for shop-floor control, and scheduling. But he also advocated the following principles:

1. Have product designers and process developers work closely together;
2. Pay careful attention to appearance in design;
3. Develop a policy of never ending improvement in the product, augmented by research and good lab facilities; have a program of new product development;
4. Stay flexible; never establish something with the idea that it is permanent; anything can be improved;
5. On mechanization: think of tools and mechanization as means of employing labor to better advantage;

6. Be precise in process design and definition; use process charts; record the know-how; balance your lines;
7. Be a bear about cleanliness; don't accept dirt as a way of life.[14]

One Japanese participant remarked at the time that Japanese management up to then had been "all Art of Management, and no Science of Management."[15] The result of this training process, however, was not to replace the old with the new, but rather to combine the two. Thus, in a sense, Japanese industry effected in the 1950s the marriage that American industry had accomplished a generation or two earlier.

Managed with these same principles, a large number of American firms like Mesta Machine enjoyed great success in the immediate postwar period. Markets were growing, their production systems were well designed and well managed, and new technology promised whole new areas of opportunity. Yet within twenty-five years many of these once vigorous manufacturers became curiously inept, with facilities, equipment, and systems that were not up to the rigors of international competition. By the 1970s Mesta Machine was an organization that had forgotten what had made it great. As new managers took over who had little direct experience with the company's customers, work force or technology, as the internal development and acquisition of new manufacturing capabilities diminished, as staff groups gained power while line organizations withered, and as a once leading-edge technical organization became second-rate, Mesta Machine's manufacturing prowess became a thing of the past.

What happened at Mesta Machine was, in microcosm, what happened to U.S. manufacturing in general. In reflecting on its slow but steady erosion, World War II now appears to be a watershed. On the production side, the very success of the war effort became the enemy of further progress. It was as if, having apparently mastered manufacturing, Americans could go on to worry about other things, safe in the assumption that production would continue as vigorous and robust as before.

When in 1958 John Kenneth Galbraith observed in his book *The Affluent Society* that America had "solved the problem of production," he reflected an opinion widely shared. To be sure, no company president stood up and announced that production, having been "solved," would henceforth no longer receive the time, attention, and resources it had once enjoyed. But in practice that is what happened. The squeaking wheels in marketing, finance, and government relations occupied more and more of the management agenda as the decades of the 1950s and 1960s wore on. It is not surprising, therefore, that many companies (particularly the larger ones) looked to people with those kinds of backgrounds and skills when selecting senior managers.[16] Seeing the upward mobility in those functions, aggressive younger managers increasingly favored them as well.

This tendency for manufacturing to become of secondary concern was not simply a matter of benign neglect. The decisions that firms make when trying to deal with problems of marketing and finance have an impact on manufacturing and the kinds of capabilities that the manufacturing organization is required to develop. As companies diversified and moved increasingly to organizational structures employing the profit-center concept as the principal means of controlling diverse entities, senior managers came to rely more and more on periodic financial reports and capital appropriation procedures for their information about the state of individual businesses. Financial measures became the principal means of monitoring manufacturing performance, identifying problems, and pursuing opportunities for growth. In the hands of an executive who had little understanding of either operations or science, a control system dominated by such financial measures as return on investment (ROI) could easily lead to a failure to invest in equipment, worker capabilities, or new technology. Likewise, developing new products without taking into account their manufacturability or the diversity of the demands they placed on manufacturing often led to unfocused facilities that tried to be "jacks of all trades"—and ended up being masters of none.

On the technology side, America's success in World War II was once again its own worst enemy. What had attracted attention during the war, both in industry and in Washington, was not so much our success in making thousands of small technical improvements that cumulatively bolstered the production of conventional war equipment like airplanes and guns but rather our success in grand large-scale projects: the Manhattan Project to develop the atomic bomb, the development of radar, the electronic computer, and jet propulsion. The dramatic nature of these efforts and the prestige accorded those who worked on them—together with tight central direction of their planning, execution, and funding—was seductive to companies. Only later did they discover that this encouraged a distancing of industrial research from practice—from markets, from factories, and from the base of experience that they represented. A similar distancing occurred in engineering schools at about the same time. Influenced by the highly publicized achievements of "big science,'' they became more and more theoretical in their orientation.[17]

With focused, large scale research projects as their model, and with government funding as an inducement, many firms established central R & D labs during the war and in the decade following. These labs were central only in terms of the amount of resources lavished on them; they were generally geographically separate from the rest of the organization, and came to be staffed with scientists whose allegiance was primarily to their scientific disciplines rather than to market opportunities or organizational needs. As one example, GM's research laboratory was first headed by Charles Kettering, a renowned entrepreneur, inventor, engineer, and hands-on researcher. Brilliant as he was, Kettering's work was closely tied to the business; he lived and breathed the automotive industry. When Kettering retired in 1947 he was replaced by Charles McCuen, an outstanding automotive engineer who had grown up in the Oldsmobile organization. In 1955, however, the pattern was broken. McCuen retired and was replaced by Lawrence Hafstad, an eminent nuclear scientist who had never before been associated with an automotive company.

This sequence illustrates the evolution of industrial research that was occurring in many American companies. Staffed initially by people who understood the technology from the ground up, and who could provide a source of ideas and assistance closely linked to market needs, industrial research was passed on to people without close ties to the product, the customer, or the business but who had good credentials in the scientific community and inclinations toward ''big science.'' Such people and such organizations were inclined to work on breakthrough projects in a laboratory setting, rather than on incremental improvements or refinements of existing concepts in the factory. Thus, the emphasis on continual improvement that had characterized the early industrial research efforts was gradually supplanted with a belief in, and a reliance on, a few carefully chosen great leaps forward in technology. It is not surprising in this context that the practical and more mundane problems of improving production processes—how to make products faster, more precise, more reliable, and more effective—received less and less attention in companies as well as professional schools, while major product innovation received more and more.

The competitive environment that evolved after the war also reinforced this emphasis on marketing, finance, and big science. With few foreign competitors, relatively strong demand (both domestically and in foreign markets) for American manufacturers' products, and ample manufacturing capacity after the war, and encouraged by national industrial unions and oligopoly-like industry structures, manufacturing practices tended to become standardized across companies in many industries. This allowed top managers to confine their competitive imagination and energy to marketing, new product development, control, and acquisitions. In that context, the technology and manufacturing legacy from the prewar era was sufficient to ensure success, at least for a while.

The Artisan and the Engineer: Two Cultures in Conflict

As the world filled with strong international competitors, however, the failure to cultivate and exploit strong connections between science and practice and the neglect of manufacturing capabilities spelled disaster. The key to American preeminence had been the meshing of the skills and traditions of the craftsman with the thought process of the scientist, the combination of experience and analysis, the mixture of systematic procedure and individual artistry. Harnessing art and science together was powerful because the two traditions helped to offset the weaknesses inherent in each.

That balance was a precarious one, however. Each side of it had a certain disdain for the other: people raised in the craftsman tradition tend to be deeply suspicious of analyses conducted by someone who "doesn't know the territory," and their skills, painfully developed through long experience, can be devalued by scientific advances that obsolete those skills. The scientist-analyst, on the other hand, tends to be intolerant of those who have "know-how" but not "know-why," viewing them as prisoners of tradition. About the only way an organization can maintain this uneasy alliance is through a central core of people who have been trained in both. Once this binding core is lost, and as one side begins to gain power over the other, no countervailing force is likely to assert itself to reestablish that balance.

This is what happened in the United States after World War II. As the generation of managers who had maintained that balance in their companies by having their feet in both camps slowly passed from the scene, American manufacturing gradually lost touch with its old-world roots. Under pressure to respond to new marketing and financial concerns and without people who understood the central role of the artisan traditions, the necessity of continual improvement, or the importance of technical leadership through in-house process development, manufacturing decisions were increasingly driven solely by financial or marketing concerns. The management approaches that gained favor were those that seemed to promise quick, measurable financial results and the maximum amount of management control. So it was that "hard" analytical approaches—management by the numbers—slowly drove out the "soft" experience-based elements of the older system of production. Without its tempering influence, U.S. manufacturers were no longer protected from the inherent weaknesses and blind spots of scientific management.

As soon as management thinking became overly mechanistic and lost its grounding in bedrock principles—a strong and shared belief in "the right way to do things," an absolutist sense of artisan integrity—key decisions came to be the plaything of marginal analysis, with its short-term trade-offs between apparent costs and benefits. Unless one had a long-term, almost organic understanding of how people, both workers and managers, reacted to certain pressures and inducements, how relationships between suppliers and customers could deteriorate or be strengthened over time, how incremental changes in products and manufacturing processes interacted and cumulatively enhanced performance, and how competitors evolved in response to attacks or opportunities, one's analysis tended to be dominated by shorter-term considerations. The attraction of near-term profits could beguile an organization into sacrificing its long-term health (or that of its suppliers) if its managers lacked a holistic perspective, rooted in experience, that enabled them to foresee how such an action might play its way out over time. In such an environment, everything became calculatable and negotiable; therefore power shifted from those who had the most experience to those who were the cleverest at analysis, the best negotiators, the most polished presenters, the most flexible and opportunistic deal makers. Analytical and scientific skills were increasingly valued, experience and artisan skills devalued. As new-world management science replaced old-world values, manufacturing organizations lost the compass these values had provided.

Bad quality no longer was regarded as an embarrassing indictment of one's skill and integrity, to be attacked and eliminated whatever the cost, but simply as another problem to be dealt with through quick fixes: rework stations, "acceptable quality level" agreements, and warranty contracts. Relationships with suppliers of key parts or materials, formerly treated as long-term, almost familial associations, deteriorated into short-term contractual liaisons that stifled cooperation and the sense of partnership in a common struggle. Workers were no longer prized for their capabilities and loyalty but were regarded as "hourly workers," mere commodities. The object became not to train them but instead to surround and eventually eliminate them with "foolproof" systems. The analysts were astonished to find that the "fools" usually won.

These weaknesses of the scientific method were already apparent in the principles and assumptions that Taylor espoused. One of his significant contributions was the emphasis on research and experimentation. Yet he assumed that learning about production (through staff analysis) and the actual making of things (by the line organization) were separable activities: both could and should be done by specialists. This sharp distinction, between learning by staff and production by line personnel, increased the likelihood that learning only took place as a result of analysis that was divorced from hands-on experience, performed by people who were both physically and psychologically separated from the workplace. However, as application of this approach revealed, unless staff people are intimately involved in production, there are likely to be many problems (and thus many opportunities for learning) that they simply do not know about.

Taylor's heavy emphasis on the importance of embodying knowledge (art) in standards (science) and using standards to control work can act to further limit an organization. As the search for knowledge evolves into the pursuit of ever greater control, both workers (who are separated from the analysis and learning process) and knowledge specialists (who are removed from the factory floor) are likely to forget that their real objective is constant improvement in pursuit of an advantage over their company's competitors.

Even worse, when control alone becomes the objective and the development of standards the central means for achieving it, learning and improvement may be further limited by Taylor's ideal of the "one best way." A production standard that is assumed to embody the "one best way" can easily become the norm for the production organization. Instead of being just the latest in a continuing progression, the standard becomes a focal point around which performance is controlled, labor contracts are defined, and production systems designed. The risk is that the emphasis on standards may lead to a static conception of the enterprise and a kind of steady-state, by-the-book mentality.

The Challenge of World-class Competition

The great risk of a purely scientific approach to the management of production lies in the creation of a rigid, static system that stifles continual learning and the building of new capabilities. And obviously this risk is amplified by control systems that discourage experimentation, where manufacturing managers are judged on the basis of short-term financial measures of performance and where the central manufacturing task is simply to meet delivery schedules and monthly budgets. If all of one's competitors are doing the same thing, this risk may not be apparent; however, when competitors emerge who use superior manufacturing capability as a competitive weapon, this risk can be transformed into a real liability. Just as over fifteen hundred years ago, the Roman army lost its effectiveness as it became more hierarchical, as its leaders were increasingly drawn from the elite on the basis of political favor rather than fighting experience, as decision making became more standardized and centralized, and as its supervisory style evolved from "follow-me" motivation to close, brutal control (including killing the messenger who brought bad news), so did American manufacturing lose its effectiveness after World War II.[18]

As many U.S. manufacturers faced up to the rigors of international competition in the late 1970s and early 1980s, they explored a variety of approaches to achieving renewed competitive vigor. Some executives sought the easy, the quick, the dramatic: new factories in new locations, new information systems, new equipment, new product designs, new procedures, new technology. Some looked in the mirror and saw the need for new managers and for new ways of managing.

Others, following the example of their new competitors, came to understand the fundamental and far-reaching changes required to create a truly world-class manufacturing organization. For these companies, the challenge was not to strike off in an entirely new direction but rather to recapture something that had been lost: to find ways to tap the great reservoir of skill, process knowledge, experience, and tradition in the manufacturing organization—in quality, in materials management, in human resources, and in technology—that originally had made them great.

A tradition of continual improvement, a commitment to technical leadership, and the integration of the mentality of the entrepreneurial craftsman with that of the careful scientist once caused "Made in the U.S.A." to be synonymous with manufacturing and technical excellence. It can do so again.

Thinking Long Term:
The Capital Investment Process

Introduction

The structure that a mature enterprise takes on at any point in time essentially represents the accumulation of a long series of prior resource allocation decisions. Opportunities to invest its limited resources arise continually, in a variety of ways, and must be acted upon by people throughout the organization. Their decisions regarding which opportunities to pursue and which to abandon, which aspects of the organization to strengthen and which to deemphasize, and how much of their assets to devote to future rather than to current needs, ultimately determine the firm's physical assets, human skills, technological capabilities, and overall competitiveness.

If these decisions are made without a coherent guiding philosophy or strategy, the organization that results will be like a stalagmite: shapeless, inefficient, and of little usefulness. If a company wants to develop in a specific direction, it must make these resource allocation decisions in an organized fashion. The major ones, of course, are generally made directly by senior managers, but there are thousands of other decisions that are too small to warrant their involvement. These are typically handled through a variety of systems, procedures, and ingrained behavior patterns—what we call the managerial infrastructure. If these systems are faulty, even though senior management decisions are made with care and purpose, the structure that results may not be the one desired. In the next three chapters we discuss some of the most important aspects of the management infrastructure, paying particular attention to its effect on an organization's manufacturing competitiveness.

No resource allocation decision is more difficult to evaluate than one that involves a proposal to invest current resources in the prospect of future returns. In resolving such issues most companies today employ some sort of formal capital budgeting system. Over time, therefore, the capital budgeting process serves to shape the facilities and equipment, as well as the skills and the capabilities, of the manufacturing organization. In this chapter we examine the central role it plays in the infrastructure that supports the development and execution of a manufacturing strategy.

Over the years scholars and practitioners have developed conceptual frameworks and analytical techniques to ensure rigor and consistency in investment decision making. Discounted cash flow analysis and other sophisticated techniques have been designed to assess the impact of various alternatives on the value of the firm. But the capital budgeting process does more than simply evaluate and select among alternatives. It also helps define projects, and influences how the organization comes to view them, thus helping to lay the foundation for later action and implementation. Finally, if it is to strengthen the firm's competitive position, it must not only generate and shape decisions in such a way that they achieve a required level of financial attractiveness; it must also spotlight and help facilitate investments that will build and sustain some type of competitive advantage. Rather than simply responding to the implied needs of a forecasted future, it should play a role in creating the future that the company desires. Otherwise, it may inadvertently foster investments that over time undermine that desired future.

We have walked through a number of old, atrociously laid out and poorly maintained factories over the past several years, and we have seen a surprising number of twenty-five-year-old machines in operation. We find it difficult to believe that the top managers of these companies have adopted a conscious strategy of competing with old equipment and run-down buildings. Nor do we ascribe all the blame for such deterioration to the current set of managers, who are desperately trying—usually with minimal success—to meet their delivery and profitability goals in the face of breakdowns, machines that can't hold tolerances, and workers who no longer care.

A variety of explanations might be offered as to why an old machine is chugging away on some plant floor, but to put them into perspective recall that it takes exactly twenty-five years to create a twenty-five-year-old machine. There is no shortcut—unless a company decides to begin with a used machine. Over that twenty-five-year period a number of investment proposals were probably studied, and well-meaning managers, at various organizational levels, must have made a series of decisions not to replace (or, worse, not even to consider replacing) that steadily aging machine. Some of the problem may lie with existing managers, but most of it lies in the capital budgeting procedures and guidelines that led them and their predecessors to accept increasingly noncompetitive facilities.

In exploring both how this might occur and how it can be avoided, we have divided this chapter into three sections. In the first, we sketch out how the capital budgeting process in most companies works today, and the theory upon which it is based. Then we present a series of three brief case histories of specific investment decisions that illustrate the way such systems often work in practice, and the problems that result. In the second section we use these case histories, as well as other examples, to identify some of the biases and blindspots in the theory that underlies most such systems. We also discuss a few of the more important issues of organization and procedure that affect the implementation of this theory. In the final section we outline an approach to capital budgeting that treats financial analysis as an element of a larger framework. This framework focuses on how a particular sequence of capital investments can both create value for customers and build an advantage over one's competitors.

The Typical Capital Budgeting Process in Operation

Whether, and how much, of one's hard-earned capital to invest in risky future opportunities is an age-old question. Over the years individuals and companies have employed a variety of ways—from intuition to formal procedures—to deal with this issue. One of the simplest and most common approaches is based on the idea of *payback*: how long does it take until the returns generated by an investment recover the amount invested? One can then compare this payback period with the expected lifetime of the investment, its riskiness, and one's financial position.

The obvious problem with this approach is that it does not consider what happens after the payback period; it is easy to construct examples in which one investment has a shorter payback than another but is clearly less attractive in a longer-term perspective. Therefore, around the turn of this century the notion of *average return on investment* began to be used in evaluating alternatives: the annual cash flows generated by the investment, averaged over some suitably long period (typically five to ten years), divided by the amount of the investment. When the income tax—and the notion of depreciation allowances to offset such taxes—began to intrude upon decision making, this approach was modified in two ways. First, the average cash was reduced by the taxes paid (adjusted to reflect an allowance for depreciation). Second, the average depreciated value of the investment over its lifetime (this usually is about half the initial investment) replaced the total investment in the denominator. The value that results from this calculation is roughly comparable to the "rate of return on book value" that became increasingly popular for measuring corporate performance during the first half of this century.

The flaws in this approach are more subtle, having to do with the fact that different patterns of cash flows can have the same average value over a period of years but some might be clearly preferable to others. Therefore, the modern theory of investment analysis based on the concept of *discounted present value* was developed and elaborated over the past fifty years. The theory is simple: a dollar received today is worth more than a dollar received at some future date. How much more depends upon the uses to which the dollar can be put. If one's only alternative is to invest the money at 5 percent interest, a dollar today is worth $1.05 after a year; if investments promising a 10 percent return are available, the comparable value is $1.10. Conversely, at a 5 percent interest rate a dollar received a year from now is worth $1 \div 1.05$, or $0.952; at a 10 percent interest rate the value is $0.909.

The extension to capital investment is straightforward: one invests a certain sum of money in the expectation of receiving a series of returns stretching into the future. Each of these returns can be translated into an equivalent amount today, and the difference between the amount invested and the sum of the discounted returns indicates whether the proposed project is more attractive than some specified alternative use of the funds. Estimates of several items are required to complete this calculation: the size of the anticipated investment, the amount and timing of the resulting cash flows, and the rate of return that could be realized if the capital project were not approved and the funds were directed elsewhere. This last figure is generally termed the firm's hurdle rate.

The simple theory outlined above has been expanded and complicated through the incorporation of approaches for dealing with a variety of issues, such as choosing an appropriate discount rate and estimating future returns. However, the basic approach of forecasting future cash flows and discounting them to create a present value is firmly entrenched in finance textbooks,[1] and widely institutionalized in the operating procedures that companies have adopted for generating and evaluating potential investments. Although these procedures differ from company to company, they have important common elements. Taken together, these elements constitute an approach to investment decision making that we shall refer to as the modern capital budgeting paradigm.

In this paradigm, investment proposals are generated by the operating divisions or plants in a "bottom up" process. Proposals are considered on a project by project basis and are reviewed at several levels in the organization, depending on their size. Working under guidelines established by a corporate staff, the operating divisions frame their proposals in a standard format—e.g., a Capital Authorization Request (CAR), or its equivalent. Operating divisions are instructed to follow standardized procedures in estimating a CAR's revenues, costs, and cash flows, and in calculating the net present value of the future cash flows using the appropriate discount rate (which may vary depending on the type of investment). The CAR is the focal point of analysis and decision making in the typical company's capital budgeting system, and the basic theory of discounted cash flow analysis is its organizing framework.[2]

In attempting to implement this approach to capital budgeting, one usually confronts two kinds of problems: (1) the allocation of capital resources occurs in an organizational setting where information and incentives differ from division to division and from level to level, and where the way one chooses to define and analyze a given situation can have a profound influence on the outcome of the project; and (2) investment opportunities differ in a variety of ways, some of which call into question certain assumptions of the simple theory. As a result, the traditional investment decision process is subject to certain subtle but systematic biases. To illustrate the range of these problems, we now examine three representative case examples. The first concerns an investment in a new technology, the second in a new product, and the third in a new factory.

Amalgamated Metals: The Continuous Heat Treating Line
Faced with a capacity constraint in the Coated Products Group's heat-treating operation in early 1981, the manufacturing group at

Amalgamated Metals examined several options for adding capacity. After a preliminary study by the engineering staff and a series of meetings with marketing, manufacturing staff, and plant groups, the vice president of manufacturing directed the staff to draft a Capital Authorization Request for the expansion of the number 2 line's heat-treating capacity. The proposed new Continuous Heat Treating Line (CHTL) combined two novel features: a continuous flow process and a computerized control system.

The preparation of the CAR was assigned to Tom Rollins in Amalgamated's industrial engineering group. The centerpiece of the CAR was a discounted cash flow analysis of the project's financial value. This analysis (using standard forms and a computer program) was prepared under guidelines laid down by the corporate staff. Though Rollins coordinated the development of the CAR, the actual work of estimating revenues and costs was performed in different departments of the division. As the work proceeded, it became clear that major uncertainties surrounded sales volumes and profit margins.

The CHTL appeared to produce materials that had higher strength and greater consistency than was possible with the existing process, but it was unclear whether customers were willing to pay a premium for this. Although most customers expressed some interest in the new process, and a few actually encouraged Amalgamated to make the investment, they were unwilling to commit themselves to specific orders for the new material or to pay a price premium for it.

Working under a tight deadline, Rollins used estimates provided by manufacturing, marketing, and engineering, together with some of his own assumptions, to calculate the project's annual cash flows. Sales and marketing were only willing to commit to sales projections over a four-year horizon after start-up. Since the useful life of the equipment was assumed to be twenty years, Rollins extended the fourth year's sales and margin numbers through the remaining sixteen years. He excluded any benefits arising out of the new products that might be facilitated by the CHTL. He felt that it would be difficult to justify these potential benefits to the corporate staff.

Rollins's draft CAR, including the formal financial analysis, was approved by the vice president of manufacturing, but the division general manager asked for a second look. He felt that the investment's financial attractiveness (an internal rate of return of 13 percent) was not sufficient, given the degree of uncertainty attached to its profitability and sales estimates.

Rollins went back to the drawing board and came up with new

assumptions about profit margins and sales volumes. The proposal went back up the line with a more attractive set of numbers. (See Table 3-1 for the financial analysis.) Then the group vice president submitted the CAR, with a cover letter, to the Office of Financial Analysis (OFA), which reviewed all proposals before submission to the executive committee.

After reviewing the proposal, the OFA took issue with both the sales estimates and the investment figures. It felt that the former were too optimistic, and that the investment should be increased to take into account possible changes in the coating line that would probably have to be made once the CHTL came on stream. Since these changes would cause the project to fall short of the corporation's financial hurdles, a great deal of discussion ensued. In the end, the vice president of manufacturing successfully argued that changing the coating line was a decision that should be considered separately. The corporate staff toned down the revenue estimates a bit, and the proposal was sent on to the executive committee.

Table 3-1 Amalgamated Metals, Financial Analysis of CHTL Line ($ in thousands)

Year	Investment	Pretax Cash Flow	Operating Total After-Tax Cash Flow*
1	$ 7,200	$ 0	$− 7,200
2	35,200	0	− 35,200
3	36,000	0	− 36,000
4	1,600	18,080	9,440
5	0	20,480	12,240
6	0	24,160	14,080
7	0	25,840	14,920
—	—	—	—
—	—	—	—
—	—	—	—
23	0	25,840	14,920
Total investment	$80,000		
Present value at 10%			$ 26,869
Internal rate of return			15%

NOTE: Cost of capital: 10%
Depreciation: straight line
Tax rate: 50%
Depreciation life: 20 years

*After-tax CF = (Pretax CF − deprec.) (1 − tax rate) − investment + deprec.

The executive committee was primarily concerned about how customers would respond to the output from the new line. Its members had much experience with investments of this sort, and they realized that it was difficult to predict customer reaction. Within the committee the proposal was championed by an executive vice president. He argued that the new line was exactly the kind of process technology that Amalgamated needed to develop to remain a leader in its industry. Moreover, he felt that one of the most important elements of the new technology was the significant capabilities that it added to the organization, particularly in developing new products.

After lengthy discussion, his arguments carried the day. Thus, even though the project appeared marginal on financial grounds, the executive committee approved the proposal, and it was submitted to the Board of Directors. The Board approved it with very little discussion.

The continuous line was introduced in September of 1983 and came on stream in record time. However, reaction in the marketplace was neither as swift nor as positive as expected. While customers were impressed with the first products they saw off the line, most were unwilling to pay a premium for the product; initial sales revenues were therefore less than the marketing organization had anticipated.

Twelve months after the original start-up, the CHTL was operating at about fifty percent of capacity. The marketing organization had made some progress selling existing products, whose performance characteristics were widely accepted, off the new line. It had more problems, however, selling products whose performance characteristics were not as well established in the marketplace, particularly those which required customers to make changes in their own operations. Moreover, the engineering organization so far had had little success in developing new products based on the unique capabilities of the CHTL.

The managers at Amalgamated Metals followed the modern capital budgeting paradigm fairly closely. The way in which they went about it, however, raises a number of questions about both the decision-making process they followed and the quality of the project's implementation. For example, several potential advantages of the continuous line, including the value of the new products and new knowledge that could be generated with a computer-based process, were excluded from the formal analysis. In part, Rollins ignored such considerations because they were hard to quantify. But more important, the norms of the organization seemed to run against incorporating soft data into a capital authorization request. The corporate financial staff had a tendency to treat all investment proposals with skepticism, so Rollins felt that the inclusion of this kind of data in the CHTL proposal might trigger suspicion. Those doubts, he worried, might spill over to the rest of the analysis and discredit the whole proposal.

In theory one should take into account only those costs (or revenues and investments) that change as a result of the proposal being accepted. This principle sounds deceptively simple; putting it into practice is far from easy, however. For example, the corporate staff wanted to charge the project for the follow-on costs required to upgrade the coating operation, whereas manufacturing was opposed. The corporate staff argued that changes in heat treating had always been followed by investment requests in the coating lines, either to take advantage of the new opportunities it created or to correct resulting problems in the coating lines. The manufacturing organization, in order to make the CHTL investment proposal appear as attractive as possible, wanted those coating investments treated as a separate decision. We see a similar type of behavior in the next case, an investment analysis that took place at the General Foods Corporation.

General Foods: The "Super Project"

This proposal, dubbed the Super Project, called for an investment of almost $400,000 in 1967 to introduce a new instant dessert that would compete with Jell-O.[3] Capital budgeting at General Foods was quite sophisticated, employing a multiyear planning horizon, use of both payback and return on average assets as criteria, and different hurdle rates for different types of investment.

Initial analysis provided strong support for the project. It estimated a payback of less than seven years and an after-tax return on assets of over 30 percent—both well within the guidelines established for this type of investment—but raised several questions. For example, the new product would make use of an agglomerator that was also used in producing Jell-O. Since all the costs of this machine had already been fully charged off against Jell-O's revenues, no cost was assigned to its use for the new product. If, however, the proposed new dessert were charged a portion of the agglomerator's initial cost (representing the fraction of its capacity that it was expected to consume), its rate of return would be reduced below General Foods' guidelines.

One might argue that including this allocated cost would not be correct, since the money associated with purchasing the Jell-O agglomerator had already been spent and would not change if the new product were introduced. On the other hand, other new products might be developed in the future that could also use the capacity of that machine. If it were fully utilized by the new instant dessert, however, these other products would have to bear the full cost of an additional agglomerator, which might very well reduce their ROIs below General Foods' criteria. Yet these products might actually be more attractive than the Super Project if the cost of additional machine capacity were not included.

Similarly, no provision was made in the analysis for an increase in divisional overhead costs if the new product were to be introduced. There was no clear reason why overhead costs should increase (there was no plan to hire additional supervisors or managers), yet over the years overhead costs at General Foods had risen roughly proportionally with sales—and the new product was projected to increase sales. Should an increase in the overhead cost be incorporated in the analysis?

Finally, if the new product proved to be successful, it was likely to cannibalize the sales of Jell-O. Therefore, the initial analysis deducted the profit contribution that would be lost because of Jell-O's reduced sales from the profit generated by the new product. In other words, it credited the new product only for the *incremental* profits from the sales of both products. This appears plausible until one considers the possibility that one of General Foods' competitors might introduce a similar new product, even if G.F. decided not to. Such a competitive product would very likely reduce the profits of Jell-O whether or not G.F. brought out the new product. Should not G.F., therefore, evaluate the new product on the basis of its own internal profitability, and ignore the possibility of reduced Jell-O sales?

Such issues, raised both by the Super Project and the CHTL, illustrate that determining what is "relevant" depends on what the alternative is. Whether explicitly or implicitly, the evaluation of any investment proposal must be based on a comparison with what is called the *base case*: a description of what would be expected to happen to costs and revenues if the proposed investment were *not* undertaken.

At Amalgamated Metals, as is the practice at most companies, Rollins implicitly assumed that the base case was a continuation of current costs and current revenues. This avoided the need to forecast what would happen to the Coated Products Group if it did *not* invest in the CHTL. There was no consideration of a possible deterioration of Amalgamated's sales or cost position without the investment in new technology or capacity.

What is hidden by this approach is that the firm is actually comparing alternative futures. Some investments have futures that are simple and highly predictable. But if the future is more complicated, a poor definition of the base case and a narrow focus on a single project can lead to a weakened competitive position.

Carborundum: The Ceramax Capacity Decision
These issues are illustrated by a decision faced in the late 1960s by the Carborundum Corporation regarding how much and where to expand production capacity for Ceramax, a specially treated high-porosity ceramic material with remarkable filtration properties.[4] Sales of this product had been growing at over 15 percent per year, and Carborundum had reached capacity at its only manufacturing plant. Three alternatives for increasing Ceramax capacity were under consideration:

1. The low investment, minimum disruption option: add five thousand tons of capacity at the existing Lockport, N.Y., plant;
2. The lower freight cost, closer to customers option: add twelve thousand tons capacity at a renovated plant in Lebanon, Indiana (in the middle of Ceramax's largest geographic market area); and
3. The high investment, latest technology option: add twelve thousand tons capacity at a new plant in Birmingham, Alabama (the heart of the smallest, but fastest growing market).

Using modern capital budgeting techniques and a sophisticated computer simulation model to estimate market shares and growth rates, Carborundum staff members calculated the net present value of the cash flows associated with each alternative. In making these calculations, the analysts used a five-year time horizon and a discount rate of 15 percent. In addition, they calculated the present value of a base case that assumed no additional capacity would be provided anywhere. The results (summarized in Table 3–2) indicated that the cash flows from doing nothing had the highest net present value of any of the alternatives.

The fact that this financial analysis suggested that Carborundum not expand capacity for one of its most profitable and rapidly growing products puzzled top management. Note that while the analysis attempted to be "objective" ("let the numbers speak for themselves"), it was actually highly arbitrary. Consider the use of a five-year time horizon: Was it a fair way to compare major investment alternatives that have very different objectives? The Birmingham alternative, for example, was a bet on the long-term development of the southeast market. Using a five-year time horizon would seem to penalize that alternative. On the other hand, if one were to project cash flows out over ten years (a procedure that favored the Birmingham alternative) one would penalize the Lockport alternative, which was expected to reach its capacity limit within four years.

By focusing on the various expansion proposals one by one, and evaluating each over a short time period, the analysis ignored a number of the strategic aspects of the situation. Thinking through alternative scenarios involving different actions and counteractions over time would have yielded additional insight and provided a better guide to action. For example, while expanding its existing Lockport plant was the safest alternative in the sense that it required the least investment and had the lowest probability of competitive reaction, it ran the highest risk of losing Carborundum's competitive momentum. What would have happened, for example, if Carborundum had expanded at Lockport while its largest competitor built a ten-thousand-ton plant in Birmingham (saturating the demand in that region) and the southeast market continued its vigorous growth? Carborundum would soon have found itself short of capacity at Lockport and probably losing customers, with no place to put additional capacity except the north-central region, where its competitors would have become even more entrenched than they already were. How could these implications have been built into its investment decision process?

Problems with the Modern Capital Budgeting Paradigm

Compared with uninformed hunches and seat-of-the-pants intuition, the advantage of the modern capital budgeting paradigm is presum-

Table 3-2 Summary of Financial Analysis of Capacity Expansion Options for Carborundum's Ceramax Product

			Expansion Options	
	Do Nothing	Expand Lockport	New Lebanon Plant	New Birmingham Plant
Capacity addition (tons per year)	0	5,000	12,000	12,000
Investment ($ millions)	0	0.720	1.880	2.355
Present value of net cash flows at 15% ($ millions)	3.314	3.011	2.290	2.077
Present value of net cash flows plus residual value ($ millions)	4.210	4.373	4.366	4.363

SOURCE: Carborundum, Inc. (1972).

ably its objectivity and rigor. But even dispassionate, sophisticated methods require critical judgmental assumptions that often affect the result. Sometimes the correct assumption is obvious, but there are often gray areas where the choice of assumption may depend in subtle ways on the organization's view of the world.

The three case examples presented in the previous section illustrate many of the kinds of problems that companies run up against when they attempt to apply the modern theory of capital budgeting to important investment proposals. Some of these are primarily problems of implementing the theory correctly; others raise questions about the theory itself. In this section we step back from our case-by-case analysis and try to gain perspective on these various problems.

Problems of Implementation

The implementation difficulties that companies experience typically fall into two categories: those incurred because inappropriate numerical values are employed in the various calculations, and those resulting from the way the decision is processed within the organization. The former category includes such issues as the choice of the base case, the determination of the relevant costs, the incorporation of hard-to-quantify data into the calculations, and the choice of the discount rate to be used in calculating present values. The latter relates to which groups get involved in processing an investment proposal—and in which sequence—and how their interaction influences the outcome.

Choosing the Base Case. As was pointed out in the last section, one cannot begin to calculate what the relevant costs of a particular proposal are until one chooses a base case against which the costs and revenues associated with that proposal can be compared. Too many companies, in their attempt to be objective (i.e., not introduce personal judgment into the analysis), make the same error that Amalgamated Metals, General Foods, and Carborundum all did: they assume that the base case is a continuation of the status quo. But companies today are locked in fierce battles with competitors who are continually jockeying for position, introducing new products, attacking new markets, and adopting new process technologies. Therefore, the choice of a base case must reflect a company's best assessment of what it, its competitors, and its customers are likely to do if the proposal is not adopted.

If Amalgamated did not introduce the new heat-treating process and its competitors did, for example, its sales revenues would eventually be affected. Similarly, General Foods' profits from Jell-O might well be undercut by a competitive offering, whether or not the new super dessert were introduced, and Carborundum's competitors would very likely be encouraged to add additional production capacity in the mid-central and southern sales regions if Carborundum decided not to expand capacity there itself. Assuming that the status quo will continue if an investment is not made not only biases the financial evaluation against most investments; it reflects the lack of any attempt to understand competitors' strategies and likely reaction to one's decisions.

Consider, for example, the case of two firms who share the market in a price-sensitive industry. Initially, both firms employ similar production processes and have similar cost structures. Suddenly a new manufacturing process appears that, although expensive, promises to reduce variable costs substantially. Firm A, for whatever reason, rejects the investment as being insufficiently profitable, while firm B decides to purchase the new equipment.

Both firms have performed similar financial calculations to weigh the advantages of the proposed investment but, because of different cash flow and opportunity rate assumptions, have arrived at different conclusions. Both firms should be satisfied with the results. But suppose that firm B, once its new equipment is in place, decides to compete aggressively for market share by lowering prices? Its new manufacturing process, after all, makes possible lower variable costs only if it produces at a higher volume. Will firm A be able to respond? Its outdated equipment places it at a distinct competitive disadvantage. Moreover, its competitor's price reductions may so reduce A's profitability that the investment required to upgrade its facilities would look even less palatable than before. Firm A will probably lose market share, and could even be driven out of the business entirely.

One reason that companies so often become trapped in this sort of disinvestment spiral—deferred investment leading to reduced profitability, which further reduces the incentive to invest—is that unless the long-term competitive impact of a delay, or a decision not to invest, is explicitly included in the analysis, the standard present value calculation implicitly assumes that an investment is "reversible."[5] That is, if one sells an asset, it can be bought back, or an investment can be delayed with no penalty other than that contained in the discount rate. A company cannot, however, always recover lost ground quite so easily. To regain its position, it may actually have to expend far more in the way of resources than would have been necessary if the investment had been made when first proposed. As time passes, downward spirals become more and more difficult to arrest; some companies never fully recover.

This irreversibility is partly rooted in the dynamics of human organizations. Companies are not simply collections of tangible assets; they are also collections of people, interlinked by complex bonds and loyalties that reflect understandings and commitments developed over a long period of time. Included in these linkages are their employees, suppliers, customers, and communities. The bonds joining them cannot readily be turned on and off; once allowed to dissolve, they must be regrown. Forgone opportunities may be difficult to reclaim.

For this reason investment is much like a self-fulfilling prophecy: if a firm does not believe that a particular business has a promising future, it will withhold investment—and reap the future it expects. As the manager of one European chemical company put it, "No one knows that will happen over the next five to ten years, but we want to be there when it does."[6] Companies that invest tend to drive out companies that don't—no matter how sophisticated these latter companies' capital budgeting systems may be. For a while a company may delude itself into thinking that it was right not to invest because of its resulting high return on assets. The most profitable time for a company often occurs between the time it stops investing and when it goes out of business.

Assessing the Relevant Cash Flows. Once the base case has been established, one can begin to estimate the financial implications of a proposed investment, as well as the likely reaction of one's competitors to it. Our three cases illustrate several of the kinds of problems that organizations encounter when trying to do this.

Many companies appear to adopt what we shall term a "mechanistic" perspective when making projections about the future. That is, they assume that nothing will happen without an identifiable cause, and that if this cause results from a future decision, the analysis of that future decision can be decoupled from the analysis of the current decision. This kind of logic was apparent in Amalgamated's decision to separate the CHTL analysis from the follow-on investment that would be required in the coating line; it also underlay General Foods' initial decision not to attribute any cost to using the underutilized agglomerator and floor space, and not to incorporate increased overhead costs into their financial evaluation of the Super Project. Since there was no concrete proposal either to put the agglomerator capacity to alternative use or to add overhead personnel, the analysis treated such possibilities as if they were separable decisions.

As pointed out in Chapters 1 and 2, however, there is another view of the world that is based on what we call an "organic" perspective. It assumes that there is a certain inevitability to the way events generate other events within an enterprise, and that such events are reasonably predictable once the process is set in motion. Therefore, the existence of underutilized machine capacity and floor space will probably eventually motivate some manager to find an alternative use for them. Similarly, the kinds of forces that led to the need for additional overhead personnel when sales increased in the past will probably operate in the future as well, and the new dessert product's success will probably encourage other companies to introduce similar products.[7]

Incorporating Nonfinancial Considerations. Such considerations essentially require the quantification of some very qualitative factors, as well as the development of various scenarios describing how a company and its competitors are likely to evolve whether or not a proposed investment is made. But there are a number of other "soft" considerations that often must be taken into account when evaluating a proposed investment. To leave them out of the analysis simply because they are not readily quantifiable or to avoid introducing "personal judgment," clearly biases decisions against investments that are likely to have a significant impact on such important considerations as the quality of one's product, delivery speed and reliability, and the rapidity with which new products can be introduced. Notice that these are precisely the attributes of many of the new computer-assisted manufacturing technologies, such as Computer-Aided-Design/Computer-Aided Manufacturing (CAD/CAM), Flexible Manufacturing Systems (FMS), and Computer-Integrated-Manufacturing (CIM). The reluctance of many U.S. companies to adopt these new technologies, therefore, may reflect gaps in their capital budgeting processes as much as it reflects a lack of understanding of the capabilities of these technologies and the impact that they are likely to have on an organization.[8]

The same problem affects investment proposals that have major strategic implications. In such cases, however, the importance of the decision causes most companies to short-circuit their standard capital budgeting process and resolve the issue through open discussions among top managers. Although this approach makes it less likely that such strategic investments will be choked off by standard procedures because they do not meet traditional financial criteria, it tends to insulate lower levels of the organization from strategic issues, and it is highly dependent on the selection process that separates "strategic" from "nonstrategic" investments.

Unfortunately, most companies treat the choice of manufacturing technology as a nonstrategic issue. Therefore, proposals to purchase new equipment are generally required to pass through the standard capital budgeting process, as at Amalgamated Metals. But some of the new computerized manufacturing technologies are fundamentally different, in that they are likely to have a significant impact on the kind and number of products that can be produced, the tolerances that can be obtained, the speed with which products can be manufactured, and the rate at which changes in their design can be made. At the same time, they may not be able to do certain things as well as existing equipment. Therefore, although proposals to invest in such technologies may not satisfy standard financial criteria (in that it is difficult to show that investing in them is clearly superior in financial terms to retaining the existing manufacturing technology), they have the potential to change the way the manufacturing, engineering, and marketing organizations interact, and how the company as a whole interacts with its customers—that is, they can have a tremendous strategic impact. We suggest how this strategic impact can be factored into an investment analysis in the last section of this chapter.

Choosing the Opportunity-Hurdle Rate. Despite the declines in interest rates that occurred during the early 1980s, American managers do not appear to have made a corresponding reduction in the opportunity-hurdle rates they employ in their capital budgeting procedures. These rates tend to be high—often in the range of 20 to 30 percent—and there is some evidence that they are often higher for smaller investments than for large ones.[9] Going back to our case examples, remember that Carborundum was requiring an after-tax 15 percent return on investment within a five-year planning horizon, even though the company's return on equity over the preceding decade had averaged less than 10 percent. Similarly, for projects requiring new facilities for a new product, General Foods required a pre-tax return on average investment (over a ten-year planning horizon) of 40 percent. The prime interest rate during the time of both these investments was in the vicinity of 5 percent.

As a result, the hurdle rates used by many firms today bear little resemblance either to their long-term cost of capital (even after appropriate adjustment for differences in risk) or to the actual rates of return that they can reasonably expect to earn from alternative investment opportunities.[10] Three reasons are usually offered for this discrepancy. First, companies claim that a rate higher than the actual cost of capital is required to protect them against uncertainties of various sorts, such as unforeseen reductions in predicted cash throwoffs because of competitors' actions, unexpected increases in investment costs due to inflation, and "number fudging" by subordinates anxious to have a project approved for various noneconomic reasons. Second, high hurdle rates are often considered to have motivational value. Managers are thought to perform better when challenged with a difficult-to-achieve target than they would if given a lower (and more realistic) hurdle rate. Third, firms that want to raise their average ROI often try to do so by accepting only higher return projects in the future. Today's *average* ROI, therefore, becomes the *minimum* acceptable return for tomorrow's investments.

As attractive as these explanations might be to practicing managers, they make the financial theorist distinctly uneasy. The hurdle rates used by many companies appear to incorporate unreasonably large risk components. Moreover, using artificially high hurdle rates to put pressure on managers completely undermines their value as a basis for evaluating investment opportunities. For one thing, they tend to discourage investment in existing, lower margin businesses—which one knows something about—while directing it toward businesses which appear to offer higher margins but whose risks are less well understood and are therefore felt to be less difficult to overcome.

Unfortunately, as is frequently the case with arbitrary numbers that are built into a company's systems and procedures, these hurdle rates are often utilized without question. One of the authors, for example, recently spent a day visiting a well-known semiconductor manufacturer in Silicon Valley. In the morning he met with the CEO and his chief financial officer and discussed the tremendous competitive pressure that the U.S. semiconductor industry was facing from Japan. Both men argued vigorously that their Japanese competitors had a number of advantages over them, particularly a lower cost of capital (they estimated that it was less than 10 percent in Japan at that time, versus about 20 percent in the United States).[11] That afternoon the author walked around one of this company's facilities with two of its process engineers. "What's your required payback for investment in facilities?" he asked. "Six months, before tax," they responded. "Why so short?" he inquired. "Because money is tight and the company is spending almost all the new investment funds it has building a new factory."

As he compared the morning and afternoon discussions, it occurred to the author that a six-month payback before tax implied a return on investment in the vicinity of 100 percent—dwarfing the supposedly critical difference between 20 percent and 10 percent. The author also marveled at the company's willingness to spend vast amounts of money on a brand-new facility, while perfectly good old ones were being allowed to deteriorate. It was hard to accept the argument that the company was short of investment funds; the price of its stock was going up, and he suspected that the company could probably raise a lot of money if investors could anticipate a 100 percent ROI and payback within a year!

Problems with the Underlying Theory

The preceding points can all be characterized as problems of implementation, in that the modern capital budgeting paradigm will lead to correct decisions as long as the "right" numbers are incorporated into the analysis. As we have seen, however, it is often extremely difficult to decide what these numbers should be, and even experts who espouse the paradigm often disagree as to how it should be applied to actual situations—such as the three case examples summarized earlier. Moreover, the way these issues are handled in most companies imparts a narrow, nonstrategic bias to investment decisions.

There are additional difficulties with the paradigm, however, that are not so easily blamed on poor implementation. The theory itself appears to break down when attempting to deal with them. Such difficulties include the number of projects that should be evaluated simultaneously, the length of the planning horizon, and the learning content of a proposed investment. Although, as we shall show, all three issues are often interwoven, we begin by considering them separately.

Combinations of Projects. The standard capital budgeting approach, as described earlier, assumes a project-by-project analysis, each with its own CAR. Often, however, a single investment project cannot be considered separately from other projects. Some of these investments may already have been made, as in the case of General Foods' agglomerator; others may not arise until some point in the future, as with the modifications in Amalgamated's coating machine that were likely to be triggered by the new CHTL, and the follow-on facility investments that Carborundum would face after demand growth outstripped the capacity of its current expansion project.

Unfortunately, the capital budgeting paradigm does not readily accommodate these kinds of interdependencies between investment projects. Although there is no reason why several projects cannot be treated as one big project and evaluated together, as the interdependencies between projects get more numerous and complicated it is difficult to see where to stop. Taken to its logical extreme, one should combine each new project with all previous and future projects.

This, in fact, is one reason why many companies are finding it so difficult to justify the expenditure for some of the new manufacturing technologies. Each individual CAR—for a parts rationalization system, say, or a computer-aided-design system, a flexible manufacturing system, a plant floor data collection and information system, or a customer communication system—may not meet the corporate profitability criteria. The full benefits only materialize when *all* these advances are in place, just as Federal Express's overnight air parcel delivery system could only function properly after all the spokes emanating from its Memphis hub were in operation.

Choosing the Planning Horizon. As we have seen in the Carborundum case, it can be extremely difficult to compare investments having different lifetimes. When projects have similar lifetimes, present value calculations favor those with shorter payback periods; when projects have unequal lifetimes, those with longer lives will usually appear, on a present value basis, to be more attractive than those with shorter lives. On the other hand, few investments are considered to be "doomsday projects": ones for which there is no successor. One usually assumes that at the end of the current project's lifetime, another project, involving similar activities, will begin. One should therefore be careful not to focus exclusively on initial projects alone but also take into account the follow-on investments with which they will be replaced.

For example, narrow use of the present-value criterion will almost inevitably argue for expanding in place—for adding on to an existing facility rather than building an entirely new plant in a different location. Less initial investment is typically required; the risks are lower and the returns more immediate. Over the long run, however, a series of such decisions—each backed by its own impeccable logic—can lead to ponderous, outmoded facilities that are easy prey for the smaller, more modern, and better focused plants of competitors.[12]

A few years ago, for example, one U.S. manufacturer of transportation equipment was wrestling with the deteriorating condition of its home plant. This plant complex consisted of a collection of over forty separate multilevel buildings that produced a tremendous variety of low-demand items using equipment that dated back before World War II. Rather than undertaking the task of rationalizing and modernizing this complex, whose poor condition was the consequence of a series of management decisions over a long period of time, the company reluctantly closed it down.[13]

The important point here is not only that this kind of analysis may contain blind spots but that in many cases one must frame the analysis in terms of the *alternative futures* each investment proposal may create for the firm. In the case of Carborundum, one must think in terms of the alternative expansion strategies that might have been followed. Should it have planned to add capacity in several small chunks, for example, or in just a couple of big chunks? Alternatively, should it have made a large expansion initially (at Lebanon, say) and have utilized the Lockport expansion as a filler later on, or should it have pursued a more conservative strategy: adding larger increments only after the Lockport plant had been rounded out and the market had grown to the point where it could absorb larger units more easily?

Framing the investment problem in terms of alternative capacity strategies would have required that Carborundum examine several possible investment paths. For example, it should have compared compound investment possibilities, such as "Lockport now—Lebanon later" with other compound alternatives, "Lebanon now—Lockport later" over a longer time horizon.

In examining the relative merits of such alternatives, one needs to take into account not only their estimated financial consequences but also the likely competitive reaction. Pursuing the "Lockport now,

Lebanon later'' strategy, for example, might have allowed one of Carborundum's competitors to take the offensive with a major expansion. This would have been particularly dangerous if this competitor's facility incorporated the most advanced (and lowest cost) technology available. Moreover, expanding Lockport first would have led to lower sales and market share if total demand rose faster than expected. What is required is a management decision, based on a clear strategic conceptualization, about whether one investment alternative is preferable to another in terms of its impact on the long-term health and vigor of the enterprise.

Incorporating the Learning and Option Content of an Investment. One might argue that it is perfectly feasible to use the discounted present-value approach to evaluate a sequence of investment projects stretching off into the future, despite the implementation problems associated with deciding how far into the future one should project demands, prices, and costs, and how many possible investment sequences should be considered. The theory begins to crack apart, however, when such sequences facilitate learning in an organization and so create new options for later action.

To understand this better, consider a textile company that is contemplating a capacity expansion using standard equipment—another hundred looms, say, to supplement several thousand others that the company has been operating for several years. The costs of operating these new looms are well understood, the revenues to be expected from their operation are based on considerable market experience, and the capabilities required to operate them effectively are already in place. Buying them is unlikely to require anything from the company beyond the money they cost, and their operation is unlikely to provide anything beyond the revenues they generate.

Now suppose that the company is also considering spending an equivalent amount of money on an R & D project—experimenting with a new type of synthetic fiber, say. The technical and commercial potential of the new fiber is highly uncertain.

These two investments differ in fundamental ways. In fact, they are at opposite ends of an investment spectrum. Figure 3–1 displays that spectrum and identifies the major differences between the two investments. The new looms, on the left-hand side of the spectrum, represent an investment whose costs and returns are relatively certain; very little is likely to be learned from operating them. The R & D project, on the other end, represents an investment whose

Figure 3-1   A Spectrum of Investment Decisions

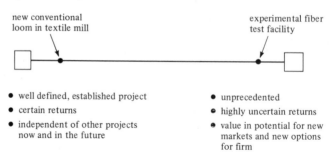

• well defined, established project	• unprecedented
• certain returns	• highly uncertain returns
• independent of other projects now and in the future	• value in potential for new markets and new options for firm

returns are highly uncertain and which has a high option content—that is, its ultimate value will depend on other investments made sometime in the future. Much might be learned from it, but it is not clear what new knowledge might be gained or how it could be employed.

The differences in the two kinds of investments suggest a need for very different methods of evaluation. It is clear, for example, that they make very different demands on the organization, generate very different kinds of business opportunities, and create value in very different ways. The experimental facility can create new knowledge and new capabilities; the new looms simply replicate existing operations and provide an increment of capacity in a well-established line of business.

The loom investment fits the assumptions of modern capital budgeting theory almost perfectly; a well-executed discounted cash flow analysis would be both easy to complete and a sound basis for decision making. But the R & D facility poses significant problems. Most important is that it deals not with uncertainty but with the unknowable. There are no clearly identifiable future cash flows. Both the degree of interaction with other projects and the nature of the risks incurred are almost impossible to estimate in advance. Most of the value of right-side projects comes either from new knowledge or from uncovering profitable opportunities for later investments.

If cash flow estimates are fuzzy and much of the potential value of the investment is contained in the new knowledge it can provide, applying modern capital budgeting procedures can be a meaningless exercise. The point is not that right-hand side investments are impervious to analysis of any sort. Many textbooks contain a variety of suggestions for analyzing such projects. But making decisions about investments in things like basic R & D should be based less on analytical techniques than on a more organic understanding of the nature of the information that might be provided and how it can be expected to lead eventually to some form of economic value.

Most companies recognize the difference between investing in pure R & D and investing in projects like the looms. Unfortunately, they often fail to realize that most investment proposals fall somewhere between these two extremes. As a result, they contain elements of both kinds of projects. The capital budgeting systems in use in most companies, however, treat everything like the looms.

Projects that generate a high degree of learning in an organization are likely to lead to revised expectations about technologies and markets, as well as to the generation of new investment proposals. Therefore, rather than assuming that a specific follow-on investment will be made at some prespecified point in the future (as with the modifications in the coating line required by Amalgamated's CHTL), consider the complications that are introduced if, at any point in the future, new investments may be generated and evaluated in the light of the information existing at that moment. Some of these options may be known when the initial investment is considered; others might not even be defined until some time has passed and after the organization has assimilated the learning provided by the initial investment.[14] In this sense, some investments resemble the ante in poker: one doesn't expect any return from the ante itself; it simply allows one into the game.

Going back to the earlier case examples, a decision by Carborundum to build a large plant incorporating the latest production technology in the small but fast growing southern region might have been expected to have a high learning and option content. The company probably would have learned greatly from that experience and could then have been able to strike off in a variety of directions. Doing nothing, on the other hand, would probably have boxed it out of existing markets and restricted its future options. Both alternatives, however, were evaluated in exactly the same way by Carborundum's capital budgeting process.

The Human Side of the Capital Budgeting Process

Up to this point we have been focusing primarily on some of the more important technical issues that companies must deal with as they decide whether or not to make an investment. But it is important to keep in mind that companies are collections of people, and how these people conceive and define an investment proposal, and then interact to move that proposal through the capital budgeting process, is at least as important as the technical manipulations that are performed during its evaluation. In the three earlier case studies, it was possible to catch glimpses of each organization's internal workings. Now, however, we need to examine these issues directly and highlight some of the pitfalls that following the traditional capital budgeting paradigm may lead a company into.

An Emphasis on Staff Analysis.   To begin, the use of complex and sophisticated analytical tools may limit the number of people who understand the assumptions on which they are based, while the apparent precision of their results may provide a false sense of security to those who do not. This sophistication, when combined with the multilevel review process usually followed, provides a strong incentive for senior managers to create and rely on a specialized staff group to scrutinize and revise proposals prior to their final review.

Interposing such a staff group may insure that financial expertise is applied, but it may also lead to significant problems in implementation. In many companies it has caused the investment process to become staff dominated: the divisions develop their own staffs (proposal advocates) to deal with the corporate staff (protectors of the purse). These staff groups often engage in an almost ritualistic mating dance. In the conflict of their parochial interests important information—in particular, a broad, general management perspective grounded in the overall needs of the organization—often gets lost.

Moreover, as we have seen in the case histories, many investment proposals have a strategic content that may not be adequately depicted in their CARs or taken properly into account in the review process. Everybody assumes that the investment's strategic implications will be understood and incorporated into the final decision when the proposal rises to the senior management level. Depending on the quality of the information available to them and the depth of their experience, senior managers may well be able to compensate in this fashion—if the proposal is attractive enough to slip through the financial screen and large enough to attract their attention. This fortunately was the case at Amalgamated Metals, where the executive vice president recognized the potential value of the new product capability that would be created by the CHTL, even though the possibility of new products had been excluded from the proposal's CAR.

Deemphasizing the Role of Operating Groups. But the failure to include such benefits (or costs) in the analysis, and the failure to involve lower levels of the organization in their examination, may also hide important implementation and coordination issues. For example, to create and exploit the CHTL's new product flexibility, the various parts of Amalgamated's organization needed to be made aware of how they could contribute to (or impede) this flexibility, and their efforts had to be coordinated. If different functional groups within an organization do not understand the purpose and nature of a proposed investment, they are not likely to develop either the necessary systems and procedures or the appropriate supporting skills required to utilize the new capabilities it provides. It is unlikely that the CHTL's increased new product potential would have materialized simply by putting it into place, and this should have been recognized early on.

A Bias toward Big Projects. Over the years, despite these problems, most companies have developed great confidence in their capital budgeting process: It is based on a well-established theory that, until recently, has not been subjected to serious criticism. It has been refined and tested over hundreds of proposals, and the obvious bugs in the system have been eliminated. Its procedures have become standardized, and people throughout the organization have become accustomed to them. It may not be a fair game, but everyone at least understands its rules. Moreover, it's the only game in town.

As a result, the very effectiveness of this process, and the degree of control that it gives top management over investment decisions, has caused many companies to gradually place more and more confidence in it. Unfortunately, in a variety of subtle ways it has encouraged in companies a preference for big projects—the kind that require the preparation of a CAR and are subjected to detailed analyses—over small projects. As we will see in later chapters, however, the secret to building world-class manufacturing capabilities often lies in making numerous little investments over a long period of time. Such investments tend to bubble up, in an entrepreneurial fashion, from lower levels in the organization. Neither senior managers nor their corporate staffs are likely to get involved in such projects; in fact, most of them are almost invisible above the factory level because they are paid for out of operating budgets. This lack of visibility, together with their reliance on the personal, subjective judgment of lower-level managers rather than on the objective, rigorous analysis that is applied to formal CARs, causes many top managers to regard them with suspicion.

As a result, many companies have come to deemphasize what has been called "vineyard economics."[15] One of the authors remembers admiring a small, terraced vineyard perched precariously on a steep slope overlooking a small valley. He asked the owner how much it would cost to duplicate the vineyard: the strong retaining walls (reaching over twenty feet in places), the irrigation and drainage systems, the stone steps and paths that had been painstakingly constructed up to and through the vineyard, the endlessly worked soil, and finally the vines themselves—carefully purchased, grafted skillfully onto existing roots, patiently nurtured over several years before producing their first fruit, and then lovingly cultivated for years thereafter. If one started with a bare hillside, the author was told, it would come to the equivalent of several million dollars.

This was astonishing, since an equivalent amount of uncultivated land could be bought in the vicinity for less than a couple of hundred thousand dollars. Nor could the owner point to any major investments that he had made in it recently. "But you see," he said, "I didn't build this all at once. My great-grandfather began it, and my grandfather and father after him; now it's my turn. Every year I cover all my expenses and make a comfortable profit. Some of my time, and a little of that profit, goes back into repairing the damage that occurs during the year and into making further improvements. I have never been in debt; I make a good living, and every year my vineyard becomes more and more valuable."

Too many companies, we fear, are encouraged by the rigor of their capital budgeting systems to focus on major investments, such as buying an existing vineyard or having one built for them, rather than on putting it together, stone by stone and vine by vine, over a long period of time. They tend to focus too much attention on the investment itself rather than on the long-term implications of that investment. For example, most companies examine investments in new production facilities very carefully. They try to cut costs here and there, explore a variety of possible modifications, and endlessly seek to justify trying to make do with existing facilities.

But a new factory doesn't actually cost very much. It only looks as if it costs a lot because all the money is spent at one time. For example, a new facility that costs $10 million to build, say, often generates over $25 million in sales revenue and $20 million in manufacturing costs each year. The materials that it consumes annually will probably be worth more than the plant itself. The cost of these materials, the value of the human resources that will be required, and the sales revenues that are at stake deserve far more attention than does the plant investment itself. Companies tend to agonize over that investment, however, because they see that money going out all at once rather than bit by bit, day after day.

Capital Investment for Competitive Advantage

In pointing out some of the blind spots and biases that characterize the capital investment process adopted by most companies today, we do not intend to imply that the solution is to abandon that process altogether and return to the kind of informal approaches that were in use a hundred years ago. Rather, we would advocate expanding the focus of capital budgeting so that it can be viewed in a larger framework.

This larger framework places the company in the context of a competitive environment and demands that new investments not only achieve a satisfactory financial return but also maintain, if not improve, the company's competitive position. It combines financial evaluation with an analysis of customer behavior, organizational capabilities, and competitive strategy. An understanding of customers gives insight into how the investment creates value, and an understanding of the new capabilities it provides is essential to assessing the competitive advantage it might lead to. A strategic analysis, on the other hand, provides insight into what must be managed well if the firm is to achieve that competitive advantage.

Customers and the Product Profile
One usually thinks of products in terms of the basic functions they perform. But in a competitive environment it is important to see the product in terms of a profile of the characteristics that influence customer choice: its performance, reliability, cost, availability, and so forth. In practice, defining the important characteristics of the product requires a careful understanding of both the firm's customers and the product's technical dimensions. The first step in analyzing how a capital investment might create a competitive advantage, therefore, is to gauge how the investment affects the company's products and capabilities.

Figure 3-2 presents a product profile analysis based on information from the Amalgamated Metals CHTL proposal. The old and new heat-treating processes are positioned along several continua relating to their technologies and impact on customers. We have also indicated the CHTL's likely future development path. It is clear from this analysis that the new process has only a modest impact on production costs, delivery, or product variety. Its advantage over the old process lies in superior material characteristics, higher reliability, and greater new-product capability. Moreover, these advantages are likely to grow over time.

The second step in this kind of competitive analysis is to determine how the new investment will affect the firm's commercial and technical capabilities. This will suggest how difficult it will be for competitors to achieve the same results. It also affects what must be managed well to get the new investment implemented effectively. In Figures 3-3 and 3-4 we divide the firm's capability into two domains—technical and commercial—and evaluate the impact of the new invest-

Figure 3-2   Investment and the Product Profile: The Continuous Heat
Treating Case

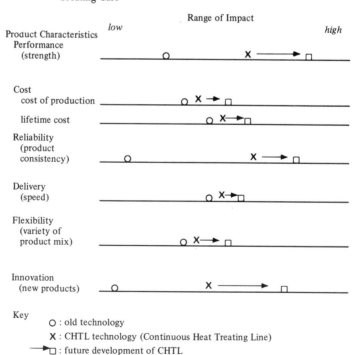

Key
O : old technology
X : CHTL technology (Continuous Heat Treating Line)
→□ : future development of CHTL

Figure 3-3   Impact of CHTL Investment on Capabilities: Technical Domain

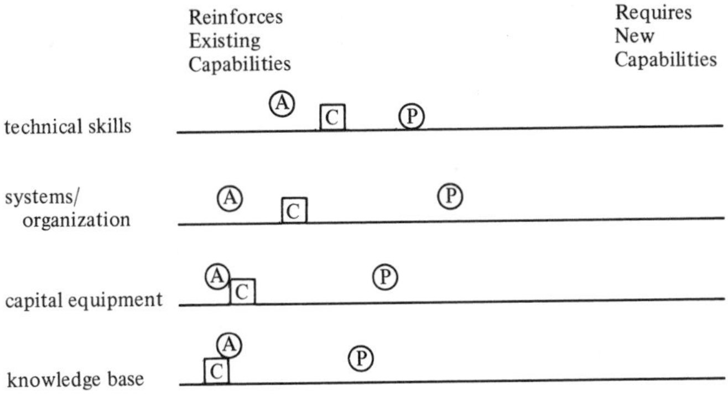

Key

Ⓐ : Amalgamated (whole firm)

ⓒ : Competitor

Ⓟ : Amalgamated (plant in which CHTL
     is to be installed)

Figure 3-4   Impact of CHTL Investment on Capabilities: Commercial Domain

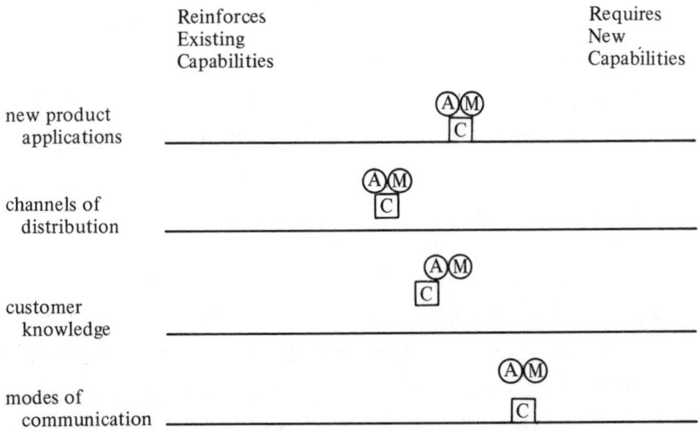

Key

Ⓐ : Amalgamated (whole firm)

ⓒ : Competitor

Ⓜ : Sales/marketing organization

ment on several dimensions within each domain. There is a continuum of effects. On the right-hand side of each continuum are those investments that are so different that they displace or disrupt established capabilities. In fact, in some instances the new investment may render established capabilities obsolete. On the left-hand side are investments that refine, build on, and strengthen established systems and capabilities.

Not only should a company take into consideration the impact of the investment on existing capabilities, it should also compare them with competitors' capabilities. Thus, in Figures 3–3 and 3–4 we look at what the CHTL would mean for different operating groups (such as the plant in which the CHTL is to be installed and the corporate sales force) within Amalgamated, as well as for its toughest competitor. Including the operating units can suggest where implementation problems might lie; looking at its toughest competitor can help it gauge how enduring any advantage provided by the CHTL might be.

In applying this framework to the CHTL, we find that the investment builds on existing capabilities in both the firm and the industry. Both Amalgamated and its competitors are in similar positions. The equipment to be used is provided by an outside vendor, and a significant base of operating knowledge and skill exists within the company. At the plant level, the CHTL's impact is somewhat different. For example, although Amalgamated has skills in software development at the corporate level, as well as some expertise in developing systems that link sensors, capital equipment, and microprocessor-based controllers, the expertise in these areas at the plant level is less extensive. Mobilizing the appropriate skills and the systems capability will therefore be a central problem in implementation.

This analysis of the CHTL's technical side suggests that Amalgamated will create little competitive advantage simply by acquiring the basic machine. Any edge it gets will rest on more subtle changes: equipment modifications, control systems, and operating practices. In the commercial domain, however, there is considerable potential for advantage. If Amalgamated exploits the new process to create new, high performance products, it will need to develop a new set of commercial capabilities. Figure 3–4 suggests that neither Amalgamated nor its competitors have the commercial skills that are likely to be required.

Whereas customers previously adjusted their designs and processes to fit the standardized specifications of the existing material, they now can request a material that has been tailored to their specific needs. This is likely to call for new skills in applications engineering and technical sales support. Moreover, Amalgamated will have to educate customers about the advantages of using customized materials. Developing such skills may create advantages that Amalgamated's competitors will find difficult to duplicate.

Integration

Working through the product profile and the investment's implications for capability development provides insight into how it might be expected to create value, what must be done to manage its implementation, and how difficult it might be for competitors to acquire similar capabilities. The firm then needs to integrate these insights to arrive at an overall assessment of the investment's attractiveness. This integration must contain three elements. First, there must be an understanding of the interaction between the technical and commercial domains, and between the firm's capabilities and its customers. It is not enough to know what new marketing capabilities or what new technical skills will be required. One must also understand how those new capabilities might interact to create additional value.

In the case of the CHTL, for example, it is clear that the ability to segment customers and create market niches will be essential to exploiting the potential of the new process. Developing new products will require, in turn, what we call "nimble" manufacturing: the ability to produce small quantities efficiently and to change product mix relatively easily and quickly. The challenge for manufacturing is to be able to react quickly to new possibilities in the marketplace and to support the new product development effort with new hardware and software.

The second element in this integration is an analysis of what the investment means for the financial health and vigor of the enterprise. This financial summary might make use of traditional approaches, including the derivation of cash flows and the calculation of paybacks, present values, and rates of return. Note, however, that the purpose of the analysis is not to calculate a final, decisive number but rather to generate insight into the financial implications of alternative courses of action. Cash flow estimates, for example, provide a useful "sanity check" on the project. Given these, one can ask questions such as (1) Given the investments required, what pattern of returns do we have to achieve to make this an attractive (or breakeven) proposition? and (2) Given what we know about the product profile and customer needs, is that pattern of returns realistic? In the Amalgamated Metals case, for example, a review of the financial calculations showed that the attractiveness of the investment depended heavily on achieving higher profit margins and customer acceptance rapidly. Because of the heavy up-front expenditures, any significant delay in revenues would render the financial returns marginal.

The third element in an integrated analysis is an examination of how the investment program fits with the strategic directions of the business and its major functional areas. Amalgamated's CHTL, for example, when combined with new process capabilities, marketing skills, applications engineering, and nimble manufacturing, would provide the foundation for a new business: creating product niches in high-performance, high-reliability materials. Whether or not its customers would buy the materials produced by the CHTL during the first three or four years of the system's life was important financially but was ultimately less important than whether this process pointed in a strategic direction that the company wanted to pursue. The concept of manufacturing strategy outlined in Chapter 1 provides a useful framework for examining this question of fit: it requires that the company decide how it wants to compete and how it wants to implement this choice through a coherent set of manufacturing structure and infrastructure decisions.

Even if Amalgamated's management had decided that the overall direction did make sense, the CHTL's impact on individual functions should have raised issues of implementation. Since the basic mission of the sales organization had been to sell high volumes of standardized products, the new investment implied significant changes. The company needed to develop a whole new set of marketing and manufacturing capabilities. As a result, both marketing and manufacturing were likely to find that they needed new people, new systems, and new functional strategies.

Conclusions and Implications

Many investment decisions involve more than simply acquiring and installing new capacity. Each of the investments considered in this chapter requires a set of supporting capabilities and may create additional opportunities beyond those that are immediately obvious. An investment proposal should therefore be viewed as part of a sequence of investments and opportunities that will take the firm down a particular strategic path. This may sound obvious, but it is all too rare in practice.

Our framework emphasizes that capital investment involves the development, nurturing, and replenishing of the firm's productive and creative capabilities. Its application, therefore, depends on a thorough understanding of the business, the way that the firm currently competes, and how it intends to compete over the longer term. But the framework also creates a language and a process that can assist general managers in communicating the firm's mission and purpose throughout their organization.

Moreover, this same framework can help each of the functional groups within an organization assess their roles in implementing the new investment. Achieving a shared understanding of the investment's purpose and requirements is essential, as it allows people in marketing, sales, manufacturing, R & D, and finance to communicate with one another and participate in the development of a holistic understanding of how the investment relates to their competitive mission. In fact, unless that competitive mission has been articulated and communicated throughout the organization, the right kinds of investments may not even come up for discussion.

| 4 |

Organizing the Manufacturing Function

Introduction

Much of the writing about manufacturing managers and management tends to focus on the success or failure of certain key decisions, such as the choice among competing process technologies, plant locations, and capital investments. As every experienced manager knows, however, a handful of "right" decisions plays only a relatively small part in making a company ultimately successful. To be effective, decisions must be interpreted by and implemented through people—people who are often geographically distant from one another, have different skills, job descriptions, educational backgrounds, career expectations, and who sometimes speak different languages. Somehow the strength, intelligence, and allegiance of this mass of diverse individuals must be harnessed and directed toward the common goals. Therefore, the most critical task confronting a senior manager is not simply to acquire the best resources and make the right decisions but to *build and operate through a purposeful organization.*

This task is particularly difficult and important for the manufacturing function, because it usually contains the great majority of the company's people. These people are largely unaware of the way their organization shapes and constrains their activities (it is said that the last thing a fish discovers is water); but as a company's strategy and manufacturing mission change, most of them will have to make some change in their job assignments and behavior if consistent priorities are to be maintained. Again and again we have found the root cause of a "manufacturing crisis" to be that a company's manufacturing policies and people—workers, supervisors, and managers—are no longer compatible with its competitive needs. Even more subtly, the manufacturing organization that attempts to coordinate them all is no longer doing its job effectively. In a sense, the manufacturing organization should be the glue that keeps manufacturing priorities in place and welds the manufacturing function into a competitive weapon.

The way manufacturing chooses to organize itself also has direct implications for the relative emphasis placed on different competitive dimensions. Certain types of organizational structures are characterized by high flexibility, others encourage efficiency and tight control, and still others promote dependability. Poorly designed organizations do not run smoothly and tend to be "accident prone," just as poorly designed machines tend to experience malfunctions that cause inefficiency and frustration. Unfortunately, problems in a company's manufacturing organization often surface at about the same time as problems in other parts of the company, and they surface in a variety of ways. For example:

• Company A, a fast-growing, high-technology company had quadrupled in size in a ten-year period. Its manufacturing organization was essentially the same at the end of that decade as before—dominated by a powerful manufacturing VP and a strong central staff—despite the fact that its product line had broadened considerably, the company was beginning to make many more of the components it had formerly purchased, and the number of plants had both increased and spread into four countries. A sluggishness and sense of lost direction began to afflict the manufacturing organization, as overhead and logistics costs soared.

• Company B operated in a market where competition was on the basis of quality and service rather than price. Its manufacturing organization was highly decentralized and adept at new product introduction and fast product mix changes. Then severe industry overcapacity and price competition caused corporate sales to level off and profits to decline for the first time in its history. Manufacturing efficiency and dependability clearly had to be improved, but there was fear of "upsetting the corporate culture."

Why did these companies' manufacturing arms get into trouble, and how much of their problems grew out of their organizational structures?

Over the past half dozen years we have observed a number of manufacturing companies implement a variety of productivity and quality improvement programs. Often, under tremendous competitive pressure, they have attempted to make major improvements simultaneously in several areas: reduced labor and material costs, lower reject rates and inventory levels, compressed production cycle times, and a more rapid rate of new product introduction. The very survival of some of these companies was in question. In almost all of them, top management was strongly behind these efforts—at least initially.

Yet many of these programs failed, often despite apparent initial success. The desired improvements came more and more grudgingly. Difficult problems and trade-offs appeared. Management support waned as the organizational costs of these programs began to outweigh their perceived benefits. Both workers and managers began to lose confidence in the new approaches; morale plummeted. Eventually, with an almost perceptible sigh of relief, they were abandoned. Different (usually more traditional) goals and approaches were reinstated, the more ambitious ones discredited, and the opportunity for major improvements lost. Why?

As we investigated these failures, as well as some of the successes that had experienced serious difficulties, we were surprised at the degree of internal resistance these campaigns had generated. They were often perceived as attacking, in fundamental ways, the basic working of the organization: its administrative processes, its approach to managerial control, its performance measurement and reward systems, its management selection and promotion system—just like the human body perceives and rejects an organ transplant that is essential to its survival. Ironically, these measurement, management development, and organizational approaches were often quite "modern," in that they were largely based on philosophies of management that became popular in the United States after World War II.

We have divided this chapter into three sections. We begin by identifying two basic principles that have pervaded recent thinking about organizational design and suggest how they have contributed to the kind of problems that many manufacturing companies are experiencing today as they try to respond to competitive pressures for vastly improved quality, productivity, and market responsiveness. We conclude this first section by describing some of the ways that companies have tried to overcome these organizational impediments. Next we look at the various roles that central manufacturing staff groups can play, and the ramifications that different roles have for personnel selection and assignments.

Decisions regarding how the manufacturing function of a company should be organized and the appropriate role and composition of the manufacturing staff cannot be made in a vacuum, of course. Therefore, in the final section we describe two polar extremes for organizing the manufacturing function, outline the different demands they place on line and staff personnel, and suggest the circumstances under which each is appropriate. We also explore how each type is affected by various forms of growth.

Modern Principles of Business Organization

The underlying principles of organizational design seem to be agreed to rather widely, whether for a manufacturing or any other type of organization. For this reason we begin this section by reviewing two of these principles and their application to a manufacturing-based company. This leads into a discussion of a few of the approaches companies are using in trying to overcome some of their negative consequences.

Divide and Conquer

The first "modern" principle is not modern at all. Julius Caesar enunciated it over two thousand years ago, and even then it was an ancient principle of warfare: Divide and Conquer. As applied to business organizations, it accepts the fact that few people can perform a wide range of tasks equally well. Therefore, specialization is necessary: the various tasks associated with running a complicated enterprise are divided up, carefully defined (through job descriptions), and parceled out to individuals or management groups.[1] The resulting allocation of responsibilities is typically formalized in an organization chart.

This principle underlay both the functionalization of business (different groups were specialized according to whether they designed, made, or sold a product) that began taking place in the United States over 100 years ago, and the separation of line activities from staff activities that began to occur at the turn of this century.[2] What is more modern is a third type of specialization, divisionalization, which swept corporate America after 1950. Divisionalization typically took place along product group, market segment, or geographic lines and reflected the fact that, as different segments of a business became more and more dissimilar, it became increasingly difficult for a single top management group to direct them all effectively. Therefore, it was necessary to push responsibility down in the organization so that those closest to a given market or region would be able to respond appropriately to its "local" needs.

This process of divisionalization both accompanied and encouraged the differentiation of tasks within companies: organization charts became more and more elaborate, responsibilities further divided, and job definitions more and more narrow. As a result, the job of monitoring and integrating all these disparate activities became progressively more difficult. Figure 4–1 suggests the complexity

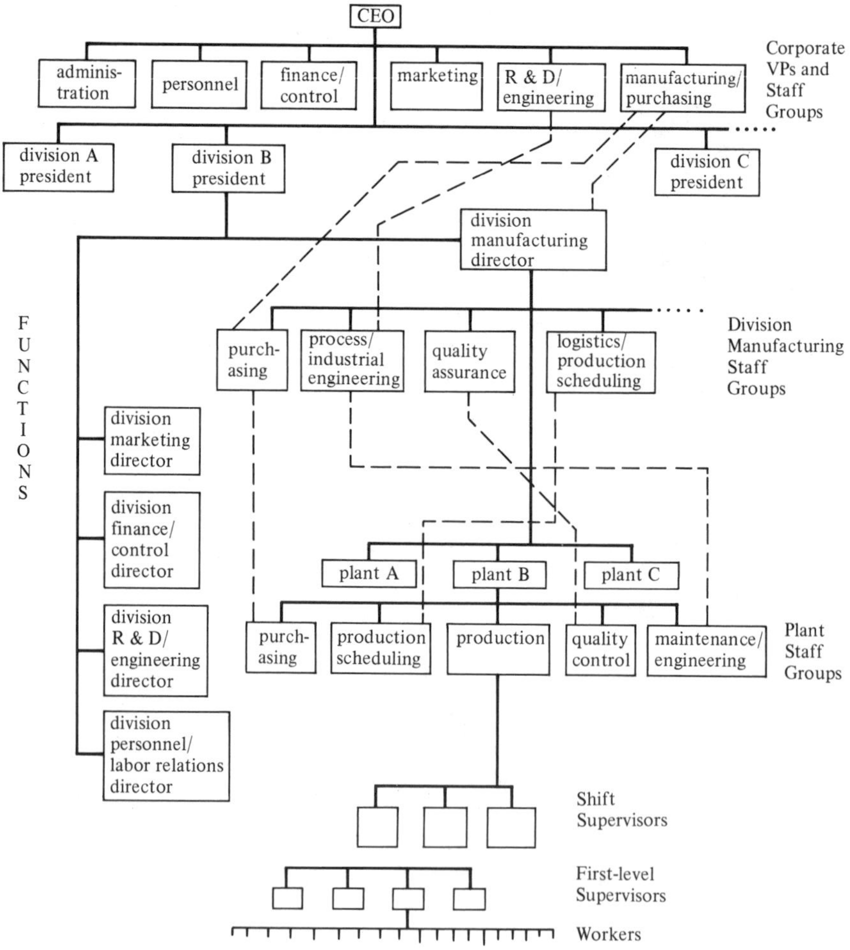

Figure 4-1   Organization Chart for a Typical U.S. Manufacturing Company

of the organization chart for a typical U.S. company that has resulted from these three trends.

At the top of each divisional manufacturing organization is a director of manufacturing (sometimes designated a division vice president) who usually has roughly equal authority—although in many companies not equal influence, status, or remuneration—to the heads of the divisional marketing, finance, control, and R & D groups. Normally the manufacturing director has a staff of specialists reporting to him or her. These specialist groups typically coordinate the activities of their counterparts at different facilities and manage the "plant network"—accumulating data about performance, evaluating and compensating managers, reviewing major capital investment and process technology decisions, and coordinating the interlinked activities of groups of plants.

Finally, and most important, we have the line activities: those that actually involve the production of goods and services in the various operating units. Each has its own staff group to support a line organization consisting of a production supervisor, one or more shift supervisors, a number of first-level supervisors, and the workers themselves—all under the direction of a plant manager.

Note that various staff groups, which contain both specialists and integrators, are often replicated at three levels in such an organization: at the corporate level, within each division, and at each plant. Moreover, there are likely to be three or more levels of management between workers and their plant manager, and five or more between them and the top corporate officer. Notice also the lack of horizontal linkages; information and control paths are almost exclusively vertical. Therefore, a worker or first-level supervisor who wants to communicate with his or her counterpart in another plant, with an engineer in the divisional R & D group, or with a salesperson has no natural channel for doing so.

Responsibility Equals Authority
The second major principle of modern organizational design is that, as far as possible, a manager's *responsibility* should equal his or her *authority*. That is, a management group entrusted with the responsibility for a certain task should have the authority to take the steps and commit the resources necessary to carry it out. Moreover, the accomplishment of this task should be measurable. Since it would not be fair to measure the group's performance along dimensions over which its management has little or no control, customized per-

formance measures must usually be developed. The narrower the task, the narrower the measure used, and usually the shorter the time frame employed.

While this principle seems "fair," firms often encounter almost intractable problems putting it into practice. Suppose, as is often the case, a certain activity (the manufacture of a product, say) involves several organizational units that have different areas of specialization and share certain resources. Should one unit be given primary responsibility yet not have complete authority? Alternatively, should responsibility and authority be divided up as best as possible, with a corporate staff group given oversight responsibility (but limited authority) over it?

Further, suppose that performance measures can be defined for each subunit and that they are carefully tracked and utilized. Will this ensure accomplishment of the overall objectives? If it does not, as is often the case, should those who achieved their targets be rewarded even though the entire organization falls short? If this occurs frequently, should the organization respond by further refining and customizing individual performance measures, by adding additional measures, or simply by attempting to discover why those submeasures don't tie in to the overall performance goal?

The Consequences of These Organizational Principles

To understand better the consequences of these two principles in operation, consider the bottom portion of Figure 4–1, the organization chart for a typical U.S. manufacturing facility. As shown in more detail in Figure 4–2, the purchasing group is responsible for acquiring the raw materials required, and its performance is measured by their cost, quality, and timeliness of delivery. The materials group is responsible for the movement of materials through the manufacturing process and their storage, and its performance is measured by its ability to service demand and the cost of the inventories maintained. The production group is responsible for the actual conversion of raw materials into finished goods, and its performance is measured by the cost (usually as compared with some standard cost), quality, and timeliness of this conversion. The quality group is responsible for the quality of the finished product and is evaluated by how successful it is in preventing defective parts from entering the conversion process and defective goods from leaving the factory—as well as by the cost of performing this function. The maintenance group is responsible for maintaining and upgrading the equipment used and is evalu-

Figure 4-2 A Representative Plant Organization

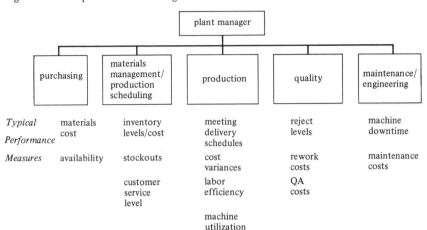

ated by the cost of this activity and the percent of unscheduled machine downtime that is experienced.

Other groups are responsible for process design, process engineering, labor relations, and so on, and have their own measures. Several of these groups may not even report to the plant manager. For example, purchasing may report to a central purchasing staff group, quality to a central quality group, and manufacturing process development (if it exists) to a central engineering group.

Such an organization may operate quite satisfactorily in a stable environment, where pressures on any one of these subgroups to make marginal (5 to 10 percent, say) improvements in performance—improving quality, reducing inventory, shortening delivery times, introducing new products at a faster rate, and so on—can be handled largely within the subgroup. Other groups may be asked to cooperate by adjusting their behavior slightly, but such adjustments are likely to have little impact on their own performance measures. Problems do arise, however, when *major* improvements—simultaneously along several dimensions—are called for.

For example, in recent years a number of American manufacturing firms have found that to be competitive they must improve their overall labor productivity by 30 to 60 percent, reduce inventories at least 50 percent, and reduce defect rates by a factor of 10 or more. Such improvements simply cannot be achieved by each of the subgroups—production working on productivity, materials on inventory reduction, and quality on the reject rate—operating independently. Worse, the things that one group may be called upon to do to help another group make such dramatic improvements are likely to impair its own performance, as reflected by the customized measures created for it.

In attempting to make a significant reduction in inventories, for example, many companies have found it necessary to move to the kind of "just-in-time" system described in Chapter 7. Instead of accepting large quantities of purchased materials every week or month, they demand daily or even more frequent deliveries of smaller quantities in the attempt to reduce raw material inventories. This is usually facilitated if the firm works with just a few suppliers who, either because of their flexibility or location, are able to meet the desired delivery schedule. Yet these suppliers may not be able to match, at least initially, the low costs offered by other suppliers who specialize in larger delivery quantities.

Similarly, production supervisors often seek to ensure that they will meet their delivery schedules by maintaining backup inventories of parts and partially completed products. Reducing these inventories will probably increase the likelihood that the production group will miss its delivery promises, causing that performance measure to decline; moreover, workers and equipment may be temporarily idled because of a lack of materials, leading to a drop in other performance measures.

The upshot is that while the performance of the materials manager may improve, the performance of the purchasing manager and that of the production supervisor will appear to decline. The same kind of conflict arises during attempts to improve reject rates or new process or product introductions (see Chapters 8 through 11). Again, all subgroups must cooperate, yet this is likely to reflect poorly on the measures used to evaluate some of them. Faced with interlinked problems, the organization attempts to respond with segmented solutions and isolated experiments. It is not surprising, therefore, that many companies experience considerable resistance when they embark on such ambitious improvements. Organizational infighting tends to worsen the more performance measurement is based on individual results and the shorter the time period.

A "Prisoner's Dilemma"

Managers in such situations find themselves caught in a "prisoner's dilemma." This refers to a hypothetical situation in which two people are arrested on suspicion of having collaborated in committing a major crime. Each is questioned separately and confronted with the following choice: the person can either confess to the crime and implicate the other person, or deny guilt. The consequences of each course of action will depend on what the other person decides to do:

	B's options	
	don't confess	confess
don't confess	1, 1	10, 0
confess	0, 10	6, 6

(A's options labels the rows: don't confess / confess)

The numbers inside each quadrant refer to the number of years in prison that prisoner A will get, followed by the years that prisoner B will get for each pair of decisions. Therefore, if prisoner A confesses and B does not, A will be set free while the authorities will "throw the book" at B, who can look forward to ten years in prison. On the other hand, if neither confesses, each will be charged with a lesser crime and only spend one year imprisoned.

Clearly, both prisoners would be better off if each, independently, decided not to confess. That would put them in the upper left-hand corner of the matrix. But that is not what is likely to happen. Consider what you would do if you were prisoner A, confronted with such a choice. If you knew that your fellow prisoner was going to confess, you would be better off confessing as well, because the years in prison that await you (6) are less than if you don't confess (10). But even if prisoner B does not confess, prisoner A is better off confessing, because he or she still gets fewer years in prison (0 versus 1) by doing so. Hence, the best strategy for prisoner A, whatever B decides to do, is to confess.

Prisoner B faces exactly the same choices and the same projected outcomes and should arrive at exactly the same conclusion. As a result, both prisoners are likely to be induced to confess and thereby end up worse off than if they both decided not to confess. The structure of their predicament encourages adversarial behavior, even though both would be better off if they cooperated.

This kind of dilemma is common in business and economics. It underlies, for example, situations in which a choice must be made regarding whether or not to escalate the commitment of resources: "If we throw another 100,000 men into the battle (or dollars into advertising) and our opponent doesn't, we can win; but if our opponent matches or surpasses our increase, we will evolve into a new deadlock at a higher commitment of resources."

Within manufacturing, the carefully subdivided organization shown in Figure 4-2, with clear alignment of responsibility and authority, often finds itself unable to respond to the need for major change. For example, if the materials manager makes a substantial effort to reduce inventory buffers, his or her performance measures will improve only if concurrently the production supervisor can reduce setup times and the maintenance manager can improve machine uptime. If some of them make such improvements but others do not, the performance measures of those who do may actually get worse (while the others will see no significant change).

The risks to the manager making a major change are magnified in practice by the fact that getting the payoff requires not just that all managers *attempt* to make reinforcing changes; they must actually achieve the intended results. Thus, if managers don't trust or respect the abilities of their counterparts in other parts of the organization, they are unlikely to venture wholeheartedly into such improvements. Furthermore, if the measurement system is unable to track improvements very precisely (a topic addressed in Chapter 5) but serves to spotlight failures (such as a machine without material or a worker without an operable machine), managers are likely to be reluctant to pursue improvements that require joint efforts.

Overcoming Organizational Barriers

How can organizations configured in this fashion overcome such internal resistance? Different companies have employed different approaches, but most are characterized by some means of breaking down the organizational separation and adversarial behavior that have been built into their organization and control systems through the adoption of the modern principles of organization described earlier. One approach relies on personal leadership, another on various types of organizational restructuring, and a third on building a corporate culture that emphasizes and rewards cooperative behavior. The order in which they are presented reflects the time frame typically required for each of them to be operative.

In some organizations, the glue that keeps different functions, divisions, and levels working together despite the naturally divisive forces at work is the personal leadership of a single person. Often this person is the founder of the company; in others he or she may initially be thrust into a leadership position during a time of crisis, when the organization's very survival is at stake. Examples include England's Winston Churchill in World War II and Lee Iacocca at

Chrysler in the late 1970s. In still others a leader may be able to instill altruistic behavior simply through extraordinary competence or force of personality. Such direct personal allegiance is often reinforced by a conscious dissolution of organizational demarcations by eliminating organizational charts, for example, or by continually shifting people around within the organization so that one's functional or divisional loyalties never become too deep-seated.

Too few companies, unfortunately, are endowed with leaders who have the ability to command this kind of personal loyalty. What is more alarming is that many organizations actually seem to impede the flowering of such leadership in those who might develop it—or worse, cause them to go elsewhere. When it appears necessary to break down the organizational barriers that promote adversarial behavior, therefore, most companies are forced to resort instead to some kind of organizational restructuring. One approach is to centralize control. Responsibilities that were previously separated are pulled together and placed under a single person, or lines of authority are redrawn. For example, purchasing, production scheduling, and distribution may all be put under the control of a single materials manager, or the plant manager may be given authority over functions (such as quality or process engineering) that previously reported directly to divisional or corporate managers.

Alternatively, some companies decide to move in a very different direction: deintegration. That is, they spin off small portions of their total production to relatively small independent outside contractors. Ironically, they often find that they can achieve better cooperation with an outside organization than with an in-house group, because they are thereby able to prevent their activities from impairing the performance measures of any internal groups (as described previously).

We see much of this kind of restructuring going on in U.S. companies today. For example, in the past few years Johnson & Johnson, 3M, Digital Equipment, and Hewlett-Packard—all of which had long prided themselves on their highly decentralized organizations—have moved toward more centralization and sharing of key resources. All have given as their reason the need to coordinate their activities better. The big U.S. auto companies, on the other hand, have been moving in the opposite direction.

Both these approaches have their shortcomings. The problem with personal leadership is that it is generally too dependent on that person, and that moment in time. Thus, one often sees a company that seemed to have great cohesion under its founder, or when faced with a crisis, dissolve into factionalism when the founder leaves or the crisis is over. The problem with the second is that such organizational restructuring is usually highly disruptive; therefore, a long time often is required before the desired effect is achieved. Worse, changes in the formal organization may never be fully effective if the informal organization—the web of personal relationships, individual abilities, and informal sources of influence (arising, for example, out of special relationships with key customers, suppliers, or senior corporate managers)—is very powerful. In addition, when organizations restructure, they seldom change their performance measurement and reward systems at the same time. The result is that those old systems, possibly embellished with some new wrinkles, serve to mitigate the potential impact of the restructuring.

If that is the case, then the only approach that is ultimately effective may be the longest term and most difficult one of all: the informal organization must be changed, and everyone in it must assimilate a new set of shared values in which cooperative behavior and interpersonal loyalty are uppermost. This appears to be the essence of the notion of "corporate culture" that became the subject of much popular discussion in the 1980s.

In brief, a corporate culture that is conducive to productivity growth emphasizes overriding organizational objectives over narrow personal interests. It encompasses a set of shared values and common assumptions about the "right way" to achieve organizational success. The organization is viewed as a community, inextricably bound together by a sense of belonging and a common fate. Employment contracts are looked upon as subordinate to informal understandings and long-lasting personal commitments.

Strong, although often quite subtle, pressures and controls are placed on members to conform to these values. New members are selected carefully and then undergo a process of socialization that both inculcates the organization's norms and assumptions, and assesses whether the new member "fits" the culture; those who don't fit are encouraged to leave. A common vocabulary is transmitted, as is a body of folklore that provides examples of individual behavior that is considered "good" or "bad." Performance measurement and reward systems are biased toward group, rather than individual, results.

These values and behavior patterns are not only deeply felt and enduring; they may seem to outsiders to be unreasonably rigid. It is interesting that modern management theory tends to regard rationality (or reasonableness) as such a desirable characteristic in organizations. When an *individual* is described as "totally rational," on the other hand, there is a tendency to be a bit suspicious; it suggests unprincipled, opportunistic behavior—a lack of character. Many of the most successful organizations down through history, where success is measured in terms of their capacity to endure and grow, are often somewhat irrational. They accept unswervingly a certain mode of behavior, even in situations where that behavior appears to be dysfunctional.

A corporate culture that encourages cooperative behavior serves to discourage the kind of organizational infighting that we described earlier. But its very stability may lead to another kind of problem. As we will stress in later chapters, productivity growth (or any other kind of improvement) requires continual ongoing experimentation and changes in behavior. A corporate culture that does not place a sufficiently high value on such improvement and the assimilation of new skills may block progress just as effectively as one that is at war with itself.

The Roles and Responsibilities of a Manufacturing Staff Group

As companies become larger and more complex—as they expand the number of markets they try to serve, the number of geographic regions in which they operate, and the number of stages in the value chain that they try to encompass—the percentage of total employees involved in staff activities tends to grow. The larger the number of activities, the more specialist expertise is called for and the more coordination among them is required. As pointed out earlier, staff groups tend to replicate themselves at various levels within the company, and additional staff personnel are therefore added to coordinate these groups' various activities. This process has led many companies to the point where over half their total manufacturing personnel fall into the category of staff.

In most manufacturing organizations, moreover, there is considerable tension, if not almost overt hostility, between line and staff groups. Although line personnel, deep in their hearts, usually recognize the intrinsic value of a staff group (just as the average motorist recognizes the intrinsic value of a radar-equipped police force—as long as it confines its attention to other motorists), they often consider the costs of such a group to outweigh its contribution. Line managers often work in remote locations, in factories and offices that are at best stark, whereas the staff are pictured as luxuriating in well-appointed air-conditioned offices and hobnobbing with the "top brass" in plush after-hours watering holes. Yet the line group feel that *they* are responsible for the actual creation of value in the organization, and the staff are simply (to use the older, more pejorative, term) "burden"—a group of people dedicated to the creation of complex systems that will justify their own existence.

The combination of this self-induced internal tension and increased competitive pressure led much of American industry to undertake a massive reduction in staff personnel during the 1980s. Some staff groups were simply downsized. Other companies eliminated the staff groups attached to one or more of their organizational levels. Still others, by restructuring themselves into relatively autonomous business units, were able to eliminate the need for many corporate staff activities.

But it is important to keep in mind that these staff groups did not spring out of thin air. They were consciously created to meet specific needs. Therefore, while many companies allowed such groups to grow beyond the size necessary to fulfill those needs, one must be careful when paring them back not to sever a necessary support system for an important line activity. Chopping staff arbitrarily, like cutting inventories or workers' salaries, is a simple solution to a complex problem. Like most simple solutions, it can create more problems than it solves.

There are at least ten essential roles that staff personnel can play within a manufacturing organization. Many of these roles are interrelated, so any decoupling is artificial. But the following brief descriptions at least provide a sense of the range of tasks that must be performed if the organization is to function effectively.

Auditing. Over time the company develops standards, goals, and procedures that prescribe how various activities ought to be carried out: quality control procedures, personnel management, equipment maintenance, safety measures, "good manufacturing practices" in general, and so on. Part of the responsibility of the manufacturing staff is to oversee the proper carrying out of these activities. This requires regular visits to the plants, and inspections that are similar to the inspections of financial records that are carried out by accounting auditors.

Review and Evaluation of Operating-unit Performance. As was mentioned earlier, one of the key tasks of the manufacturing staff is to collect data relating to the performance of differing operating units and evaluate their effectiveness in carrying out their assigned responsibilities. In some organizations, only the performance that results from the accumulation of individual decisions is evaluated; in others, the major decisions themselves are scrutinized.

Communications. In a large, geographically dispersed organization, communication becomes a problem. Not only must the decisions and policies made at corporate or divisional headquarters be transmitted and explained to line personnel in the field, but also the ideas and approaches that have been developed by and tested out in one operating unit should be communicated to other units so that the organization can learn through shared experience. Finally, relevant information from outside the company—relating to competitors' actions, governmental regulations, and technological developments—should also be disseminated.

Coordination. Most plants utilize products or services that are produced by other plants within the total organization and in turn produce products and services for other plants. For the total system to operate smoothly, these interplant flows must be coordinated by a group that is in possession of the "big picture" and is above the rivalries and self-interest of individual plants. This coordinative role often also includes services and decisions that are better done centrally than by a number of individual plants: purchasing, management recruiting, equipment selection, and so forth. Another function of the corporate staff in many companies is to monitor the proposed hiring and layoff plans at different plants and facilitate the transfer of people or equipment from one plant to another so as to minimize the number laid off and bring skills to the points where they are needed most. Finally, corporate staff often provide coordination between manufacturing and other functions in such areas as sales forecasting, product planning, and distribution. This is necessary either because the manufacturing group doesn't align naturally with other functions, because of its lack of proximity to them, or simply because it is "too busy."

Consulting. Most plants need expert help on various problems from time to time but cannot always afford to employ such experts on a full-time basis because they are needed for only a short time.

One alternative is for them to utilize the services of outside consulting firms. Another is to set up a group within the manufacturing staff that does consulting for the individual plants. Not only can the company as a whole sometimes achieve a high utilization of the time of these internal consultants, but also, through repeated exposure, they become intimately familiar with the production processes, equipment, and people within the company. Therefore, they may be able to achieve a higher level of specific expertise than is obtainable from a consulting firm that services a broad variety of clients. Finally, the movement of such consultants from plant to plant facilitates the auditing and communication functions described previously.

Management Training and Career Development. Just as new people must be selected, acculturated, and trained, so must the skills of the existing people in an organization be enhanced. Usually the manufacturing staff is entrusted with coordinating the training and development of the people in the manufacturing organization as a whole. This might range from simply distributing information about "approved educational programs" provided by outside institutions, to authorizing and monitoring the performance of the individuals who attend them, to designing and staffing instructional programs of its own, to taking an active role in moving individuals from one set of management responsibilities to another as part of a conscious career planning process. Often this training role is integrated with the consulting and coordinating roles and may include the selection and hiring of entry-level managers who (in subsequent assignments) may move into the line organization.

Special Programs. From time to time, special needs arise that do not fit comfortably into any existing category of responsibilities. Examples include the energy conservation programs that many companies set up after the first oil crisis in 1974, special safety programs that arise in response to an increase in the accident rate, and job enrichment programs. Starting toward the end of the 1970s, many companies instituted productivity- and quality-improvement and inventory-reduction programs that were developed and "sold" by corporate staff groups.

Representing Line Management in Corporate Financial Reviews. Major requests for funds (plant expansions, new equipment, etc.) must often go through an elaborate review process, as described in Chapter 3. The staff often works with line managers in formulating these requests, reviewing them for accuracy, putting them into the proper format, assembling the necessary supporting data, and (assuming it is satisfied with a proposal's viability) shepherding them through the corporate review process and defending them in various corporate forums. These activities often overlap with performance review, communications, and consulting activities.

Advanced Process Development. Line managers, especially when they are being evaluated primarily on the basis of financial performance (profit, ROI, etc.), are often reluctant to undertake major process development activities because the cost does not sufficiently outweigh the potential benefits to their own group. Such process development projects include both the development of management systems (for production scheduling, inventory control, capacity planning, etc.) and the development of new equipment or ancillary devices.

Profit center managers often see themselves as incurring the risks and expenses of such projects all by themselves, while the rest of the organization shares in the rewards of the ones that are successful. If each waits for another profit center to take the plunge, nothing might get done. Therefore, the corporate staff often feel that they must take a lead role in choosing which kinds of projects are pursued, either carrying them out themselves or funding their development in selected operating units.

Guru Wisdom. The manufacturing staff often becomes the repository of highly skilled senior people, whose familiarity with the company's technology, products, and personnel is developed over a long period of time. As a result, their knowledge and counsel are sought by a broad range of people, both within the manufacturing organization and in other functional groups. The titles and responsibilities of such gurus may appear to be highly specific, but their reputations transcend their particular job description of the moment. They spend much of their time answering questions, giving advice, and overseeing the spontaneous flow of information throughout the organization. In some organizations they perform the role of technological "gatekeepers": through their long experience with the technology of their industries and their wide acquaintanceships with people who work for suppliers, customers, and competitors, they are often the first to learn about potentially important new technological developments. In other organizations they may become the personal adviser to the CEO on "matters of manufacturing."

The importance of such gurus should not be underestimated. One company, for example, after requesting a study by a well-known consulting company and conducting a nationwide search, created a new position of manufacturing vice president a few years ago and filled it with an extremely able person. Following the consultant's advice, this person set up a traditional corporate manufacturing staff. As he was proceeding with the development and guidance of this group, he became aware of a certain sense of disappointment among some of the senior corporate officers. Further investigation revealed that the major impetus for the consulting study and the creation of his own position was the loss, through death, of a senior vice president in the company.

This person had been trained as an engineer and had spent many years in the company's manufacturing function. Even though his later career had taken him into general management and then into the top echelon of corporate management, he remained the "expert" on matters relating to technology or manufacturing. Even though the new manufacturing vice president was "doing all the right things," he had not structured himself or his group to fill the need that was, subliminally at least, the real driving force behind the creation of his position. What the top management in the company really wanted, it turned out, was another guru.

The preceding paragraphs provide a brief indication of the variety of functions and roles that have to be performed in a typical manufacturing organization. Notice that they involve very different skills and usually require very different kinds of people. Good auditors and financial analysts are not necessarily good communicators, and good consultants do not necessarily make good managers of special projects or programs. Gurus are gurus, and may not be good for anything else.

Nor do all these functions have to be performed by a corporate staff. If the company is highly diversified and decentralized, it may be inappropriate, if not impossible, for any central group to provide the kind of specialized skill and coordination that would be possible in a more centralized company. Perhaps some of these tasks should be carried out by "lead" divisions. Or, if the company has created large, specialized plants, it may make sense to locate certain roles (such as providing technolocial expertise) there rather than at some central location.

It is important to keep in mind that most organizations over time develop informal approaches to all these tasks. Individuals, motivated by their own interests or previous work experiences, undertake some of them as labors of love. Individuals or groups are assigned to perform others on a one-time basis and then over time find themselves gradually spending more and more of their time on them. Other functional groups, because of their own needs, develop the capability to perform others. Thus, recognized or not, coordinated or not, the work usually gets done—somehow, somewhere.

Molding and Adapting the Manufacturing Organization

The job of the manufacturing vice president is to create order out of this potential chaos. This requires that he or she decide exactly whether and where (at what level and location) in the total organization each of these tasks should be performed, and who should have responsibility for seeing that they are defined and performed properly.

The subsidiary problem then becomes, given the widely differing personal characteristics required for these tasks, how to attract and manage the people who will be given responsibility for them. The usual idea is to "promote" people out of the line organization to fill staff positions requiring the expertise that they have acquired through hands-on experience. But some roles (auditors, communicators, and program managers, say) might require very different backgrounds and skills. Where do these people come from and, probably more important, where do they go? That is, where are their opportunities for advancement in the organization?

In making these decisions and in choosing among alternatives that seem to be equally plausible, a company should be guided by one central principle: the staff is a *support* group, not the aristocracy of the manufacturing organization. Most organization charts (including the one depicted in Figure 4–1) promote this latter impression: the staff is on top and the line organization is at the bottom. But if the role of the staff is really to support line operations, their positions should be reversed: the organization chart should look more like a table than a pyramid. Unfortunately, it is not always easy to maintain this notion of the proper relationship between line and staff because two "laws of organizations" can combine to thwart the best intentions.

The first has to do with the natural tendency of people to want to do a good job and then to expand their responsibilities:

> A strong central staff will find something to do and will eventually decide that what it wants to do is sufficiently important that it justifies interfering with what somebody else wants to do.

An important corollary to this law is that weak managers will be glad to let somebody else deal with their problems and let that person share responsibility for the consequences. The implication is that if one chooses a strong, aggressive person to head a staff function, one should not be surprised to see it grow larger and more powerful over time.

The second law relates to the natural tendency of staff organizations, as they become larger, to become more bureaucratic. When managers want to increase their control over the activities for which they are responsible, they often decide that it's necessary to increase their staff. But often this has precisely the opposite effect. When they increase their staff they insert a screen, in effect, between themselves and the reality they are entrusted with managing. Hence:

> Large staffs, composed of ambitious and overprotective people determined to justify their existence, make work and make trouble. They cut off the executive from the line organization and the line organization from the executive.

This statement of the "law of bureaucratic behavior" is paraphrased from Arthur Schlesinger, Jr., who described its operation in government:

> Franklin Roosevelt had three rules about [his] staff: He did not want more special assistants than he could deal with personally; he did not want his assistants to interpose themselves between him and the heads of departments and agencies; and he did not want them to build up staffs of their own. . . . He fought the worst depression in American history with fewer high paid officials on the White House payroll than the President's wife has today, and he fought the greatest war in American history with fewer high paid officials than the Vice President has today. The problems he faced were much greater than any faced by his successors, but he was free from

the delusion that he could tackle them more effectively if he increased the number of bodies in his immediate entourage.[3]

But if adding staff is likely to create more problems than it solves, how can one maintain control (and consistent corporate priorities) when confronted with a broad and changing mix of products, product specifications, process technologies, production volumes, skill levels, and customer demand patterns? And what mix of roles, drawn from the preceding set, is appropriate for staff personnel? This is where organizational design becomes key, since it largely determines which tasks will be easy (natural) for the manufacturing function to carry out and which will be difficult (unnatural).

In framing an answer to these questions, we will begin by differentiating between the administrative burden on the managements of individual plants, and that on the central manufacturing staff. Different ways of organizing a manufacturing system will place different demands on each of these groups. In a rough sense, the same amount of "control" must be exercised over the system, no matter how responsibilities are divided between the two.[4]

At one extreme, one could lump all production activities for all products into a single plant. This makes the job of the central staff relatively easy, but the job of the plant management becomes horrendous. At the other extreme, one could simplify the job of each individual plant (or operating unit within a given plant) so that each concentrates on a more restricted set of activities (products, processes, volume levels, etc.); in this case the coordinative job of the central organization becomes much more difficult.

Although many companies begin by adopting the first approach, either by design or by default, in our experience it becomes increasingly unworkable as more and more complexity is put under one roof. At some point a single large plant, even a contiguous plant complex, breaks down as more products, processes, skill levels, and market demands are added to it. As they have come to understand this, many companies have reversed direction by applying the concept of "focused manufacturing": dividing up the total manufacturing job into a number of *focused* units, each of which is responsible for a limited set of activities and objectives.[5]

But this leads to another problem: given such an approach, how should the central manufacturing staff be organized so that it can effectively manage the resulting diversity of units and tasks? It must somehow maintain the total organization's sense of priorities and manufacturing mission, even though individual units may have quite different focuses. To help think about the variety of ways in which this can be accomplished, we will consider two polar examples: a "market/product-focused organization" and a "technology/production process-focused organization." Both are depicted in Figure 4–3. What should be the major responsibilities of the central manufacturing staff and of the plant managers in each situation?

The corporate staff clearly has to play a much more active role in making the second kind of organization work. Logistics movements have to be carefully coordinated, and a change in any of the plants (or the market) can have repercussions throughout the system. Only the plant manager at the last stage (process C) can be measured on a profitability basis, and even that measure is highly dependent on negotiated transfer prices and the smooth functioning of the rest of the system. The managers within each stage will not have much opportunity to exercise their independent decision-making capability, since most variables under their control (capacity, output, specifications, etc.) will affect everybody else. Each plant will therefore prob-

Figure 4-3   Two Extreme Options for Organizing Manufacturing

Type I. Market-and-Product—Focused Organization

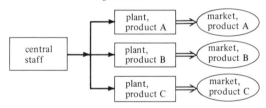

Type II. Technology-and-Production Process—Focused Organization

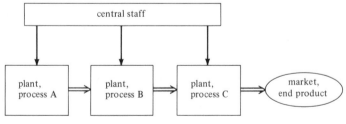

Key:

⟶ Organizational relationships

⟹ Physical flows

ably be regarded as a "cost center" and be measured in large part on its ability to work smoothly within this highly interdependent system.

The distinction between such product-focused (Type I) and process-focused (Type II) manufacturing organizations should not be confused with the difference between traditional "divisional" and "functional" corporate organizations. In fact, it is entirely possible that two divisions within a divisionally organized company would choose to organize their manufacturing groups differently. The important distinction has to do with how the manufacturing organization works.

Given this brief overview, let us turn to a more complete description of these product and process-focused organizations.

Type I: The Product/Market-Focused Organization
Authority in the product-focused organization is highly decentralized, which tends to make it more responsive to market needs and more flexible when introducing new products. Each product group is analogous to a separate company and thus can react quickly to market shifts and customer needs. A product focus tends to be better suited to less complex, less capital-intensive process technologies, where economies of scale do not demand large common production facilities, and where flexibility and innovativeness are generally more important than careful planning and tight control. Profit, or ROI, is usually the primary measure used to evaluate performance. Such organizations appeal most to companies whose dominant orientation is to a market or consumer group, rather than to a technology or a material, and who have a high need and tolerance for diversity.

The responsibility for decisions on capital investment, technology, and product development are thrust down from the corporate level to lower levels of management. A product/market focus demands talented, market-oriented junior managers, so considerable emphasis must be placed on recruiting and developing them. Junior managers have to be tracked carefully through the system, implying a sophisticated evaluation and reward system.

The corporate-level manufacturing staff in such organizations is well removed from day-to-day operations, but it is instrumental in communicating and coordinating across product groups regarding such issues as personnel policies, manpower availability, special services (from computer assistance to training programs), capital appropriation requests, and purchasing leverage.

Type II: The Process-Focused Organization

Within this kind of organization, individual plants are typically not dedicated to individual products or product lines but rather to one or more process stages. Sometimes a product is produced in its entirety by a single plant in such an organization, but more often that plant is only one of several that contribute to the product's manufacture. Responsibilities throughout the plant, as well as throughout the upper management hierarchy, are delineated not by product line, but by manufacturing process stage. Plants tend to be cost centers, not profit centers, and measurement is based on technologically derived standards.

A process focus tends to be better suited to companies with complex (and divisible) processes that are highly capital intensive, like those for producing chemicals and semiconductors. Decisions involving capacities, material flows, and technological change are critical and absorb much of top management's energies. A process focus is not conducive to the rapid introduction of new products, since it does not assign authority along product lines. Nor is it very flexible in altering the output levels of existing products, because of the "pipeline momentum" in the system. But it can facilitate low-cost, highly dependable production by exploiting economies of scale and large concentrations of technical expertise.

A process-focused organization requires that tremendous attention be placed on coordinating functional responsibilities, to ensure a smooth response to changes in the product mix. Staff groups are intimately involved in coordination, communication, facility evaluation, problem solving and consulting, and assisting in the financial justification of the large capital expenditures that are periodically requested. Moreover, because control is exercised centrally, young managers must serve a long and generally more technical apprenticeship—usually with less decision-making responsibility. This places a burden on upper-level management to keep junior managers motivated and learning, while gradually developing their interest and ability to assume greater responsibilities.

Product or Process Focus: Which Is Best?

Despite the economies of scale and the strong centralization of control in a process-focused organization, it may not have lower total manufacturing costs than a well-managed product-focused organization. The central overhead and logistics costs required by a process focus can sometimes offset whatever cost reductions are possible through tight control and economies of scale. A product focus, on the other hand, is generally easier to manage because of its smaller size and total responsibility for a particular product or customer. This usually results in shorter cycle times, faster response to market changes, less inventory, lower logistics costs, and, of course, lower overhead.

Technologically based plants tend to be staffed with people who are highly expert and up-to-date in that technology. They will be aware of technological trends, the strengths and weaknesses of the latest processing alternatives, the research being conducted around the world, and the operating problems that different companies are having with a particular process. Operating people in such a plant often are more likely to move to a similar plant in a competitor company than they are to transfer to a different process stage within their own company.

In a product organization, on the other hand, each product-plant complex may involve a number of technologies, and there may not be a sufficient mass of technical expertise in such a complex to keep abreast of the latest developments in that technology. This becomes, then, more a responsibility of the corporate staff or, possibly, the responsibility of a separate research group in the corporation— which may not even be under the control of the manufacturing organization. For this reason, businesses that utilize highly complex and evolving technologies often gravitate toward organizing themselves by process stage.

Purchasing is another area that a process organization tends to manage more carefully than does a product organization. If purchasing becomes too fragmented as a result of decentralization, the company as a whole may not be able to exploit potential advantages: many small orders placed by several small purchasing departments and held in various locations tend to be much more costly than centralized purchasing and storage. On the other hand, centralized purchasing tends to be more bureaucratic and less responsive to local market needs, so many companies evolve to a combination of both, where the product organizations are delegated responsibility for certain purchases while a central purchasing department handles the remainder.

In summary, a process-oriented manufacturing organization demands a strong central staff group to make it function properly. Moving to a product orientation does not just change material flows between plants; it should also affect the size, power, and responsibilities of the central staff. One's whole philosophy of plant management is altered in fundamental ways:

1. The type of people who should be assigned to be plant managers (product-oriented rather than technology-oriented; profit-oriented rather than cost-oriented; strong leaders rather than "good soldiers");
2. The amount of responsibility and autonomy that should be given them, and the performance criteria that should be used in evaluating and rewarding them; and
3. The kind of expectations placed on them by (and the protection given them against the demands of) marketing and finance.

Although the amount of central coordination that has to be done will decrease, the job of monitoring and evaluating individual plants may increase. The central group must also take a more active role in keeping abreast of technological developments and encouraging the introduction of new processes and approaches into the appropriate product-oriented plants. Similarly, as plants move to more reliance on outside suppliers and ordering becomes more decentralized, the central staff must act to coordinate these orders so as to maintain consistent relationships with suppliers. Finally, it will probably have to be more active in management development: identifying potential plant managers and grooming them for increased responsibilities. Figure 4–4 contains a brief summary of the important differences between product-focused and process-focused organizations.

An Either/Or Choice
It is obvious that these polar examples of manufacturing organization—product focus versus process focus—place fundamentally different demands on both line and staff organizations: different policies and practices, different measurement and control systems, different managerial attitudes, different kinds of people, and different career paths for them. Therefore, the choice of manufacturing-organization structure should essentially be a choice *between* them: either a product focus or a process focus. Just as individual plants should each have a clear focus, so should the organization that binds them together.

A mixed, or composite, organization will only invite confusion, as staff groups and plant managements seek to define their responsibilities and relative authority on various issues. If some manufacturing groups within the company preserve a product focus while others

Figure 4-4 Important Differences between Alternative Manufacturing Organization Structures

Exhibit III

Differences between product-focused and process-focused manufacturing organizations

	Product focus	*Process focus*
Profit or cost responsibility: where located	Product groups	Central organization
Size of corporate staff	Relatively small	Relatively large
Major functions of corporate staff	(a) Review capital appropriation requests (b) Communicate corporate changes and requests (c) Act as clearinghouse for personnel information management recruiting purchasing used equipment management development programs (d) Evaluate and reward plant managers (e) Select plant managers and manage career paths-possibly across product group lines	(a) Coordination with marketing (b) Facilities decisions (c) Personnel policies (d) Purchasing (e) Logistics-inventory management (f) Coordination of production schedules (g) Make versus buy, vertical integration decisions (h) Recruit future plant managers (i) Review plant performance, cost center basis
Major responsibilities of plant organizations	(a) Coordination with marketing (b) Facilities decisions (subject to marketing) (c) Purchasing and logistics (d) Production scheduling and inventory control (e) Make versus buy (f) Recruit management	(a) Use materials and facilities efficiently (b) Recruit production, clerical, and lower management workers (c) Training and development of future department and plant managers (d) Respond to special requests from marketing, within limited ranges

Source: Reprinted by permission of the *Harvard Business Review.* An exhibit from "How Should You Organize Manufacturing?" by Robert H. Hayes and Roger W. Schmenner (January-February 1978), p. 112. Copyright © 1978 by the President and Fellows of Harvard College; all rights reserved.

have a process focus, they should be kept as separate as possible. To see more clearly what we mean, consider some mixed organizational focuses and the difficulties they might lead to:

A process-focused factory supplying two product markets: In this instance, the organization chart might look something like Figure 4–5. Here the corporation is trying to serve two distinct markets and product lines from the same factory, whose process technology appears to meet the needs of both (it may, in fact, consist of a series of linked process stages operating under tight central control). If the needs of the two markets are very different this kind of organization will almost inevitably lead to confusion; a plant that tries to service the needs of both at the same time is unlikely to serve either well. An organization that utilizes the manufacturing facilities of one of its product groups to supply a major portion of the needs of another product group would be risking the same kind of confusion.

An in-house supplier serving two separate product divisions: A more subtle problem arises with the kind of organization depicted in Figure 4–6. In this instance a corporate staff oversees two independent product groups, which serve two distinct markets, *and* a component plant that supplies both of them. The usual argument for a common supplier plant is that economies of scale are possible from combining the requirements of both product groups. The supplier plant, however, must be coordinated by the same staff people who oversee the product groups, requiring them to switch back and forth between their product- and process-focused roles. Alternatively, a captive supplier plant within one product group may be asked to supply a major portion of the requirements of another product group's plant.

How should a company organize around such situations? The im-

Figure 4-5   A Process-Focused Factory Producing
for Two Product Groups

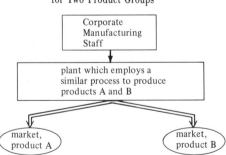

Figure 4-6 A Product-Focused Factory Supplying Two Product Groups

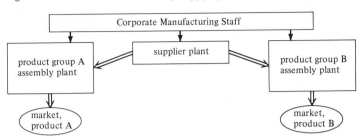

portant principle to keep in mind is that a factory that has configured itself to meet the priorities required by a certain competitive strategy is likely to prefer suppliers who exhibit the same priorities. This suggests that a company try to erect managerial dividing lines between its product-focused and its process-focused manufacturing segments. In particular, the transfer of products between product-focused and process-focused plant groups should not be coordinated by a central staff group but handled through arms' length bargaining—as if, in effect, they had independent "subsidiary" relationships within the parent company. Such an in-house supplier would then be treated like any other supplier, able to resist demands that violate the integrity of its manufacturing mission just as the customer plant is free to select suppliers that are more attuned to its own mission.

Such an arrangement may appear to be needlessly complex and to add to manufacturing's administrative overhead without clear financial benefits. These, of course, are the classic arguments for consolidating and centralizing any business activity, and they must be balanced by the classic counterargument: combining two dissimilar activities into one does not reduce complexity; it simply hides it and is likely to destroy the focus and distinctness of both. Our position is not that both product and process focus cannot exist within the same company but simply that separating them as much as possible will result in less confusion and less danger that different operating units will work at cross purposes.

Many companies, consciously or unconsciously, have evolved toward precisely this kind of separation. In some cases it is explicit, with two or more different staff groups operating relatively autonomously within the manufacturing organization; in others, although a single central staff appears on the organization chart, subgroups within this staff operate independently. One way for a company to test the degree of organizational focus in its manufacturing arm—and whether adequate insulation between product-focused and process-focused plant groups exists—is to contemplate how it would separate itself if forced to do so (by an antitrust decision, say). A focused organization should be able to divide itself up cleanly and naturally, with no substantial organizational changes.

Growth and Its Impact on the Manufacturing Organization

A company's manufacturing function should organize itself in such a way as to reinforce the priorities that the company has placed on certain competitive dimensions, while maintaining consistency with the basic attitudes, values, and traditions that shape and drive the rest of the company. But companies are dynamic—they change and grow over time. Unless a manufacturing organization is designed so that it can adapt to this growth, it will become increasingly unstable and inappropriate for the evolving needs of the company. This is basically what happened to the two companies described at the beginning of this chapter. Therefore, simplicity and focus are not enough; the organizational design must also be able to accommodate the kind of growth the company is likely to experience.

Growth, in fact, can subvert a healthy manufacturing operation: not all at once, but bit by bit. When growing quickly, top-level managers are faced with a rapid series of investment and deployment decisions: new factories, new product and process technologies, new suppliers, and new people. As they grapple with such issues, they are likely to pay less attention to existing plants. Lacking their guidance, the plants can lose direction.

How, then, can a company cope with growth? First, one must identify and understand the type of growth desired or being experienced, and the kind of difficulties it creates. Growth can have several forms:

1. A broadening of the product lines being offered;
2. An increase in the span of the production processes performed for existing products (i.e., vertical integration);
3. An increased demand for existing products within the existing market area; and
4. An expansion in the geographic regions serviced.

These types of growth are very different. Distinguishing among them is important because the design of the manufacturing organization should reflect the *kind* of growth confronting the organization, not simply the fact of growth. Let us look at the types of growth we have enumerated:

1. If growth is due primarily to a broadening of product lines, a product-focused organization is more likely to meet the increased need for flexibility that results. Once organized in this way, other aspects of the manufacturing organization—such as the production of the original product lines—can go on as before.

2. If growth occurs principally from increasing the span of the process, a process-focused organization can probably best introduce and manage the added segments of the full production process. Not only will it be easier to coordinate the separate pieces of the process, but the confusion associated with new stages can be confined to specific linkages that are under management's control.

3. If growth results from the natural maturation of a product toward "commodity" status, the company will typically face pressure to reduce its cost. This forces it into more specialization of equipment and tasks, an increasing ratio of capital to labor expenses, and a more standard and rigid process flow. The management of such kinds of changes is probably best accomplished by an organization focused along process lines, and willing to forsake the flexibilities of a more decentralized product focus.

4. Growth realized through geographic expansion is more problematic. Sometimes such growth can be met with existing facilities. Frequently, however, expansion in foreign countries is best met with an entirely separate manufacturing organization, organized along either product or process lines.

Recognizing and Avoiding the Pitfalls of Growth
The unrecognized consequences of growth often surface with the apparent breakdown of the relationship between the central manufacturing staff and division or plant management. For example, many companies that built their manufacturing organization around a strong central staff group find that as their markets and product offerings grow in size and complexity the staff is no longer able to cope as effectively with the demands placed upon it. The company senses this loss of effectiveness, and a tenuous mandate appears for changing the manufacturing organization.

Sometimes the response is to break out product divisions. The natural inclination in most companies with strong central staffs, however, is instead to strengthen the central staff. As the central staff becomes stronger, siphoning ever-increasing authority and people from the plant organization in its attempt to regain control, the decision-making capabilities of plant managers diminish. In short, the strong tend to get stronger, and the weak weaker. At some point this vicious cycle breaks down under the strain of increasing complexity, and when it does a simple executive order will not be sufficient to accomplish the profound changes—in people, policies, and attitudes—that have to take place.

On the other hand, it is sometimes dangerous to delegate too much responsibility for capacity expansion decisions to product-oriented managers. In the interests of keeping their own jobs as simple as possible, they may tend to "expand in place"—continually expanding current plants or building nearby satellite plants. Over a period of time they may create a huge, tightly interconnected plant complex that exhibits the tight central control and inflexibility of a process organization—despite the fact that the corporation as a whole continues to emphasize market flexibility and technological opportunism. Such a situation can be remedied either by dismembering and reorganizing this product division, or by decoupling it from the rest of the company so that it has more of an independent status.

Conclusion

The purpose of an organization is to weld people together in a common purpose, while allowing various individuals and groups to focus their attention and expertise on specific tasks. Yet too many companies have organized themselves in such a way that they drive people apart, channeling their competitive instincts against each other rather than against their outside competitors. And rather than integrating their expertise, they stifle its development and restrict its transfer.

There are a variety of ways a company can choose to organize itself; each approach will influence how its different subgroups communicate with one another and coordinate their activities. It also affects the roles that various staff groups should play and how they interact with line activities. A company's organization structure should reflect both its competitive strategy and its technological constraints. But organizations tend to evolve in unpredictable ways and, like a river delta that gradually builds up until it diverts the river into another channel, they can come to thwart the purposes for which they were created. Unless these dynamics are understood, apparently innocuous alterations can accumulate into an organizational monstrosity—a Rube Goldberg device that absorbs all the energies of its participants without producing any significant output.

| 5 |

Measuring Manufacturing Performance

Introduction

Most of the assets of a typical industrial company are invested in its manufacturing organization. That is also where most of its people and managers are found, and most of its costs incurred. Its prosperity—even survival—lies in its ability to control those costs and use those assets effectively. Following Lord Kelvin's famous dictum: "When you can measure what you are speaking about, and express it in numbers, you know something about it; but when you cannot measure it . . . your knowledge is of a meager and unsatisfactory kind," most companies develop elaborate and pervasive accounting systems to record costs, shipments, and revenues. These systems measure the performance of specific activities and managers and compare them with what had been anticipated. In the process they have a profound effect on human behavior, because people are more likely to do what you *inspect* than what you *expect*.

Such measurements can provide useful information to managers who are trying to identify the sources of their problems or the reasons for their success. But most measurement systems in place today do not provide the kind of information needed by companies that seek to create a competitive advantage through manufacturing. That information is of two kinds. The first is insight into the direction and rate of improvement in performance over time, answering such questions as, Are we getting better at the things that are most important to our manufacturing strategy? and What is our rate of improvement? The second kind of information has to do with competitors. Most systems compare performance against some form of internal budget or standard. But a competitive advantage in the marketplace is revealed only by how one measures up to one's competitors; in other words, the right "standard" to apply in measuring performance must be an external one. A measurement system, therefore, must be outward looking, providing accurate information regarding how the capabilities that are key to a company's success compare to the best in the world.

Putting in place a measurement system that supports a manufacturing advantage involves more than minor adjustments to traditional accounting systems. To understand the nature of these differences, in both concept and practice, and to lay the foundation for our discussion of alternative approaches, we begin the chapter by reviewing some of the basic concepts behind traditional systems for measuring factory performance, including a bit of their history. We then describe an approach for measuring the rate of improvement in manufacturing performance that is based on the concept of "total factor productivity." Next we describe an approach for evaluating a manufacturing company's competitive position, focusing on the capabilities of its key competitors. We conclude with a brief discussion of the implications of this approach.

The Measurement Tangle

Modern manufacturing accounting systems have long historical roots. From the time of the earliest factories in medieval Europe, accounting systems have been evolving to meet an increasingly complex set of demands. When managers collect data from a manufacturing process, they have a variety of purposes in mind, falling into three basic groups:

1. *Process management:* How long will it take to produce and deliver a given order? How much material must be ordered and when? How many people and machines must be assigned to produce it? When should they begin? How much assistance will they need from supervisors and specialists?
2. *Business management:* What products should be developed? What price should be assigned to a given product? How should this price be affected by the volume ordered? Should a product be dropped from the line? What wages can be paid workers and managers? How much and which kind of equipment should be bought to assist them? How much factory space is required to house these people and equipment?

3. *External reporting:* How much profit was made during the most recent reporting period? What are the values of the various stocks of raw material, partly finished goods, and finished goods that are being held? What is the value of the buildings and equipment assigned to production?

These three sets of issues can be thought of as dealing with progressively longer time horizons. Process management is essentially concerned with scheduling and staffing decisions that generally are reviewed and changed rather frequently. The important costs are almost entirely variable, depending on the rate of production, and can be directly assigned to specific products, materials, machines, and people. Those costs that cannot be directly assigned are not particularly relevant to making the kinds of decisions that process managers are concerned about.

On the other hand, the time frame over which pricing, wage, and facilities decisions are expected to endure might cover several years. Costs that look fixed in the short run, like the supervisor's salary—or even "sunk," like the cost of the plant and its equipment—become more and more variable (that is, subject to management influence) in the long run. The numbers that are relevant in making such decisions, therefore, include both the direct costs of production and the indirect "overhead" costs associated with staff specialists, product designers, and top managers. These costs must somehow be assigned to specific products for pricing purposes, and to specific activities for the purpose of deciding whether to increase or reduce the investment in those activities.

Reporting is somewhat more difficult to classify. Even though one might be required to report on the performance of a given manufacturing unit quite frequently (monthly or even weekly), the rules that govern this reporting must not be allowed to change very often or the information reported will not be consistent—either across companies or over time. In addition, because all revenues and costs must be accounted for, including corporate overhead allocations, there is no place for the concept of "fixed" costs. Reporting, therefore, can be considered to have the longest time frame of all.

This ordering also reflects the historical emphasis placed on these sets of issues. In the early days of the industrial revolution the concerns of process management and control dominated data collection; hence the title "controller," which is today something of an historical residue. Questions relating to pricing and equipment purchase were made on the fly, and largely on the basis of intuition, by the managers most closely involved with the decision. And the basic reporting instrument—as it is in most small firms today—was the cashbox: if it held enough at the end of every week to meet the payroll, pay one's suppliers, and provide a comfortable living for the owner, the business was a success.

Later, as companies expanded in size, number of locations, breadth of product line, and the complexity of the production process—and as top management and its staff groups became separated from line personnel within a complex hierarchy—management decision making began to demand more and more data collection activity. Over the past fifty years or so, the increasing importance of public ownership, government taxation, and a variety of forms of regulation (together with the resulting emergence of a powerful accounting profession) have tilted the emphasis of most companies' accounting systems toward the external report of costs and revenues in periodic financial statements.[1]

It does not take much reflection to come to the conclusion that the three different types of issues just described are likely to require the collection of very different data and the preparation of entirely different reports. In fact, one might easily infer that to do a really good job at all three one really needs three entirely different data collection and accounting systems. If the needs of only one set dominate the accounting function of a company, as financial reporting dominates in most companies today, one might expect that the other needs would be poorly served—just as one might expect that the needs of financial reporting might be poorly served by a cost reporting system that is set up primarily to assist in short-term scheduling decisions.

Perhaps an analogy would be useful here. Consider the origins of modern accounting systems: voyage accounting as it was practiced 500 years ago. A ship owner would hire a captain and crew, buy merchandise and load it on the ship, and then send it on its way (accompanying it himself or sending a representative) to some foreign port. When—and if—it arrived the merchandise would be sold at whatever price could be obtained, new merchandise purchased (based on the price and availability of goods at that port at the time, as well as on the owner's sense of the demand at home), and the ship would return. If it arrived safely the new merchandise would be sold, the captain and crew paid, and whatever was left over was the "surplus,'' or profit, from the voyage. Accounting was essentially confined to bookkeeping.

But suppose an emissary approached the ship's captain two months after leaving his home port, halfway to his destination—in front of him only open ocean and unseen dangers, the uncertainty of what prices might be obtained for his merchandise and what goods would be available for purchase, the perilous return trip, and the uncertainty as to the revenue that might be received for this new cargo —and said, "The owner is curious: how much money have we made so far?" How should he answer? On the one hand, no money has been made; only costs have been incurred. On the other, the ship and its cargo are closer to the completion of their voyage, and therefore must be worth more, than when they first left their home port.

That is the question that financial reporting requires be asked in today's business environment; one must estimate the profitability over an arbitrary time period, before all the results are in, of a complex web of voyages (i.e., equipment and products) that encompass a variety of destinations and are sometimes expected to last several years. Attempts to assign lumpy costs and revenues to any given short time period (as compared with the length of the average voyage) will almost inevitably lead to questionable estimates, because the expenditures that have been incurred and the revenues that emanate from them have to be arbitrarily assigned.

Moreover, the insistence on the use of standard approaches, based on generally accepted accounting principles (GAAP), in preparing such reports, although giving them the appearance of consistency and objectivity, robs them of their ability to measure the nuances of performance in ships that are carrying different cargoes and following very different courses to different destinations. If one is competing on the basis of delivery speed, it seems obvious that one would use different measures of performance than if competing on the basis of lowest delivered costs. Yet the influence of the highly conservative GAAP, policed by the accounting profession, together with limited information collecting and processing capabilities (which, until recently, made it both costly and confusing to keep multiple sets of accounts) has led most companies to adopt similar measurement and reporting systems no matter what their competitive strategy or approach to production.

Finally, whatever answer is given to the emissary's question, one can be sure of only one thing: it is of little use to the captain as he tries to stay on course, evaluate the performance of his ship and crew, or decide whether and how to react to the changing winds and currents. Our focus in this book is on the needs of that captain, today's business manager, as he or she attempts to deal with the problems of managing operations and making effective business decisions.

Cost Accounting's Increasing "Reality Variance"
To price their products and evaluate the efficiency of their various operations, most manufacturing companies today employ a methodology called cost accounting. Initially developed in the late 1800s for the purpose of attributing the total costs of operating textile mills, railroads, steel mills, and retail stores to specific products, departments, and activities, the cost accounting systems now in place are increasingly showing their age.[2] Not only are they providing inadequate or misleading information to managers (and indirectly to investors); they are leading to bad decisions. In addition, because they communicate distorted information about performance, the rewards and punishments they give rise to affect motivation and morale at lower levels of the organization in dysfunctional ways. In this section we will explore why this is happening.

The basic cost accounting methodology is simple. The costs of operating a manufacturing facility are collected and divided into two categories: those that vary directly (variable costs) with the production of an identifiable part or product—such as direct labor, materials, and energy—and those that do not but are required in order for the production of any product to take place. These include the cost of the buildings and equipment used, the salaries of supervisors, managers, and support groups, and ancillary costs such as taxes and insurance. Because they do not vary directly with the production of any particular item, but instead tend to reflect commitments (such as salaries, interest and depreciation expenses) that cover specific time periods, these are typically called period, indirect, or (in order to juxtapose them more clearly with variable costs) fixed costs.[3]

One cannot properly evaluate management performance using these measures alone, of course, because it is difficult to say whether a given measure indicates good, bad, or average performance unless one can compare it with some appropriate reference value. This reference value may be an historical figure (making it possible to measure the trend in performance over time), a budgeted figure (permitting the evaluation of a manager's ability to forecast and control the operations under his or her control), or a "standard" determined in some objective manner: time-and-motion studies, industry data, engineering calculations, or the concurrent performance of other plants within the same company.

Given such reference measures it then becomes possible to perform "variance analyses": separating the total deviation of an aggregate performance measure from its reference value (between, say, a product's measured cost per unit and its standard cost) into its various components. Was an apparently above-standard performance due to a low usage or cost of materials? A higher-than-expected production rate? Higher machine efficiency (perhaps due to new equipment)? Or higher direct labor efficiency? The answer is, Probably some combination of the above. But the exact combination can give one better insight into how much of the outcome was due to good management rather than good fortune.[4]

Although this kind of analysis allows one to assess the efficiency of the various activities that take place in a factory, it does not help the manager establish the selling price for a given product, decide whether to retain it or replace it in the product line, or determine which managers, departments, or products are deserving of particular credit for the facility's overall profit. To answer these types of profit-dependent questions it is necessary to factor in *all* the costs of producing each product, including the so-called fixed costs.

The Impact of Changing Cost Structures

When cost accounting was in its infancy, factoring in fixed costs was not a particularly difficult problem, since the great bulk of the total costs of production were variable costs, primarily direct labor and materials. Therefore, elaborate systems were developed to measure and evaluate them. The fixed costs, which represented only 10 to 20 percent of the total, were then allocated to specific products and activities in some reasonable way. Usually this was done by identifying (or simply asserting) a strong relationship with one or more of the direct costs and then distributing the fixed cost on the basis of the amount of that direct cost. For example, if supervision and factory support costs were small compared with direct labor but there was a clear relationship between the two—for example, an operating policy that there should be one supervisor for every ten workers—then the cost of supervision could be attributed to a specific product by measuring the ratio between supervisory costs and direct labor hours *over all products* and multiplying that "supervisory burden rate" by the number of direct labor hours consumed.

The fixed costs in different circumstances might be driven by a variety of direct costs, including the consumption of a critical material or the number of machine hours required. But because of the historical importance of direct labor, as well as the existence of systems for measuring it quite precisely, it became by far the most prevalent means for allocating most fixed costs.

Relatively few American companies base their overhead allocation on materials consumption, on the other hand, even though materials account for more than 50 percent of the total manufacturing cost in most companies. What they call "materials consumed" is often, instead, an estimate derived by multiplying a product's standard material cost by the amount produced. Periodically, typically every few months, this estimated consumption is reconciled with actual material usage, based on a physical count. Even when actual (rather than standard) materials transactions are recorded, they are typically recorded in dollar, rather than in physical, terms.[5]

Returning to our history, as companies began substituting equipment for labor, investment costs became increasingly burdensome to the small, cash-poor company of the time—which still tended to finance itself out of its cashbox. This led to the development of another set of systems for evaluating capital investment—the capital budgeting system (the subject of Chapter 3), and one for measuring the effectiveness with which existing capital equipment was being utilized. As a result, the internal accounting systems of most companies today are dominated by mechanisms for measuring direct labor and machine utilization. These measures, developed with great precision (but often too late to guide effective decision-making), then serve to drive their cost allocation schemes, capital budgeting systems, and, ultimately, management evaluation systems.

It is our position that this approach to cost accounting and capital budgeting is increasingly afflicted with a new and dangerous type of adverse variance: a "reality variance." This new variance owes its existence to a variety of causes but is essentially due to the application of a set of tools developed in an early twentieth-century context to today's very different technological and competitive environment. For example, the cost of direct labor in a typical high-technology company today seldom exceeds 10 percent of total costs; increasingly it is under 5 percent, as are depreciation charges. Indirect factory

costs—particularly materials control, quality assurance, maintenance and process engineering, and software development—have
been growing rapidly, on the other hand, and in many companies
now add up to five to ten times direct labor costs. As a result, the
cost accounting systems such companies are using to measure performance, and which influence their behavior, devote three-quarters
or more of their energies to measuring costs that are likely to account
for less than 15 percent of the total. By focusing attention on less
important factors in today's production environment, they distract
managers from other factors that are more critical to their success.

As the so-called fixed costs become a larger and larger component
of total costs, as product life cycles shorten, and as shared activities
become more and more critical to competitive success, one might
expect that the traditional means for assigning them to products
would start to break down. Indeed, it can lead to quite bizarre behavior if managers are deluded into thinking that costs constructed in
this way actually bear some relationship to the true costs of making
a product or operating a process. For example, if a company uses
indirect workers for equipment changeovers and setups but it allo-
cates indirect costs on the basis of direct labor hours, almost inevitably it will underestimate the cost of producing low-volume products
while overstating the cost of high-volume products.[6]

We know one high-tech company whose overhead costs add up to
almost ten times its direct labor costs, which come to roughly ten
dollars per hour. Managers in this company are motivated to buy a
part from an outside vendor, if at all possible, instead of making it
internally because in so doing they reduce the costs for which they
are responsible (which include the allocated costs) by $(1 + 10) \times$
$10, or $110, for each direct labor hour saved. Managing an increasing volume of subcontracting, however, requires additional overhead
personnel. Therefore, this company finds that its direct labor costs
are decreasing, while its overhead costs are increasing—which drives
up its overhead allocation rate for the remaining products and motivates its managers to subcontract even more. While extreme, this
company is not atypical of many today that are being driven in unanticipated directions by the apparently innocuous mandates of their
accounting systems.

Not only are overhead costs increasing as a percentage of the total,
but many companies today are finding that direct labor costs are not
as variable as they used to be, and as their cost allocation schemes
assume. Seniority rules, the fear of permanently losing especially

good workers or particularly valuable skills in the event of a layoff, and the increase in worker motivation and worker-manager interaction that come from various forms of "lifetime employment" have made labor costs almost as fixed as management costs in many companies today. Nor are the fixed costs quite as fixed as they were assumed to be. As was pointed out in Chapter 1, the increasing pressure of foreign competition has led a number of companies to make substantial reductions in their management and investment costs in the past several years. Just as all costs are variable in the long run, in today's sophisticated manufacturing environment they are increasingly fixed in the short run. And as companies discover how complicated the interplay is between reject levels and factory throughput time, between product design and manufacturing productivity, between purchasing and equipment maintenance and work-in-process, the notion that one can somehow separate all these interrelated costs into tidy packages on a monthly or even quarterly basis becomes somewhat ludicrous.

Moreover it is dangerous. Not only does it tend to blur what is really going on in a factory—while giving managers a false sense of accuracy and completeness—it may induce companies to pursue the mirage of increased profitability (as depicted in their financial reports, prepared according to GAAP) by avoiding actions and investments that are essential to their long-term survival. They become dependent on external suppliers for critical skills and parts, a process that has come to be called the "hollowing out" of corporations, and then watch indignantly as these suppliers evolve into competitors. They choose to use an older machine to make a given part rather than a more modern machine, even though it produces higher quality and requires less setup, because the old machine is fully depreciated.

Almost as bad, as pointed out in Chapter 3, they delay investing in advanced manufacturing technology because their traditional approach to measuring its costs and benefits suggests that it will not offer as high a return on investment as they are used to, since it does not take into account the profound changes that the new technology can make in their cost structure, flexibility, and relationship with customers. They overinvest in hardware and underinvest in the software development and worker training essential to extracting the full potential from that hardware (see Chapter 6), because hardware can be depreciated over several years but software and training expenses reduce profitability immediately. They avoid splitting up oversized, bureaucratic factories into small, entrepreneurial units with limited product lines and responsibilities because their traditional cost models suggest that this will lead to higher overhead costs without any effect on variable costs. Many companies that have carried out this kind of refocusing, however, have found both assumptions to be incorrect.

Today's accounting systems for measuring manufacturing performance thus have become an impediment to competitive advantage. Their preoccupation with variances from internal standards and annual budgets obscures the importance of continual improvement. And without clear ties to one's competitive environment or strategy, or references to comparative manufacturing capabilities, the numbers generated by them can lead to poor decisions and competitive weakness.

As a result, many companies (and even a small but increasing number of academics) have begun the search for other approaches to measuring and evaluating manufacturing performance. Some are experimenting with more satisfactory ways of allocating overhead costs, perhaps based on different "cost drivers," such as machine hours, the number of customer orders or jobs scheduled, factory throughput times (or the amount of work-in-process inventory), and the number of parts produced. Others are exploiting the capabilities of new computerized manufacturing technologies to capture detailed data about a given job or process on a real-time basis, thereby allowing individual operations or transactions to be assigned to specific support activities. Still others are attempting to develop entirely new types of performance measures—such as customer perceptions of quality or service satisfaction, time to launch new products, or process throughput times—and new ways for combining them.[7]

Measuring Improvement in Manufacturing Performance

If a firm thoroughly dominates its markets, controls the basic technologies in its products and processes, expects little change in the demands of its (satisfied) customers and has little actual or prospective competition, it may get along quite well doing what it always has done. For everybody else, long-term success depends on getting better and better: continually learning and applying new knowledge to improve performance. This requires a clear conception of where the organization has been and where it is going. Manufacturing therefore needs a measurement system that provides perspective on its direction and rate of improvement. Traditional accounting systems rarely do this.

The last thing most manufacturing managers need, however, is another new statistic or report added on to all the others they have to deal with. The typical factory, in fact, has too many measures and reports, generated over time for a variety of purposes: internal control, pricing of special customer requests, inventory valuation, capital budgeting requests or audits, governmental mandates, special studies, and on and on. Like the number of products in a product line, or the number of personnel in a staff group, measurements and reports seem to have an ability to grow of their own accord.

Many of the reports that routinely get produced in a company have been developed in response to the needs of the company's external reporting system and therefore reflect the concerns discussed in the preceding section. In the case of others, the original reason for developing the report may either have been forgotten or is no longer relevant. Many are likely to violate one or more of the three criteria every report should satisfy:

1. It should be tailored to the satisfaction of a specific, important need (and one not met by other reports), in a timely fashion.
2. It should be based on the most relevant and objective information available.
3. It should be simple enough to be widely understandable, credible, and usable within the organization.

By making report generation easier and faster, the advent of powerful computers, low-cost storage devices, and high-speed printers have tended to accelerate report proliferation. Moreover, rather than centralizing and standardizing their preparation, modern technology tends to encourage the development of different reporting and measuring systems for different plants within the same plant system, making it difficult for them to properly compare their performance or to learn from each other's experience. As a result, the complaint of factory managers in many companies is not that they do not have enough data but rather that they are inundated by a *blizzard* of reports—each conveying a somewhat different message depending upon the measures used and whether performance is compared against standards, last year's results, budgets, or industry (or sister plant) averages.

Rather than helping to bring blurry data into clearer focus, these reports often tend to obscure and distort the operating realities that managers have to understand. What they need are detailed, accurate data about the important activities that are going on in their plant and some way to combine those data together so that one can answer such questions as, "How effectively is the plant operating, overall?" "What activities within it are operating particularly well or poorly?" and "Are we getting better at the things that are really important to strengthening our competitive position?"

In this section we will describe an approach to answering these questions that a number of companies are beginning to experiment with. It requires the calculation of the efficiency (productivity) with which the plant converts key resources into outputs, an analysis of the behavior of these productivities over time, and then a procedure for tying them all together into an overall total factor productivity (TFP) measure of performance. This is the approach used in Chapter 6, where we discuss the management characteristics that seem to spell the difference between high-performing and low-performing factories.[8]

Single-Factor Productivity
In essence, productivity is a measure of the efficiency with which physical inputs are translated into physical outputs. This focus on *physical* transformations is in contrast to the usual *financial* measures of performance, which assess the effectiveness with which monetary inputs are translated into monetary outputs. In practice, however, as will be discussed, physical inputs and outputs are often difficult to deal with, so one is forced to use approximations based on monetary values.

If adequate physical measures (units, tons, gallons, etc.) are available, however, one can begin to estimate a company's overall productivity by calculating the single factor productivity (sfp) of each of the important resources (labor hours, material, management time, etc.) that are used in the production of its products:

$$\text{sfp}_{A,2} = \frac{\text{output of product A}}{\text{input of resource 2}}$$

Note that $\text{sfp}_{A,2}$ is *not* equal to the amount of resource 2 that is used in producing each unit of product A (which is the basis of most product cost analyses); instead it is the *inverse* of that number—the average amount of product A generated per unit of resource 2.

Unless the process is exactly specified by the design of the equipment it uses or by the physical or chemical laws that underlie it, there is seldom any way of determining whether the value of a partial productivity ratio is good or bad. That is, although it is usually possible to estimate how many worker hours were consumed in producing a given product, it is difficult to say how many *ought* to have been consumed. Industrial engineers can perform time-and-motion studies to estimate the number of hours that an "average" person working at a "normal" work pace using a given method and tools should need to produce a given amount of a certain product, but the industrial engineers at one company may arrive at a very different estimate than would those at another company which produces a similar product using a different process. Therefore, lacking any objective measure of what a given ratio ought to be, companies usually confine their attention to determining how it is changing over time.

Consider the following simple example. A company produces the same product, using the same raw materials, during two time periods. The specific inputs and outputs during these two periods are as follows:

Table 5-1 Resources Utilized in Producing Product A

| | Period 1 | | Period 2 | |
Output	Amounts	sfp	Amounts	sfp
Units produced (thou.)	22.14		24.78	
Inputs				
Materials used				
material 1 (lbs)	25.99	0.852	29.08	0.852
material 2 (sq ft)	19.41	1.141	20.95	1.183
Energy (mill. of BTUs)	51.30	0.432	56.19	0.441
Labor (thou. of hrs.)	4.73	4.681	5.31	4.667
Equipment (thou. of hrs.)	3.22	6.876	3.60	6.876
Working capital (thou. of $)	68.75	0.322	78.64	0.315

If a single factor productivity has increased between period 1 and period 2, it indicates that more output has been produced per unit of that resource than in the earlier period; conversely, a smaller ratio indicates decreased productivity. The actual productivity changes are therefore as follows:

Table 5-2 Productivity Changes Between Period 1 and Period 2

Resources	Single Factor Ratios		Ratio	Productivity Change (%)
	Period 1	*Period 2*		
Material 1	0.852	0.852	1.00	0
Material 2	1.141	1.183	1.0368	+ 3.68
Energy	0.432	0.441	1.0208	+ 2.08
Labor	4.681	4.667	0.9970	− 0.30
Equipment	6.876	6.876	1.00	0
Working capital	0.322	0.315	0.9780	− 2.2

Measuring Productivity Using Value Added

In the attempt to simplify the calculations required and reduce the impact of changes in material prices on their productivity measure, many companies prefer to base their productivity calculations on the concept of "value added" rather than on sales output or revenues, where

$$\text{Value added} = \text{Sales revenue} - \text{Cost of purchased materials and services}$$

Some companies, in fact, define productivity as "value added per employee." The problem with this measure is that it does not take into account the effect of price changes on either value added or wage rates. Therefore, these companies can be lulled by ever-increasing values of value added per employee into thinking that their labor productivity is increasing when, in fact, it may be decreasing.

This approach has two additional drawbacks. First, it eliminates the possibility of determining how much of a company's total productivity improvement is due to more efficient use of purchased materials. Second, it takes the productivity improvement that *is* due to purchased materials and attributes it instead to more efficient use of energy and labor. For example, the 0.3 percent deterioration in labor productivity calculated in Table 5-2 might be converted into an apparent *increase* if output were measured in terms of value added rather than units produced and if materials comprised the bulk of total input costs. Appendix B contains further details about productivity measurement and how to deal with some of its problems.

Total Factor Productivity

Normally, as in the example in Table 5-2, single-factor productivities do not change at the same rate. The productivity of material 2, for example, has increased, while the productivity of labor hours has decreased. How can one determine whether this trade-off is favorable or unfavorable—that is, whether the *overall* process is operating better or worse than before? Managers generally have to rely on their informed judgment in evaluating such trade-offs, but some are so critical that specific procedures are mandated. The capital budgeting system in place in most companies (and described in Chapter 3) is the usual means for making the trade-off between the productivity of capital and that of labor and other factors. Its function is to determine whether the increase in investment in a particular machine or project (which will cause capital productivity to decline, if output does not rise sufficiently) is justified by the reduction in the usage of other inputs (causing their productivity to increase).

Looking at just one or two productivities, as do companies whose accounting systems focus attention primarily on direct labor and machine utilization, can seriously bias management evaluations and lead to dysfunctional game playing within an organization. Consider the consequences of adopting total sales per employee as one's primary measure of productivity. If managers are being measured by the value of that ratio alone, they would be tempted to begin purchasing more and more parts and services from outside vendors. Or they might shift their emphasis to products whose costs are dominated by purchased parts or materials or require very little labor. They might even—if the manufacturing organization is given credit for everything produced, whether it is sold directly or goes into the finished-goods inventory of some downstream distribution organization—emphasize long runs of simple products rather than incur the time-consuming setups and additional process steps required for producing more sophisticated products in frequent, small batches.

To determine whether the overall productivity of the process that transforms all these resources into product A has increased or decreased, one has to find some way for combining the productivities of different resources (hours, pounds, BTUs, etc.) into an overall TFP. Similarly, if one wants to determine the overall productivity of the factory or department that produces several products, it is necessary to combine their individual TFPs in some way. The easiest way to do this is to take a weighted average of the different productivities of different resources or products, where the weights reflect the monetary value of each resource or product. Similarly, assuming that the price of a product reflects changes in its quality over time, weighting the number of units produced by their market price allows one to adjust for different quality (or product performance) levels from one year to the next.

If one introduces monetary values into one's calculations, however, at some point one will have to correct for the impact of whatever price changes have occurred between two periods. Otherwise, one's single factor productivity ratios will reflect the changes that have occurred in prices as well as in efficiency. For example, the conclusion (from Table 5–2) that the productivity of product A's working capital decreased between periods 1 and 2 rested on the assumption that a dollar of working capital in period 2 was equivalent to a dollar in period 1. If the value of a dollar in period 2 were only 95 percent of the value of a dollar in period 1, however, then only $74,710 (= .95 × $78,640) worth of period 1 dollars was used for working capital in period 2, implying that the productivity of working capital *increased* by 3 percent in period 2.

Using (inflation–adjusted) monetary values to reflect resource consumption makes it possible to estimate the aggregate change in TFP between periods 1 and 2. For example, again using the results of Table 5–2, if material 1 accounts for 40 percent of the total cost of product A, material 2 for 20 percent, energy for 5 percent, labor for 25 percent, and equipment for 10 percent,

$$\frac{TFP_2 - TFP_1}{TFP_1} = (.4)(0) + (.2)(3.68) + (.05)(2.08) + (.25)(-.30) + (.10)(0)$$
$$= 0.77\%.[9]$$

Using a measure like TFP to track factory performance gives managers an integrated perspective on performance. But it also lays the foundation for understanding the dynamics behind where the plant has been, and where it is going. Figure 5–1 graphs the behavior of TFP over a ten-year period in a plant that we have studied in some depth. Until 1982, this plant had tracked performance using cost variances and comparisons with annual budgets, focusing considerable attention on direct labor. According to these measures, the plant had performed quite well. But no one had ever looked at a measure that was as comprehensive as TFP, and no one had ever looked at any measure over the entire history of the plant.

Figure 5–1 shows that the plant has had an uneven history. The

Figure 5-1 Total Factor Productivity Index: Plant B

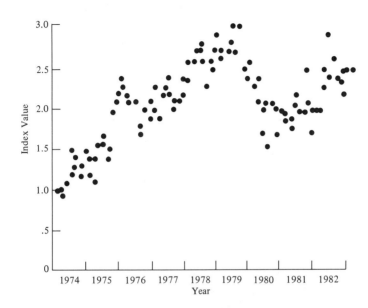

TFP data document a significant increase in performance over the period, but they also suggest that much of that improvement came in the early years of the plant's history. After strong improvement during a start-up phase that lasted into 1976, TFP went through a long up-and-down cycle; performance in 1982 was only somewhat above that of 1976. Investigation showed that only part of this pattern could be explained by cyclical changes in demand. Much of it reflected changes in capital investment, and in particular, the way the plant managed equipment introductions; we return to these issues in Chapter 6. Given such a perspective, plant managers are in a much better position to gauge changes in performance, and to focus their efforts on improving TFP over time.

As this example suggests, TFP can be a useful way to measure factory performance. Most companies already collect the basic raw data required but need to develop a new way to process and report these data. This can be surprisingly difficult, since most companies find it much easier to build factories in remote locations, master new technologies, and enter new markets than to change the derivation and arrangement of the numbers in their accounting reports. But unless an organization finds some way of measuring productivity directly, rather than using existing surrogates (such as gross margin, machine utilization, and labor variances), the people in it will probably perceive any attempts to improve manufacturing performance to be simply the latest in a long history of cost-reduction programs. Such a perception can cause them to fall back on traditional approaches for reducing costs, as measured by their familiar accounting reports, in the short run.[10] In so doing, they may miss opportunities to uncover the real sources of superior performance and competitive advantage in their organization.

Conducting a Manufacturing Competitive Analysis

The central question that any system of measurement must answer is, How are we doing? For captains of ships as for captains of industry, the necessary follow-on question is, Compared to what? We have already suggested that a look at a factory's (or a firm's) history is essential. But in creating a competitive advantage in manufacturing, the only standard of comparison that really matters is the performance of one's best competitors (actual or potential). Thus, an effective performance measurement system must provide insight into how a company compares with its best competitors with respect to the manufacturing capabilities upon which its manufacturing strategy is based.

Such a competitive analysis contains three elements. The first is an objective review of the company's fundamental decision patterns in manufacturing, to see whether and how they translate into manufacturing capabilities and competitive advantage. The second is an analysis of manufacturing's impact on overall sales, investment, and profitability. The third is a compilation of benchmark data for evaluating key manufacturing activities; this indicates the potential for improvement.

Decision Patterns in Manufacturing

Behind a firm's manufacturing capabilities and performance lies a pattern of structure and infrastructure decisions: capacity, facilities, technology, sourcing, work force, quality, production planning and control, and organization. A manufacturing analysis that does not include an understanding of these decision patterns and the forces that drive them is incomplete. Similarly, a competitor's decision patterns implicitly define its manufacturing strategy and provide a framework within which to analyze its behavior.

The first step in the approach we recommend for analyzing competitive manufacturing decision patterns (see Table 5-3) is to identify a relatively small number of competitors who are representative of the major modes of competition in the industry. Many pharmaceutical firms, for example, separate their competitors into two major groups—ethical and generic. The first do research on, and develop, proprietary drugs sold under a brand name. The second develop and produce drugs that are not protected by patents and are sold under a generic label.

Let us examine a representative company in each group: Merck (ethical) and Zenith (generic). These two companies are both successful, and good information about their manufacturing strategies is available.[11] The following brief comparison—based both on information about the policies each company has followed in each of the decision categories and on an assessment of the forces or attitudes that drive those decisions—suggests what one can do with publicly available information, examined within the framework of Table 5-3. This second step requires insight into each company's basic values (such as Merck's overriding commitment to customer service) or strategic objectives (Zenith's insistence on carrying a broad line), since its intent is to discover what the company's competitive capabilities are, and how those capabilities are likely to evolve in the future.

Table 5-3 Competitive Analysis of Manufacturing Decision Patterns

Step 1: Establish Structure
    A. identify major modes of competing
    B. generate complete competitor list (actual and prospective)
    C. select a representative subset for study

Step 2: Data Analysis for Selected Competitors
    A. manufacturing strategy by element: evidence, sources, drivers
    B. insights from each element

Step 3: Overall Competitive Assessment
    A. comparison of firms
    B. comparison of modes of competing
    C. across firms and modes (self versus full range of competitors)

Step 4: Manufacturing's Competitive Response
    A. conclusions from above
    B. implications for one's manufacturing strategy
    C. plan of action

Table 5–4 presents a summary of our analysis of the decision patterns at Merck and Zenith. The dominant themes that run through Merck's manufacturing decisions are quality and customer service. The mission of manufacturing, which is integral to Merck's strategy, appears to be, Never fail to deliver a high-quality product to a customer whenever that customer demands it. Thus, Merck's efforts to become a leader in manufacturing technology, and its significant investment in internal processes and software, were driven more by a desire to create higher-quality products and faster response to customer demands than by a desire to cut costs.

In contrast to the coherence and integration found at Merck, Zenith's manufacturing decisions demonstrate some conflicting tendencies. It is influenced most strongly by the heavy cost pressure it faces in its markets. Decisions about capacity (pursue high utilization), technology (minimize R & D; invest for cost reduction), and work force (low wages) all seem to be driven by a desire to produce products of acceptable quality at low cost. However, Zenith also tries to produce a broad line of products and to introduce new products frequently. Thus, its main plants are not focused, it carries high inventories, and it has little control over its sources of supply. There is little evidence that Zenith has been able to develop a manufacturing strategy that will create the capabilities it needs to deliver a high variety of products at low cost. In the meantime, manufacturing's mission seems to be, Produce a broad line, but run as lean as possible.

Once information about representative competitors has been developed, a company needs to compare its decision patterns in manufacturing with theirs (step 3). Top management must ask itself: "How well does manufacturing support our business strategy?" and "In what ways does manufacturing create a competitive advantage for us?"

Given such an assessment of decision patterns, a manufacturing organization will have a more realistic sense of what is possible and where it stands. It will understand both its own tendencies and those of its competitors, and it will have a clearer sense of the threats and opportunities it faces. As interesting as such an analysis may be, however, it will have little impact if the organization does not act upon it.

The capstone of a competitive measurement system, therefore, is step 4: developing a competitive response for the manufacturing organization. For example, after looking at Merck and Zenith, one of their competitors might come to the conclusion that achieving production flexibility (defined as the ability to produce a wide variety of products at a competitive cost) is critical in their business. Such a comparison may also reveal that its own plants are poorly focused, its broad product line has been achieved only at the expense of very high overhead costs, and that failure to act will leave it vulnerable to competitors who are able to develop a more flexible, less overhead-intensive system. Such implications become the starting point for a plan of action.

Manufacturing's Impact on Business Profitability
An analysis of comparative manufacturing decision patterns provides one type of insight into the nature of different competitors' manufacturing strategies. But an effective competitive measurement system also needs to provide information about how decisions in manufacturing combine to influence the performance of the business. The second element in our manufacturing competitive analysis, therefore, is a financial analysis of manufacturing's role in the profitability of the business as a whole.

In Appendix A we describe a method for decomposing the profitability of a business unit (measured by return on assets) into four determinants: the profit margin on sales, the ratio of break-even sales to capacity, the capacity utilization rate, and the ratio of sales to assets. Breaking profitability down in this way enables one to learn something about manufacturing's financial impact on the business, since manufacturing decisions and capabilities principally affect costs, capacity, break-even sales, and asset intensity. With comparative information one can thus gain insight into how different approaches to manufacturing affect profitability.

For example, a manager who wants to improve the ROI of his or her business can follow one or more of the following approaches:

1. Increase one's production volume if this can be done without reducing selling prices to the point where the reduction in profit margin offsets the increase in capacity utilization.
2. Decrease the business's fixed costs (which serves to reemphasize that "fixed" costs are not fixed in the long run), thereby reducing its break-even sales level.
3. Increase the profit margin by increasing selling prices, by reducing variable conversion costs (approaches for improving labor, materials, and energy productivity are the subject of Chapter 6), or by selectively culling low-contribution products from the product line; or

Table 5-4 Comparison of Manufacturing Strategy Decision Patterns in the Pharmaceutical Industry

Decision Category	Company	
	MERCK	ZENITH
Capacity	maintain excess capacity; avoid stockouts; build new capacity ahead of market demand	past: match demand; expand by working overtime or adding shifts current: lead demand, but try to achieve high utilization
Facilities	bulk (active ingredients): traditionally focused, now moving to multipurpose, modular pharmaceutical: multiple products, strategically located near markets	pharmaceutical: broad product lines produced in all facilities
Technology	manufacturing technology leader; internal development of both software and hardware for automated processes; focus on improved quality and customer service	follower in technology; standard off-the-shelf equipment; introduce automation only if justified by cost savings
Vertical integration	high level of vertical integration, from packaging to direct sales	low level of integration; purchase packaging and active ingredients from many suppliers

Work force	"We hire the best." Above average pensions, generous fringes; substantial in-house training and support for education; union relationships legalistic, adversarial	hourly workers paid less than industry average; senior level executives have significant industry experience
Quality	product quality is top priority; company quality standards set higher than regulatory requirements of *any* country	exists at "razor's edge" of FDA regs; 33 recalls in 1986—but major effort to upgrade quality under way
Production planning	centralized production scheduling using MRP II system; maintains high finished goods inventory: will meet any demand with 24-hour delivery	short production runs, many changeovers, many products make scheduling a "nightmare"; very high finished goods inventory, but very low work-in-process
New product development	heavy R & D investment, focused on proprietary products and applications over a broad range of categories	minimal investment in R & D, focused on generic versions of established products, and formulations that permit lower cost
Performance measurement	tied to quality, dependability, and image of the firm	focused primarily on manufacturing cost
Organization	functional, process-focused organization; centralized control; technically oriented leadership; decision-making is cross-functional, and collaborative; strong communications system	flat organization; decentralized decision-making fostering entrepreneurial spirit; reporting structures at operating level are a loose matrix

4. Reduce the asset intensity of the business by improving capital productivity and reducing work-in-process inventories.

By observing how a management group chooses to maneuver its way through this thicket of possibilities, one can learn much about manufacturing's role in the business.

The basic information needed to estimate these components of profitability can often be obtained through some creative digging into public documents (such as annual reports, prospectuses, government studies, and trade journals), and discussions with suppliers, customers, employees, and consultants. The following example demonstrates the kind of insight that can be provided by this approach. Three business units, all making similar products, generated comparative financial statistics over three two-year periods as are shown in Table 5-5.

Business B had historically been regarded as the industry's best, whereas business C was a "dog" that had been acquired by a new management group in 1976 and appeared to have been "turned around." How good, in reality, is business B, and how good a job have the new managers of business C done?

An analysis based only on the data in Table 5-5 suggests that business C's major problem is its profit-to-sales ratio, while business B's profitability has been both strong and stable. More insight is provided in Table 5-6, where other measures are provided.

What becomes clear, given this additional detail, is that all three businesses are achieving similar contribution levels (although business C's has actually *fallen* significantly under the new management). Business C's major problem, or at least the major difference between it and the other businesses, appears to be in its fixed costs,

Table 5-5   Performance Measures for Three Manufacturing Businesses

Business	Year	PBT/Sales	PBT/Net Assets
A	1983–84	.033	.11
	1981–82	.008	.02
	1979–80	.030	.08
B	1983–84	.034	.16
	1981–82	.032	.12
	1979–80	.036	.15
C	1983–84	.013	.05
	1981–82	(.010)	(.03)
	1979–80	.019	.10

Table 5-6 Performance Measures for Three Manufacturing Businesses

Business	Year	Contribution (%)	B-E Sales/Capacity	Capacity Utilization (%)	PBT/Sales	Sales/Assets	PBT/Assets
A	1983–84	.23	.74	.86	.033	3.3	.11
	1981–82	.29	.69	.71	.008	2.5	.02
	1979–80	.26	.75	.85	.030	2.7	.08
B	1983–84	.25	.77	.89	.034	4.7	.16
	1981–82	.24	.78	.90	.032	3.8	.12
	1979–80	.27	.75	.87	.036	4.3	.15
C	1983–84	.25	.90	.95	.013	3.8	.05
	1981–82	.31	.81	.79	(.010)	3.1	(.03)
	1979–80	.35	.76	.81	.019	5.2	.10

which have driven its B-E sales up to 90 percent of capacity. Interestingly enough, this figure has also deteriorated under the new managers. Their major accomplishment appears to have been that they increased substantially the volume of production. Upon investigation it was found that they achieved this largely by pulling back from subcontractors some small-volume, nonstandard products that formerly had been farmed out because they had been felt to interfere with the normal production flows in the business. The net effect was to increase the variable costs of the operation but spread its fixed costs over a substantially greater volume. As a result, the profit/sales ratio of the business increased.

This, together with a write-off of some apparently obsolete equipment, enabled the new management group to leverage a modest PBT/sales figure into a barely acceptable return on assets. The questions that arise out of this analysis are, Have business C's actions really constituted a "turnaround," and have they enhanced or impaired its future profitability in the process? Our analysis suggests a quite different answer to these questions than the initial performance data indicated. Clearly their actions have caused a short-term improvement in the business's profitability. But the business is vulnerable. Unless real improvements in cost or differentiation occur, the situation in business C is likely to deteriorate.

Competitive Benchmarking

For operating managers in factories, engineering departments, laboratories, and distribution centers, information about things like market share or the ratio of corporate sales to assets is interesting but not particularly helpful in creating the kind of operating capabilities that make a difference in the marketplace. What is needed are data on competitive performance in specific activities that are central to the operation's mission; this is the purpose of a technique called competitive benchmarking.

The experiences of two very different companies, Chaparral Steel and Xerox, illustrate how benchmarking can work. Chaparral started in 1975 as a minimill producing simple reinforcing bars. Today it manufactures a wide range of structural shapes and special quality bar steel; production in 1987 was 1.5 million tons. From the day that it opened its doors, Chaparral set out to be the best in its business. And that meant that it had to identify who were the best makers, rollers, and finishers of steel in the world and compare itself against them.

Chaparral therefore established relationships with steelmakers in Europe and Japan and began regular visits to observe and learn from them. Typical practice is to send a small team (an operator, a supervisor, an engineer, and a maintenance technician) to talk with their counterparts at the target site. The team gathers data on specific parameters like equipment cycle times, yields, and inventory levels. But they also examine practices and methods to get some understanding of what lies behind the performance observed. Similar visits are made to equipment manufacturers to learn about the latest developments in technology.

The data developed in these benchmarking trips are compared with existing practice at Chaparral and then translated into higher targets for the operating groups. These targets are credible to operating personnel because they have observed comparable performance in other companies and understand that if they don't achieve them, their business will suffer. As each target is reached, Chaparral people watch for new developments in key companies, and for the emergence of new leaders. Recently, for example, Pohang, the Korean steelmaker, has become the benchmark for landed cost in the United States. Gordon Forward, CEO of Chaparral, has therefore stated, "Our objective is to get our labor costs below the cost per ton of the ocean voyage from Korea. That way, they can pay their people zero and we can still meet them at the unloading docks with a cost advantage."

Benchmarking has also played an important role at Xerox.[12] Faced with declining market share and eroding profitability in its basic copier business, in 1979 Xerox began a searching examination of its methods and practices. Beginning with an engineering examination of competitive products, including a study of Fuji Xerox, its partly owned subsidiary in Japan, Xerox managers uncovered strong evidence of a sizable cost gap between it and its major Japanese competitors. The lower Japanese costs replaced the traditional annual budgets as targets for Xerox manufacturing.

Xerox soon found that even deeper insight could be achieved by looking at similar activities in companies with which it did not compete. A particularly interesting example is the benchmarking relationship that Xerox developed with a retailer and mail-order house for outdoor goods. Eager to improve its warehousing and distribution operations, the logistics and distribution organization at Xerox assigned a staff member to find a prime candidate for benchmarking. After searching in trade journals and discussing warehousing

systems and performance with consultants and logistics profession-
als, he recommended L. L. Bean of Freeport, Maine. It had developed a strong reputation for customer service, and the distribution
problems it faced were similar to Xerox's.

A visit to Freeport by a small group of Xerox managers uncovered
both similarities and differences in practice and performance. Although Bean's operations were largely manual, it had achieved a
high level of productivity. Table 5-7 compares 1982 labor productivity in L. L. Bean's warehouse operation with a proposed operation
at Xerox. Much of Bean's superiority could be explained by differences in methods: arranging materials so that fast moving items were
closer to stock pickers, choosing storage locations to minimize fork-
lift travel distance, and batching orders to minimize travel distance.

Xerox incorporated these findings into the performance targets
and systems being proposed for its modernized warehousing operations. This kind of benchmarking against similar activities in non-
competitor companies has won widespread support at Xerox and has
become standard practice in the operating groups responsible for implementing change. Xerox senior managers believe that it has been
an important factor behind their significant improvements in performance over the last nine years.

Although Chaparral and Xerox do benchmarking somewhat differently, there are common themes in the methods they use and the
philosophy that guides them. Table 5-8 briefly summarizes these
commonalities and the way information is developed and used. Perhaps the most important element is the involvement of operating
personnel in identifying target companies and collecting data. Members of the benchmarking team must be well trained; but if they do
their job well, the data collected will be relevant and the changes
suggested will be implemented successfully.

Table 5-7 Comparison of Productivity in Warehouse Operations, 1982

Productivity Measure	L. L. Bean	Xerox (planned)
Orders per worker per day	550	117
Lines[a] per worker per day	1,440	497

[a]A line is a standard measure of travel distance for one trip to a storage bin.
SOURCE: Tucker et al. (1987).

Table 5-8   Methods for Benchmarking

Step or Objective	Source or Method
1. Identify superior performance in critical activities (in both competitors and noncompetitors).	Trade journals; consultants; professional meetings; annual reports.
2. Expand information through direct contact.	Visits to selected firms by small multifunctional operating teams.
3. Prepare reports and communicate findings.	Summarize key findings; define benchmark levels of performance.
4. Develop and implement action plan.	Turn benchmarks into targets; change practices and procedures to achieve targets.

Summary and Implications

For the ship's captain in the midst of a long and uncertain voyage, the central questions a measurement system must answer are not how much money was made during the previous month or quarter but whether the ship is being guided and operated properly: Is it on course? Are the crew and vessel performing well? A measurement system should also raise strategic issues: Is the destination that has been chosen still appropriate? Is the course correct? What winds and currents are likely to be encountered? Is the crew prepared for the emergencies that are most likely to occur?

Like ship captains, captains of industry need systems of measurement that give them information about how they are doing compared both with their own history and with their toughest competitors. The approach to measurement that we have outlined in this chapter—using TFP to capture dynamic performance in the factory, breaking down an overall performance measure into its component parts, and conducting a competitive analysis to assess one's position relative to competitors—provides perspective and insight into capabilities, opportunities, and vulnerabilities. To be useful in supporting the creation of a competitive advantage in manufacturing, one's measures need to be both broad and integrated.

Too many managers try to steer their ships using accounting data that are narrow in focus and static in perspective. We suggest that a more dynamic perspective is necessary, and that the scope of the measurement system be broadened. Understanding output and input patterns over time is an important first element. But managers also need an external perspective—a comparison of competitive capabilities. An understanding of competitors not only can provide insight into one's own manufacturing strategy but it can also reveal relative strengths and weaknesses and how competitors are likely to react to various changes.

A dynamic and broadly based system of measurement will generate information that can be used at different levels in the organization for different purposes. Benchmarking, for example, can provide information that is useful both at the operating level, to improve the yields in a particular operation, say, and to top managers who want to assess their manufacturing organization's overall position. These dual requirements—relevance and timeliness at an operating level, and integration at a strategic level—have implications for the way the measurement system is organized and managed.

Any new measure (such as TFP), moreover, must provide information that is both accurate and credible. Operating groups should participate in defining and monitoring the system, because the information collected is more likely to be relevant and put to good use if the people who are going to use it are involved. This suggests that measuring manufacturing performance must be largely a line responsibility. Technical specialists may provide assistance, but the responsibility for defining the system, getting the right information, and putting it to use rests with the general manager.

| 6 |

The High-Performance Factory

Introduction

A manufacturing advantage that can stand up to international competition must be built upon high-performance factories: factories that can offer high quality, rapid on-time delivery, and low delivered cost. Superior performance is not achieved through new equipment, skillful management, or highly motivated workers alone; it is also the product of sustained concrete action on a very practical level. The challenge is to make real factories—one's *own* factories—whether new or old, work better than one's competitors'.

Comparing factories within the same industry around the world, one often finds huge differences between the best and the average. Even within the same company one often observes widely differing levels of performance among plants that produce similar products and employ similar manufacturing processes. Consider, for example, the performance of the five plants depicted in Figure 6-1. These plants produced the same product—an identical consumer packaged good—using the same manufacturing process. Moreover, they all belonged to the same company, and operated under the same corporate accounting, procurement, materials management, and compensation systems. Using the concept of total factor productivity (see Chapter 5 and Appendix B), we measured their performance over the same time period. Why are some of these factories so much more productive than others, what caused the changes in their productivity over time, and what can be learned from the high-performance ones?

These are the questions that motivated us to embark on a multi-year research project on manufacturing performance. Our work has taken us to plants in Japan, the United States, and Europe, covering

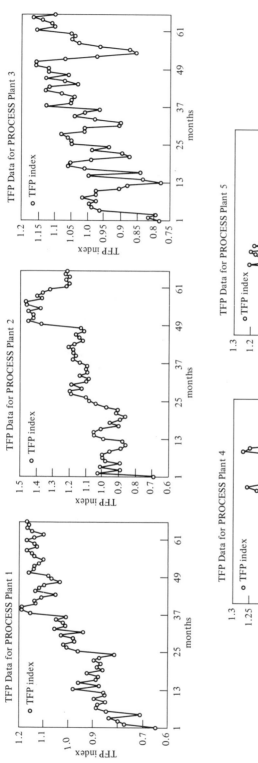

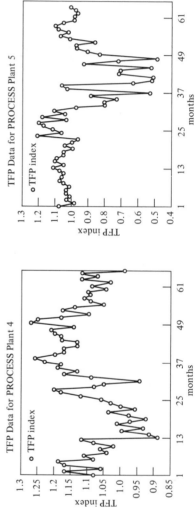

Figure 6-1   Productivity Comparison of Five Plants Producing Consumer Packaged Goods

a wide range of industries, including automobiles, semiconductors, electronics, steel, textiles, consumer packaged goods, pharmaceuticals, medical products, advanced ceramics, chemicals, and many others. Much of this work has been captured in case studies of specific situations. In twelve of the plants, moreover, we collected detailed monthly data on factory performance and management practices over several years. These plants belonged to three companies, but within each company different factories produced very similar products. Focusing on factories belonging to the same company—all facing similar technological and competitive environments—allowed us to concentrate on the impact of management policies and practices.

In this chapter we identify the central managerial themes that seem to make a significant difference in manufacturing performance. We first describe the key performance dimensions we focused on, and discuss how the measurement issues raised in Chapter 5 were handled in the factories we studied. We then discuss our major findings. The chapter concludes with a brief summary and interpretation of our results, followed by an introduction to Chapters 7 through 9 which explore these themes in more depth.

We found no magic answers; as in the golden years of American manufacturing, high performance today is built on a solid foundation of effective capital investment, thoughtful product and process design, and operating clarity and precision. There is one other common denominator in high-performance plants: an ability to learn—to achieve sustained improvement in performance over a long period of time. When assessing a manufacturing organization, learning is the bottom line.

Measuring Performance: Through the Glass Darkly

When we embarked on this study, we knew that a factory's performance would be affected by its company's competitive strategy, the nature of its product and process technologies, the requirements of its customers, and the behavior of its competitors. Therefore, we examined a variety of dimensions of performance. Our purpose was not, however, simply to catalogue the impact of various specific management practices on different performance measures but rather to isolate a few general principles that appear to have great impact on two key dimensions of performance: quality and productivity.

Our definition of productivity was the same as that in Chapter 5: the quantity of good output produced per unit of each resource (input) used. We measured quality by the degree to which a product conformed to the specifications laid out in its design.

Not only are productivity and quality important in their own right, we discovered that how an organization thinks about quality, how it goes about improving it, and how it relates quality to productivity was one litmus test for high performance. Productivity and quality were once thought to be in fundamental conflict: higher quality could only be achieved through more inspection, more processing, or tighter tolerances—all of which lowered productivity. Recent experience in a number of industries, however, has shown that this conflict is not inevitable. Indeed, in the high-performance organizations that we studied we found that higher quality and higher productivity went hand in hand; in fact, they reinforced one another.

To be able to say something concrete about management and performance, we needed hard data about a factory's quality and productivity, and how both had changed over time. Our need for data brought us up against the measurement issues discussed in Chapter 5. Working through those issues, however, provided a number of insights into the task of managing a factory, and why some managers were able to achieve relatively high performance in their factories. The issues, and our approach to them, are illustrated by the in-depth analysis we made of the twelve factories.[1]

The three companies that own them belong to three different industries. One of them employs a manufacturing process that is highly connected and automated. On the continuum from "job shop" to "continuous process," it is closest to the latter; therefore we refer to it as the PROCESS company. Another employs a batch manufacturing process based on a disconnected line-flow work organization; we refer to it as the FAB (fabrication and assembly) company.[2] The third company produces electronic equipment using a manufacturing process that ranges from process to fabrication and assembly and is characterized by very rapid changes in products and manufacturing processes; we refer to it as the HI-TECH company. All of the five factories of the process company and three of the four factories of the fabrication-and-assembly company are in the United States (the fourth is just across the border in Canada). Of the three factories belonging to the high-tech company, one is in the United States, one is in Europe, and one is in Asia.

The managers in these companies were surprisingly supportive of our research. This stemmed in part from the pressure that they were under to improve their organization's performance in an increasingly fierce competitive environment, but it also reflected their dissatisfaction with traditional tools and approaches. For many of these managers the usual periodic profit and loss statements and variance reports did not provide adequate up-to-date information about what was really going on in their factories. Although they routinely made comparisons and evaluated performance, cutting through the welter of detail to identify the policies and practices that really made a difference was quite difficult for them. Instead of clarifying their understanding, their performance measures often obscured their view—like looking through a thick, slightly fogged window. Thus, one of our first findings was how inadequate were the prevailing systems of performance measurement in most factories. And one of our first tasks was to develop a measure of performance that gave a clearer perspective on factory performance.

Measurement in Practice
What is it about traditional approaches to factory measurement that gets in the way of managerial efforts to improve performance? All the systems we encountered in our field research were based on the approach discussed in Chapter 5. Each month, plant controllers collected and reported data on the estimated costs incurred during the month for different types of inputs, such as labor, materials, and energy. They also reported the costs that would have been incurred if their workers and equipment had performed at a predetermined "standard" level. Actual costs were compared with standard costs, and variances were highlighted for management action. Different departments in the plant kept track of a multitude of items: the number of employees, the number of engineering changes, the value of assets in place, material and process reject rates, and so forth.

In theory this system is supposed to take the incredibly diverse range of activities in the plant and summarize them in a useful way. Yet we found that instead it often masked critical phenomena and distorted management's understanding of them. The problem is less in the basic, raw data that were collected and more in the way these data were processed and interpreted. For example, each month factory managers received a pile of reports, detailing cost variances, labor efficiencies, utilization rates, shipments, and so on, but were given no integrative measure of efficiency. Such a measure is not hard to calculate, however. Given the data generated by these factories' normal measurement systems, we were able to track, on a monthly basis, the production of each product manufactured in the factory, and all the labor, capital, energy, and materials that were consumed in its production. Then, as described in Appendix B, we converted these individual measures of productivity into one overall measure of Total Factor Productivity (TFP).

There were several aspects of our TFP data that appealed to the factory managers we worked with. Perhaps the most striking was that we presented data to them in constant dollar terms. Most accounting systems collect and report current dollars, which leads to distortions during periods of high inflation (such as the late 1970s and early 1980s). Consider the situation at FAB plant 1, depicted in Figure 6-2. According to its financial reports, production volumes at plant 1 fluctuated between $45 and $70 million from 1974 to 1982. After eliminating the effect of inflation, however, we found that there had been a fairly steady decline in output. In presenting this fact to the plant's staff, several executives initially expressed disbelief at the magnitude of the decline. They had come to think of their plant as a "$50-million plant"; their accounting system had masked the fundamental changes taking place. When we eliminated such distortions, we provided plant managers with data that were more useful and intuitively appealing to them than those contained in their usual reports.

Figure 6-2   Real vs. Nominal Output, FAB Plant 1

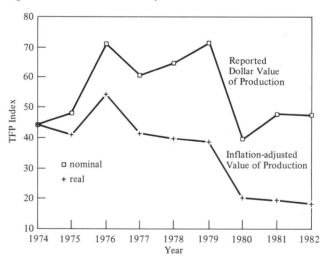

Another important advantage of our TFP approach is that it integrated and summarized the contributions of all the factors of production (according to their contribution to total cost). By incorporating the trade-offs made between quality and various costs, for example, or between capital and labor productivity, it provided a balanced perspective of overall performance. In contrast, traditional systems usually provide great detail but seldom integrate. To illustrate, one of the PROCESS plants was proud of the success achieved by a key department in reducing its labor hours and costs. Yet our data revealed that much of the "improvement" had been obtained simply by spending money on equipment that did little more than replace people. In focusing primarily on reducing direct labor, that department's managers had neglected to develop the management skills and systems needed to utilize this equipment effectively. As a result, the TFP (overall efficiency) of their department, which integrated labor productivity and capital productivity, had improved very little.

As was noted in Chapter 5, our twelve factories tended to be preoccupied with the cost of direct labor. Not only did their managers focus considerable attention on it, but their systems for measuring direct labor were generally more detailed and extensive than those for other inputs. This was true even in situations where direct labor was only a tiny fraction of total costs. In HI-TECH, for example, direct labor accounted for only 5 percent of total costs, but far more resources, time, and attention were directed at measuring direct labor than at any other aspect of factory performance. Using sophisticated bar-code scanners, HI-TECH managers could track the activities of line operators by the minute. In contrast, they had difficulty identifying even the number of manufacturing engineers working in the same department. Yet the cost of manufacturing engineers was more than five times that of direct labor.

Just as surprising, all the companies we studied paid relatively little attention to materials consumption and productivity. Often this blinded or distorted their performance evaluations. Early in our study we asked one of the FAB plants for information about the materials consumed in production during a series of months. When we used these data to estimate the productivity of these materials, we got results that were quite irregular. On investigation we discovered that this plant (and many others in our study) kept very good records of materials *purchased* but did not keep track of the materials actually *used* in a month. What it called "materials consumed" was, in fact, only an estimate derived by multiplying a product's standard material cost—which implied that the materials productivity was constant from month to month—by the number of units produced and adding an adjustment to reflect price changes.

The systems used to collect other kinds of data also frequently fostered serious misinterpretations—gaps between the meanings conveyed by the words used to describe various data and what those data actually measured. In one of the plants, for example, the plant controller reacted with surprise and annoyance to our analysis of the number of engineering changes that had been implemented. "We do not have anything like this level of engineering changes in this plant," he argued. "My office tracks and signs off on all engineering changes that go through this place, and I can tell you that your number is wrong." There was a brief silence; then the engineering manager quietly informed the group that only very large (in dollar terms) engineering changes were reviewed by the plant controller, and that our data were quite accurate. This revealed that one of the plant's key executives had been tracking something called "engineering changes," thinking that it meant "all engineering changes," when in fact it meant only "major engineering changes."

We found other examples of the bias and distortion introduced by traditional measurement approaches, as well as other, more subtle, problems that were created by the way certain measures were used in managing the plant. Consider, for example, the time horizon implicit in most performance data. In contrast to a cost system that is geared to an annual budget and a monthly or weekly variance report, our TFP data were presented in such a way that it was possible to gain a perspective on a factory's behavior over a period of several years. Few managers are able to develop this kind of perspective from the data provided by traditional measurement systems. Their time and attention are focused on variances that are inherently static in perspective and short-term in orientation. Moreover, their own tenure in a particular job or location is generally restricted to a few years. As a result, there tends to be little collective "memory" at the plant manager level. Our TFP measure, on the other hand, provided a more dynamic perspective on the manufacturing managers' mission: a sense of where their plant had come from, where it was, and where it was going. The managers thus found our approach useful and credible; we found it to be a solid basis for learning why some factories are more productive than others.

The Major Findings

Not surprisingly, our study of a variety of plants and companies highlighted the importance of the role played by management. As our work progressed, similar findings turned up again and again. Although different industries and technologies required different kinds of managerial skills, there were certain managerial activities, certain policies and practices, that characterized all the high-performance operations we studied. Good management really seemed to make a difference—much more than was reflected, in most cases, by plant managers' compensation or prestige in their companies.

The Power and Paradox of Capital Investment

It is widely believed—by economists, by public-policy makers, and by managers (including most of those in our study)—that the key to productivity improvement is investment in new equipment. Our analysis confirmed that capital investment plays a powerful role, but one that is far more complex and paradoxical than is commonly understood. It is clear from our data on these twelve factories, and from the experience of many other firms that we have observed, that capital investment is essential to sustained growth in performance over long periods of time (i.e., a decade or more). Managed poorly, however, new equipment can actually reduce performance significantly. Simply investing money in new facilities does not guarantee improvement. Long-term growth in productivity and quality is not primarily attributable to advances in raw technical capability, embodied in new machinery. Of greater significance is the impact that capital investment plays in driving continual improvement throughout the production organization.

Two examples illustrate the importance of investment-supported learning:

> In the PROCESS company, substantial investments were made in new equipment (designed in-house) to produce a new product whose sales were growing rapidly. In conjunction with these investments, the company's engineers and the operating team responsible for the product made myriad small changes to the product's design, the machinery, and operating practices. All these investment-related changes led to increased production capacity, improved products, and significant growth in TFP.

The FAB company attempted to expand the market for an established product by redesigning it, and subsequently invested in new production equipment. Although the new equipment was similar to the plant's existing machinery, the introduction of the new product created opportunities to make changes in work flows, testing procedures, and other operating practices. As volume increased, plant management discovered ways to make the new configuration accommodate expanded production without a proportional increase in the work force. Moreover, even the older equipment seemed to run more efficiently. TFP expanded significantly during this period.

In both of these examples the new equipment provided immediate first-level benefits because it was more advanced than the old. But the major impact on TFP came through the search for second-level performance improvements that were triggered by the opportunities created by the new equipment. The initial investment made it possible for the managers in these plants to uncover and exploit those opportunities. Moreover, they stimulated the search for, and the application of, better understanding of their production processes—the fundamental source of long-term growth in performance.

These examples illustrate that investment is an essential factor in progress; it unfreezes old assumptions, encourages the development of new ways for improving efficiency, and expands the factory's skills and capabilities. Figure 6-3 documents the importance that learning and capital investment had on long-term productivity growth at FAB's plant 2. We estimate that over the period from 1973 to 1982 its TFP increased by almost 96 percent. Some of that increase, of course, was related to changes in capacity utilization and to the introduction of new technology. Yet our analysis shows that about two-thirds of its TFP growth was explained by learning: improvements in operating efficiency that were not due to these factors. And fully three-fourths of that learning was related to capital investment. Without capital investment TFP would probably have increased, but at a much slower rate. Taking into account the second-level effects, we estimate that capital investment accounted for about two-thirds of the plant's long-term TFP growth.

It is important to add, however, that these long-term benefits are not obtained without some cost—and this cost is often greater than most people think. We found that the indirect costs associated with installing new equipment in a factory were sometimes staggering in their impact—often exceeding the cost of the equipment itself. Fig-

Figure 6-3 Capital Investment, Learning, and Productivity Growth in FAB Plant 2 (1973-1982)

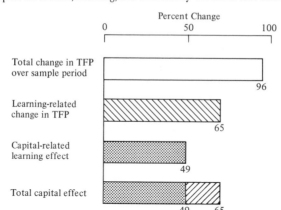

NOTE: These estimates are based on two regressions that each seek to explain TFP in plant 2. The first is a regression of TFP on time and cumulative volume. We define "learning-related change in TFP" as the amount of TFP growth (measured in percentage points) accounted for by cumulative volume. In the second regression we add the capital stock as an additional explanatory variable. The total capital effect is the amount of TFP growth accounted for by the capital stock in the second regression. The "capital-related learning effect" is the difference between the impact of cumulative volume on TFP in the first and second regressions. It provides a rough measure of how much of the overall learning effect was related to changes in the capital stock.

ure 6-4 illustrates the magnitude of the short-run impact of introducing new equipment in two of the FAB plants. In plant 1, for example, we estimate that a $1 million investment in new equipment imposed an additional $1.75 million cost, in terms of lost total factor productivity, on the plant during the first twelve months following installation. In plant 2, the costs imposed by the same level of investment were only $0.63 million. Looked at another way, if plant 1 had managed the introduction of new equipment so that these indirect costs were cut in half, TFP would have grown an additional 5 percent in the year following the change.

The fact that new equipment can lead to operating problems is not surprising. One might expect some initial loss of efficiency while the equipment is installed and workers learn to use it effectively. But, like throwing a stone into a pond, the ripple effects of new equipment are soon felt throughout the factory in the form of increased inventory, lower equipment utilization, higher reject rates, more downtime, and higher material waste. As a result, TFP is often reduced substantially. Again and again we found evidence that these TFP-related costs often exceeded the cost of the new equipment.

Figure 6-4   Short-run Impact of Capital Investment on Cost and TFP in Two FAB Plants

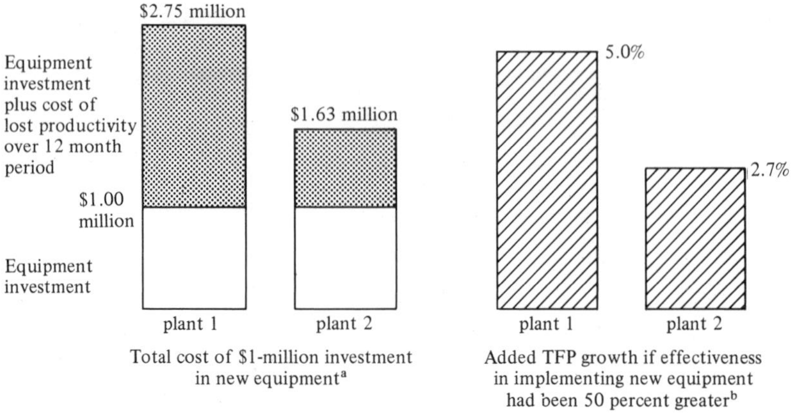

Total cost of $1-million investment
in new equipment[a]

Added TFP growth if effectiveness
in implementing new equipment
had been 50 percent greater[b]

[a]The second-level cost of investment is defined as the increase in total production cost caused by the new investment in the twelve-month period after installation. It is estimated using regression analysis, with log TFP as the dependent variable, and a twelve-month distributed lag on new investment (as a percentage of the capital stock), time, and capacity utilization as independent variables.

[b]The impact on TFP growth is estimated as the growth in TFP that would have occurred over a twelve-month period if the plant had been able to cut the cost of confusion and disruption (lost TFP) associated with introducing new investment by 50 percent.

Moreover, negative aftereffects on TFP often persisted for up to a year after the equipment was installed.

Although capital investment has a negative impact on performance in the short run, the size and duration of that impact depends on how the introduction of new equipment is managed. In the PROCESS plants, for example, we found that implementation difficulties were strongly influenced by the degree of process knowledge within the operating groups. In cases where supervisors and line operators were broadly trained and relatively independent of corporate or plant staff support services, introductions were more effective. We also found that capital investment was more disruptive in those plants where the objectives and priorities of the operating departments were at odds with those in process engineering.[3]

This, then, is the paradox of capital investment. It is essential to long-term productivity growth, and its impact can be quite powerful. Yet in the short term, depending on the way it is managed, it can reduce TFP and impose substantial costs on the production organization. The important implication of these two findings is that it is very difficult for a company to "invest its way out" of a productivity problem, at least in the near term. By itself, putting in new equipment will create confusion and make things worse for a number of months; moreover, unless coupled with a commitment to exploit the second-level opportunities for improvement created by the investment, the net benefits are likely to be small and slow in coming. Yet many companies seem to be attempting to deal with their competitive problems by relying almost solely on the first-level benefits of new equipment and new plants. Our results suggest that there are other things that they ought to be doing first—things that will be much less expensive, will take less time to show results, and will lay the foundation for extracting the full potential from capital investment when it occurs.

Designing for Manufacturability
The foundation of sustained improvement and high performance is made up of several building blocks. Of these, none is more important than product design. Our work in a variety of industries has uncovered numerous examples of the impact—for better or worse—of product design on quality and productivity. From the experience of companies that have been able to improve their manufacturing performance significantly through better design, two approaches stand out: reducing parts complexity and integrating process design with product design.

Design complexity is a function of the number of components in a given product, and the number of different components and parts required to build the product line as a whole. Complexity is the enemy of consistency, and process consistency is essential for high-quality production. Further, complexity lowers productivity and creates control problems that use up time and resources. Reducing complexity through product design, therefore, can lead to improvements in both quality and productivity. If not managed carefully, however, design can create far more complexity than the product really requires.

Take, for example, the situation observed in company R, a manufacturer of refrigerators. Operating in a very competitive market, company R had developed a relatively broad line of refrigeration products, ranging from large freezers to small tabletop models. Beset by problems of quality and cost, the company compared its approach to manufacturing with that of its toughest competitor. In the course of this analysis, it discovered that although its competitor's product line was just as broad, it required far fewer parts and components. For example, company R had to produce and manage seventy-eight different types of storage shelves, while its competitor had only twenty (and R concluded that even twenty was probably too many!). Similar problems showed up in plastic parts, door hardware, and cooling system components. Some of the diversity reflected a conscious attempt to differentiate the product, but much of it seemed to have neither rhyme nor reason.

Company R found, as have many other firms with complex parts structures, that it could reduce the complexity of manufacturing while still offering a wide range of product choices to the customer. One way to do that is to develop a restricted list of standard components and modules that must be drawn from when designing any new product. In the case of refrigerators, one might treat the cooling system as a module, with standard components from product to product. Instead of designing a different system for each product, the design engineers would choose from among a small set of cooling system modules. Further, within each module or system, just as within the product as a whole, there should be ongoing efforts to reduce the number of parts.

Our evidence suggests that design modularity and simplification can have a significant impact on performance. To illustrate the kinds of effects we have seen, Table 6-1 presents the results of a redesign effort on a major hydraulic system by an equipment manufacturer. Using value engineering to reduce the number of parts, together with a modular design, the equipment producer cut customer rejects by more than half and increased labor productivity by 52 percent.[4]

We have found many other examples of companies where product redesign efforts led to similar improvements in manufacturing performance. But reducing the number of components alone does not

Table 6-1   Impact of Modular Product Design and Value Engineering—
Hydraulic System

	Before	*After*
Time to market (months)	15	5
Number of components	63	9
Labor productivity index	100	152
Product-quality indices		
inspection costs	100	18
field returns	100	47.5

exploit all the potential that better product design has for improving the production system. Product design interacts with process design in a variety of ways; taking advantage of those interactions requires that they be managed in tandem. To illustrate the impact this can have on management behavior and results, consider the experience of PLUS Development Corporation when it designed and developed the Hardcard®, a hard disc drive incorporated into a single expansion board for an IBM personal computer.[5]

PLUS developed the Hardcard® in partnership with JEMCO, a Japanese company that believed strongly in the importance of integrating product and process design. The design engineers at PLUS had long been accustomed to a more arm's length relationship with manufacturing; working hand in glove with the JEMCO manufacturing engineers therefore took some getting used to. Whereas PLUS designers were used to rough specifications ("less than 10 mm"), the JEMCO team wanted detailed precision ("9.8 mm"). PLUS engineers designed for functionality and then looked for manufacturing problems; the JEMCO team wanted to design parts and components to exact specifications, anticipating and eliminating problems before going into production.

Putting the JEMCO approach into practice meant that both product designers and process engineers had to learn to communicate with and accommodate each other. For example, at one point the JEMCO engineers decided that a gap between two pieces of etched glass in the optical encoder could not be maintained within the desired tolerance limits during volume production. Given that information, PLUS engineers were able to loosen the tolerance required from 0.002 to 0.010 of an inch. At another point, the JEMCO team suggested that a metal plate guarding the drive be designed to fit into place without screws; it did not want the production worker to have to use any judgment in aligning the part.

Implementing these two suggestions (and numerous others as well) required a significant amount of engineering effort. The JEMCO engineers believed that such effort would be well rewarded, both in the form of higher yields and productivity and in a more reliable and maintainable product. But the product itself was not the only thing that changed under the JEMCO approach; the process was being designed at the same time and was modified several times to accommodate product requirements. For example, to get parts that would meet demanding specifications yet still could be made simply, JEMCO engineers invested time and money developing a special tool for each part. They also designed and built special-purpose machines, such as one for installing the optical encoder, an operation that previously had been done by hand.

The result of this kind of design integration was a product that respected the limits in the process, yet made maximum use of its capabilities. The process, in turn, was targeted on the product and provided the capabilities it needed. PLUS was able to put the product into volume production very quickly, and achieved yields in the first few weeks of operation that its traditional process had never been able to attain even after years of production. Of course, skillful product and process design is only part of the secret of high-performance manufacturing, but it is an essential part. We return to this topic in Chapters 10 and 11.

Eliminating Waste

It is not surprising that we found that waste, in the form of scrap or rejected material, was inversely related to the level of product quality. After all, reducing a product's reject rate implies both higher quality and less consumption of materials and labor. What is more interesting is that reducing materials waste often improves productivity far beyond what one might expect from the material saving alone. Studies of a number of Japanese firms have shown, in fact, that lowering defect rates well below those that have long been considered reasonable has led to a substantial improvement in TFP.

These findings have triggered a close examination of the experience of an increasing number of U.S. firms where the same phenomenon has been observed. In the high-performance plants that we studied, we found that waste reduction was grounded in a philosophy of creating value for customers. The notion is simple: any activity that does not produce added value for the customer is waste—be it wasted materials (due to scrap or overproduction), unnecessary motion, waiting time (worker or product), or machine malfunctioning. It is this philosophy, and the actions that follow from it, that link waste reduction and overall productivity.

The most dramatic evidence on the impact of waste in our study comes from the PROCESS company. Consider the experience of department C, as outlined in Table 6–2. It suggests that changes in the waste rate (in this case measured by the ratio of the cost of wasted material to total cost, expressed as a percentage) can lead to dramatic operating improvements. For example, reducing waste in plant 4's department C by 10 percent from its mean value (which by itself

Table 6-2 Impact of Waste on TFP in Department C at PROCESS Company

Plant	Average Waste Rate (%)	Waste Rate Impact on TFP[a]	Degree of Uncertainty[b]	Effect on TFP of a 10% Reduction in Waste Rate (%)
C-1	11.2	− .011	.009	+ 1.2
C-2	12.4	− .014	.000	+ 1.8
C-3	12.7	− .016	.000	+ 2.0
C-4	9.3	− .033	.002	+ 3.1
C-5	8.2	− .010	.006	+ 0.8

NOTES:

[a] This impact is the coefficient of the average waste rate in a regression of log TFP on the waste rate, utilization, and time.

[b] The degree of uncertainty is the probability that a higher waste rate actually has a positive effect on TFP.

would reduce total manufacturing costs by only half of 1 percent) appears to have been accompanied by a 3 percent improvement in total factor productivity. Discussions with plant managers suggest that these estimates may even understate the ultimate impact of changes in equipment and operating procedures that are triggered by efforts to reduce waste.

The strength of this relationship is even more surprising when one considers that in PROCESS factories "waste" material is a direct substitute for new raw materials and is recycled within the factory. Furthermore, the proportion of waste generally increases with the speed of the process. Therefore, an increase in the production throughput rate (which might be expected to cause TFP to increase, because labor and capital costs are largely independent of the throughput rate) would tend to be associated with higher waste ratios. This should cause TFP and the percentage of waste to increase together. The fact that they do not indicates the powerful impact that reducing waste has on overall productivity.

Reducing Work-in-Process

Many factories around the world operate with what is called a "just-in-case" inventory system: they maintain a large amount of Work-in-Process Inventory (WIP) to keep equipment and workers busy "just in case" something goes wrong. In theory, this WIP inventory buffers each stage of the process from its neighbors so that problems in one area do not spread to others. And it lowers setup costs by permitting machines to produce long runs.

There is growing recognition, however, that reducing WIP may be a vital element in the creation of high-performance manufacturing. Having a lot of WIP around appears to create a smoothly running operation only because it covers up problems—but it thereby also obscures opportunities for eliminating them. In our statistical analysis we found a strong negative relationship between the level of WIP in a factory and its TFP. This impact was greater than could be explained simply by the fact that less inventory requires less working capital (assuming that production output is not affected, this alone would cause capital productivity—and therefore total productivity—to increase). Table 6-3 describes the impact of reducing WIP on TFP in the three companies. Although varying significantly from plant to plant, in every case reductions in WIP were associated with increases in productivity. In some plants the effect was quite powerful. In HI-TECH's American plant, for example, a 10 percent decrease in the WIP required to produce component D was associated with a 9 per-

Table 6-3 Impact of WIP on TFP

Plant	Unit Impact on TFP[a]	Degree of Uncertainty in the Estimate[b]	Impact on TFP of 10% Reducation in WIP
HI-TECH			
U.S.-A	− .008	.238	+ 1.15
U.S.-B	− .018	.306	+ 1.18
U.S.-C	− .070	.103	+ 3.73
U.S.-D	− .148	.003	+ 9.11
PROCESS			
H-1	− .157	.001	+ 1.63
H-2	− .429	.000	+ 4.01
H-3	− .441	.000	+ 4.65
H-4	− .634	.000	+ 3.52
H-5	− .449	.000	+ 3.84
FAB			
1	− .224	.000	+ 2.86
2	− .062	.000	+ 1.14
3	− .232	.000	+ 3.59

NOTES:
[a]Unit impact is estimated using a regression of the log of TFP on time, utilization, and work-in-process inventory (five-month moving average), expressed as a percentage.
[b]The degree of uncertainty is the probability that reducing WIP actually leads to lower TFP.

cent increase in its TFP. Lowering work-in-process inventory appears to be one of the major contributors to higher TFP in a plant.

This is another link in a growing body of empirical evidence suggesting that efforts made by Japanese (and a growing number of U.S.) companies to reduce WIP to a fraction of its traditional value can lead to major benefits. Almost invariably, lowering WIP is credited with enabling faster, more reliable delivery times, lower reject rates (because faster production cycle times both reduce inventory obsolescence and make possible faster feedback when the process starts to malfunction), and lower overhead costs. As a result, not only does TFP increase, so do other important indicators of manufacturing performance.

It is important to emphasize here that simply pulling work-in-process inventory out of a factory will not, by itself, lead to such improvements. It is more likely to lead to disaster. The WIP is there for a reason (usually a variety of reasons); it is a symptom, not the disease itself. A long-term program for reducing WIP, therefore, must work on the reasons that led to its being there in the first place: erratic process yields, unreliable equipment, long production changeover and setup times, constantly changing production schedules, and suppliers who don't deliver on time. In the presence of such diseases, a large cushion of WIP is all that stands between a factory and chaos. Therefore, when we advise companies to reduce their WIP, we are really advising them first to systematically eliminate the conditions that make WIP necessary.

Managing Change to Reduce Confusion
Although defective products and equipment, as well as excess work-in-process inventory, are detrimental in themselves, they also reflect different facets of a larger phenomenon at work in the factories we studied: confusion. A variety of management actions can confuse or disrupt a factory's operation. These include erratically varying the rate of production (or changing a production schedule at the last minute), frequently expediting orders, changing the work crews (or the workers on a specific crew) assigned to a given machine or part of the process, haphazardly adding new products or changing the specifications of an existing product, or adding to or altering the equipment used.

Of the many sources of confusion we examined, none better illustrated the impact on performance than engineering changes. Engineering change orders (ECOs) typically specify a change in either the materials to be used in producing a product, the manufacturing process employed, or the specifications of the product itself. One might expect that such changes would reduce productivity in the short run but lead to increased TFP in the long run. The short-term effect is evident in Table 6–4, where we present data on ECO activity in three FAB plants. The effects are sizable. In plant 2, for example, adding ten ECOs per month (well within the typical range of variation) reduces TFP by almost 5 percent. This is clear evidence of the expected short-term negative effect of ECOs, but we were surprised to see that their debilitating effects persisted for up to a year. Since ECOs should be one of the major means for increasing productivity over the long run, we attempted to understand what was causing this negative effect, and how it might be influenced by management.

Our data suggest that both the *average* level of the number of ECOs implemented in a given month and the *variation* in this level are detrimental to TFP. The implication of this finding is that many companies would benefit from reducing the average number of ECOs to which their plants must respond in a given period of time. That is, pressure should be placed on engineering and marketing personnel to focus their attention only on the most important changes and to "design it right the first time." Moreover, these ECOs should be released in a controlled, steady fashion rather than in bunches.

We also found that the way ECO introductions are managed may be just as important as their number. In the one plant that divided ECOs into cost categories ("major" denoted those that were the most expensive to implement), we were surprised to find that minor ECOs had the greatest negative effect on TFP. Major ECOs, on the other hand, actually had a *positive* effect. Investigating further, we discovered that departments within the plant typically were given advance warning of impending major ECOs. Recognizing that they were potentially disruptive, managers saw to it that careful preparation preceded their implementation: supervisors were warned, workers were trained, and engineers were brought in to assist. Minor ECOs, on the other hand, were simply "dumped" on the factory.

Like the short-term impact of capital investment, the impact of an ECO on TFP depends not only on the ECO itself but also on the amount of confusion it creates. And that depends on how it is managed. The same is true for a variety of other activities in a factory. Indeed, few factories fit the common image of a smoothly operating machine, where the same materials are transformed into the same products by the same people using the same methods day in and day

Table 6-4 Impact of Engineering Changes on Monthly TFP in Three FAB Plants

Plant	Unit Impact of the Number of ECOs	Mean Level of ECOs per Month	Number of ECOs in Lowest Month	Number of ECOs in Highest Month	% Impact on TFP of Increasing ECO Activity from 5 per Month to 15 per Month
1	−.0028	16.5	1	41	− 2.8
2	−.0046	12.2	2	43	− 4.6
3	−.0166	7.0	1	19	− 16.6

out. Most factories are in flux, with changes in product design, process configuration, work force, materials, and customer requirements occurring almost daily. Managed well, such change can be a source of improvement; managed poorly, it creates confusion that reduces quality and productivity.

A Look Ahead

We began our study of manufacturing performance by trying to understand why different factories that belong to the same company often display such wide variations in performance. We have identified managerial practices and policies relating to product design, capital investment, waste, WIP inventory, and engineering changes that all seem to cause such differences. Yet our investigations also uncovered aspects of factory management that deserve much more careful analysis. We were struck, for example, by the way all these elements seemed to mesh together in the highest-performing factories. It was not so much excellence in particular areas of operation that distinguished them but the power of their manufacturing systems as a whole. Therefore, although we need to scrutinize carefully the approaches these high-performance plants used to manage their material flows, process technology, and people, we also need to examine the principles that underlay those approaches and their interconnections.

A systemic perspective in factory management is important because many of the critical managerial activities we have identified share common roots. Take, for example, the problem of confusion and its impact on performance. Although we emphasized the role of engineering changes when discussing confusion, it is a more pervasive phenomenon. In fact, it appears that a good part of the differences in productivity we observed among various factories reflect differences in the amount of confusion (or, more precisely, the extent of the confusion-creating activities) in them.

A poorly designed product, for example, creates complexity that leads to confusion, and triggers demands for engineering changes. Poorly handled ECOs create wasted material as well as increased reject rates. Work-in-process, in turn, is often at least partially a function of the amount of unpredictable variation in the reject rate (necessitating backup materials in case the expected amount of good output is not produced). Moreover, work-in-process inventory is both the result of disruptions (confusion) in the plant—caused, for example, by new equipment—and the cause of confusion in itself. Confusion, in short, appears to be linked to a variety of different kinds of change. One of the most important tasks of management, therefore, is to prevent confusion or mitigate the potentially damaging effects of confusion-causing activities.

Many managers, upon reading this, may object: Are not the things that cause confusion—changing production schedules, expediting orders, shifting work crews, adding or overhauling equipment, and changing product specifications—simply what companies have to do to respond to changing customer demands and technological opportunities? But remember that much of our evidence about the impact of confusion was developed through a comparison of factories within the same company, and therefore subject largely to the same market and technological shifts. The point is that some plant management groups seem to be unusually successful at preventing this external buffeting from having as serious an impact on their factory's operations as it does in sister factories. They do this both by limiting the number of changes introduced at any one time and by carefully managing the way these changes are implemented.

Other management groups, in contrast, appear to be continually caught by surprise by such changes. They manage them in a haphazard fashion and leapfrog from one crisis to another. As a result, much of the consequent confusion is internally generated. In fact, one well-known company conducted a study of the revisions made in its production schedules during 1983 and found that fully three-quarters of them were generated by its sales department, without any change in customer orders. It decided to begin the process of reducing confusion by decreasing significantly this internally induced order churn.

Why do apparently simple changes seem to cause such big problems in some factories? Part of the answer seems to lie in the fact that the managers, engineers, and operators in some factories have a very difficult time predicting how a given change will affect the production process. The degree to which changes cause confusion in a factory thus is affected by the extent of its process understanding and control.

Factories that have processes under control, that have a system of manufacturing in which each of the elements work in concert, are more productive than others. Moreover, as our capital investment data make clear, a factory's current level of productivity is generally less important than its learning rate—the rate at which its productivity improves over time. A factory whose TFP is less than another's, but whose rate of improvement is greater, will eventually surpass the leader.

The importance of learning indicates the need for a much closer look at the human side of the factory. There is a tendency, when studying manufacturing, to let the hardware, the systems, and the procedures dominate one's thinking and analysis. But when it comes to achieving sustained improvement in performance, the people in the organization and the way they are linked to other elements of manufacturing should become the focus of attention.

These three issues—the materials flow and information systems, process knowledge and control, and the role of people in production—are examined in turn in Chapters 7 through 9. In each case, we present contrasting management approaches, attempt to develop some general principles, and then suggest ways to implement these principles. Although the principles themselves are fairly simple, implementing them is far from easy for most organizations. It requires changing some deeply rooted assumptions and behavior patterns, adopting new goals and approaches to performance measurement, and altering the working relationships between operators and staff personnel. But such changes appear to be the key to high-performance manufacturing. As in physical conditioning: "No pain, no gain."

The Architecture of Manufacturing:
Material and Information Flows

Introduction

The most striking thing about a factory is usually its machinery: in a steel mill, the sheer size, power, and noise of the electric arc furnace as it melts tons of scrap; in an automobile assembly plant, the rhythmic operation of the automated welding system; in a computer plant, the virtuosity of the assembly robots. But our research on high-performance manufacturing suggests that for all its sound and fury, the equipment, or hardware, by itself is rarely the primary source of a factory's competitive advantage. What matters is how that hardware is used, and how it is integrated with materials, people, and information through software—the systems and procedures that direct and control the factory's activities.

The "architecture" of a manufacturing system—which includes its hardware, its material and information flows, the rules and procedures used to coordinate them, and the managerial philosophy that underlies them all—largely determines the productivity of the people and assets in the factory, the quality of its products, and the responsiveness of the organization to customer needs. Indeed, two factories with almost identical hardware may perform very differently if they have different system architectures. Just how differently is demonstrated by the experience of Mazda, the Japanese auto firm, in the mid-1970s.

The New Production System at Mazda

For Yoshiki Yamasaki (head of automobile production) and his production staff, 1976 was the year of the new production system (NPS). The oil shock of 1973 had cut sharply into Mazda's sales, and in 1976 the company was deeply in debt and still losing money. Sumitomo Bank, its main creditor, effected a reorganization of the company in early 1976. The mandate for Mr. Yamasaki was straightforward: achieve dramatic reductions in costs, shorten lead times, and significantly improve quality—and do it all without spending much money.[1]

Yamasaki responded to the challenge by proposing a radically different approach to production. Throughout its history, Mazda had sought manufacturing leadership through advanced hardware. It prided itself on being the first to introduce such equipment as advanced material handling systems, sophisticated forging presses, and computer-controlled processes. Yet its labor and asset productivities were still only about half those of its principal Japanese competitors. Closing that gap, without new hardware, was the goal of the new production system. It focused instead on the basic architecture of the manufacturing system. A project manager described its underlying philosophy as follows: "The ideal form of the new system is analogous to a water pipeline through which water flows smoothly. In the actual production lines, this translates to the elimination of floats (in-process inventory), enabling synchronized production with a given cycle time."

Synchronizing departments and integrating operations required changes in the location and sequencing of equipment, reductions in setup times, faster, more accurate information about production problems, and improvements in process quality. Production scheduling changed as well. It shifted to a "pull" system in which the production of components and subassemblies was triggered by final assembly. All these changes were accompanied by new work assignments, new responsibilities, and new training programs at all levels in the company.

Without significant capital investment, Mazda was able to achieve dramatic improvements in performance because of these fundamental changes in its manufacturing system. Table 7–1 and Figure 7–1 document some of these changes. Between 1976 and 1980 output per employee went from 19.3 to 43.8 vehicles per year. This improvement in operating performance reflected improvements in equipment utilization, more effective use of people, and a dramatic drop in work-in-process inventory. By 1981 it had almost caught up with Nissan and was within striking distance of Toyota.[2]

Mazda's experience underscores the power and strategic significance of a manufacturing system's architecture. This system archi-

Table 7-1 Manufacturing Performance at Mazda, 1976–1980

Factor	Before New Production System (1976)	After New Production System (1980)
Setup time[a]	6.5 hr.	13 min.
Float[b]	1,000 pieces in process	60 pieces in process
Downtime[c]	10%	3.8%
Labor productivity (vehicles per person per year)	19.3	43.8

[a]gear cutting
[b]machining of steering knuckles
[c]cylinder block casting line

SOURCE: Toyo Kogyo Ltd. (1982).

Figure 7-1 Productivity and Work-in-Process: Mazda, Nissan, Toyota (logarithmic scales)

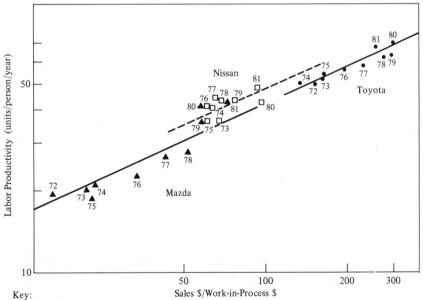

tecture affects not only the factory's potential for improvement, but how the people within the manufacturing organization (workers, managers, and support staff) think about themselves and their role in the overall success of the business. These self-perceptions and expectations, in turn, influence how others view the manufacturing organization and the contribution it is expected to make.

The system's effect on the product and the customer is pervasive. Even tactical decisions like the production lot size (the number of components or subassemblies produced in each batch) and department layout have a significant cumulative impact on performance characteristics. These seemingly small decisions combine to affect significantly a factory's ability to meet the key competitive priorities (cost, quality, delivery, flexibility, and innovativeness) that are established by its company's competitive strategy. Moreover, the fabric of policies, practices, and decisions that make up the manufacturing system cannot easily be acquired or copied. When well integrated with its hardware, a manufacturing system can thus become a source of sustainable competitive advantage.

In this chapter we first examine the concepts behind the design of a manufacturing system's architecture and then compare the systems at work in two very different factories. Our focus includes both what goes on within a factory and how that factory is linked to its suppliers. In the next-to-last section of this chapter, based on our comparisons of factories A and B, we draw some conclusions about the principles that underlie the most effective manufacturing architectures. How to implement these principles is the subject of the chapter's concluding section.

The Challenge of Factory Management

Developing an architecture for manufacturing begins with an assessment of the basic tasks that the factory must perform. A production process consists of a sequence of steps, typically assigned to separate departments, that take various inputs (such as parts, components, and subassemblies) and convert them into desired outputs. For example, a factory making electronic instruments might have such departments as incoming materials, component test and inspection, printed circuit board insertion, wave soldering, power source assembly, optical subassembly, final assembly and test, packaging, and finished goods warehousing. Each of these departments would perform a series of conversion steps and then transfer the resulting output to the next department.

Each task performed by the various departments in a factory accomplishes one or more of three things: it converts inputs into outputs, it moves material from one location to another, or it transfers information. *Conversion activities* add value to the product by transforming materials, components, or subassemblies into a higher level of component or assembly. *Material flows* refer to the movement of materials from one department (location) to another. Because of the number of conversion steps, the material volumes, and the distances involved in most factories, such movements are both numerous and extremely important. *Information transfers* serve not only to coordinate conversion steps and material flows but also to provide the feedback necessary to make improvements in the factory's procedures, process technology, and operating characteristics.

Within the factory, various activities are directed toward accomplishing a variety of goals. One set of goals is concerned with the design of the product itself, its function, features, and appearance. But a factory also has internal goals with respect to output volume, cost, quality, time and location of delivery. Many of these goals are broken down into subgoals that define short-term operating targets: product specifications, inventory turns, standard costs, times and quantities, and daily shipment requirements. Others express longer-term objectives, such as the speed of new product introduction, defect reduction, and the rate of productivity improvement.

The challenge for the manufacturing organization is to integrate all these tasks and align them with the company's chosen goals—and to do so better than most or all of its competitors. Making that happen is not simple. Although it takes only a few paragraphs to describe a factory's basic tasks and goals, in reality they can become very complex, very quickly. For example, in an electronic instrument factory with ten departments, the information and material flows within and between departments could amount to hundreds of transactions for each batch of each product. With dozens of batches entering the factory each day, there are likely to be thousands of flow transactions every week.

Recognizing the sources and implications of such complexity is key to making flow management a source of competitive advantage. One source of complexity arises out of the differences between the departments within the factory. Individually, each department represents a collection of activities that are somewhat homogeneous and closely related. Thus in an instrument factory, the wave solder department is organized around the commonality of the technology and equipment used to apply solder to circuit boards. Similarly, the circuit board insertion department is defined by the set of tasks associated with loading a circuit board with components and preparing it for wave solder.

As illustrated by this contrast, departments within a factory often differ widely in the technologies of their conversion processes, their economics, the way in which they are organized, the skills required to run them, the managerial approaches that are critical to achieving successful performance, and a variety of other dimensions. In large part because of these differences, traditional factory flow systems incorporate buffers of excess resources between departments—buffers of inventory (waiting or idle materials and products), of information, of equipment, and of people. These buffers serve to partially decouple one department from another and thereby simplify their management. These buffers, together with substantial interdepartmental differences, add to the complexity of flow management in a factory.

Uncertainty is often an even more important contributor to a factory's complexity than are departmental differences. Uncertainty comes in many forms: uncertainty regarding costs, the quantity and quality of output from a given department or supplier, the lead times associated with material transfers among departments, the production setup or changeover times, and production run times. All these within-factory uncertainties are compounded by such external uncertainties as the demand for one's products and the availability of critical materials or capital. As with departmental differences, traditional manufacturing systems typically employ buffers as the primary mechanism for softening the impact of uncertainty.

The complexity and uncertainty that complicate the lives of manufacturing managers have led over the years to an array of tools, techniques, programs, and principles for designing different manufacturing architectures, each with its own set of acronyms. Many of these ideas are quite powerful. But rather than embark upon a theoretical discussion of these tools and techniques, it might be more instructive to try to understand their use by considering what goes on in real factories. Seeing firsthand how factories operate is essential to understanding the realities their managers must cope with, and how different behavior patterns reflect the philosophy, flow patterns, and decision rules used by the organization.

Getting inside a factory to find out what makes it tick, what makes it distinctive, what makes it effective, is something we enjoy doing. Here, and in Chapters 8 and 9, we will visit and compare two factories that serve similar markets and employ similar technologies but are managed very differently. We use these visits both to illustrate basic principles and to underscore the interconnections between the myriad decisions and policies that managers make in directing factory operations. Our purpose is both to provide a better understanding of the nature of the tasks performed by a manufacturing organization and the problems faced by the people who work there, and to bring into sharper focus the way that managing factory operations can affect a company's ability to compete.

Comparing Two Contrasting Architectures: Factory A versus Factory B

Both factory A and factory B belonged to firms that designed, manufactured, and marketed equipment for industrial customers. The production processes used in both included metal stamping and bending, parts machining and finishing, subassembly of major modules, the addition of electronic controls and connection cables (sourced from outside suppliers), and final assembly and test. A finished unit consisted of more than a thousand different components that could be combined in an almost infinite array of combinations. This equipment sold at prices ranging from fifty to one hundred thousand dollars.

Factory A was organized by process stages (stamping, machining, subassembly, and so forth), and parts and components moved through the departments in batches. Except for final assembly, each department produced in response to a forecast of expected demand. Parts and subassemblies were stored in a central inventory and delivered to final assembly by material handlers. Products were customized to meet specific order specifications in final assembly, largely through the addition of various subassemblies.

Our visit to factory A brought us into contact with people who had been in the forefront of the application of computers to factory management. Roger White, director of materials management, had played a major role in the development of factory A's systems: "We had our share of disasters with the computer systems, but we believed that the investments we were making would pay off. And I think we were right. We have so many parts and products, there's no way we could manage it without the systems we have."

Two trends had driven factory A's choice of manufacturing systems. First, both the number of its product offerings and the number of the components and materials required by its product designs had grown continuously. As a consequence, the volume of data with which factory A had to deal had grown exponentially over the previous decade. The second driving force was the decline in the cost of computing power. By the late 1960s management had concluded that computers offered the best means for coping with the factory's increased complexity.

The development of computer-based systems had been led by a group that was now called Materials Management. It included such subgroups as master scheduling, inventory control, shop floor control, and procurement. In the mid-1980s this group was a major force within the factory. In fact, both the plant manager and its materials management director reported directly to the corporate vice president of operations.

Over the years the materials management department had developed specialists in inventory control, scheduling, and procurement. These people were complemented by a number of computer and systems specialists who helped design and implement the computer systems needed to perform these tasks.

Allen Whitby, inventory control manager, commented on the systems in place:

> We have what I would call a class A system. It's basically an MRP (Materials Requirements Planning) system, but we have made a number of changes to the standard version. All of the departments are tied into a master schedule, and the system generates all the reports and information needed to run those departments. I've made a number of presentations to APICS (American Production and Inventory Control Society) about our system, and the response has been very favorable. People have been impressed with the way we've optimized batch sizes in the departments. The algorithms we've developed are pretty sophisticated.

The factory operated under the philosophy that materials management was responsible for getting the input materials and information (job orders, sequences, dates, etc.) to individual factory departments, while manufacturing was responsible for managing the labor and equipment required to perform the conversion tasks within the departments and for passing information on task completion back to the materials management group. Materials managers generally felt that good systems were now in place, and their current challenge was getting the manufacturing organization to use those systems more effectively.

Over the previous decade, the evolution of the materials management system had made significant changes in the character of factory A's information flows. There were now large amounts of centralized data, which provided tremendous detail about every aspect of the factory's operations. Along with the centralization of data, there had been a tendency over time to centralize more of the key decisions. For example, individual departments no longer determined the order in which jobs were to be processed, the sequence of tasks within each job, batch sizes, or how mistakes in incoming materials or orders should be dealt with; these were now all handled centrally by materials management. The materials management group felt that, as a result, issues like batch size were being handled more effectively than they had been in the past.

The availability of sophisticated computer systems had also increased the amount of data provided to the factory. One area where this had stimulated change was in procurement. Factory A had long followed a policy of securing multiple vendors for most purchased parts. Contracts with vendors were negotiated on an annual basis, and suppliers were chosen on the basis of price, quality, and schedule performance. New information systems had been designed to provide purchasing agents with detailed information about supplier performance, including incoming inspection results and delivery reliability. This information, and the ability to do comparative analysis, had been quite useful in annual contract negotiations. Several procurement specialists felt that the system had been instrumental in achieving price reductions and improvements in delivery.

The ability of suppliers to meet delivery targets had been enhanced by tying them into the factory's master scheduling system. Some of the suppliers were actually on-line, with terminals in their factories linked directly to factory A. All suppliers regularly received copies of the monthly master schedule and its updates. Over the years the amount of data provided to suppliers, as well as to departments within factory A, had grown significantly. It was not unusual, for example, for factory visitors to come upon stacks of computer printouts alongside stacks of parts and components. In fact, the monthly master schedule was referred to as the "hernia book" because of its weight. Its size was due not just to the steadily increasing product line (which materials managers had designed their system to accommodate) but also to increasing attempts to track what was going on both within and between departments.

As computers had gotten faster and cheaper, there had been a tendency to regenerate the master plan (and all of its detail for the individual departments) at more frequent intervals. Thus, it was now not unusual for a department to get a new work schedule two or three times a week, whereas previously one had been provided only once every week or two. Clearly, except for the hourly workers who performed the actual material handling on the factory floor and in the stock rooms, the materials management group had become primarily information handlers. The manufacturing departments, on the other hand, had become largely dependent on the information provided by materials management.

In spite of everybody's best efforts to work around the two major sources of complexity at factory A—differences between departments and uncertainty—things had not always gone smoothly. In fact, there seemed to be a continuous flow of complaints centered around a handful of issues. One was that there still was too much inventory in the factory. Another was the poor accuracy of sales forecasts. Third was that vendors' response times were often longer than the lead times requested by customers. Still another was that engineering changes (which had a direct impact on product bills-of-material) were slow in moving out onto the factory floor. Thus, what was actually getting built was often different from what the information system assumed would be built. Finally, the accuracy of the data coming back to the materials department was not good. The workers just did not seem to see the necessity, or have the discipline, to report back all the information that the systems required.

These were the ongoing concerns of the materials group, but factory A's manufacturing group saw things from a somewhat different perspective. Bart Morrison, plant manager, commented: "From a production standpoint, the real issue in materials management is shortages of parts. Even when we think we have the materials, people and equipment that we need, the mix isn't right, or the quality's off, or we don't have enough of some key item. It's pretty frustrating, and it kills our utilization rates."

Because of all this uncertainty, the factory's departments were constantly in a fire-fighting mode—trying, under pressure, to meet each day's schedule and customer expectations. The short-term focus of manufacturing was reinforced by the fact that materials management discouraged factory personnel from making process changes.

These added uncertainty to its task, and necessitated changes in its data base. Initially, at least, such changes would probably result in more shortages and more headaches for materials management. Production managers saw this issue differently: failure to make such changes served to lower morale and the motivation to improve.

Thus, at factory A, although business was good and the factory was profitable, all was not calm. We sensed an undercurrent of tension in the organization, but over time both materials managers and manufacturing managers had come to regard this tension as an unavoidable fact of factory life. Thus, while everybody complained about their problems, nobody had any great hope that they would ever really go away. New computer hardware had been installed a few months earlier with the expectation that it would eliminate many of these difficulties. But the problems of getting that system up and running were taking much longer to overcome than expected, and the results so far had not been nearly as dramatic as hoped for.

Factory B

At factory B, belonging to another company, we found a very different manufacturing architecture, and a very different approach to the management of flows within the factory. Factory B had also seen an increase in product variety, although not quite as fast as at factory A, and it too had benefited from the availability of lower-cost computing power. However, the approaches it had taken to the management of factory operations were quite different.

In the 1960s, factory B had found itself short of capital. This forced it to restrict capital investment and led its management to pay close attention to equipment purchases and to inventory levels. As a consequence, the factory had developed capabilities to modify and enhance its own equipment. In addition, instead of organizing product flows by process stage, factory B had set up what were called "production units." These were departments that contained the equipment necessary (e.g., machining, finishing, testing) to make a complete component or subassembly. The final assembly area was divided up into four short lines, each dedicated to a specific product family. Harry Cowles, plant manager, commented on the setup: "We've been running like this for as long as I can remember. I think Hank Schneider was the one who set it up. He had this thing about trying to get rid of inventory. We have worked continually on ways to restructure departments and rearrange equipment, in order to reduce stock and simplify materials handling."

Manufacturing management (responsible for conversion activities) at factory B had drawn closer to materials management (responsible for the handling of material flows as well as the information required for coordination and improvement) over recent years. Rather than having separate directors of materials and manufacturing, factory B simply had a plant manager to whom all department heads reported; within each department there were both materials people and production people. Factory B did have a small manufacturing systems group, but its assignment was simply to provide the basic framework of key systems; it was up to the individual departments to adapt these systems to their own needs. In fact, any new factory system was always developed initially under the direction of a task force headed by a line manager from one of the production units.

Although the factory had begun using computers in the early 1970s, its simplified layouts and production flows had made it unnecessary to use large-scale information systems to manage production on the shop floor. Each department worked with a monthly master schedule, but actual daily production was tied to activity in final assembly. The factory used a simple reorder-point system to trigger production: when the inventory of some part was reduced below a critical point, a reorder ticket was sent to the department that produced it. This was the signal to produce a standard lot size of the part, based on that month's master schedule. Great efforts had been made to reduce setup times and changeover costs, so that each part could be produced in small batches, thus minimizing inventory.

The use of a sophisticated computer system for high-level scheduling but simple manual systems for shop floor control was consistent with factory B's philosophy of decentralizing decision making. No centralized data existed other than the master schedule and the bills of material for finished products, components, and subassemblies. They were incorporated into an MRP system used for longer-term planning. Coordination information was not kept centrally but was passed quickly along to affected departments. Those departments had considerable freedom to manage their internal flows of materials and information and, on the basis of their own "microview," could decide which improvements to make in materials movements and production processes. The major constraint they faced was the need to produce exactly what the final assembly schedule required, within specifications and on time.

The same philosophy governed supplier relationships. Suppliers were tied into factory B through the master schedule, but they too were on a reorder-point system. Martha O'Toole, director of the manufacturing systems group, commented on the suppliers:

> When I first came here I was surprised by the way we treated suppliers. We have a much smaller number of suppliers than I expected and most of them are located within a two hours' drive of the plant. In addition, there are a lot of family ties involved, and I was worried about the problems that can create. But, for the most part, our suppliers have tremendous skills, and they've been pretty responsive.

The importance of discipline, commitment, and responsiveness came up several times during our visit, whether in connection with meeting promises made between departments within the factory, between the factory and suppliers, or between the factory and its customers. To some extent this reflected the fact that there was general agreement within the organization as to what kinds of commitments were appropriate; once made, such commitments obligated the entire organization to deliver on them. We also noticed that the amount of information directed at improving basic processes, procedures, and systems was similar in magnitude to that required to coordinate current activities. Information flows for both needs were characterized by rapidity, simplicity, and directness. The factory utilized visual systems like signal lights and color-coded reorder tickets for much of the shop floor information transfers. Consequently, the current status of specific orders and work stations was readily apparent to everyone involved.

We also found that factory B had an interesting mix of capabilities. As a result of the low changeover times and tight tolerance levels that had been achieved, conversion activities were quite flexible, both in terms of flow paths and product changeovers. This flexibility had been achieved without the necessity for high buffer inventories. In fact, throughout our tour we were struck by the fact that there simply wasn't much work-in-process inventory anywhere. Not only were people and equipment highly utilized, but parts and materials were also seldom idle.

In spite of its many strengths, factory B confronted several challenges. One of these was an inability to capitalize on all the opportunities that arose for improving processes, material flows, and information. At the same time, there was occasionally the sense that processes were being changed too often and not allowed to stabilize sufficiently. There was always the question of balance between too much change and not enough. Capital investment was another challenge. The factory always seemed to generate more attractive proposals than it could implement at one time. These included numerous market development and product development projects that arose out of the strong working relationships it enjoyed with its customers. Finally, there were three items that had always been on management's list of desired improvements (and probably always would be): production cycle times in the factory were still felt to be too long; inventories were still too high; and suppliers were still not regarded as being sufficiently integrated with the factory.

The Principles Underlying These Alternative Architectures

Factories A and B are similar in many ways. They have the same basic goals: meeting customer commitments, reducing product costs, increasing resource utilization within the factory, and improving the factory's capabilities over time. They use similar manufacturing processes and buy some of the same equipment from the same vendors. Both have comparable computer software (a version of materials requirements planning) for long-term planning and scheduling. However, the manufacturing systems they use to manage their hardware and to achieve their goals are significantly different. Factory A has developed a system run by different groups of specialists (materials managers versus production managers). It has substantial expertise in each subarea, but the subareas do not interrelate well. Factory B, on the other hand, has less sophisticated systems (as judged by a specialist), but seems to have been more effective at integrating them and meeting its overall objectives.

The manufacturing architectures of these two factories can be contrasted on a number of important dimensions. Perhaps the most striking is the basic structure of their process flows. To illustrate this difference, consider Figure 7–2. The top panel portrays a process flow like that found in the departments of factory A. Batches of product move through conversion activities (e.g., forming, mounting, connecting, etc.), are inspected ("check"), and then stored as work-in-process for subsequent processing. In the bottom panel, the same equipment has been arranged to permit a process flow like that found within each department of factory B. In-process storage areas

Figure 7-2   A Comparison of Process Flows at Factories A and B

Factory A

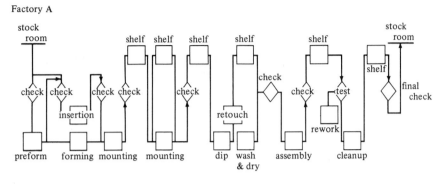

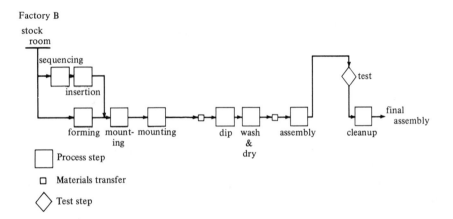

Factory B

and checkpoints have been eliminated, and work-in-process inventory has been cut dramatically. The whole process is more integrated and streamlined. Far fewer transactions are required to manage it, and fewer material handlers are needed to move material through the process and in and out of storage areas. The result is a much faster (three days versus four weeks) and more efficient production cycle.

These differences in basic process structure are accompanied by different approaches used in managing the system of flows. There are sharp differences, for example, in the scope of the responsibilities of the operating groups. In factory A the materials management group coordinates information and materials flows, while the manufacturing group concentrates on conversion activities and equipment maintenance. People within factory A tend to focus on short-term problems and on what each group considers its primary area of responsibility. In factory B, the scope of each department is much broader, extending from meeting specific customer commitments to systematically improving the capabilities of the factory. The breadth and integrated nature of these responsibilities align the majority of factory B's activities much more closely with its competitive objectives than is the case at factory A.

Another major difference between these two factories is what each management group accepts as "given" and what each seeks to change. In the case of factory A, much of the uncertainty which it confronts, as well as the differences between departments, are regarded as facts of life by the materials management group. Since its sphere of responsibility does not include changing the things that create those uncertainties and departmental differences, it seeks to cope with them by accumulating information and creating systems that buffer factory operations from their impact. That is, it tries to accommodate complexity so that it does not interfere with meeting shipment schedules.

In factory B, on the other hand, uncertainty and departmental differences are viewed with equal concern but are considered to be open to modification over time. Management's focus is on reducing uncertainty and on eliminating the differences between departments so that they no longer hinder overall factory performance. This attitude clearly influences the behavior not only of managers but also of direct and indirect workers as well.

The assignment of responsibility for performing various tasks and ensuring successful operations is also very different in the two factories. The centralized nature of factory A's approach leads naturally to the centralization of more and more tasks, and at least implicitly, of more of the responsibility. Thus, the manufacturing floor increasingly feels constrained, both in its scope of responsibility and in its authority to make desired changes. In factory B, in contrast, both responsibility and authority are consistently pushed down to the lowest levels. Thus, there is a sense of expanding control and competence at the department level within factory B.

Given these differences in scope and responsibility, it is not surprising that the two factories tackle implementation problems differently. The centralization of control and the separation of information and material flows from manufacturing conversion activities make implementation in factory A a matter of getting the factory (manufacturing) to carry out what the staff (materials management) has decided is the right way to deal with a problem. In factory B, problem analysis and solution go hand in hand, and both the solutions and their implementation are very likely to come from the department level. Whereas in factory A there is a continual search for the "complete solution" to a massive underlying problem, factory B regards success as coming more from an ongoing series of incremental solutions to a continually evolving sequence of little problems.

In summary, each of the factories has developed a distinctive manufacturing architecture. The philosophy, pattern of flows, and decision rules differ in nature and emphasis. In factory A, the emphasis is on creating a set of procedures to manage flows and then putting into place tracking systems to signal when those procedures are not being followed. The central task, as viewed by those primarily responsible for managing factory flows (i.e., materials management), is to get the factory's actual activities to conform to the planned activities. In factory B, on the other hand, the primary emphasis is on establishing, and winning allegiance to, a basic set of principles throughout the factory. Selecting the appropriate systems and procedures, and the performance of day-to-day activities, is left to individual workers and managers within the departments.

The role of the operating departments, and the general orientation of the managers in running each factory, are mirrored in its relationships with suppliers. In factory A, the basic aim of the purchasing staff has been to reduce the price paid for purchased parts and materials, while assuring a steady supply in the face of uncertainty and diverse vendor characteristics. The primary buffers used to compensate for these sources of complexity have been multiple vendors and large raw material inventories. The use of formal, short-term, arms-length contracts makes it possible to reward or discipline vendors by changing the volume of purchases awarded them.

Supplier relationships in factory B are quite different. In the first place, factory B has many fewer suppliers (250 versus over 1,000), and many of its parts and components are sole sourced. Moreover, many of factory B's suppliers are medium-sized local firms that have considerable manufacturing and engineering expertise. These suppliers have often been given responsibility for designing and engineering specific components. They have worked with factory B in reducing its work-in-process inventory and in improving customer delivery performance. Although contracts exist, factory B's suppliers seem to be bound to it more by personal relationships at several levels in the organization. Further, there is a sense of partnership and joint destiny not found in factory A.

These two approaches to supplier relationships have something of the nature of a self-fulfilling prophecy: suppliers tend to become what buyers assume they are. Whereas factory B assumes that suppliers are capable and valuable partners, factory A assumes that they are interchangeable (and therefore expendable) sources of parts. Faced with the prospect of having business pulled away from them when their short-term contracts expire, factory A's suppliers have become reactive and defensive. They seek to make factory A dependent on them by restricting the information passed on to it, thereby becoming (in its eyes) mere vendors of parts. Forced by their customer to take a short-term view, they concentrate on fire fighting and fail to develop the capabilities that might create a competitive advantage for factory A over the longer term.

The manufacturing systems used to manage flows within each factory and the relationships they have developed with suppliers have produced very different results. Factory A is fighting to maintain control in the face of increasing product complexity, parts and vendor proliferation, and shortening delivery lead times. Factory B is continually making small (but cumulatively significant) improvements in such areas as production cycle times, flexibility, resource utilization, and manufacturing processes. Factory B's in-process inventories are one-fifth the levels in factory A, as are its cycle (throughput) times; its productivity and quality levels are significantly higher.

As these comparisons suggest, an organization that commits itself to a major sustained effort to restructure the basic architecture of its production system, as did Mazda in its development of the New Production System, can powerfully enhance its capabilities and performance. Our research indicates quite clearly that the principles underlying the architecture adopted by factory B are far more effective than those that shape the behavior of factory A.

Implementing the New Architecture

The comparison of factory A and factory B suggests that the most important elements in an effective manufacturing architecture are the principles and philosophy that guide it. These create a sense of direction that shapes the actions people take and determines the enduring character of the factory. Our studies have led us to identify a few major principles that underpin the architectures of world-class factories. These principles echo several of the themes that we had raised in our discussion of high-performance manufacturing in Chapter 6.

The first principle is that a factory's primary purpose is to *increase value* for the final customer. It is essential to distinguish between activities that make life in the factory easier, or enable it to operate more smoothly, and those that really affect the value provided to the customer. For example, neither the flows of information within the factory nor material flows in and out of inventory generally create value for the customer. Only the conversion activities add value. Adhering to this principle means continually searching for ways to eliminate activities that do not add value (ranging from scrap and rework to parts waiting time to underutilized equipment and people), so that more of the factory's activities can be directed toward improving the products and services delivered to customers.

Creating a factory that is a distinctive source of value for customers requires that problem solving be pervasive. Its intent is to remove or reconfigure those things that hinder the creation of value. The factory, therefore, must be willing and able to change process conversion steps, setup procedures, and plant layouts as opportunities to enhance value added and to reduce waste are identified. What goes on in the factory is not cast in concrete but is continually being modified.

The second principle is *strict discipline*. The promises made between departments, between the factory and suppliers, between the factory and product development engineering, and between the factory and the sales organization (and eventually the customers) should be sacred. The factory must know what it can and cannot do; it has to inform the upstream and downstream groups with whom it works about those capabilities and constraints; and then it must deliver what it agrees to deliver. The absence of such discipline locks the factory into a vicious spiral, where everybody makes promises they know they can't keep and hopes for the best, and no one expects these promises will be met, so accumulates information and materials for protection when they aren't.

The third principle is *simplicity*: taking flows, processes, and information and making them clear, direct, and reliable so that complexity is reduced. Departments within the factory should be reconfigured to reduce supply lines and eliminate unnecessary materials handling. Sources of equipment and process uncertainty must be eliminated. This includes unpredictable variation in cycle times, quality levels and yield, and setup and run times. Finally, information flows must be timely, accurate, and purposeful: each piece of information should have a purpose and that purpose should be directly related to creating value in the factory. More information is not necessarily better than less; it may simply serve to confuse people. The real objective is to have the necessary information in the right place at the right time.

Following this set of principles can lead to a manufacturing architecture of great power. It not only makes possible effective day-to-day operations; it lays the foundation for ongoing improvement. It empowers a factory to do things its average competitors can't do. The recent popularity of techniques like just-in-time and total quality control (that embody similar concepts) has led many companies to begin to experiment with these principles.

Many firms have divisions or individual factories that, with a minimum amount of investment, have been able to reduce inventory levels and cycle times by a factor of five or ten, changeover times by a factor of twenty or more, and rejects to one-hundredth of their previous levels. Although such individual pockets of improvement show what can happen when the principles just outlined are applied consistently, the real payoff comes when all the departments and factories involved in making a given product (and eventually upstream suppliers and their factories) follow them as well. This is an order of magnitude more difficult, however, than doing so as an experiment in a single volunteer factory. The real challenge for management is how to make it happen: how to start, how to sustain the effort, how to keep it on track, and how to build momentum.

First, management must recognize that the changes required to achieve such improvements in performance demand a completely new architecture, and a new set of guiding principles. It is not simply a matter of changing a few things; almost everything must be changed, and changed dramatically. Those changes will affect how materials are stored, tracked, and allocated to the factory floor; how production processes are organized and linked; how accounting systems monitor performance and allocate costs; how the work force is trained and assigned; how information systems are altered and improved; how engineering defines its role; and how facilities are designed and upgraded. Such extensive and pervasive changes require change in the forces that drive those detailed actions. It is not enough for management to intervene on a case-by-case basis and modify individual proposals. The old forces that taught people that the way to succeed was to hedge information and hoard materials must be replaced with new forces that teach them that reducing uncertainty and eliminating complexity are the keys to success.

Beyond recognizing the need for, and the nature of, the changes that are required at all three levels, the next step is simply to begin. Starting in a single department or corner of a factory has worked for many companies. The organization needs to experience the realities of these new principles, flows and procedures, and how they are intertwined, and needs to build commitment to them. The experience of Hewlett-Packard's factory in Vancouver, Washington, illustrates how one can start in a single department, spread the system to include all departments, and eventually even take the system to suppliers.

Confronted by stiff competitive pressure in the early 1980s, H-P's Vancouver plant went through a searching reexamination of the basic principles that it was using to manage manufacturing. Through discussions with other H-P divisions and visits to other manufacturers, the Vancouver management team became convinced that the principles outlined here had to be implemented in their operation. They also recognized that not only would full-scale implementation change the factory itself in fundamental ways; it would change the way the factory interacted with other functional organizations.

Beginning with one department, the Vancouver team focused on three areas: the flow structure, the procedures for scheduling production, and worker involvement. Two changes were critical in creating a new pattern of material and information flows. The first involved the sequencing and layout of equipment so as to shorten lines of supply and reduce material handling. The second focused on compressing setup times, so that batch sizes could be reduced and manufacturing cycle times shortened. These two changes combined to sharply reduce work-in-process inventories.

The next major thrust was to change the way production was scheduled. For as long as anyone could remember, a typical month at the factory ended with a great flurry of activity to meet the monthly shipment schedule—the so-called end-of-the-month syndrome. Something like half the month's shipments would typically take place in the last week of the month. This caused all sorts of problems, including inventory buildup, stockouts, poor quality, missed deliveries, and excessive overtime. Under the new system, the factory sought to achieve "linearity" (one-fourth of the monthly shipments were scheduled each week) and trust in the production schedule.

Because these changes were limited to one department, the problems the team encountered were manageable. One thing it discovered was that reconfiguring the flow structure required changes in the tasks its people had to perform. Thus, the change process grew to encompass an iterative adaptation of both people and systems as its impact spread. This necessitated training programs to provide additional skills, including problem-solving techniques and how to handle multiple tasks. Equipped with such skills, factory personnel could deal with the problems that surfaced as the inventory used to buffer operations from one another was reduced.

After a successful pilot operation in one department, the new approach rolled through the plant over a twenty-four-month period. Once the production system was in place and the factory was performing in a manner consistent with the new set of philosophies and principles, factory management went to work on the linkages between the factory and other groups—accounting, personnel, and division top management. Cost accounting and reporting, employee evaluation, and overall factory performance measurement were found to be particularly important. Putting their own house in order, and in the process achieving significant improvements, gave credibility to efforts to change these systems, but it still was not easy.

The same was true for the last phase of the new production system: changing supplier relationships. In mounting that effort, the management team had to go through much the same kind of process at each supplier as had taken place within the Vancouver plant. But because the team had already gone through the process of changing its own factory, it had developed an appreciation for the importance of changing the basic architecture of manufacturing. It understood that a new set of supplier relationships would require similar changes in suppliers' principles, flows, and procedures.

Changing supplier relationships has been an early, important focus of many companies' attempts to cope with increased competitive pressure. Unfortunately, such efforts have often taken the form of the old wolf in new sheep's clothing. Instead of hammering away on price, the purchasing departments in these companies begin to hammer away on reducing inventory, shortening delivery times, and improving quality—but without price increases. A supplier who has been working under the traditional approach will see such efforts for what they are. Thus, the reaction of one supplier faced with an old-wolf purchasing department: "They want us to carry their inventory and swallow the added cost. They think that this will allow them to reduce their costs, but they won't get away with it. We may get squeezed in the short term, but they'll pay eventually."

The basic problem with the old-wolf–new-clothing scenario is that the buyer has changed the emphasis placed on certain criteria, and perhaps some individual decisions, but has not changed its basic flow patterns or the philosophy and principles that underlie them. What is needed is a new manufacturing architecture. Inevitably, that means a substantial process of education, sharing, and learning; there is no quick fix. Changing the manufacturing philosophies of buyers and suppliers that have grown up under the traditional approach and assumptions takes lots of time and effort. Our experience suggests that only those factories which have created a new architecture for their own operations, and which commit significant resources to sharing what they have learned with their suppliers, have a chance of successfully creating a supplier network that has the characteristics they desire.

To reduce complexity, eliminate sources of uncertainty, and reduce conflicts between their factories and their customer's, it is essential that suppliers change from arm's-length adversaries to comakers. Under the comaker view, the buyer organization seeks close working relationships with a few key vendors over the long term. The success of one's vendors is regarded as being integrally linked to one's own. Small vendors are potentially as good as big ones, particularly if they are located nearby. The nature of the close, interactive relationship that develops is such that information is shared freely, multiple contacts are maintained at several organizational levels, buyer and supplier work jointly to solve common problems and to design new products, and everyone is treated with mutual respect. Requests by both parties reflect self-discipline and are therefore credible. Table 7–2 highlights some of the differences between this comaker view and the traditional view. These differences are based on the same principles outlined in the previous section but have been phrased here in terms directly applicable to vendor relations.

The central assumption underlying the comaker approach is that the best vendor-producer *team* will win. Capable, dedicated, vigorous vendors provide a sort of armed guard that reinforces one's own manufacturing organization. Under the comaker view, one is not just buying parts from a vendor; one is buttressing oneself with additional information and capabilities. The comaker relationship is

Table 7-2 Contrasting Views of Vendor Relations

	Traditional	Comaker
Selection/qualification criteria	buyer wants multiple sources	buyer wants few sources
	suppliers fight for business	best suppliers are sought out and retained
	price is primary criteria for selection	nonprice criteria (delivery, quality, etc.) given equal or higher weight
Vendor's production processes	arm's length relationship	works closely with buyer
	focus is on final test	focus is on process control
	stability is the goal	improvement is the goal
Pricing	buyer wants lowest possible price	buyer expects to provide fair return
	leverage-based	trust-based
	short-term agreements	long-term agreements
Schedules	extreme flexibility expected	realistic commitments that *must* be met
	constant changes in schedules	credible promises
		joint effort
		continued improvement
Quality expectations	vendor's responsibility	early vendor involvement
	acceptance levels	
New products	late vendor involvement	vendor design skills highly valued
	vendor not responsible for design	
Information transfers	minimal: exceptions only	substantial and regular
	no news is assumed to be good news	problem-solving information constantly passed back and forth
	single buyer-vendor contact points	multiple levels, two-way contacts

built on the notions that each party to the relationship has unique things to contribute and that their combined success is greatest when they work as one. The extent of the changes required to install such an approach to vendor relations should not be underestimated, however; they are generally greater than those required to alter the management of flows within one's own factory.

When such changes are firmly in place and integrated with one's own factory, however, the result is often a substantial competitive advantage. This advantage is reflected in significantly lower inventories, faster overall response times, higher quality, and lower total costs. Perhaps most important, the new architecture encourages continued improvement in processes and procedures, and superior new products that take advantage of those capabilities.

Experiences at Mazda, at H-P's Vancouver plant, and in many other operations around the world underscore the power of a manufacturing architecture based on the principles we have outlined here. Yet many companies and factories hesitate, reluctant to change their traditional approach. Among the most common excuses:

- Our suppliers won't support us by making deliveries in small batches on a daily basis.
- We will always have back orders in our factory, so we will constantly have to expedite if we are to make up shortages and complete products for shipment. If we pursue these principles, the line will always be shutting down and our production will always be late.
- Our batch-oriented materials planning group and the control system they operate under won't allow us to operate in this mode. We have to change all of our systems before we can change the way we manage the flows in the factory.
- If we adopt this new approach to managing factory operations, we won't be able to track materials through the factory with work orders, so we'll lose control of job status and inventory.
- We're a low-volume job-shop operation, so we can't really benefit from these principles. (That is, everything we do is custom made, and there are no consistent patterns.)
- Our factory is already operating satisfactorily. We don't need to convert to this new approach.

Plausible as they sound, each of these excuses can be shown to be largely a result of a misunderstanding, either of the principles underlying this new architecture or the potential results from their application.[3] Given the performance improvements that have been observed when such principles have been adopted, the issue for many companies really comes down to whether it is wise to wait until a competitive opportunity becomes a competitive necessity.

| 8 |

Controlling and Improving
the Manufacturing Process

Introduction

Chapter 7 dealt with different approaches to controlling the flow of materials and information in a factory. In this chapter we turn to the conversion process itself, through which materials and information are transformed into final products. We describe four different philosophies that companies can adopt in attempting to control such processes, one of which is nicely illustrated by a dramatic approach that we encountered several years ago.

The vice president of manufacturing for a large midwestern producer of sophisticated industrial equipment managed eight plants in the Michigan-Ohio-Indiana region. This man—whom we shall call Marv—was particularly proud of his "tight control" over his organization. A helicopter called the *White Tornado* played a central role in Marv's version of control. To him, control meant quick and decisive action to get a process back on track if it ever got out of line. He had designed an information system that allowed him to keep very close tabs on daily developments at all eight plants. If the operating performance (costs, overdue deliveries, process yields, product quality, etc.) at any of them got "out of line," the *White Tornado* was ready to fly. Marv could be at any of his plants within a short time; his dramatic arrival and fiery personality tended to galvanize plant managers into action. As a result, Marv himself became known as the White Tornado.

When the White Tornado showed up at a plant, he was usually successful in bringing the problem back "under control" within a short time. Although we admired his apparent effectiveness, we were bothered by some nagging questions. Could this organization really be in control if the vice president of manufacturing regularly had to swoop around in his helicopter to keep things in line? Moreover, Marv's style tended to permeate the plants, influencing the behavior of the plant managers even when he was not around. Thus, life in the plants was a series of special task forces, crash programs, and major efforts sparked by one crisis after another. The White Tornado only saw the problems that were so big that plant managers could not hide them from him long enough to solve them themselves.

Our research has convinced us that effective process control does not arise out of the kind of dramatic interventions epitomized by the White Tornado. Sustained process control and improvement are rooted in a deep understanding of the principles governing the conversion process itself. When effectively applied, such understanding creates capabilities that make possible superior productivity, quality, flexibility, delivery, and innovativeness.

We begin our discussion of the principles that govern the control and improvement of production processes, as we did in the last chapter, by comparing the approaches to process control taken at factory A and at factory B. This comparison raises a number of issues that we then incorporate into a framework for thinking about process control. This framework is organized around four levels of control and the kinds of knowledge that support each. The final section of the chapter describes how one company achieved sustained improvement in factory performance through the application of a similar framework.

Two Approaches to Process Control: Factories A and B

The approach that a factory's management takes in trying to achieve process control reflects some fundamental assumptions about the nature of production systems and the sources of performance improvement. Factories A and B illustrate two different approaches to process control—indeed, two different philosophies of management—and underscore the important choices that manufacturing managers must make when designing process control systems.[1]

Factory A

Factory A was proud of its new computerized quality tracking system, installed in early 1987. The system stored, tracked, and classified data on product quality—as measured both on the line and in the Quality Assurance (QA) laboratory. Ellen Corby, QA manager, explained the system to us: "We designed the software to allow the QA staff to analyze a variety of different characteristics. We use a bar-code system that allows us to trace the product to specific shifts, specific operators, specific pieces of equipment, and specific vendors."

When asked where the idea for the system came from, Ellen smiled and said, "Well, it all started when Bart Morrison (factory A manager) was going through the February plant status report a couple of years ago."

The monthly plant status report was a collection of reports from each of the major staff groups, comparing performance against objectives for the previous month. Although the reports contained detailed financial information as well as cost and usage variances, production statistics, direct labor utilization, and quality data, Morrison tended to focus on only a few key indicators. As he sifted through the quality report in mid-March, 1983, the data for product 45, a new product introduced eight months earlier, caught his eye.

This product had experienced a final test reject rate of 15 percent in February, about twice the acceptable level and three times what Morrison had expected. The high defect rate had caused the plant to miss its shipment target—and, as people in the plant knew only too well, anything that affected shipments got Bart's attention. After checking back through the reports for previous months, he discovered that product 45 final test rejects had varied between 7 and 9 percent over the previous six months. The jump to 15 percent signaled a major problem.

Ellen Corby remembered Morrison's reaction clearly: "Bart went through the roof. Product 45 was an important product, and he wasted no time in getting the senior staff together. The meeting was very productive, probably because we had done it so many times before."

Harry Augden, director of product testing, recalled the discussion: "A number of my people thought that the 15 percent number was an aberration. But Bart was worried that something fundamental had gone wrong. The problem could have come from several things: from materials, from assembly mistakes, even from the test procedure itself. But Bart was mostly concerned about assembly."

Mary Pompalo, an assembly supervisor, was surprised when she found out about the problem: "We did a good job on product 45, so I was upset when my boss told me that Bart was worried that we were making serious mistakes. We gave the assembly operators very detailed instructions and we watched them very carefully. I made sure my people did exactly what the procedures called for.''

Morrison set up a product 45 task force with himself as chairman. Procedures were rechecked, inspectors made additional in-process checks on the line, and supervisors met with technicians and operators to make sure that procedures were followed to the letter. After several days the task force still had not uncovered any serious errors in the assembly process, nor could they find significant problems in incoming materials. But final tests still showed that about 15 percent of the finished units were defective.

Frustrated, Morrison discussed the problem with Earl Lander, vice president of quality assurance (QA) for the corporation. Lander sent two of his staff members to the plant for a few days to work with its QA group in trying to track down the problem. Soon they shifted their attention to the subassembly areas. After some experimentation they found that changes in certain machine settings substantially reduced the defect rate.

Later, one of the technicians in the subassembly area talked about the product: "I knew there was something wrong with the way that machine was set up for that job. I couldn't put my finger on it, but I felt it wasn't right. Nobody asked me what I thought, so I just did what the supervisors told me to do.''

Working at a feverish pace the task force was able to identify and implement a process change that brought reject rates back into the acceptable range (6 to 7 percent). This experience motivated Morrison to request a detailed quality tracking system that would provide earlier warning of product problems. Thus the quality problem with product 45 triggered the development of the new computerized tracking system.

Factory B

During our visit to factory B we discovered some of the reasons for its reputation as a high-quality producer. At one point, we met Ed Stepanek, team leader in the heat treating area. He showed us a bulletin board tacked to a partition in the middle of the work area and explained the different charts. "The team keeps track of five different process parameters in this area. The chart we are most proud of is this one on furnace temperature variations. We came up with it several months ago when working on a reliability problem.''

The temperature chart had its origin in a conversation between

Fred Sparks, a heat treating technician, and Larry Moss, a quality assurance engineer. Fred was looking for information about product performance that could help his heat treating team improve its operation. Larry showed him some competitive data on reliability that the QA group had pulled together. The data indicated that their product was losing some of its reliability advantage in the field, even though internal test results had not changed; competitors' products evidently had improved. Larry and Fred decided that heat treating might be a good place to look for improvements.

Fred reported on his conversation at the next meeting of his team, and the group decided to mount a problem-solving effort. The approach they followed had been developed over a number of years; it began with generating ideas about how heat treating might lead to different kinds of field failures. Then the team collected data to narrow the possibilities, making liberal use of what Stepanek called "the five whys." Fred Sparks explained:

> We have all been through a lot of training on problem solving, and it has become second nature for us to ask *why* five times, whenever anyone suggests a possible cause for a certain problem: Why did that problem arise? Why did the thing that caused *it* occur? And so on. We figure that the five whys should lead us pretty close to the true source of the problem. After you have worked here awhile, you learn that Harry Cowles (plant manager) really cares about quality. He's always talking about "quality at the source."

The team was the focal point of the problem-solving process, but it received a lot of help from QA. A QA staff member attended team meetings, collected and analyzed data, and was instrumental in helping to narrow the options. The idea for concentrating on temperature differences in the furnace came from an operator, Randy Logan, whose responsibilities included monitoring the furnace. Team discussions triggered recollections of previous problems that had occurred with products that had been placed in the back of the furnace.

Billy O'Donnell, a manufacturing engineer, helped the heat treating team install sensors and measurement equipment:

> Ed told me about his team's work on reliability and asked me to work with them in some experiments on temperature variation in the furnace. I helped them rig up sensors in four different parts of the furnace. We only did it on one of the furnaces to see if we could spot a problem. The experiment really worked well. We not only

found temperature differences but we found that they often changed during the shift.

The team traced the source of the temperature variation back to the equipment (sometimes a residue built up that affected temperature in the back of the furnace) and to load-unload procedures. Then it instituted a procedure to track the temperature differences within each of the furnaces. Stepanek commented:

> We have a pretty good procedure now, but what I'd really like to do is regulate the temperature automatically in different zones in the furnace. I don't think it would be that hard to do, and I'm pretty sure that management would put up the money for the system. Harry is always telling us that it's better to invest in preventing problems than in detecting them.

Comparing Factories A and B

Factory A and factory B differ in fundamental ways in their approach to process control and improvement. These differences are not a matter of inherent skill or competence. The people who work in both factories are equally capable and motivated in doing what they have been assigned to do. The differences arise because of fundamental differences in assumptions and structure; these are briefly summarized in Table 8-1.

Perhaps the most fundamental difference between the two factories concerns process control. At factory A process control means control of people. Supervisors at factory A define as clearly as possible what workers should do and then spend a good deal of their time making sure that the workers adhere to specified procedures. Control at factory B is much different; it focuses on the fundamental process used to produce the product. People are the means by which control is achieved, not the thing to be controlled. "Quality at the source" is far more than a slogan; it represents a basic goal: to achieve control over critical process parameters.

Both factories use staff groups in achieving process control, but their functions are quite different. As illustrated by its handling of the problem with product 45, factory A's various staff functions—such as quality assurance, manufacturing engineering, and materials management—are responsible both for collecting critical information about process behavior and for diagnosing and solving problems. Although first level supervisors are supposedly responsible for

Table 8-1 Process Control: Factory A versus Factory B

Item	Factory A	Factory B
Focus	control people; follow instructions	control the process; quality at the source
Line/staff role	line: supervise operations; meet shipment targets staff: collect and analyze data; direct responsibility for control	line: primary responsibility for process control staff: technical excellence; support line organization
Data collection	many detailed reports; data collected by staff groups; long lags in response	track a few key variables at local level; line operators are directly responsible
Source of information/action	centralized data processing/decision making; minimal involvement of floor-level operators	decentralized data processing; decision making done primarily at floor level
Standard of comparison	comparison against budgets and engineered standards	comparison against customer needs, competitors, and own history
Role of management	detailed analyses/decision making; always in the loop	set direction; establish commitment, marshal resources; direct involvement is rare

maintaining control, they play a subordinate role to the staff groups when problems arise.

Staff personnel play a less central, but no less important, role at factory B. They act essentially as expert consultants who serve and support the line organization. Achieving and maintaining control over the process—including collecting basic process information and identifying, diagnosing and solving problems—is the line's responsibility. However, as the heat treating example suggests, staff people provide significant expertise and often collect specialized data when specific problems are encountered.

With active staff groups generating a variety of detailed reports on factory operations, factory A's Bart Morrison felt that he was being kept fully informed. Of course, he was not the only one to receive that information; the plant was awash with reports, memos, and computer printouts containing detailed information about financial performance, cost and volume variances, and quality. Although a great deal of data was generated each month, much of it was essentially obsolete in that it described where the process had been several weeks earlier.

Harry Cowles received far fewer reports each month about the condition of his factory. In fact, much less paper moved around factory B. The important data in the plant were monitored by the operators themselves, through charts that tracked the performance of a relatively small number of critical process parameters. This information was collected on a real-time basis in order to identify where special attention was needed or opportunities for further improvement existed. Thus factory B's managers did not need to wait for a monthly report to keep abreast of developments inside the factory. Reading the control charts located around the factory provided up-to-date information about its status.

Information collection and processing were highly decentralized in factory B: responsibility was vested in the team leaders in each of the factory's operating departments. In contrast, information processing in factory A was highly centralized: information flowed up to the top for review and analysis, and instructions flowed down through the ranks of management before being executed by the operating groups. This flow structure implied that the plant manager and his key staff members in factory A were always involved in problem identification and solving. In fact, the organization could not really focus effectively on a problem until senior management "got in the loop."

Top management's role in process control at factory B was much different. It was difficult to determine, for example, what role Harry Cowles played in solving the reliability problem that the heat treating team investigated. In fact, at factory B it was not unusual for several process improvement projects to be going on without the plant manager's awareness. The role of factory B's senior management was to set direction, to articulate fundamental principles, and to provide resources to support and sustain the efforts going on at the operating level.

A Framework for Process Control and Improvement

Our comparison of factories A and B underscores the range of issues that must be faced when developing an approach to process control and improvement. The approaches taken by the two factories grew out of fundamental differences in the definition of control and how one should go about achieving it. In this section we develop a framework for categorizing various forms of control and thinking about the managerial skills and systems called for by each. Figure 8-1 provides the starting point for this discussion.

The vertical axis in Figure 8-1 measures a specific process or product characteristic, while the horizontal axis tracks the sequence of

Figure 8-1 A Framework for Process Control

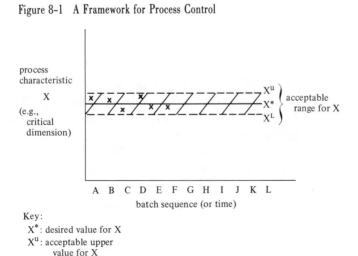

Key:
X^*: desired value for X
X^u: acceptable upper
    value for X
X^L: acceptable lower
    value for X

production batches over time. In this example, a certain process characteristic, indicated by X, is being tracked. Although X* is the desired value for X, the final product's design can accommodate some variation around X*. As long as the process operates within certain upper and lower limits (and as long as other parameters are held within their limits), the final product will meet its specifications.

The creation of superior products, having distinctive and desirable characteristics, requires tight control over process parameters. If a manufacturing organization can do this better than its competitors, it will contribute to the creation of a competitive advantage over them. Three kinds of process capability are identifiable within this framework. The first is the ability to achieve *consistency* in X, over repeated runs of the process. This capability is illustrated in the first several batches in Figure 8-1, where all the observations fall within the acceptable (hatched) range bounding X*. Improving the consistency of the process—that is, increasing the proportion of observations in the acceptable range—may affect several competitive dimensions: fewer defects, improved reliability, and lowered costs of manufacturing and field service or repair.

A second and closely related capability is the degree of *precision* in the process. This capability is illustrated by the width of the hatched range. The narrower the range within which the process operates consistently, the more precise it is. This precision may simplify and reduce errors in downstream processes and interact with other parts of the product in such a way as to improve product performance.

A third capability, not shown in Figure 8-1, is related to the *potential* performance of that type of process. Given existing materials, tools, equipment, skills, and procedures, the process cannot consistently operate beyond this frontier. Being able to expand the frontier of a process (e.g., its speed) may have a powerful competitive effect. Not only can it lead to lower costs and delivery time; it may affect the performance of the product itself.

Achieving process consistency, increasing its precision, and expanding its performance frontier—each requires a different level of control. Improving consistency and precision, for example, requires understanding and controlling the major causes of variation in the process, of which there are two basic forms.

The first is what we call *normal* variation. Small differences in materials, people, equipment, environmental conditions, and procedures may produce small differences in X, even when the process is operating as designed under expected environmental conditions. Instead of running at a thickness of exactly X*, for example, the process may run at X* plus 1 percent in batch 1 and at X* minus 1.02 percent in batch 2. But processes are also subject to what we call *abnormal* variation. Abnormal variations arise through unusual events that produce process characteristics falling outside the acceptable range. They may be due to gross errors in procedure, to major changes in materials or the environment, or to other kinds of contingencies that disrupt the normal operation of the process.

Most attempts to achieve process consistency focus simply on controlling abnormal variations and employ what we call *reactive control*. They concentrate on putting into place "early warning systems" to tell plant management when abnormal variation has occurred so that they can initiate corrective action. Marv and his White Tornado, as well as the less dramatic approaches in use at factory A, illustrate the application of this type of control. Some amount of reactive control is necessary in most operations, of course, since performance may suffer long-term damage if the organization does not have in place a means of recognizing major disruptions—machines failing unexpectedly, deliveries not arriving on time, and off-spec materials received from suppliers—and responding quickly to counteract their effects. When fires start, the factory needs a way to spot them and put them out.

Reactive control alone, however, will not be able to improve the consistency or the precision of a process. An effective system of reactive control may return a wayward process to acceptable limits, but only until another abnormal variation strikes. Preventing operations from exceeding designed limits requires that one eliminate the sources of abnormal variation. Thus, whereas reactive control focuses on returning the process to its acceptable range when it strays outside, *preventive control* focuses on identifying and removing the underlying source of abnormal variation within the process. The primary question it seeks to answer is not whether but *why* each failure occurred; then it tries to prevent that failure from occurring again.

The relationship between reactive control and preventive control is illustrated by an incident observed during a visit to factory B. Noticing a flurry of activity around one of the large machining centers, we watched as a small team of operators and technicians discussed an obvious malfunction in the equipment. One of the machine's cutting tools had shattered, causing some minor damage to the equipment. Once the problem was diagnosed, the operators fixed the equipment, replaced the tool, and had the machine operating again fairly quickly. Had they stopped at that point they would have demonstrated reactive control of that process.

Later, however, we discovered that the operators had continued to pursue the reasons behind the tool's shattering. They identified a variety of possible sources of failure, including improper alignment, poor product design, inappropriate process specifications, and a fault in the tool itself. After some experimentation they determined that the fault in this case lay with the tool. Working with its supplier led to improved tools, providing additional control over this particular source of variation.

Whereas reactive control is full of starts and stops, preventive control requires continuous activity. Operators, managers, and engineers must doggedly pursue the sources of abnormal variation in the process. Over a long period of time such activity results in a process that operates within established limits on a consistent basis. Preventive control is the basis for producing things "right the first time." As we saw in Chapter 6, reducing waste through consistent operations can significantly improve overall factory productivity.

The same approach and persistence can also make possible greater process precision: what we call *progressive control*. Whereas the intent of both reactive and preventive control is to ensure that the variation in the process stays within an acceptable range, progressive control seeks to shrink that range—that is, in Figure 8–1, the hatched area bracketing X^*. Not only is the ultimate goal of progressive control different from those of the two previous forms, but so is its focus: rather than seeking to react to or prevent abnormal variations, it seeks to establish progressively tighter control over *normal* variation in the process.

As was noted earlier, this normal variation is due to such fundamental product and process characteristics as the design of the product, the ability of equipment to hold certain tolerances, operator skills, and the quality of materials. Narrowing those limits, therefore, usually requires changing basic elements in both product and process design. Moreover, as a manufacturing organization attempts to shrink the limits around X^*, it will uncover new sources of variation, as well as subtle interactions between them and the original process parameters. Progressive control demands that such nuances be identified and understood. Engineers, operators, and managers must go after second- and third-order effects and their interactions with the same kind of persistence that other organizations exhibit when exercising reactive control.

The difference between preventive and progressive control is illustrated by an episode that occurred in factory B's polishing operation. Through careful control over the location and speed of the polisher heads, the polishing team had been able to achieve a target degree of surface smoothness on a consistent basis. But the development of a new product required even greater precision than before and led team members to work on narrowing the acceptable range of smoothness. Working with the engineering group, they began to investigate possible sources of normal variation. One of the things they discovered was that tiny vibrations in the polishing equipment, previously undetected, produced slight variations in the surface characteristics of the material. After some experimentation, the engineers installed a stronger, more rigid support structure for the equipment, which eliminated these vibrations. Other sources of variation were also uncovered and examined as the group pushed to increase the precision of the process.

A factory that pursues both abnormal and normal variation with the same vigor, and that learns from each experiment, will be able to achieve increasingly consistent and precise operation. The three levels of control discussed thus far, however, assume that a single procedure (or formula) is being followed. The ultimate level of control is to be able to make changes in this formula and still maintain the critical process characteristics within acceptable (and narrowing) limits. We call this fourth level *dynamic control*. Achieving dynamic control may entail new equipment, new procedures, new information, different product designs, and higher levels of operator skills and organizational capabilities.

The transition from batch to continuous annealing of steel sheet illustrates the difference between progressive and dynamic control. In the traditional batch process, large coils of steel sheet are stacked three or four high in a large silo-shaped furnace and baked at a specific temperature for several days. Baking changes the microstructure of the material, making it stronger and more suitable for further processing. The nature of the process (wrapping the steel sheet into coils, stacking the coils one on another, and heating them in a cylindrical furnace) imposes limits on the potential strength and consistency of the sheet. Achieving higher-strength steel and greater control over its microstructure calls for a different process.

Developing such a process required an understanding of the fundamental determinants of the sheet's microstructure, the basis for dynamic control. Research had shown that this microstructure is influenced by the specific sequence of heating and cooling operations that the steel undergoes. Achieving dynamic control of annealing, therefore, required equipment and systems that would enable one to manage the heating and cooling operations in a far more precise manner than is possible in the batch process.

In continuous annealing, an uncoiled sheet is passed through a sequence of heating and cooling operations on a continuous basis. Each heating and cooling zone is monitored by sensors that provide precise information about the conditions (such as surface temperature, tension, and pressure) prevailing in that zone. Backed by a computer-based mathematical model of what happens to the steel as it passes through various zones, engineers and operators have developed procedures for determining the impact of different variables on the characteristics of the steel. Hence, continuous annealing—achieved only through the development of the science underlying the annealing phenomenon—makes it possible to achieve a much higher level of control over sheet steel characteristics.

Knowledge: The Foundation of Process Control
The four types of process control—reactive, preventive, progressive, and dynamic—characterize the different levels of mastery that a manufacturing organization can achieve over process and product characteristics. Moving from merely reacting, when trouble occurs, to control over fundamental sources of variation in performance requires successively uncovering, exploring, and applying deeper layers of knowledge about the process. Then one must apply this knowledge effectively through people, equipment, systems, and procedures. Knowing what actions to take to achieve a desired result is not just "know-how," it is "know-why." Table 8-2 summarizes the different levels of knowledge, the linkages between knowledge and process control, and the domains within which knowledge is applied.[2]

Reactive control rests on two kinds of knowledge. First, it requires that an organization be able to distinguish good product from bad. Without this rudimentary kind of knowledge, the organization cannot begin to differentiate between normal and abnormal variation. One can, of course, exercise reactive control with little systematic process understanding, by using trial and error and other brute-force

Table 8-2 Control and Knowledge in the Factory

Level of Control	Degree of Knowledge	Characteristic Skills, Links to Process	Domain of Application
Reactive	can identify key output characteristics (tell good from bad); measure key variables	make problems visible; quick action; develop a repertoire of solutions and decision rules to counteract abnormal variations	current operations; direct work force; small ad hoc teams
Preventive	understand the direction of the cause and effect relationships embodied in rules and procedures; identify sources of abnormal variation	pay attention to detail; exercise care and discipline; develop better procedures to eliminate abnormal variations	current operations; environmental and internal variables; direct work force with engineering support
Progressive	strength of cause and effect relationship defined; second- and third-order parameters defined and understood; process capable of quantitative description; sources of normal variation increasingly identified	detailed engineering analysis/ testing; equipment, software, process development to establish control over sources of normal variation	changes to existing process: machinery, control mechanisms, operating sequence, product design; requires partnership with product and process engineers
Dynamic	full-system model of process; identification of general principles governing science of the process	research skills: observation, experimentation and analysis; integration of science and engineering; process designed to maintain control even as the formula is being changed	science of process; new process concepts; scientists, advanced engineering departments

methods. But an organization is far more likely to recognize problems and be able to restore a process to an acceptable state if it has identified the key process parameters and developed ways to measure them.

Knowing the key variables and how to measure them enables the organization to make problems visible and develop methods for dealing with them quickly and effectively. Preventive control, however, requires deeper knowledge about cause-and-effect relationships: it requires that one understand (at least in a rough way) how different variables and their interaction affect performance and are, in turn, affected by environmental conditions. Furthermore, to achieve repeatable performance, knowledge about cause-and-effect relationships needs to be incorporated into operating rules and procedures.

Both reactive and preventive control focus on current operations and are achieved primarily through the actions of those members of the manufacturing organization who are most directly involved with daily production: operators, technicians, supervisors, and technical specialists. Achieving consistency in performance is based on discipline and attention to detail when executing procedures, and on being able to respond nimbly to the unexpected. These capabilities also lay the foundation for improving precision, but they are not sufficient. Achieving progressive control requires that the organization develop deeper knowledge about the detailed structure of the process. Although the direction of cause-effect relationships alone ("If we decrease A, B will increase") may be enough to obtain rough control over abnormal variation, gaining control over normal variation requires knowledge of the approximate magnitude of that effect. Progressive control, moreover, depends on gaining insight into second- and third-order parameters and the direction and strength of their effects.

Whereas reactive and preventive control assume that the equipment, materials, and designs are given, these become the focus of attention in progressive control. It seeks to exploit understanding of the strength of various relationships as well as of more subtle nuances in the process. Thus, the hallmark of progressive control is creative engineering: modifications to equipment, control mechanisms, software algorithms, and systems, based on detailed analysis, testing, and experimentation.

Skillful engineering and detailed process understanding are just as important in the achievement of dynamic control, but a deep understanding of the science underlying the process is also required. Being able to measure, explain, and exploit the systemic interactions and scientific principles underlying the process allows one to understand and extend the limits inherent in an existing design. Dynamic control thus requires classic research skills in observation, analysis, and experimentation, and highly trained and skilled scientists to do it. This is why the introduction of science had such a powerful impact on production in the first half of this century, as described in Chapter 2. Creating economic value out of that knowledge, however, demands in addition that scientific knowledge, practical engineering, and operator know-how all be harnessed to develop new materials, equipment, procedures, and product designs.

The Framework Applied: Factory A and Factory B Revisited

Our framework for process control applies to all processes, from entire factories to individual pieces of equipment. Within a single factory different process steps may operate at different levels of control, in part because of differing levels of knowledge. Effective process management thus requires a range of skills, from quick reaction and discipline at the operating level to creative problem solving in engineering and careful experimentation in R & D. Moreover, achieving a higher level of control requires mastery of the level below it. A manufacturing organization cannot increase the precision of a process without first developing the knowledge and the capabilities that underlie preventive control. And we have already noted the close connection between scientific knowledge and engineering know-how in achieving dynamic control. This is the primary reason that a manufacturing organization cannot skip steps in its pursuit of Stage IV; the capabilities required at each stage are essential building blocks for subsequent stages.

The cumulative nature of knowledge, and the interaction between different levels of control, underscore the importance of integrating the knowledge and capabilities of different parts of the manufacturing organization. Comparing factory A and factory B illustrates the value of an integrated perspective.

Factory A pursued reactive control through centralized, detailed tracking of product information made available to the manufacturing organization only after a substantial time lag. Although the organization was capable of moving quickly to counteract problems once they became apparent, processes could stray outside of acceptable limits for some time before the manufacturing organization was alerted that a problem existed.

Furthermore, the centralized nature of control activities and the factory's focus on early-warning systems and fire fighting made sustained process improvement difficult. Implicit in the design of its information and control system was the notion that process improvement was the responsibility of staff groups rather than of the line organization. As the product 45 story suggests, this structure often failed to make use of valuable information available at the operating level. Moreover, senior management failed to comprehend the value, or even acknowledge the existence, of preventive, progressive, and dynamic control, or the importance of fundamental knowledge about the process.

In contrast, factory B was oriented toward process improvement. Although it had achieved effective reactive and preventive control, the way it reacted to the recognition that the heat treating operation was responsible for minute product variations showed that its ultimate objective was total control over its processes. Local information on a timely basis, local responsibility for monitoring and adjusting the process, and strong top management commitment and direction provided the motivation and insight needed to attain higher levels of process understanding. Further, the heat treating team displayed great discipline and persistence in pursuing better understanding and more effective control of its process. These laid the foundation for significant improvements in process capabilities, through new sensors, new software, and computer-based process automation. Through these enhancements it was then able to achieve even greater understanding of the basic science underlying heat treating.

Knowledge in Action: Learning and Problem Solving

Our observations at factory B and other high-performance plants, within the four-levels-of-control framework, suggest that developing and systematically applying process knowledge is central to building a competitive advantage in manufacturing. Because the world is continually changing, the pursuit of improved knowledge must be ongoing. The high-performance factory, therefore, must be able both to add continually to its stock of process knowledge and to apply that knowledge to practical problems.

In contrast to the assumptions of Taylorism (discussed in Chapter 2), world-class manufacturing organizations do not divide people into those who think and those who act. Learning and applying knowledge must be high on everyone's agenda, at every level in the organization. The line organization in a high-performance factory has two fundamental, mutually reinforcing missions. The first is to operate the existing process successfully, achieving both reactive and preventive control. The second is to expand its knowledge of the process in order to improve it, and to lay the basis for higher levels of control. Other parts of the organization, including engineering groups and the R & D laboratories, share this mission.

Everybody should be included in the learning process—not because one can thereby keep everyone happy or give them a sense of involvement, but because important information and insights are found at every level in the organization. Operators working directly with equipment and systems often have the best access to information about certain aspects of the process. If well trained and endowed with the right tools, people working directly in the process can acquire extremely valuable insight. Staff engineers and laboratory scientists, on the other hand, are positioned to learn more effectively about other aspects of the process, given their training and the information to which they have access.

No matter where an individual works, there are two basic activities that underlie the creation of new process knowledge. The first is simply observation of the operation in action. In a learning organization, people pay attention to the process and look for patterns that link process variables to product characteristics. An alert observer can often spot opportunities for process improvement without going through any formal or systematic analysis. Two anecdotes capture the importance of close observation and pattern recognition.

In one large multinational organization, all new employees attend an introductory meeting with senior management. At the end of the meeting the new employees are invited to attend lunch in the company cafeteria. Before entering the cafeteria each person is handed a small three-by-five-inch card and told to examine closely the operation of the cafeteria and, at the conclusion of lunch, to write down one suggestion for improving cafeteria operations. The message in that assignment is clear: "From the day you begin work in this company we want you to pay attention, to always be on the lookout for ways to make things better."

The second anecdote comes from another company that uses a traditional assembly-line process. At each work station operators have access to a set of buttons that allow them to stop the assembly line. Operators are instructed to stop the line if they spot a defective part or if they are having trouble completing their operation. More important, they are encouraged to stop the line if they spot any opportunity for improving the process. Here again the message is clear: "We want you to not only complete your assignment; we also want you to look for opportunities to make improvements."

Problem solving is another activity that is central to the creation of knowledge. We have already noted the emphasis that reactive control places on recognizing and reacting to problems, but these same problems also provide opportunities for improving one's knowledge about the process. Some problems arise simply because of a failure to execute an existing procedure correctly. Problem solving in this context may involve reexamining the procedure being followed, additional training of the people involved, or readjustment of a machine setting. In other cases, problems may arise because of imperfect process knowledge. Pursuing solutions to such problems can lead to a better understanding of the process.

Solving all but the simplest problems requires experimentation. Some experiments arise naturally. For example, two sequential batches of product may inadvertently be processed in slightly different ways. If information about each batch's processing parameters and output characteristics is retained, one may be able to develop insight into how different process characteristics influence performance. Other experiments need to be formalized and controlled, however. If, say, a semiconductor manufacturer wants to explore the impact of a new diffusion process, it may design a controlled experiment in which a special batch of wafers are processed with the new diffusion procedure and compared to a "control" batch of wafers processed the old way. Controlled experiments of this kind can be quite powerful as long as knowledge about the process has developed to the point where the controlled batch is, in fact, controlled. If process behavior is influenced by powerful confounding (uncontrolled) variables, controlled experiments may provide little useful information The quality of the information created through experimentation depends on environmental factors, existing knowledge about the process, and the design of the experiment itself.

The Learning Cycle and Statistical Process Control

The process of learning, from observation to problem solving, involves a set of activities that we term the learning cycle. In a learning cycle, the investigator identifies a problem, develops a diagnosis of the sources of the problem, and conducts tests to determine the important relationships between these causes and effects. The learning cycle is not complete, however, until the resulting knowledge is implemented: the knowledge created through the learning process must be embodied in new procedures, changes in equipment, changes in information systems, or the training of people. What has been learned must be incorporated into the production system, and the gain in control permanently captured by the organization.

The learning process never ends; the completion of one cycle lays the groundwork for a new cycle as new problems are uncovered. Moreover, learning should occur at every level in the organization and represent an important part of everyone's mission statement. But simply recognizing the importance of continuous learning is not enough to make it happen. Individuals and work teams need a set of tools and matching capabilities. Good information management is critical because new insight must be communicated to those who can use it in operating and controlling the process. One set of tools that has been found to be particularly effective in facilitating such new insight and communication is known as statistical process control (SPC).[3]

At one level, statistical process control is a philosophy; at another, it is a set of statistical tools that can be used to identify, diagnose, and solve production problems. The philosophy of SPC shares much in common with the basic control framework laid out earlier in this chapter: to break up a process into a set of individual steps, or elements, and ascertain specific parameters for each step that will lead to the overall product or process performance desired. Its goal is to be able to distinguish between normal and abnormal variation in every important process parameter, and then pursue increasing levels of control over the process. Graphs and charts are used to present statistics (such as averages and ranges) that help identify and communicate problems and suggest corrective action.

The primary SPC tool for distinguishing normal from abnormal variations is the control chart. The top panel in Figure 8–2 presents a control chart showing the observed average hourly temperature $(\overline{X})$ of a certain production process and the long-term average of this average $(\overline{\overline{X}})$. The bottom panel shows R, the range of temperatures within each day, as well as the average range $(\overline{R})$ over the longer term. An upper control limit (UCL) and a lower control limit (LCL), indicate the bounds representing the "normal" variation for this process. As long as results fall within these limits, the process is "under control." When the results go outside of these limits, implying

Figure 8-2 Statistical Process Control: Control Charts for Average Hourly Temperature

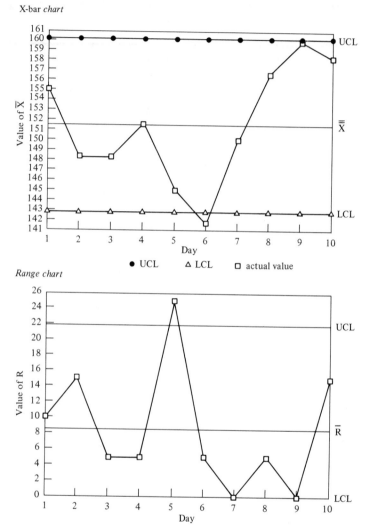

that some form of abnormal variation has occurred, the process needs to be adjusted to bring it back into control. The control chart can thus trigger reactive control. However, maintaining control charts over time can also help identify patterns of abnormal variation and serve as a means of achieving preventive control.

Through the use of control charts and other techniques, SPC plays two powerful roles in the learning cycle. First, it facilitates the collection of data that can be used to pinpoint process weaknesses and identify opportunities for improvement. Second, it provides a set of tools that can be used to analyze the data in order to develop diagnoses and possible remedies. A selection of commonly used tools and their uses are presented in Figure 8-3. For example, a fish-bone (cause-effect) diagram can help a work group categorize and systematically explore the major possible sources of process variation. Given information about those sources, a Pareto diagram ranks them by size and provides some indication of their relative importance. Two other charts—histograms and scatter diagrams—provide an indication of the frequency of different variable values over time and possible patterns of association between two variables.

Figure 8-3　Charts Used in Statistical Process Control

Fish-bone Diagram

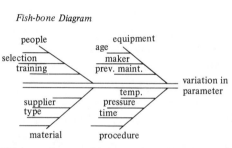

Fish-bone: shows possible causes of a problem; aids hypothesis generation

Pareto Chart

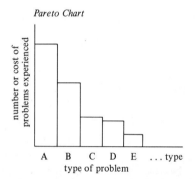

Pareto: shows magnitude of each of several effects; helps focus effort

Histogram

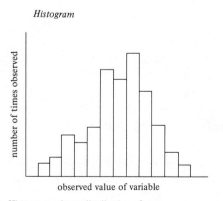

Histogram: shows distribution of some variable; helps identify patterns

Scatter Diagram

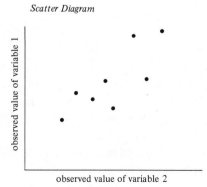

Scatter: shows association between two variables; helps to identify possible cause-effect relationship

The experience of factory B's heat treating team suggests the power such tools can have at the operating level, by helping people examine process problems carefully and logically. The same kinds of tools and techniques—control charts, fish-bone diagrams, histograms, and scatter diagrams—have their counterparts at other levels of the organization and other places in the production system. Engineers seeking to develop substantial changes in process equipment may use additional kinds of tools, as might scientists working in the R & D facility. The objective is to utilize scientific knowledge, process data, and appropriate techniques at every level so that each member of the organization is involved in a learning cycle and has the tools and skills required to do it well.

Placed in the context of the process control framework developed earlier, SPC represents part of a broad approach to process management. Collecting process data at the operating level and using well-defined procedures provides work groups with a focus and a structure for their efforts. In that sense, SPC can be an important contributor to the creation of discipline within the production organization. Discipline is not only important in reducing variability in operations; it is essential to learning.

But communication is required as well as discipline if knowledge is to be used effectively. If different parts of the organization are to communicate effectively, they must have a common language. With its graphic representations and related terminology, SPC provides such a language. Communication is facilitated, moreover, because SPC-guided learning activities are rooted in data and precise in characterizing problems and solutions. For example, the group working on temperature differences in the heat treating furnace at factory B could quite easily explain their concerns, the rationale behind their proposed solution, and their needs to staff personnel and to senior management. Finally, once experiments have been conducted and potential solutions explored, refined, and implemented, the use of SPC facilitates the introduction of those changes in other parts of the organization. Thus, the learning that takes place at the local level can be shared, becoming organizational learning that benefits a wide range of operations.

The power provided by these higher levels of control and knowledge is subtle but pervasive. In a factory that relies primarily on reactive control, even a small change in material flows and plant layout can be traumatic. On the other hand, one that has mastered progressive control can make such changes easily, without breaking stride.

This difference is often crucial when a factory tries to move to a just-in-time inventory system or install a new Flexible Manufacturing System (FMS).

An organization that relies on reactive control is likely, for example, to restrict the number of parts assigned to be produced on the FMS, and seldom changes them. It runs the FMS much like it would run any other process, thereby failing to take advantage of its full flexibility.[4] In contrast, installing an FMS in a high-performance factory enables it to change the nature of that factory's competitive advantage to one based on superior knowledge and responsiveness to customer needs. Faced with a competitive environment that increasingly emphasizes the importance of such responsiveness, companies are discovering that it requires much higher levels of process understanding and control than were necessary before. Putting ever more resources into elaborate reactive control systems is not the answer.

Making It Happen: Organizing and Managing for Process Improvement
The achievement of process control at all four levels, and the creation of sustained improvement in performance over long periods of time, require that a manufacturing organization be able to develop and apply knowledge in its production processes. Creating that kind of organization and achieving that kind of performance are not things that happen overnight. Getting from factory A, where shipment schedules dominate management's agenda, everyone is preoccupied with installing and detecting early-warning signals, and most problem-solving is reactive, to factory B, where everybody is learning and new process knowledge is continually being incorporated, requires more than just a clever slogan, a crash program, or a new technology. As we have tried to indicate in previous chapters, the high-performance manufacturing organization is a finely tuned interactive system. Getting from A to B therefore requires a change in the very foundation of that system.

Signetics Corporation's efforts in the early 1980s to change its approach to process control and improvement illustrates the nature of that challenge and the impact of making it happen. Realizing that a continuation of its traditional methods of quality control were unlikely to meet the challenge of its Japanese competitors or the demands of its own customers, in 1980 Signetics' senior management took the first steps toward a new approach. Table 8-3 compares the old and new approaches.[5]

Table 8-3 Product and Process Quality Philosophy at Signetics

Before	After
Screen for product quality.	Plan for product quality.
Product quality is a staff responsibility.	Product quality is everyone's responsibility.
Mistakes are inevitable.	Zero defects are possible.
Quality control means inspection.	Quality means conformance to specifications.
Scrap and rework are the major costs of poor process quality.	Disappointed customers and lost market share are the major costs of poor process quality.
Process quality is a tactical issue.	Process quality is a strategic issue.

SOURCE: Adapted from Harwood, 1984.

Signetics had historically employed what we have termed reactive control. It relied on inspection to sort good product from bad, and fire fighting to deal with emergency problems. Process control was a staff responsibility. But in 1980 process control became a line function, zero defects became the goal, the notion of going after root causes to eliminate sources of variation became a guiding principle, and improvement in process quality became everyone's responsibility.

The significant change in attitude, behavior, and practice that this philosophical sea-change called for necessitated extensive training, the development of new systems for collecting data, new measures of performance, and a senior management commitment to make quality considerations play a central role in every manager's objectives. There was also a change in organization structure to transfer responsibility for quality and process control to the line organization. Yet watchwords, guiding principles, training seminars, and reorganization alone did not create improved quality. Signetics' senior management discovered that real change came only through changes in basic operating practices, new patterns of communication, new capabilities, and new levels of commitment. Chuck Harwood, president of Signetics, summarized the situation after a year of effort:

> We had planted some seeds, set up some models, passed down the word; we expected this to flower in the rest of the company. What happened? Not much. . . . I was not happy with our progress. A survey at the end of 1980 showed that some people thought the new

program was great; others thought it was baloney; and others knew that, if they just hunkered down, this program would go away.[6]

Words and surface actions were not enough. So top management continued to deepen its commitment to a new way of managing processes, and fundamental changes began to occur at the operating level. Part of this came through a new relationship with a key customer, an automotive parts manufacturer. This customer forged an agreement with Signetics that required it to achieve (over a specified period of time) a defect rate of two hundred parts-per-million (ppm) in their processes—in some cases implying a reduction in defects to less than one-hundredth of their previous levels. Moreover, since the product had to be delivered at relatively low cost, this improvement could not be achieved simply through 100 percent testing. The only way to achieve this goal was for Signetics to eliminate the root causes of poor quality in its processes and products. That, in turn, would require a level of integration of fabrication, assembly, engineering, and design that was unprecedented in Signetics' past experience.

After a slow start, during which time the manufacturing organization debated the merits of implementing the full program—statistical process control, line responsibility, a goal of zero defects (was it possible? would it pay off?)—the program slowly gained a foothold and began to show some improvement. Yet over the next few months the organization confronted some difficult decisions that raised the stakes for the entire program. Given competing demands for scarce resources, Signetic was essentially forced to decide just how committed it really was.

For example, at one point the automotive manufacturer uncovered a tendency for Signetics' components to fail during accelerated environmental testing. The problem was traced to the tiny gold wires connecting the integrated circuit to the package housing it. Under certain stressful conditions, some of these wires would crack or break. Signetics had never focused much attention on this problem. Along with many other U.S. IC manufacturers, it had never considered the problem serious enough to worry about. Now, in the light of its two-hundred-parts-per-million commitment, the manufacturing organization had to decide how to deal with this problem (known as wire creep), as well as other similar types of problems that began to become visible.

Extensive discussions produced a set of options for dealing with wire creep. In microcosm, these proposals captured the choices facing the company as a whole. The issue, what level of process control to pursue, could be summarized in three options:

1. Identify the key variables in the wire-bonding process, and establish limits for them.

Option 1 would give Signetics the basis for achieving reactive and then preventive control over the bonding process. But its engineers worried that the limits might have to be set so tight that, without some change in the basic process, the cost of eliminating wire creep would be unacceptably high. Thus, option 2:

2. Deepen knowledge of the wire bonding process so that changes could be introduced that would lower, not raise, costs.

Greater knowledge, combined with process modification, would allow the organization to move toward progressive control over the bonding process. The promise of reduced costs made this a more attractive option, but there was a more fundamental approach that became option 3:

3. Determine the cause of wire creep at the molecular or atomic level.

This would involve developing a scientific understanding of the interaction of product design, material, and process. Such knowledge would allow Signetics to achieve dynamic control; when captured in equipment, procedures, and systems, it would eliminate wire creep entirely.

Signetics recognized that option 3 would need to build on options 2 and 1, but even starting down that path involved a commitment of resources with uncertain benefits. Each of the options required the time of people who might otherwise have spent it on a variety of other pressing problems. Signetics had no way of knowing what problems were most critical, nor a process for allocating scarce resources among competing problems. Furthermore, option 3 would involve laboratory analysis, as well as work by process engineers, product designers, operations, and the quality and reliability staff. Signetics had no experience administering such cross-functional coordination, and all the financial resources in the company were allocated by function. Two of the departments that would be involved in a full-scale program had already indicated that they lacked the necessary resources.

Taking a problem like wire creep all the way to dynamic control would thus involve significant changes in organizational processes, resource allocation, performance measurement, and basic operating systems. As more and more of these kinds of issues began to surface under the drive for two-hundred-parts-per-million defect rates, Signetics began to learn what commitment to superior quality and process control really meant. For senior managers it meant participating in training programs, getting involved in process details, and doing the right thing when hard choices arose (such as stopping lines and not shipping product when the process went out of spec). For functionally oriented engineers and managers, it meant learning to work with other colleagues, learning to pay attention to production line details, learning to go after root causes, learning to ask, *Why*. It meant major investments, assigning many of the organization's best people to solving problems (rather than to making products), and changing everyone's performance objectives.

Over a period of four years, Signetics developed new approaches to meet these requirements. It began at the top by instituting a training program whose first students were the top twenty-five officers of the corporation. The development of a corporate statement of policy followed, as well as the creation of improvement teams in each business unit, led by the unit general manager. At the operating level, the company instituted statistical process control and created what it called "corrective action teams": cross-functional ad hoc teams pulled together to work on significant problems. These teams, as well as the regular line organization, were supported by an upgraded technical staff that had responsibility for failure analysis, maintenance of data on field reliability, and training. The engineering organization developed a system for qualifying new products and processes, and producibility became an important criterion in the design process.

These new systems and approaches had dramatic and somewhat unexpected effects. Signetics solved the wire creep problem, and went on to solve many other problems as well. It met the ppm goal in the automotive project, and a "parts-per-million" mentality took root. Process quality improved significantly: by the mid-1980s the rate of electrical, mechanical, and visual defects had fallen from a level of 10,000 to 100 parts per million. Moreover, the program had affected other dimensions of performance, including cost and delivery. In one of the wafer fabrication plants, where the full program had been implemented first, yields had risen from 85 to 95 percent, and productivity had increased by 50 percent. Further, on-time delivery throughout the corporation had gone from 65 to 70 percent to over 95 percent of shipments.

All these improvements confirmed the power of process control in improving performance, but there was another (and somewhat unexpected) result as well. What Signetics top management had viewed initially simply as an opportunity to reduce costs and improve reliability was eventually found to create an advantage in the market place. As a result, the company changed its fundamental goal—to quality leadership in products and processes. That commitment to process quality became a corporate objective, part of its image in the marketplace, and an important element in its communication with customers.

In its drive for superior process control and quality, the Signetics experience illustrates the basic premise of the framework laid out in this chapter: process control creates the capabilities that build competitive advantage. It also underscores the challenge of getting there. Higher levels of control, and the superior performance that go with them, demand fundamental change; higher levels of control provide powerful benefits, but there is no free lunch. That realization has sunk in at Signetics; in lighter moments the people there talk about the three tools for achieving process control: the wheelbarrow, the hammer, and the mirror.

The wheelbarrow signifies commitment and comes from the story of a tightrope walker who walked along a wire stretched across the Grand Canyon, pushing a wheelbarrow. After each trip she asked the audience if they thought she could do it again. After the third trip, everyone shouted "Yes!" She then pointed to a particularly vocal member of the audience and invited him to ride in the wheelbarrow during the next trip. The moral: talk is cheap; commitment is demonstrated only by personal involvement.

The hammer symbolizes attention to detail, persistence, and follow-through. Every time a problem pops up, you have to hammer away at it. Finally, the mirror signifies focus. When improving process quality, the way to start is by staring at yourself in the mirror. One cannot look to others to provide the new attitude, the new sense of discipline, and the new level of commitment. The person in the mirror must be prepared to walk down the same path. Changing one's own attitudes and practices is often the most important first step in making the improvement process work. And it is senior management's job to make sure that the right people are looking into the mirror. The right people, given the right skills and the right kind of support and leadership, can achieve superior process control, superior factory performance, and a sustainable competitive advantage.

| 9 |

People Make It Happen

Introduction

Superior performance is ultimately based on the people in an organization. The right management principles, systems, and procedures play an essential role, but the capabilities that create a competitive advantage come from people—their skill, discipline, motivation, ability to solve problems, and capacity for learning. Developing their potential is at the heart of high-performance manufacturing. Moreover, it allows a manufacturing organization to differentiate itself in ways that are extraordinarily difficult for its competitors to copy. Both good news and bad are associated with this fact: the reason it is so difficult to emulate the human resource management practices of another company is precisely because such practices are so difficult to change.

Effective management of a factory's human resources requires continuity and consistency across many decisions and throughout all levels of the organization. The multiplicity and pervasiveness of these decisions, and the fact that no single manager can be involved in all of them, make it extremely difficult to maintain this kind of continuity. It depends much more on shared values—a common philosophy of management—than on superb analytical techniques. Although almost all companies create systems and policies to help structure specific kinds of decisions and actions, they often fail to put in place the philosophy and principles that provide a clear sense of direction to the people who operate those systems.

Yet once established, philosophies and values are much more difficult to alter than a factory building or a blast furnace. Creating a coherent, integrated approach to managing people is a long-term proposition. It cannot be purchased in any market or quickly revamped as new competitive threats appear. It can only be created, and nurtured into a lasting advantage, through consistent and painstaking effort. On the other hand, it can be quickly undermined by a few inconsistent, thoughtless actions. In that sense, it is hard to do but easy to undo.

We begin our discussion of the management of people, as before, with a look at factories A and B. We identify some of the issues associated with managing people in a factory setting and analyze two quite different approaches that can be taken. The third section of this chapter draws on this comparison in advocating a few principles of human resource management, together with examples of their application. These principles include restructuring the jobs in the factory, building technical competence broadly throughout the organization, developing and giving free rein to people's problem-solving abilities, reducing artificial inequalities, and encouraging continual learning.

The fourth section explores how the application of these principles can lead to a competitive advantage. We examine how people interact with some of the new manufacturing technologies, such as flexible automation and computer-based process control, and describe how a handful of companies have attempted to tap the potential of these technologies. We conclude with a summary of the major points made in Chapters 6 through 9.

Two Approaches for Managing People:
Factory A and Factory B

A factory's top managers, its personnel (or human resources) staff, and the people on the shop floor all view human-resource management from different perspectives. Employees are concerned about feedback and performance evaluation, compensation, working conditions, employment security, and promotion opportunities. In addition to its concern with these issues, the personnel office is involved in job design, recruiting, training, and development.

Manufacturing managers bring a different perspective. They are concerned with how people interact with the manufacturing process, and how changes in that process affect these people's job assignments and organizational roles. Getting a factory to operate effectively requires flexibility, dependability, and certain levels of various skills, as well as both physical and mental effort. Moreover, since people perform (or preside over) the conversion steps and material flow activities in a factory, controlling those tasks requires control over people. This raises issues of performance measurement, supervision, the assignment of responsibilities to line or staff groups, and making sure that everyone in the factory has the information needed to do his or her job properly.

Each of these perspectives addresses different elements in the human-resource management system. The people in the factory focus on operating procedures and policies, while the personnel staff focuses on human-resource policies. The factory manager often gets involved in both but should be more concerned with basic principles underlying them. Unfortunately, no matter what a company says publicly, all too often its day-to-day responses to random problems result in de facto policies. Understanding all three elements—principles, policies, and procedures—how they interact, and how to achieve consistency in them is essential to managing a factory's people effectively. The importance of this was brought home to us in our visits to factories A and B, which we have already partially described in Chapters 7 and 8.

Factory A

On the surface, factory A has achieved a solid record in the management of human resources. Although it has long been unionized, it has had only one strike (lasting one week) in the past twenty years. Absenteeism and turnover, among both blue- and white-collar personnel, are low; morale (as measured by employee surveys) is very satisfactory; and union-management and management-work-force relationships are fairly good. Yet below the surface, people at all levels expressed concern about their company's situation and prospects. The factory's financial performance has not been outstanding, and its competitive position appears to be slowly deteriorating.

Although only the hourly work force is unionized, all employees have been affected by the way jobs and pay are structured in the collective bargaining agreement. Salary levels throughout the factory are tied to the hourly wages negotiated with the union, and (like union wage rates) they are tied to specific job classifications. Over the years, jobs have grown to be defined quite precisely and narrowly, and the pay rates associated with them have attempted to reflect the skill required and the amount of responsibility involved.

There are eighty-five job classifications for the hourly work force, and fifteen salary grades covering engineers, technicians, and administrative personnel.

The factory's average compensation level is at the high end of that prevailing in its community, and its reputation as an employer is good. Lonnie Riggs, a supervisor, commented on his experience: "I've been here for ten years. It's a good place to work. The pay's good and people treat you decent. There are a lot of rules, just like any place. But you know where you stand. If you do your work, you can do real well here."

Many of the supervisors, like Lonnie Riggs, had come up through the hourly ranks. Under the collective bargaining agreement, promotion had been based on seniority. When a worker moved to a higher-level classification, he or she was expected to learn on the job whatever new skills were needed. If, after a probation period, the worker had failed to develop those skills, the job could be put up for bid again. Most of the jobs in the plant could be mastered in a relatively short time, however, so rebidding was relatively rare.

Promotion to supervisor was determined by the department superintendents. They typically chose people who were strong technically, and who were felt to be "good at command": able to provide clear instructions and make sure people carried them out. Supervisors had some discretion to make job assignments and discipline workers but generally followed the rules and guidelines established by the labor relations staff. On the other hand, they had little latitude to make changes in methods, procedures, and equipment; the engineering departments handled these.

Although people in the plant seemed generally satisfied with the factory and their role in it, factory management was concerned about the competitive situation. As Bart Morrison, the plant manager, put it:

> One of the big challenges I face is to get the people to see what competition means for them personally. We've done all right so far, but we're going to get killed if we don't get our costs down. Morale on the floor is pretty good, but people don't really understand the business, or how well we're doing. One of my management objectives this year is to set up a communications program to get information about our competitive position down to the rank and file.

Factory B
Our visit to factory B took us into a very different work environment. Although equipment and processes were similar, job classifica-

tions, organization, and management were not. It was also unionized but individual jobs were broadly defined. There were only half a dozen job classifications (including salaried jobs) in the entire factory, even though it was approximately the same size and covered the same scope of activities as factory A. The primary organizational unit throughout the factory was the work group: staff departments and operating groups on the shop floor were divided into teams of seven to ten people, with supervisors acting as team leaders. The teams were primarily problem-solving groups; their scope included process improvements, product quality, and safety.

Supervisors at factory B tended to find themselves more in the roles of advisers, coaches, and providers of support, as opposed to the more traditional roles of bosses, disciplinarians, and givers of specific assignments. Ed Rafferty, manager of final assembly, emphasized the role of the team leaders in the operation of the plant:

> From way back, this plant has operated with the principle of pushing responsibility down in the organization. That makes the team leader a key player. Being on the front line like that can be tough duty. But we put some of our best people in those jobs. They have to be solid technically, and then we try to give them all the support we can: training, engineering assistance, encouragement, whatever.

Team leaders in factory B had a good deal of flexibility to change work assignments and handle problems. Although there were clear policies and guidelines for dealing with people in factory B, they tended to be statements of basic values—having to do with trust, fairness, and shared responsibility—rather than being tied to specific tasks.

Instead of linking pay directly to an individual job, it was based on an employee's skills, irrespective of the job currently assigned. Compensation was above average for the local community. Performance evaluation was based primarily on a worker's contribution to his or her team, rather than on individual performance. Harry Cowles, plant manager, summed up his view of the compensation and evaluation system: "Today it's working pretty well for us. But this kind of plant doesn't fit everybody. This isn't a place where you can show up, put in your eight hours doing the same thing every day, and pick up your paycheck at the end of the week. We expect a lot out of our people and we want people who expect a lot from themselves."

Given the demanding nature of the work environment, training played an important role at factory B. Considerable screening and interviewing took place before a new employee was hired, and all employees spent at least two weeks a year in systematic training, both on and off the job.

In spite of factory B's obvious success in its industry, many of the people we talked to, both staff and hourly workers, emphasized the need for improvement. Employees generally were knowledgeable about the competitive position of their factory, and the challenges it faced. We found widespread agreement that factory B still had plenty of opportunity to strengthen its ability to deliver superior products and services to its customers.

Contrasting Factories A and B

Factory A and factory B are quite different, but it would not have been difficult to find two factories that were even more different in their approach to people management. Many factories are characterized by strict regimentation and highly antagonistic labor-management relationships, just as there are some where production processes are directed by self-managing, cross-functional teams of highly trained people. Still, factories A and B are at very different points on the spectrum and are representative of many that we have encountered. They differ in substance and style in four different areas: skills, employee roles, information, and control. Moreover, these contrasts stem from fundamental differences in assumptions about people and the nature of production.

Skills. Factory A regards manufacturing as consisting of a set of well-defined tasks, each of which can be optimized. The goal of factory managers and their support staff is to find that optimum, through careful analysis, and to implement it. They believe that such analysis is too specialized to be done on the factory floor, and that it should be assigned to better-educated (and higher-paid) staff personnel. This has resulted in an increasing separation of staff and line jobs at factory A; a gradual decline in direct labor costs has been more than offset by increases in indirect labor and administrative costs.

Factory A considers the key to productivity to be "adhering to best practice." Workers are cautioned against "free-lancing" and are asked to follow the job specifications that have been set out for them. As a consequence, their jobs have been defined narrowly and precisely, and many issues have been removed from their control.

This perspective contrasts sharply with that found in factory B, where managers treat manufacturing tasks as complex and changing. They do not believe in long-term optimal solutions. Although there are certainly wrong ways to do things, the factory is simply too complicated and its environment too dynamic to seek a single right way. Given this perspective, factory B's management tends to push decisions down into the organization and have analyses conducted at the lowest level possible. Staff functions have been folded into line operations as much as possible, to support low-level decision making. The key to high productivity is felt to be constant improvement, not the rigorous determination of some optimal "best practice." As a consequence, workers are involved directly in redefining the plant layout, how individual tasks and departments are organized, production processes, and their own roles.

Line Workers' Role. Managers at factory A view the work force as a variable cost (they are referred to as "hourly workers"), whose primary role is to provide physical effort. In fact, as factory staff groups upgrade its manufacturing processes, their goal is to "de-skill" (reduce the skill levels required to perform) various jobs, thereby supporting wage rate reductions. Furthermore, the engineering staff structures jobs in such a way that when a worker is absent, another relatively untrained worker can readily replace him or her with minimum disruption. Associated with this conception of the workers' role is the view that the manufacturing process should be standardized and stabilized, and altered only occasionally by the more skilled ("smarter") staff personnel and managers. Workers and supervisors are asked not to tinker with the process but simply to execute it according to the guidelines given them.

Recognizing that the same people who are asked to do repetitive, boring jobs in a factory often are extremely creative outside it—they are carpenters, mechanics, boat builders, and so forth—factory B gives its workers a much broader role. Management seeks to enhance the skills of its people and then to find ways to utilize those skills rather than to deskill jobs. In fact, from the line workers on up, human skills are regarded as an integral part of the factory's technology; broadly skilled people are essential for systematic problem solving. People add value both to products and to processes, by making them better. Factory B wants its manufacturing processes to be people dependent, not people independent. Its goal is continual improvement—in every aspect of its operation.

Information Needs. The type of information required by those working in the two factories is also very different. One of the principal concerns of factories that operate like factory A is generating the information required to coordinate all their various activities: telling people what to do and when to do it. Detailed instructions are conveyed to the factory floor indicating how people should respond under, it is hoped, every eventuality. Over the years much of that detailed guidance has become standard operating procedure and has worked its way back into the union contract, the job classification system, and the production control system. Supervisors are evaluated primarily by whether the people under them have adhered to specified procedures. The presumption is that if something goes wrong, it probably is because of poor execution, not poor planning. One experienced former line manager described this philosophy as follows:

> We had job standards which told you exactly how you were supposed to do the job. We had operating standards which told you exactly what temperatures to set and pressures to regulate. We had formula cards that told you exactly how to mix stuff. The guy before me tried to go by the book and he really fouled things up. . . . I, being new, green, decided that I wasn't going to repeat his thing so I kind of learned how to make the stuff, keeping within the limits . . . I was called on the carpet one time for violating a formula card because I couldn't get my active ingredient at the right level, so I had calculated something else to make it right. . . . How can you get good products out of an organization such as this, with all of these constraints, [and machines] that aren't standard? Every [machine] in the company was different, yet we have so-called standard settings. . . . How can you make products when you're limited by all those kind of things, and in an organization where it's a long way from the bottom to the top? The other question is, how can you have well-motivated people? We had layer on layer of people who really weren't even needed.

At factory B, less information is processed purely for coordination purposes, because its systems are simpler, more visual, and controlled locally. Substantial information is needed on the factory floor, however, to recognize operating patterns, identify cause-and-effect relationships, and diagnose and eliminate problems. In addition, rather than trying to prespecify responses for every possible circumstance, those directly involved have great flexibility to respond to situations as they arise, to develop better approaches to their jobs, and to seek out and remove the root causes of recurring problems. Finally, the performance at factory B is judged primarily by its success in its marketplace, not by whether it has properly followed standard operating practice.

Control. Managers at factory A collect detailed accounting information and use it to analyze variances by department, by individual pieces of equipment, and by operator. This analysis is performed in a central staff group, not by people within the operating department. The same information is also used by department supervisors to evaluate the performance of individual workers. A boss is expected to know more than the workers about what should be done and how to do it. A clear understanding of management's responsibilities, authority, and prerogatives is reinforced throughout the organization.

At factory B supervisors do not presume to have all the answers. The direct supervision of various tasks is less important than at factory A. Instead, second-order control (established through systems and procedures) and even third-order control (acting according to common norms and values) guide behavior. Management's job is to provide the training, information, and support required to solve problems. Directing the factory is a team effort, involving far fewer managers and technical support personnel.

The paradigm that governs the management of people at factory A is "command and control."[1] It is top-down, characterized by clear functional responsibilities, and very much in the tradition of Frederick Taylor. Factory B has adopted a different paradigm—one that can be called continual learning—which emphasizes problem solving at all levels. It is cross-functional, combines top-down and bottom-up approaches, and violates most of Taylor's assumptions about human behavior and motivation.

The two paradigms are summarized in Table 9–1. Some of the assumptions that underlie the continual learning paradigm (the command and control counterpart for each of which is easily imagined) include the following:

1. All employees are responsible, thinking adults who inherently want to do their best.
2. Human resources are too valuable to waste or to leave untapped.

Table 9-1 Contrasting Views of Human Resources in the Factory

	Command and Control	Continual Improvement
Assumptions underlying the manufacturing architecture	optimize defined tasks productivity: adherence to best practice decisions deferred to higher levels narrow job definitions staff over line	improve evolving tasks productivity: develop better practices decisions pushed down to lower levels broad job definitions line over staff
Role of the work force	physical effort minimize skills (deskill) process should be worker independent maintain process stability (changes made only by staff groups) coordination (what and when)	mental effort maximize workers' skills (both technical and problem solving) worker can add value to the process by improving it process improvement is everybody's job (many made by workers) problem solving (cause-effect and problem elimination)
Information needs	fixed responses to problems through standard operating procedures performance evaluation based on adherence to procedures	flexible responses to problems as they arise performance evaluation based on success of the business
Management control	direct control (variance analysis, direct supervision, and inflexible procedures) boss knows the answer strict hierarchy and status	second-order (systems and procedures) and third-order (norms and values) control boss supports and helps peers working as a team

3. Creative talents and skills are widely distributed at all levels of an organization and society.
4. Workers will surface important problems and concerns if they feel the organization will respond appropriately.
5. Work is more interesting when people are challenged in performing it.
6. People take pride in training others.
7. Better performance occurs when artificial differences in how people are treated are removed.
8. Real responsibility motivates high performance.
9. People make better decisions, and implement them better, when they work together.

For an organization facing a very stable environment, with limited opportunity for improvement, the command-and-control mode may well be an effective way to operate. In today's volatile markets, however, where competition is vigorous and fluid and significant opportunities exist to improve factory performance, continual learning is the more appropriate mode.

Basic Principles and Their Application

Realizing the full potential of the people in the factory is critical to high-performance manufacturing. Indeed, a production system in which buffers are removed to force integration and higher levels of process control are being sought will fail without skilled, motivated people. What managers do to create that skill and motivation will differ from industry to industry. The practices and programs that make sense in a steel mill may not have much application in a semiconductor plant. Differences in technology, in local labor market conditions, and in business circumstances will lead to different approaches. But we believe that there are some general principles that can guide managers in managing the people in the factory. These principles have to do with the structure of jobs, technical competence, problem-solving skills, organizational inequality, and continual improvement.

The Structure of Jobs

A fundamental principle of high-performance manufacturing is the dual nature of everyone's job. People are responsible both for performing a current assignment and for learning from their experience so that they can improve the performance of that task in the future. Their ability to fulfill this dual mission is largely a function of the breadth and depth of the jobs that they are assigned. A job's breadth is measured by the number of *physical* (operating) tasks a person performs, such as converting inputs into outputs and moving materials. Its depth is measured by the number of *thinking* (managerial) tasks performed. These include troubleshooting, problem-solving, and planning. Making a job broader is often called job enlargement; making it deeper is job enrichment.

All jobs have both dimensions, but the relative importance of each can be quite different. Figure 9-1 depicts two different jobs in terms of their breadth and depth. Job 1 reflects Henry Ford's statement to the effect that he wanted to create a production system in which each worker did only one thing and could do that thing without thinking. Pursuing that dictum (as factory A has done) leads to narrow, shallow jobs and people. The span of physical tasks in job 2 is somewhat broader, but its depth is much greater. People's minds are engaged as well as their bodies; they are asked to think about their job and how it relates to other jobs in the factory, thus developing a sense of responsibility that encourages learning.[2]

Giving workers broader and deeper jobs does not always lead to

Figure 9-1   The Structure of Manufacturing Jobs: Breadth and Depth

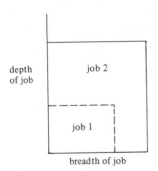

Aspects of Depth

Types of Tasks:
- process design
- methods improvement
- scheduling
- accounting and control
- maintenance
- planning, problem solving, and troubleshooting
- dealing with uncertainty
- processing information that is not proceduralized

Aspects of Breadth

Types of Tasks:
- machine operation
- equipment monitoring
- materials handling
- quality checking
- preventive maintenance

better performance, however. For example, Volvo, the Swedish automotive firm, learned that radically expanding the breadth and depth of jobs worked very well with workers who were hired with that kind of job structure in mind. Its "stall built" system, where teams of four or five workers performed the majority of the assembly tasks on a single automobile, worked well in new plants with new workers. In older plants with established work forces, however, its results have been mixed, leading in at least one case to a return to narrower jobs. On the other hand, Procter & Gamble has recently achieved some success in converting traditional factories into those reflecting the principles of factory B.

In many traditional factories, specifying the scope of jobs is considered the exclusive realm of the industrial engineer. As both breadth and depth are extended, it becomes increasingly important that those who will perform a job are involved in defining its scope. At one Cummins Engine plant, for example, workers not only defined their jobs but prepared a videotape to show prospective workers what kind of jobs and responsibilities to expect if they were hired.

The nature of manager's jobs is equally important. Increasing the breadth and depth of middle-management jobs typically confers greater responsibility on them and encourages the development of a mixture of line and staff skills. This usually results in fewer layers of management and practically no specialized staff. Moreover, the supervisor's job is much different.[3] The factories we know of that have practiced these ideas in their management ranks for several years tend to be lean and mean, and characterized by extremely competent and broad managers at all levels.

Building Technical Competence

Most manufacturing activities have a significant technical component. In traditional factories, how much a person needs to know about the basic technology depends on his or her specific assignment. Great technical expertise is required if one's job is to develop new equipment, whereas only a basic knowledge of how the equipment works is required if one simply is assigned to run it properly. But if competitive superiority is the goal and learning is everyone's mission, technical competence is important for every job. Building technical know-how at all levels of the organization is essential to achieving manufacturing's full potential. Developing that technical competence begins with the selection and hiring process. The people coming into the organization must be willing to learn and master the technical aspects of the business. Often, this is more a matter of attitude and aptitude than of experience. Two examples illustrate the point.

In the 1970s, when demand began to outstrip BMW's production capacity, it decided to build a new German auto assembly facility. One of its basic choices was whether to staff the new plant, which would employ roughly ten thousand workers on a two-shift basis, with guest workers (low paid and generally low skilled workers from southern and eastern Europe) or with German workers (who would expect higher pay and be more highly skilled). It finally decided to build the new plant in Dingolfing, a rural town of one thousand people in southern Germany, and staff it with German workers. Rather than seeking to expand the size of the town, workers were brought by bus from up to sixty miles away. These workers constituted a very stable group who needed additional income (their small farms could no longer provide the standard of living they desired) and who were good both at working with equipment and solving the kinds of problems that arose in the course of keeping their small farms running. By the mid-1980s, the Dingolfing plant was one of BMW's most productive. In fact, it was one of the best auto plants in Germany, in large part because of the technical competence of its work force.

Chaparral Steel, a steel producer located just south of Dallas, Texas, provides another example of the importance of selection in building technical competence. When it hired its first workers during the early 1970s, the company had clear expectations as to the degree of technical competence it hoped to build but did not want people who thought about factory work and steelmaking in traditional ways. Therefore, only a handful of workers were hired who had experience in the steel industry. The remainder were screened by state agencies, Chaparral's personnel office, and then by the factory superintendent and department supervisors. The hiring decision was based on an assessment of whether the candidate had the right attitude and the ability to learn the technical skills required.

Once workers are hired, they must be trained. Many U.S. factories grossly underestimate the importance of training in building the technical competence of their people. They generally assume either that such competence is not needed or that the worker already has it when hired. As one experienced manager put it:

> Talk about tapping into the hourly resource, they can do all kinds of things for you, [such as] take out the old equipment, install the new, including working with engineering and developing the draw-

ings and specifications, putting it in and doing the related project engineering work. . . . We haven't, or most of us haven't, scratched the surface of what they can do. They can do anything if their managers have taken the time to develop and train them through the years, year after year, not . . . discarding [them] when there is a budget constraint.

Like BMW, most German companies place great emphasis on technical training. Major German companies (including many German subsidiaries of American firms) typically sponsor apprenticeship programs, in which workers spend up to two years learning both the theory and practice of a trade before they actually make a product to be sold to a customer. There is tremendous competition to enter such apprenticeship programs, and much of the skill base in German industry is provided through it.

One U.S. company that has its own apprenticeship program is Lincoln Electric of Cleveland, Ohio. It makes arc welding equipment and has essentially only two entry-level positions: hourly worker and field sales engineer. Both kinds of employees start by going to welding school, where they learn the basic technology of their business. The former then go on to learn how to make the product, while the latter learn how Lincoln's customers use its products and how welding technology can help solve their problems. Everybody builds on their common technical understanding as they move to other parts of the organization.[4]

Another example is provided by the German chain saw manufacturer, Andreas Stihl GMBH. When its manufacturing VP decided that his entire manufacturing organization needed more technical strength (although many outsiders might have felt that it already was strong technically), he hired four Ph.D.'s to direct the major departments of the factory. (In the United States, one would be hard pressed to find any U.S. companies, except the most technical, hiring Ph.D.'s for line management jobs in the factory.) These Ph.D. line managers were able to focus more of their organization's resources on building technical competence and developing superior processes. By the mid-1980s, Stihl's technical capabilities were the envy of its industry.

Building technical competence at all levels of the organization not only requires the right type of day-to-day activities, but a very thorough and far-sighted planning activity. Most human resource departments are familiar with *head-count* planning, which is aimed at making sure that the organization has the right amount of workers of various types to meet its projected production levels. But we have in mind a different kind of planning, one that focuses on providing the right levels of technical competence. One of the most interesting approaches we have seen for doing this was described to us by managers at Siemens, in Germany. They referred to it as *head-content* planning.

In the early 1970s Siemens became increasingly concerned that the capabilities of the people in its factories (in terms of their education and areas of expertise) would not match its future requirements. This concern was amplified by the stability of its work force: factory personnel tended to stay at Siemens throughout their careers, yet the rate of technological change was increasing. Siemens's response was to develop "head content," or qualitative, human resource planning. This approach looked at the gap between future skills requirements (based on projections of the evolution of products and processes) and the existing skills base. Having estimated that it takes five to seven years to change a worker's technical competence, the company started making plans for selecting, hiring, transferring, and retraining workers, based on ten-year projections of skill requirements.

Problem-solving Capabilities

Many people argue that worker participation is good simply because it makes people feel better about themselves and their work. If looked at from the perspective of building a competitive advantage, however, the important thing about engaging people in thinking about their work and looking for improvements is not just that it makes them feel better but that it also leads to better solutions and much faster rates of improvement. A manager cannot get the people in a factory to work together to solve problems simply by announcing a new policy, however. They have to be trained in problem-solving techniques and given the necessary tools and assistance.

Statistical process control (discussed in Chapter 8) is representative of the kinds of tools people need to identify and diagnose process problems. Once trained in applying such tools, each worker can make a significant contribution to improving processes. But since most of the important problems in a factory involve more than a single worker, effective problem solving also depends on the organization's ability to stimulate and coordinate the ingenuity of many people, working together. A factory's problem-solving capability, therefore, represents a mixture of its human skills, its repertoire of techniques and tools, and its effectiveness in encouraging joint efforts.

Setting up problem-solving teams, like those found in factory B, is one approach to organizing for problem solving. They have been introduced in many companies, under a variety of labels: employee involvement groups, productivity teams, and (most recently) quality circles. Although quality circles have been spreading in Japan for more than twenty-five years—their roots can be found in the management courses taught by U.S. occupation personnel, as described in Chapter 2—their appearance in the United States, under that name, has occurred only in the past decade.

A quality circle generally consists of eight to twelve employees who work together on a regular basis and are organized into a team to address problems and issues arising in their normal work environment. Circles generally meet two to four times each month for an hour at a time, often under the guidance of an outside facilitator. In many companies quality circles are organized on a volunteer basis and begin with five to twenty hours of training in how to run meetings, how to function as a group, and how to apply specific tools and techniques to solving problems. The problems to be worked on are generally chosen by the team, with management approval.

Although some companies pay bonuses for the improvements suggested by quality circles—just as they do for individual suggestions—more commonly circles are simply given recognition, and perhaps the opportunity to attend a conference, for particularly effective proposals. Employees are usually compensated at the normal hourly rate for the time spent in formal circle meetings, and it is counted toward the standard hours worked during that pay period.[5]

Although many U.S. managers are aware of quality circles and have even tested and experimented with them in their own factories, most such efforts have been halfhearted, rather than serious attempts to fully exploit their potential. In ascertaining the level of commitment an organization is making to quality circles, one revealing question is, "What would you consider to be success in your QC effort?" If the answer is "Workers who feel better about their work and are making suggestions," the effort is probably only experimental. If, on the other hand, the answer is "Workers making significant contributions to improving their manufacturing processes and capabilities," the effort is probably serious.

There is much that must be done to lay the foundation for achieving the full potential of such teams. Improving a factory's basic housekeeping, correcting its known shortcomings, building its technical competence, establishing a philosophy of continual improvement, getting workers' inputs to process design issues, and more should precede the establishment of quality circles. To illustrate, in late 1982 Professor Robert Cole of the University of Michigan surveyed the five Japanese-owned TV plants in the United States at the time: two owned by Sony, two by Matsushita, and one by Sanyo. In all five instances the parent company made extensive use of quality circles in its Japanese facilities but had yet to begin using them in its U.S. factories. The reason given for this was that "they [the U.S. factories] are not yet ready." These companies' view was that such team efforts were something that should come late in the process, after the prerequisite philosophy and capabilities were firmly in place.[6]

But, once this is done, problem-solving teams can be astonishingly effective. For example, Nippondenso, a Japanese manufacturer of automobile components, has used ongoing problem-solving to greatly simplify its manufacturing process. In one factory that makes gauges for instrument panels, each production line has been defined as a series of steps; each step consists of positioning a part, performing a task, measuring to ensure that the task was performed correctly, and providing feedback to correct any process errors. Thus, conceptually, the process is made up of building blocks that can be continually improved or simplified, either individually or in groups. Quality circle teams have played a central role in subsequent improvements.

A similar approach to problem-solving has led to substantial process improvements at Hewlett-Packard. In one of its wave-solder operations, H-P has taken the rate of defects from several thousand (per million solder connections) to only a handful. This was accomplished through a variety of problem-solving efforts aimed at simplifying processes, systematically analyzing the steps in those simplified processes, identifying the sources and causes of problems, and developing approaches to eliminating them. The kind of SPC charts that were described in Chapter 8 proved to be very useful in H-P's problem-solving effort. Such charts not only provided an incentive and a means for identifying further improvements; they also served as effective communication devices between people on different shifts and across departments.

Eliminating Artificial Inequalities

Realizing the potential of a factory's human resources requires both enhancing their technical competence and expanding the breadth and depth of their jobs. But even these changes, wrenching as they may be for many companies, will not be sufficient unless a company also cultivates a spirit of camaraderie and a sense of equality. In companies preoccupied with static control, the lack of access to certain information creates a sense of inequality at lower levels; financial data, for example, are often reserved for managers and only distributed to those down in the organization on a need-to-know basis. Broadening people's perspective and engaging them in the competitive task facing their organization, however, requires that such information be shared widely. This is particularly true of data about one's competitive position and the new developments taking place in the market, but it also applies to information that helps establish a context for individual jobs.

One of the best examples of information sharing we have seen occurred at General Electric's refrigerator operation. The manufacturing manager at that factory decided that he needed both to communicate basic business information more broadly and to teach his organization how to interpret and use it. A series of weekly "birthday meetings" were held, through which he met with all three thousand people in his factory in groups of thirty to forty. The ostensible purpose of the meeting was to celebrate the birthdays of one or more group members, but in the process he discussed how the business was performing, how customers were responding, and what competitors were doing. Job security was also addressed in these meetings: the only real long-term form of job security, he pointed out, was success in the marketplace. Information about competitors, ranging from their new products to their capital investment plans, was also shared. The result was a better understanding of the forces that drove the business, and better agreement as to what constituted success for the entire organization. An individual or a small group could not say that it had performed satisfactorily unless the whole business was successful.

A more subtle but equally important form of inequality is that between line and staff personnel. Too often even well-meaning staff groups, such as those at factory A, use their access to information to secure and preserve their power in the organization, parceling out only what they think line managers "need" and "can handle." Just as tight materials control requires that orders be pulled through the production process, tight information control implies that information should be pulled from the production process by the line organization, with staff personnel acting simply as facilitators in this process.

Sharing information also helps individuals understand how they fit into the big picture. Take, for example, the approach developed by John Madden, the former professional football coach. During the ten years Madden was coaching the Oakland Raiders, his team won more than 85 percent of its games. This is an amazing record, considering that the mechanism for drafting players in the National Football League is designed to spread talent equally across all the teams to make them as competitive as possible. In spite of this leveling process, Madden's team's were usually at the top of their league.

Madden called his approach "whole-part-whole," and it is illustrated by how he taught the team new plays. He would start by bringing the entire team (the whole)—coaches, water boys, players—together and explaining the play. This would include communicating its purposes, the times when it might be used most effectively, the results it was intended to achieve, and the factors critical to its success. The next step was to split into subfunctions (the parts), such as the backfield, the line, and the ends. Each group would practice the actions required of it in order for the play to be successful. The final step was for the entire organization (the whole) to reassemble and put the parts together. As a result, if the play was used in a game and something went wrong, each individual would "naturally" adjust in ways that might not have been attempted had the players understood only their own part and not the whole.

Good information, both about the parts and about the whole, gives people the basis for working together as a team. But teamwork also requires equality of status. This does not mean that every department or function has the same budget, or that everyone gets the same salary. It simply means that each group within the factory, and the importance of its contribution, is understood and valued equally by everyone. This kind of equality is facilitated by minimizing status differences based on physical separation, titles, and perks—such as special dining rooms, parking places, office decor, and dress. Such inequalities inhibit trust, respect, communication, and cooperation.

Equality of status must apply to engineers, managers, and support staff, as well as to hourly workers. Although a person's status often reflects relationships in the larger society, companies often reinforce these differences through their policies. Figure 9–2 details the salary

Figure 9-2   Salary Grade Differentials within an Electronics Factory

	Director of Manufacturing		
Management Level	Engineering Manager (E13)	Maintenance Manager (E10)	Manufacturing Manager (E11)
Direct Report Level	E11	E09	E08
Next Level	D 25–E07	D 25–E07	E05–E06

NOTE: E refers to salary grade, GD to hourly technician grade.

grades for managers in one electronics company we have studied. It shows that this organization's design engineering managers had substantially higher status (including pay and job rating) than did manufacturing managers, who in turn had higher status than maintenance managers. Similar differences existed throughout the company. Such inequalities impede extracting the full potential of an organization's human resources.

Pursuing Dynamic Improvement

In traditional factories, reorganizations and changes in specific job assignments are usually disruptive. As a consequence, most organizations are reluctant to make such changes. The status quo becomes a reference point, an anchor for the organization. In contrast, the principles discussed here place primary emphasis on the need for constant change in the organization and individual assignments. This is particularly necessary if one wants to capture the full benefits of an improved process or product design.

Consider, for example, the approach taken by one paper company. The introduction of a new information technology at one of its paper mills made it possible for teams of workers to broaden the span of their activities; they could also undertake tasks that had previously been done by support staffs and middle managers. In a sense, the operating groups took over the information system and used it to improve their performance. Management eventually had to decide whether to take advantage of those changes, by eliminating a layer of management and some support functions, or to take back control of the information system from the workers. Following the former course led to an aggressive restructuring of the organization and the redefinition of job assignments. These changes made it possible for the full benefits of the new information system to be realized and became a springboard for further improvements.

Real uncertainty is created in people's minds by the kind of changes we have described. Line workers must feel comfortable about what will happen if their productivity improves and fewer people are needed for a particular activity. Similarly, middle managers must not feel threatened about what will happen as workers' jobs are expanded, so that fewer middle managers are needed. Therefore, a commitment to job security and retraining people whose jobs have been eliminated plays an important role in facilitating continual change.

When this kind of commitment exists, even more significant restructuring becomes feasible. Chaparral Steel has recently implemented two such changes. First, factory workers now are asked to respond directly to any customer problems that arise. It was felt that they knew better than anyone else how to correct such problems and that this would also facilitate their learning how to prevent reoccurrence. The other change was to eliminate the field sales force for high-tech forging steel (they were retrained and given other jobs) and to assign sales and service responsibilities to the quality and reliability group for that product. These people were already doing much of the sales development work with customers and, since that was often the basis of the buying decision, were in a better position to capture the benefits of close customer relationships. The results were fewer people and increased productivity. More important, that product category's sales tripled within a few months.

Obviously, a company would be reluctant to invest in expanded job definitions, technical training, and problem-solving skills if it faced high turnover among its people. Adopting the principles outlined in this section makes retaining people extremely important. As one manager put it, "for my organization, the greatest loss in productivity occurs when someone leaves." Fortunately, the above principles seem to foster commitment and stability on the part of workers and managers alike.

Integrating People with the New Manufacturing Technologies

Integrating people, systems, and hardware has always been the foundation of superior manufacturing performance. But its importance, and particularly its human dimension, is likely to grow in the future. Intensifying competition is combining with new developments in computer-based automation to transform design, engineering, and production in several industries. Many companies see technology as the answer to their competitive problems. The new technologies, however, demand more—not less—of workers and managers in order to achieve their potential. Somewhat paradoxically, as processes become more sophisticated and more automated, success is becoming less a matter of substituting technology for people, if it ever was. Instead, human skills must be developed simultaneously with computer software and equipment hardware, and managed in such a way that they reinforce each other.

Thus, the recent changes in manufacturing technology have become both a driving force for (without integration the technology does not work), and a facilitator of (the technology makes extensive integration possible), changing the way a company manages its people, structures its material and information flows, and controls its processes. It is also challenging traditional assumptions about how people, systems, and hardware interact. For example, in industries that fabricate parts and assemble them into products, traditional approaches to manufacturing management (like those found in factory A) had their roots in Taylor's scientific management and the efforts of industrialists like Henry Ford to achieve mass production. Traditional (hard) automation used inflexible equipment, sought to make manufacturing processes less dependent on the work force, and relied on inventories to buffer each stage of the process from other stages.

The new manufacturing systems, built around low-cost computing power, new sensors, and advanced software to link them with high-performance equipment, have changed that traditional equation. Their characteristics are more like those found in continuous-process industries. This forces major changes in the traditional fabrication-and-assembly mind-set, which has been dominated by the command-and-control mentality. Continuous manufacturing processes seek to minimize WIP inventory and tend to emphasize the importance of ongoing improvement through bottleneck removal and the incremental enhancement of equipment and procedures. This is due in part to the readily apparent economics of the continuous-flow environment: substantial leverage results from even small improvements in throughput and yield. Moreover, highly automated continuous processes have well-defined flow structures and are managed to limit the amount of "noise" in the system. As noted in Chapter 6, this makes it easier to identify and study cause-and-effect relationships, solve critical problems, and fine-tune the system for performance improvement.

In contrast, the extensive noise in a traditional fabrication-and-assembly environment, with its mass of work-in-process inventory, loosely connected departments, and poorly structured material-flow paths, complicates the interaction of the work force with the manufacturing process technology. It also conceals—and may even eliminate—the economic benefits of small improvements at any given location in the factory.

This inefficiency results in part from bottlenecks, which continually shift. Focusing attention on a single bottleneck and its elimination often does little for overall output (and cost) because another bottleneck quickly arises to take its place. Similarly, problem solving in a single department seldom benefits the entire process, since departments are only loosely connected. The vagaries of the remaining departments will often wash out whatever benefits are provided by a single department's improvements. Finally, with so much noise (often hidden by in-process inventories), cause-and-effect relationships are almost impenetrable. A noisy environment limits people's leverage over the manufacturing process, and reinforces an emphasis on executing the immediate task at hand.

Implementing the kind of manufacturing architecture outlined in Chapter 7—short cycles, simplified flows, low work-in-process— moves the traditional fabrication and assembly operation toward continuous processing. In that context, a work force that can eliminate bottlenecks, identify and solve problems, and make incremental improvements is essential. Mastering new skills encourages people to try to put them to use by taking further steps toward continuous manufacturing. Finally, it establishes the foundation for the later adoption of the new manufacturing technologies, which in turn creates new requirements and opportunities.

Many managers today still believe that automation can (and should) be used to lower skill levels. Since the new technology, and the system in which it is incorporated, contain much of the knowledge required to operate the process, they assume that skilled people are no longer needed to run it. Although that may have been true for some forms of hard automation in the past, today's flexible automation does not provide an opportunity to further deskill jobs and lower wages.[7] In fact, most of the failures that have occurred with advanced automation projects can be traced to a failure to invest sufficiently in developing the skills needed to make those processes work effectively. The factory A approach to managing people will restrain a company both from developing the full potential of its human resources and from exploiting the full power of the new technologies that are now becoming available.

Some companies have sought to use the information-processing capabilities of the new technologies to reinforce their traditional command-and-control approach to management. To the extent that they remove problem solving and decision making from the line organization (as described in the top panel of Figure 9–3), this approach increases the power of staff specialists. But as shown in the lower panel, the same new technology makes it possible to do exactly the opposite: to integrate line and staff roles, and increase the degree to which those people directly involved in the production process take on such responsibilities as quality control, production planning, computer programming, machine setup, and problem diagnosis and solving. The kinds of people and the kinds of teamwork required to make this second approach work, however, may be quite different than those found in a traditional shop-floor operation.[8]

Figure 9-3   Alternative Approaches for Using the New Manufacturing Technology

Polarization and Differentiation

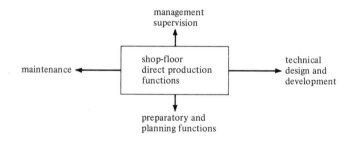

Depolarization and Integration

SOURCE: Adapted from Sorge et al., 1983.

The new information technologies enable management to expand the domain of factory-floor personnel. People on the floor can now acquire data and, with the help of computerized analysis, transform those data into improved process knowledge. Managers make a serious error, however, if they ask shop-floor personnel to take over data acquisition and information processing but do not allow them to expand the scope of their activities to include taking action. Not only is this likely to undermine their morale, but the factory will fail to exploit the technology's full potential. Once set in motion, the sequence (data collection—process knowledge—improvement planning—action) naturally repeats itself. As the factory floor learns the impact of its actions, it sees how (and what) additional data can provide more information, and how the resulting knowledge can be used to identify further opportunities to make improvements.

Through such actions, an organization that implements factory B's approach to human resource management in conjunction with some of the new computerized manufacturing technologies can reap substantial benefits. Considerable evidence suggests that factories can achieve an order-of-magnitude reduction in the number of indirect staff and overhead people required, and the elimination of several layers of management.[9] For example, Procter & Gamble has reported that the new factories that it has set up according to these principles are at least 30 percent more profitable than traditional factories making the same products. At one representative P. & G. factory, which was able to increase its profits by $17 million in one year, only $10 million of that improvement could be attributed to new equipment. The remaining $7 million apparently resulted from the integration of this equipment with the factory's social structure and information system.

Pulling the Threads Together

We have chosen to put human resources last in this series of chapters because the way people are managed in a factory determines the level of process control that can be achieved (the focus of Chapter 8), and the effectiveness of the flows and procedures that define the manufacturing architecture (the focus of Chapter 7). Superior manufacturing capabilities are the result of integrating human resource management with the management of material and information flows, and with efforts to achieve higher levels of process control.

The structure of flows within the factory, for example, has an important influence on the motivation for, and the focus of, problem-solving efforts. Streamlined material flows clarify the environment in which production takes place, reduce confusion, and help pinpoint potential problems. With less inventory to hide problems, they surface more quickly and more directly. Moreover, the motivation for eliminating a problem is heightened, because failing to act quickly has more serious consequences than it does in a just-in-case system where inventory absorbs much of the immediate impact of the problem.

Enhanced problem-solving is also an important part of process control, but its interaction with material and information flows works in a different way. Indeed, process control is an important prerequisite for the achievement of a short-cycle, low work-in-process production system. As noted in Chapter 6, most factories that have a lot of work-in-process inventory keep that inventory for very good reasons—most of them related to a lack of adequate control. Improved control allows the organization to operate with less inventory. Less inventory, in turn, clarifies the production system and identifies further problems.

A similar kind of interaction occurs between process control and human resource management. The human capacity for judgment, for pattern recognition, and for learning is absolutely essential to achieving process control. Not only does this learning take place in individuals but also in task teams, departments, and other groups within the factory. The effectiveness with which people work together, therefore, has an important influence on the organization's ability to create new knowledge and apply it in the production process. Moreover, each time an individual or team completes a learning cycle, they expand their knowledge of the process and their skill in solving problems. Thus, the cycle has two products: new knowledge that can be applied in the process, and people who have enhanced capabilities. As a result, involvement in this kind of activity creates a sense of accomplishment, motivates further attempts to improve performance, and develops new capabilities.

Management is the key to creating high-performance manufacturing and comparative advantage in the marketplace. Building an organization capable of competing with the best in the world requires extracting the full potential from materials, information, procedures, hardware, and people. In each of these areas, managers must address different kinds of issues and solve different kinds of problems. But our analysis suggests that there is a fundamental unity in the principles underlying effective factory operations. Whether in designing the architecture of manufacturing, in achieving better process control, or in managing people, the two essential tasks of management are to create clarity and order (eliminate confusion), and to facilitate learning.

Some might see a contradiction in these two tasks: since learning involves a good deal of experimentation and change, both of which can cause confusion, isn't there a conflict between orderly operations and rapid learning? Not at all. Change is not synonymous with confusion. The confusion in many plants we have studied was far greater than that required to respond to market changes or to new technology; as was pointed out earlier, such confusion is often internally generated. Confusion of this sort is like the noise (static) in a radio broadcast: it makes it very difficult to figure out what is going on. In a confused environment it is very difficult to determine cause and effect. In fact, it is hard to learn where the real problems are. Time, resources, and energy get consumed in dealing with "problems" whose solutions add little to the factory's performance. Not only does performance suffer in the short run, but people easily become discouraged and cease looking for improvements. Thus, reducing confusion and enhancing learning are not contradictory imperatives. To the contrary, they are closely related and powerful in combination.

Confusion, Capital Investment, and Productivity Growth
A factory that manages change haphazardly, that does not have its processes under control, and that is confused by the noise in its systems, is likely to learn more slowly than it should. As a consequence, it will not be able to fully exploit the strong interaction between capital investment and learning that we have argued is the hallmark of the high-performance factory. The new equipment it introduces will create confusion and short-term declines in productivity, and its benefits will be slow in coming. Major investments in new equipment are not the solution to a confused factory.

Thirty years ago, many companies, recognizing that their data-processing systems were haphazardly processing unreliable and incomplete information, decided to try to solve their problems by bringing in electronic computers. Unfortunately, they soon learned that computerizing a poorly organized and error-ridden information system simply created more problems. A new term, GIGO (garbage in, garbage out), entered the business lexicon. One should bring in a computer, companies learned through painful experience, only after one's information system has been cleaned up and systematized.

But that lesson, learned not so long ago, seems to have been forgotten by many companies today who contemplate their confused, chaotic factories, with all their complexities and uncertainties, and decide that the road to competitive salvation lies in massive investments in sophisticated new equipment and systems. This reaction reflects an instinctive propensity for attempting to deal with a system that is not working by overlaying it with another system (and often another layer of management) rather than by fixing it.

Confronted with a highly complex factory environment—dozens of production stages, products, material flow patterns and inventory locations, together with unreliable product designs, equipment, workers, and suppliers—one can react in one of two ways. Like factory A, one can attempt to develop a highly sophisticated (and usually computerized) information and control system to manage all this complexity and variability. Or, like factory B, one can set about reducing them. In effect, these two approaches concentrate on opposite ends of the control spectrum: the former on the reactive side; the latter on progressive and dynamic control.

Americans—both managers and academics—with all their technical sophistication and computer skills, seem to be attracted to the former approach; the Japanese, with their intense pragmatism, to the latter. As a result, we have spent more than a decade and hundreds of millions of dollars developing elegant Materials Requirement Planning (MRP) systems—of which, recent studies have concluded, less than a third are ultimately successful.[10] Meanwhile, world-class Japanese companies have concentrated on simplifying and clarifying their factories, eliminating error and confusion to the point where material control can often be managed manually with a handful of Kanban cards. Moreover, the same emphasis on creating clarity has facilitated the high rate of learning that has brought Japanese companies' productivity up to—and beyond—their U.S. competitors' in a number of critical industries.

Learning Is the Bottom Line

Making significant commitments to new equipment and new systems may be perfectly appropriate, even essential, for some companies. Eventually, as with computers, it will probably be appropriate for most companies. But our research has taught us that there are many things that ought to be done first to prepare one's organization for these new technologies. Managers ought to begin by attempting to reduce confusion, and by motivating and managing the learning process in their organization.

One of the barriers to such learning, as we pointed out in Chapter 5, is that plant managers are often given poor (or, at least, incomplete) measures of how they are doing, compared both with their sister plants within the same company and with their competitors. Moreover, traditional measurement and control systems tend to discourage the kind of experimentation that leads to learning. Too rigid an emphasis on standards, budgets, and exception reports encourages a steady-state mentality, a by-the-book approach to management that avoids making changes that entail risks and strives to meet short-term performance goals, whatever the cost.

But the job of plant managers is not to seek some ideal (and illusory) goal of steady-state optimality but to make persistent headway toward continual improvement in an evolving competitive environment. They must both manage effectively within existing constraints and parameters and work to change those constraints and parameters in desired directions. Fortunately, some managers seem to be able to rise above an ultimately self-defeating concern with the status quo and the near term, despite the pressures placed on them. And they are the ultimate winners. Yet they generally have to operate against the grain of their corporate control system, instead of with its heartfelt encouragement.

They also appear to operate against the grain of human nature. Again and again we have encountered managers who feel—without apparent justification—that their plants are better at some activity than any others anywhere else in the world. These managers fail to understand that learning is the key to long-term success, and that their organization will learn well only if they are learning too. As a result, they spend very little time observing firsthand how their plants compare with competitive plants. Their jobs are so time-consuming and so turbulent that they hesitate to leave them for any length of time. In most companies, for whatever reasons, their travel budgets are a fraction of those granted to comparable managers in other functions. Convinced that they are doing the best that they can, and that no one else could possibly be working harder, they fall prey to the self-deception that there is nothing they can learn from anybody else. If a sister plant or competitor develops an improved approach, they deceive themselves into thinking that it isn't really better. If the evidence of superiority is overwhelming, they argue that "it won't work here because we're different." We are chagrined to report that the not-invented-here syndrome is alive and well in American industry.

Today there is much talk about the importance of "getting back to basics." But that is good advice only if the basics aren't changing. In important respects, however, the basic tools and techniques of manufacturing are undergoing profound change in many industries, even though the fundamental principles remain unchanged. The best way to keep abreast of these changes and their relationship to those principles is to get out and see what is going on. As one highly effective manager we know has put it: "I believe in an open-door policy: open your door, and go out of it!" Managers can learn much from visiting sister plants, corporate advanced-process development labs, equipment suppliers, customers, and world-class competitors. Getting out and studying the behavior of others, and focusing attention on manufacturing performance in general, is important for the same reason that Willy Sutton robbed banks: "That's where the money is."

| 10 |

Laying the Foundation for Product and Process Development

Introduction

One can build a competitive advantage through superior manufacturing, but sustaining it over time requires comparable skills in creating a continual stream of new products and processes. Ongoing new-product development also serves to build market momentum, as well as customer and distributor loyalty. New processes solidify this advantage through lower costs, better quality and reliability, and greater flexibility.

The effective combination of product *and* process development increases the returns from each. The advantage provided by superior products is strengthened if those products can only be made with proprietary processes. Internally, effective product and process development efforts help build functional skills and interfunctional integration. Both kinds of development activities foster an organization's pride and confidence in its capabilities, encouraging their further application to new projects.

Perhaps in appreciation of this, a 1984 in-depth study of Japanese CEOs found that although gaining market share was their primary goal for the next five years, increasing the ratio of new to existing products ran a close second.[1] Furthermore, when asked how they proposed to achieve their primary goal, they cited improving their product development capabilities twice as often as any other means. In an increasing number of industries, it appears, effective new product and process development will play a key role in future success.

Not only are product design and development becoming more central to meeting the increasingly specialized demands of customers; they can also have a powerful impact on manufacturing productivity and quality, as described in Chapter 6. Moreover, process development is one of the most effective ways for increasing one's control over a production process. Managed properly, it not only strengthens an organization's technical capabilities; it fosters increasingly rapid improvement.

In the traditional approach to managing development projects, each function is expected to play a specific and limited role: engineering designs the product, manufacturing makes it, and marketing sells it. Each functional organization has developed performance criteria based on this narrow conception of its role. For product engineers, the test of a good design has typically been the reaction of fellow engineers (especially competitor engineers who have reverse-engineered the product). In today's competitive world, however, a new product should be measured against very different criteria: it must create value for customers and be difficult for competitors to manufacture with comparable cost and quality.

Unfortunately, most of the development projects we have studied fall considerably short of these goals. In fact, they often prove painful to those directly involved—sometimes even fatal to their careers—and disappointing to the rest of the organization because they fail to meet its expectations regarding timing, cost, quality, features, and market success. Whether a company is large or small, high tech or low, or whether it competes on the basis of cost or innovativeness—all appear to make little difference. One experienced manager described his approach to planning such projects as follows: "I have learned to double the [estimated] cost, halve the demand, and double the time scale. Then you will get it about right."

Many factors may contribute to such shortfalls: overly ambitious plans, technical difficulties, insufficient resources, and unanticipated competitor actions. But a failure to integrate the work of the various functions is just as important. Such lack of integration lies partly in the tendency of senior managers to treat development efforts solely as technical projects. As important as technical competence is, however, development projects are business projects and should be managed as such.

In Chapters 10 and 11, we describe some of the concepts and approaches that we have observed in firms that are particularly good at ongoing product and process development. This chapter describes the activities that lay the foundation for successful development projects. In the next section we describe various ways for measuring an organization's development performance, emphasizing the importance of its development cycle time. The third section discusses why integrating the strategies of key functional groups is so important and describes how a technique called functional mapping can facilitate this. The fourth section introduces the notion of the development funnel and describes ways to manage it. We conclude with some suggestions for developing and managing the human resources required for product and process development.

Chapter 11 focuses on the management of individual development projects, arguing that good product and process development incorporates two-way (overlapping) information flows, low-level problem solving and conflict resolution, and close interfunctional coordination. After a detailed description of the traditional approach (or paradigm) that most companies follow when managing development projects, we describe an alternative paradigm that is increasingly being used, with remarkable results. We conclude that chapter with a brief discussion of the fundamental challenge that companies face as they try to create superior new product and process capabilities: how to cultivate organizational learning over time and across projects.

A Framework for Product Development

To set the stage for our discussion, consider Figure 10–1; it arrays different kinds of development projects against the degree of product and process change involved. A project designed to create a whole new market or industry based on its own production technology (such as plain-paper copying or genetic engineering) would fall in the upper left-hand corner of the figure. A small incremental change to an existing product or process, something that could be implemented through a routine engineering change order, would fall in the lower right-hand corner.

In this and the next chapter, we focus only on the development of major "next generation" products and processes—those that fall in the shaded area. Such projects consume the bulk of the resources spent on product and process development at the business-unit level and can have significant competitive leverage. We will not discuss radical or incremental projects here, although many of the concepts and techniques we cover can also be applied to them.

Next generation development projects are often complex collections of activities involving many people over several years. To further structure the discussion of these activities, we divide the life cycle of a product or process into eight phases.

Figure 10-1   Range of Product and Process Development Combinations

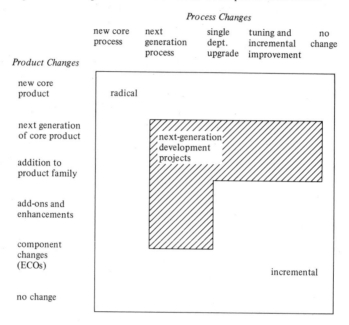

Phases in the Life of a Product or Process

Phase	Primary Activity
1	knowledge acquisition
2	concept investigation
3	basic design preparation
4	prototype building and testing
5	pilot production run
6	manufacturing introduction and ramp-up
7	ongoing enhancement
8	phase-out

Development activities encompass the first six phases. They begin with the building of knowledge and the development of a concept. In the middle phases, engineers complete a design and translate it into prototypes. After testing and refining the design, the new product or process is introduced into pilot production and then ramped up for commercial use.

It is not easy to develop measures of a project's effectiveness that are acceptable to the whole organization. Engineers, for example, tend to believe that development projects are more art than science, each being unique and thus hard to compare with each other or with initial plans. In addition, since different organizational units interact in complicated ways, it is often difficult to align a development project's performance measures with the usual assignments of responsibility and authority (as discussed in Chapter 4). But an organization needs to be able to make some rational assessment of its product and process development capabilities, and compare them with those of its competitors.

A development project should be evaluated using three primary measures: resource utilization, design quality, and development cycle time. Development resources include materials, capital equipment, and people's time. The quality of a design captures the extent to which it meets the needs of the target market, as well as its actual performance, aesthetics, and cost. Cycle time includes the total elapsed time from the beginning of the project to commercial introduction. Most firms focus their attention on only one or two of these three measures of performance; few track and manage all three. In mature industries, for example, managers tend to focus primarily on resource utilization. In high-tech environments, on the other hand, project evaluation is more likely to be based on the quality of the design. The window of market opportunity for such companies is often quite narrow, so achieving the best performance possible with each new product or process is key to success.

There are usually trade-offs between resource utilization and design quality, and those trade-offs need to be managed carefully. Although the same is true of the third performance dimension, development cycle time, it generally gets much less attention than it deserves. Many firms treat it as immutable, a fact of life in their industry. But development time can have a powerful effect on a company's competitiveness. Moreover, it has a major impact on both resource utilization and design quality.

A short development cycle allows a firm to preempt competitors in the marketplace. The speed with which a new product is introduced often spells the difference between success and failure. As Dr. Seiuemon Inaba, the founder and CEO of Fanuc, tells his engineers, "No matter how excellent a product may be . . . we will not be able to win [unless we] market it at the proper time."[2]

Furthermore, a firm that has achieved a shorter development cycle than its competitors can begin projects closer to their expected time of market introduction. Its new products can therefore incorporate a more up-to-date assessment of customer needs and technological possibilities without being late to market. Shorter cycles also foster better design quality by reducing the "moving target" problem: The longer the cycle time, the more market and design changes are likely to occur between the start of a project and its completion. A twelve-month project spans roughly only half as many changes as a twenty-four-month project. Reducing the number of changes required, in turn, makes it much easier for a project team to focus on a single project—the one it started on—instead of continually redefining it.

Finally, the cost of development is likely to be lower. This is particularly true if the shorter cycle is obtained through more effective management and organization, rather than by simply adding people. Resources are more effectively focused, and knowledge more effectively retained, when feedback loops are short and problem-solving is confined to a few people and executed quickly. Also, since a large proportion of overhead costs (which constitute the bulk of the total cost for most projects) are time dependent, the shorter the cycle time, the lower the overhead cost per project. As a result, we have found that a project completed in twelve months will often take only slightly more than half the resources of a similar project completed in twenty-four months. Fanuc's Dr. Inaba evidently agrees; he recently placed on the wall of his product development lab a clock that runs at ten times the normal speed!

The Managerial Challenge

In today's competitive environment it is not enough to achieve just low cost or high quality or a short development cycle; a company must achieve all three. Most firms pursue improvements on all three fronts primarily in the middle phases of the development cycle: design, prototype preparation, and pilot production. At first glance this might appear to make sense; these activities consume major resources and time, and they involve many of the key decisions. We have found, however, that what goes on before the actual design and development work gets underway often has just as powerful an impact on project performance.

One reason preproject planning is so important is that decisions made in the very early phases establish the direction of the project and the parameters within which subsequent work will take place. One's ability to influence the outcome of a program declines rapidly as it moves from phase to phase. Yet top managers typically pay least attention to those phases where their influence is greatest. Figure 10–

2 is based on the experience of one auto company, but we have found a similar imbalance in many other firms and industries: top management tends to get more involved when a development project approaches market introduction or process implementation, especially if problems arise or performance expectations are not being met. Yet its ability to influence what happens at that point is severely limited; the product or process has already been designed, and its cost and performance largely determined, in the earlier stages of the program.

Gaining greater leverage over the final outcome is one reason for managers to get more involved in early phases. What goes on before a project formally begins is also important, however, because of the pervasive, cross-functional character of a development program. The development of prototypes, for example, requires decisions about where to make the product, how to price it, what customers to target, what suppliers to involve, and how to service it after sale. If the various functional organizations involved have not developed a coherent strategic direction, set compatible goals, or made consistent choices, the development process will force them to confront such issues unprepared. As a result, the project unwittingly becomes the vehicle through which the organization figures out what its strategy is. Because the choices are difficult ones, they tend to slow down and complicate development; just as bad, they lead to poor product strategies.

What happens early on, even before a project begins, thus lays the

Figure 10-2 Timing and Impact of Management Attention and Influence

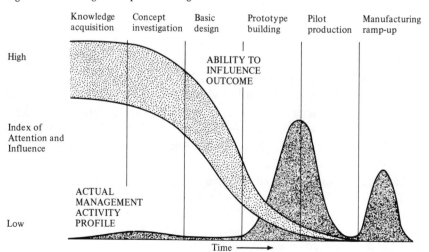

foundation for what follows. If that foundation is well grounded in market, competitive, and technical realities, the project itself can be kept simpler and better focused. In the next two sections we describe how to prepare that foundation.

Laying the Foundation with Functional Maps

Developing a new generation of products or processes is somewhat like taking a journey into the wilderness. One cannot hope to eliminate all uncertainty or develop contingency plans for all potential difficulties before the journey begins, but a little thoughtful preparation can be quite useful. One should clarify in one's mind the purpose of the journey, lay out one or two alternative courses, make sure one's equipment is in order, secure whatever maps are available, study the expected terrain, and develop some plans (and some skills) for dealing with the things that are most likely to go wrong. Such preparations reduce the journey's risks and increase the likelihood of a timely and successful conclusion.

Yet, unlike the thoughtful traveler, many companies embark on development projects without solid preparation. Although the technical details of the actual product or process may have been given careful thought, the company's basic strategy and the supporting capabilities that this strategy requires in marketing and manufacturing often have not been clearly articulated. Without strategic direction the project is likely to end up taking some wrong turns.

The saga of Apple Computer illustrates the danger of not having a clear strategic direction.[3] In the early 1980s Apple was riding the crest of its success with the Apple II personal computer. That product line was being manufactured both in Singapore and in a recently constructed facility in Dallas, Texas. Many of the peripheral components, such as disk drives and keyboards, were being manufactured by Apple in southern California, and product development, marketing, and corporate headquarters were located near San Francisco.

In 1982 Apple's CEO, Steve Jobs, initiated the development of a new product family: the Lisa-Macintosh personal computers. At least three forces motivated this project. First, Apple recognized that in addition to its historical domination of the educational market, a strong presence in both the business market and the professional personal-computer market were essential for its long-term success. It was known that IBM would shortly be entering those key segments with its own personal computer, and Apple did not want to concede them.

Second, the company had just gone through a difficult experience with the Apple III product. Intended for the business and professional user, the Apple III had been an unmitigated disaster. An inordinate number of product problems surfaced when it was first introduced, causing the eventual recall of the first several thousand units. By the time the Apple III's problems were corrected and production was running smoothly it was too late to gain a viable market position.

Third, Apple's management wanted to establish a position in the personal-computer industry that could withstand not only IBM but also the imminent challenge of several large Japanese companies. Apple personnel had great admiration for Japanese companies' success in the U.S. auto and consumer electronics industries, as well as others, and didn't want to see this duplicated in personal computers.

Against this backdrop, the Lisa-Macintosh development effort was set up as a small, dedicated team reporting directly to Steve Jobs. Its challenge was to make major leaps in both product (hardware and software) and manufacturing process development. An extremely ambitious project, developing the Lisa-Macintosh was assigned to very capable people and had the personal backing (and the day-to-day involvement) of the company's CEO.

The Lisa, priced at $8,000 to $10,000 per unit, was initially regarded as the core of the product family. Thus, it was to be developed first and was expected to provide a significant share of the family's combined profits, although not the bulk of its sales volume. It would be the family flagship, demonstating the power of its new technology and serving as the base from which to launch a derivative, but much higher unit-volume product: the Macintosh. The Macintosh was eventually to have its own production facility, but the low-volume Lisa was to be produced in the Dallas factory (which would also continue to make the Apple II).

In retrospect, this strategy for the Lisa-Macintosh was more wishful thinking than a well-thought-out plan. Although based on highly innovative design concepts, Lisa's sales never reached expectations, and the design of the Macintosh required a number of iterations before it could meet the needs of its evolving market. Such critical issues as customer segments, distribution channels, product support, and follow-on products had not been carefully examined. In addition, little thought was given (even in the later stages of product development) to how the new manufacturing facility would be coordinated with the existing ones.

The absence of strategic planning within the various functional groups created two problems: it added time, and it caused Apple to waste resources on more than one dead end. As development moved ahead in early 1983, it was clear that the original completion schedule was going to have to slip if the product's intended performance characteristics were to be met. Because superior product performance had always been Apple's driving goal, the project team repeatedly delayed the Mac's anticipated introduction in order to achieve the desired performance. Originally scheduled for introduction during March of 1983, it was rescheduled to May, then to July, and then to late fall (it was hoped, before Christmas). Volume shipments did not actually begin until early 1984.

The original goal was to have a highly automated factory for the Macintosh up and running at the time of its market introduction. The insertion of components into printed circuit boards, materials handling, final assembly, test, and packaging were all to be fully automated. When the factory was finally started up in early 1984, however, it only provided for the automatic insertion of components into one of the two printed circuit boards (the other was subcontracted), and no automation of assembly. Although there was extensive automation of material handling and testing, within eight months of the facility's opening, $7 million worth of automation equipment (one-third of the total spent on the factory) was removed because it had not proven effective.

The delay of the Macintosh's market introduction by several quarters drove Apple's earnings down dramatically and caused the stock market's valuation of the company to fall to less than half its early 1983 value. In addition, the shortcomings and disappointments of the Lisa-Macintosh development effort put the entire organization under tremendous pressure. It was one of several factors contributing to the hiring of a new president, John Sculley, and the eventual removal of Steve Jobs as CEO. It also set the stage for the major consolidation that took place in 1985.

During this consolidation, management concluded that Apple had too much manufacturing capacity and therefore decided to close the Dallas plant. Several hundred people (over 20 percent of Apple's entire work force) were let go, and substantial write-offs were incurred. The peripherals operation was also discontinued, with accompanying dislocations and write-offs. Thus, by late 1985 Apple had gone through great agony and emerged a vastly different company. Much of this had its roots in the shortcomings of the Lisa-Macintosh development effort. Although errors were certainly made during the actual execution of the project, the seeds of most of Apple's major difficulties were sown long beforehand.

The Value of Functional Maps
The problems that Apple experienced in developing the Macintosh did not arise simply because it was a highly innovative product. Although the company's competitive environment had become much tougher, it was still entering a market whose customer segments were fairly well defined and for which some distribution channels already existed. It planned to use process technology that had been introduced elsewhere several years earlier. Yet these areas caused Apple major problems. Had it clarified its marketing and manufacturing plans before launching the Lisa-Macintosh project, it might well have avoided significant investment and lost time.

How can a company go about delineating such issues and providing direction for its functional groups? An approach that we have found to be quite powerful is called *functional mapping*. A map is a chart or graph that depicts the behavior of a critical variable (or combination of variables) over time, either within the firm or in relation to competitors; *knowledge maps* summarize what is known historically about a particular variable or issue, and *strategic-choice maps* suggest alternative directions that the business or function might pursue in the future.

A set of functional maps not only can provide a useful guide for an individual development project; it helps establish a context for the stream of projects that are undertaken over time. It also ensures that all the functions share the same vision of where they are going collectively and how individual projects contribute to their common purpose. A comprehensive set of topics for such maps is shown in Figure 10–3; three or four representative maps are indicated for each of the major functions (in this example, marketing, engineering, and manufacturing).

There are two reasons why the major functions should all develop coordinated strategies before new product and process projects are undertaken. First, this facilitates the effective mobilization of all the organization's resources, capabilities, and functional groups. For most firms this implies dramatic changes in the way they manage themselves. Typically, a single functional area (usually marketing or

Figure 10-3   Relationships between Business and Functional Strategies: Functional "Maps"

engineering) is expected to lead the competitive charge, with other functions "falling into line." Maps provide a tool for guiding the development of functional excellence, and they facilitate the strategic integration of that excellence around a common purpose. Second, the increasingly global nature of competition requires that companies be more selective in targeting their investments. Top management cannot simply decide "to go global"; before undertaking major development programs it must make specific choices regarding which markets to serve with which products and which manufacturing facilities. Functional maps are a powerful tool for clarifying such choices.

Equally important, they provide a means by which different functions can communicate with one another and share their perspectives on the future. There should be ongoing discussion across the functions as the maps are developed and refined, so that the finished set represents a sort of consensus. The process of mapping thus has two outputs. The first is the maps themselves. The second is a communication process that facilitates a shared understanding of the issues facing the business, and the strategic direction each function is taking. In so doing, maps guide the development of organizational capabilities prior to the organization's actual need for those capabilities.

Each business, as well as each function, has to decide which maps are most appropriate for it. To illustrate, we will take an actual company and examine the nature of the maps it developed and how the process of mapping worked. This example comes from the vacuum cleaner business of N. V. Philips, an industrial and consumer products company based in Holland but operating worldwide.[4]

Philips Vacuum Cleaners

Marketing. A core marketing map is one that describes a business unit's primary market segments. Markets can be segmented in a variety of ways, and different approaches provide different insights into one's competitive environment and how it is likely to evolve. The map shown in Figure 10–4 subdivides the European vacuum cleaner market by price segment and by country. It indicates that the German and French markets are dominated by the high-priced segments, whereas the U.K. and Holland markets are predominantly

Price Class* (Country)		Total Market––Proportion of Sales				
		Germany	France	United Kingdom	Holland	Europe Average
		%	%	%	%	%
low	0–75	5	10	23	25	15
	76–115	15	22	39	26	22
medium	116–155	30	25	31	31	28
high	156–190	25	21	5	15	18
	> 190	25	22	2	3	17
		100	100	100	100	100

*All prices in Dutch Guilders (Dfl.).

low-priced. Note that the medium-priced segment, as a percentage of the total, is fairly consistent across all these countries.

Another useful map is shown in Figure 10-5, which looks at distribution channels by country. It indicates that Philips's marketing efforts have emphasized specialized retail outlets and department stores. Given the data in Figures 10-4 and 10-5, one also could create a map combining the information about distribution channels and price segments.

Product-positioning maps attempt to translate fundamental customer needs (features, delivery performance, reliability, and price) into product families that are directed at specific customer segments and compete against specific competitor products. The one shown in Figure 10-6 depicts the price ranges of the vacuum cleaners produced by various companies, making it possible to determine how Philips's key strengths at various price points compare with those of its major competitors.

Design Engineering. Because marketing is customer-focused, most marketing maps depict customer groupings and various means of influencing their behavior. Design-engineering maps, on the other hand, are more concerned with the dominant technologies employed by the business and how they evolve over time. Identifying the tech-

Figure 10-5 Distribution-Channel Segment Map for Philips Vacuum Cleaners

Distribution Channel	Country						Total
	France	Germany	Holland	Scandinavia	U.K.	Others	%
Specialized (household products)	* *	* *	* *	* *			36
Department stores	* *	* *	* *	* *	* *	* * *	39
Mail order			*				6
Discounts			*				6
Electrical product specialists						* *	6
Door to door							0
Others							7
Total (%)	23	18	12	6	12	29	100

NOTES: Increasing number of asterisks indicates increasing Philips strength.
Percentages shown are based on Philips' sales.

Figure 10-6   Product-Positioning Map for Philips Vacuum Cleaners

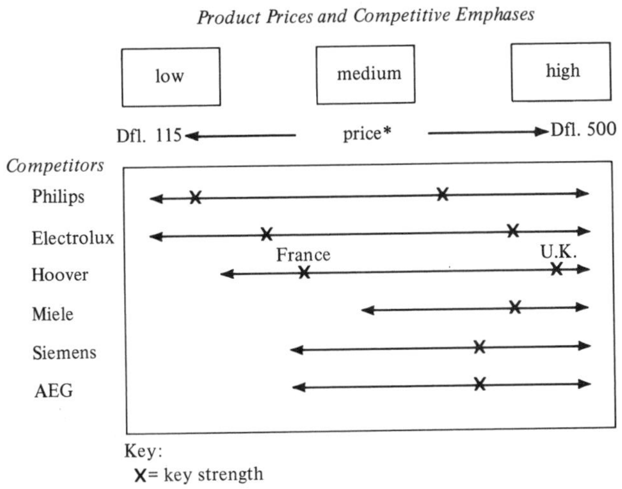

Product Prices and Competitive Emphases

Key:
X = key strength

*Prices in Dutch Guilders (Dfl.).

nological trends that drive product and process changes can help guide product improvement, cost reduction, and new-product proposals. Moreover, they may suggest what kinds of new technical knowledge and critical skills are needed to exploit potential new product and process opportunities.

A good place to begin is with a product-generation map, which breaks product families into different generations and their offshoots. For the Philips vacuum cleaner business, the product-generation map in Figure 10-7 plots the development of several major product families over time, indicating how they have evolved into follow-on and hybrid products. Indices reflecting the relative prices of various products are also presented; these suggest that Philips has been shifting from low-priced vacuum cleaners to medium-priced ones and now appears to be moving toward more high-end products. A similar, although not as dramatic movement, is seen to be occurring in Philips's "second brands" (private-label products). In addition, the number of major product families and the number of total products have both expanded rapidly.

Another kind of useful design-engineering map is a product-characteristics-and-technology map, presenting information about their evolution. Figure 10-8, for example, describes the relationship between vacuum cleaner volume (product size) and weight for Philips and three Japanese competitors (three data points, represent-

Figure 10-7   Design-Engineering Product-Generation Map for Philips Vacuum Cleaners

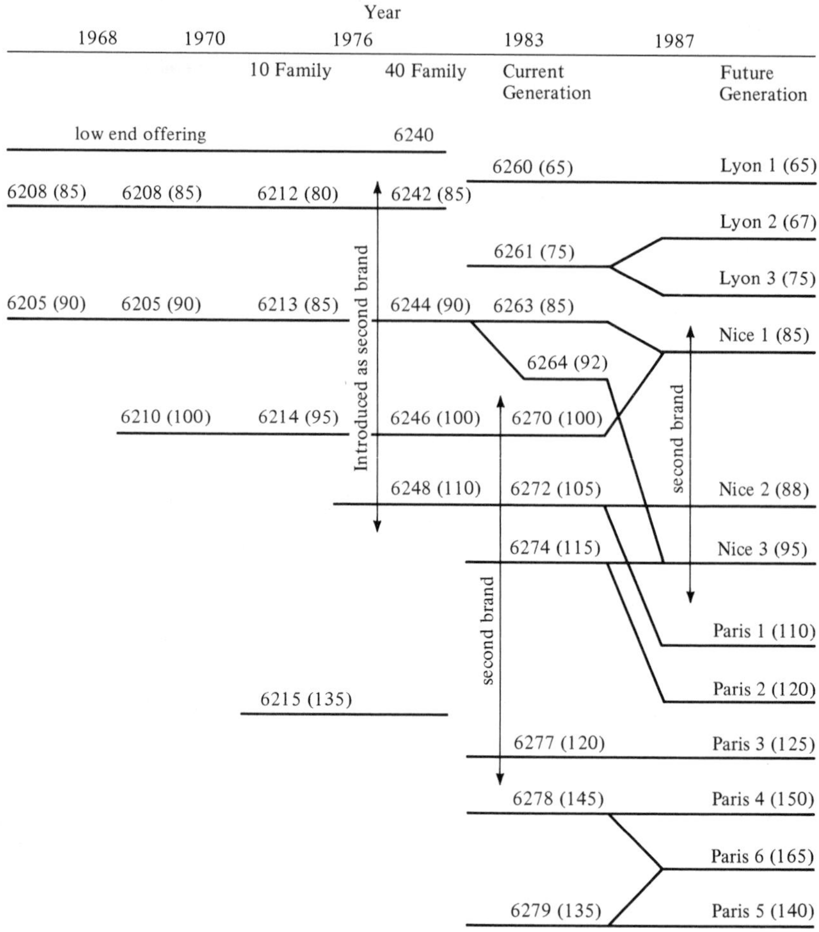

Year				
1968 1970		1976	1983	1987
		10 Family 40 Family	Current Generation	Future Generation

low end offering   6240

| | | | 6260 (65) | Lyon 1 (65) |

6208 (85)   6208 (85)   6212 (80)   ↑ 6242 (85)

Lyon 2 (67)

6261 (75)

Lyon 3 (75)

6205 (90)   6205 (90)   6213 (85)   6244 (90)   6263 (85)

Nice 1 (85)

6264 (92)

Introduced as second brand

6210 (100)   6214 (95)   6246 (100)   6270 (100)

6248 (110)   6272 (105)   Nice 2 (88)

second brand

6274 (115)   Nice 3 (95)

second brand

Paris 1 (110)

6215 (135)   Paris 2 (120)

6277 (120)   Paris 3 (125)

6278 (145)   Paris 4 (150)

Paris 6 (165)

6279 (135)   Paris 5 (140)

NOTE: Indexed prices shown in parentheses.

ing the range of 1983 products, are provided for Philips). These two product characteristics are important to customers and are heavily dependent on design and materials technology choices.

A third type of map that can facilitate the development of a design-engineering strategy depicts the likely evolution of critical skills over time. This kind of map is particularly useful when product technologies are undergoing profound change—such as a shift from electromechanical to electronic designs or from metals to plastics—requiring new skills in design engineering. The skills map for the Philips's vacuum cleaners product-development group is shown in

Figure 10-8   Product Characteristics-and-Technology Map for Philips Vacuum Cleaners

Size and Weight Trends

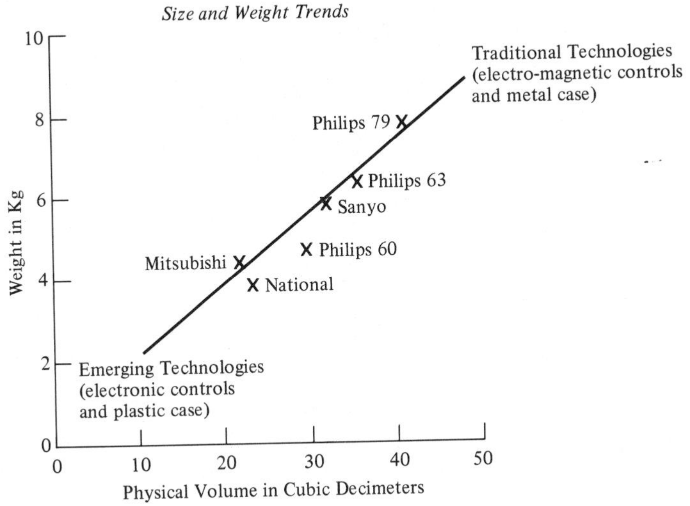

NOTE: One cubic decimeter is approximately 60 cubic inches.

Figure 10-9. It indicates how the mix of design capabilities—quiet operation, electronics, plastics, and so forth—has changed and is likely to continue to change over time.

Manufacturing.   Manufacturing often finds itself squeezed between marketing and design engineering, its role limited to reacting to their initiatives. But the possession of exceptional process capabilities can also drive one's competitive strategy, and maps can help a manufacturing organization integrate the opportunities and constraints of process technology with those of engineering and marketing. By clarifying the direction it is taking and communicating that direction to other functions, it can strengthen its overall role.

A core manufacturing map is the process-generation map, shown in Figure 10-10. This map summarizes the transition of the different product generations of Philips vacuum cleaners (see Figure 10-7) from labor-intensive to more automated assembly processes. Closely related to it is a facilities map (Figure 10-11), which indicates the focus of individual manufacturing facilities (or subparts of facilities). This map could be expanded to include competitors' facilities. Other manufacturing maps could be based on the evolution of critical manufacturing resources, such as machine technology, vendors, and human resources.

Figure 10-9   Design-Engineering Critical-Skills Map for Philips Vacuum Cleaners

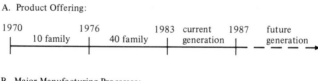

Figure 10-10   Process-Generation Map for Philips Vacuum Cleaners

A. Product Offering:

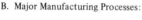

B. Major Manufacturing Processes:

1) Material

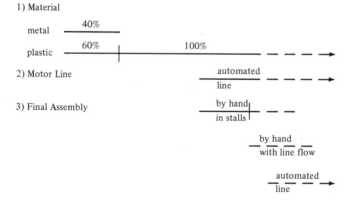

2) Motor Line

3) Final Assembly

Figure 10-11 Manufacturing Facilities Map for Philips Vacuum Cleaners

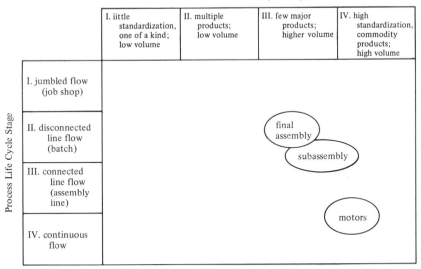

NOTE: See Hayes and Wheelwright, 1984 (Chap. 7).

Using Maps: The Apple Case Revisited
Our discussion of Apple's development of the Lisa and the Macintosh illustrates the problems that can occur when product and process development projects are launched without clear strategic direction. We have suggested that mapping can provide such direction. But would the existence of such maps have made any difference to Apple? Did information exist from which it could have gained valuable insight through a mapping process? We believe it did. In fact, the Apple case provides a good example of the power of functional mapping. Each of Apple's three main functions—marketing, design engineering, and manufacturing—confronted issues in the development of the Lisa-Macintosh product line that maps could have helped clarify.

Marketing. The Lisa and the Mac were viewed as primarily engineering projects. Marketing issues received secondary attention, yet they turned out to have a profound influence on both the designs of those products and their ultimate sales. Marketing thought of the Lisa as a high-end office product, and the Mac was slated to serve the lower end of that market, with some application to education and home use. The phrase "appliance for the knowledge worker" summarized its basic concept. Yet information available in 1982 indicated that this concept ignored several important issues.

Figure 10–12 describes the major personal-computer market segments in 1982, along with the emphases placed on different criteria by each segment. Comparing the importance placed on various criteria in Apple's development program (right side of Figure 10–12) with the needs of different market segments suggests that the Lisa was a machine without a market. Moreover, the Mac appeared to be better suited to the needs of small businesses and universities, even though Apple was directing it at large corporations. The map thus highlights a mismatch between development objectives and market requirements that should have been apparent in 1982.

Design Engineering.   The Lisa was to be both a high-end machine for offices and a technology platform for subsequent products like the Mac. But little thought was apparently given to the way that the Lisa itself would evolve. Nor does it appear that the Lisa-Mac development team understood the implications of evolving component technology. Figure 10–13 is a product-generation map that shows the evolution of the Apple and Lisa-Mac product families through 1985.

The Lisa was based on the Motorola 68000 microprocessor and

Figure 10-12   Personal-Computer Market Segments and Product Development Factors, 1982

Buyer/ Development Factors	Market Segments						Development Emphasis	
	Home	Education (K-12)	University	Home Office	Small Business (and professional)	Corporate Office	Lisa	Macintosh
Performance	*	*	***	**	**	**	***	**
Price	***	***	**	***	***	**	○	***
Features	*	*	**	*	*	*	**	*
Reliability	**	*	*	**	**	*	○	**
User friendly	**	**	*	**	*	○	***	***
Connectivity	○	○	○	○	○	***	○	○
Field support	○	○	○	○	○	***	○	○
Application software	*	*	**	**	**	***	*	**

Key:
   ***: highly significant factor
    **: important factor
     *: of some importance
     ○: little role in decision; secondary factor

Figure 10-13 Product Generations at Apple

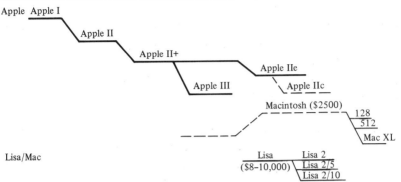

employed new concepts in software (windows, icons) and user-machine interaction (the mouse). Higher-performance models were unveiled after the initial introduction, but essentially they simply incorporated additional memory. Despite its innovativeness, the original design of the Lisa did not lend itself to future evolution and development. Not only was it very expensive to manufacture, but its use of many unusual parts and design concepts made it difficult to modify. The Mac was also based on the 68000 processor, however, and the price of memory was dropping rapidly. As a result, the Mac was soon able to provide most of the capabilities of the original Lisa at a fraction of its price. A product-generation plan, together with a forecast of the likely evolution of component technology, would have suggested in 1982 that the Lisa was likely to be a dead-end product.

Manufacturing. Apple's production experience as of 1981 had been limited largely to labor-intensive assembly in a batch processing environment. Although the Singapore facility had some experience with automation, it was a relatively recent addition to the manufacturing organization. The Lisa required only manual assembly and fit well with Apple's capabilities, but the Mac was a different story. It was decided that it should be the vehicle for developing Apple's capabilities both in line-flow (as opposed to batch) processes and automated manufacturing.

Figure 10–14 depicts the evolution of Apple's manufacturing processes, from simple manual ones to fully integrated, automated processing. It highlights the major leap that the new plant—designed to

Figure 10-14   Manufacturing-Process Generations at Apple

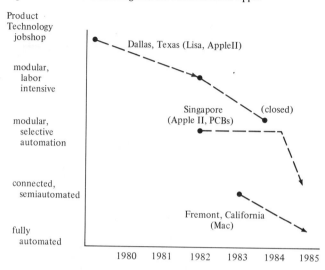

use automated materials handling, automated component insertion, and (eventually) robotic assembly—represented in manufacturing technology and systems. The plan was to make the transition from unskilled workers with solder guns to automated lines in a single step. However, the organization apparently did not have a shared understanding of what this implied, the kind of organizational capabilities that would have to be developed, or what the alternatives were.

The concerns raised in this brief discussion of the Lisa-Mac development process do not just reflect good hindsight; this information was widely available at the time and no tricks were involved in processing it. Had a set of functional maps been developed before the project began, these issues would have surfaced at Apple before it made commitments to specific target markets, product designs, and manufacturing equipment. Some decisions might have been altered as a result, but even had they remained the same, Apple would have been in a better position to manage their risks and develop the necessary supporting capabilities.

Fortunately, the lessons of this experience did not go unheeded at Apple. By 1986 it was focusing significant attention on its preproject development procedures, as well as on its project management capabilities. Each of its manufacturing facilities was well along in defining its process improvement path over time. The product development and advanced technology groups had established clear targets for forthcoming product generations and the technologies they would employ. Moreover, marketing was realigning its coverage of distribution channels and customer segments to better capitalize on the anticipated wave of new products. As a result, the introduction of several new products took place, well configured for their target markets and largely on schedule.

Managing the Development Funnel

Maps provide insight and direction, but linking them to product and process development efforts requires that a business unit establish criteria and priorities for allocating resources to a specific sequence of projects over time. The concept of the *development funnel,* illustrated in Figure 10-15, provides a framework for thinking about the generation and screening of alternative project ideas. A variety of different product and process concepts enter the funnel for investigation, but only a fraction of them progress beyond that point. Those that do must be examined carefully before entering the narrow neck of the funnel, where significant resources are expended on developing them into commercial products or processes.

Managing the funnel involves two very different tasks. First, the organization must expand its knowledge base and its access to information in order to increase the number of new product and process concepts. This is analogous to expanding the size of the mouth of the funnel. There are a variety of ways to do this, including such simple ones as mining research labs for more technical ideas and

Figure 10-15   The New Product-New Process Development Funnel

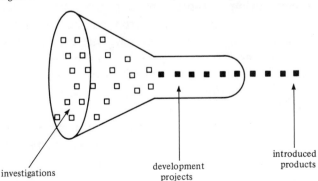

investigations

development
projects

introduced
products

soliciting creative inputs from manufacturing, marketing, customers, and suppliers.[5]

The second, and complementary, task often tends to dampen the creativity needed to widen the funnel's mouth, unfortunately. After generating a variety of alternative concepts, management must screen them and commit resources only to the most attractive ones. This is analogous to narrowing the neck of the funnel while ensuring that a constant stream of good projects is flowing down it. This narrowing process must be based on a set of screening criteria that fit the unit's technological opportunities as well as its strategic and financial needs.

Striking an effective balance between creatively widening the funnel's mouth and tough-mindedly narrowing its neck is not easy. The companies that do it best tend to combine various idea-generating mechanisms with a sequential review process. Some companies have created a group of people whose primary mission is to conceive and develop product concepts. We are not referring to such traditional groups as product planning or marketing research but to something more like basic research. New product and process ideas can be gleaned from a variety of sources, and concept development groups need considerable organizational and financial flexibility to assemble resources for nurturing the most promising ones. Unless it has the authorization to fund (or bootleg) the development of concepts at very early stages, a company is likely to miss out on many good ideas.

Honda and Texas Instruments (T.I.) are two very different companies that have implemented this kind of front-end funding mechanism. At Honda, a fixed percentage (something like 10 percent) of the R & D budget is set aside to fund new-concept development. Anyone in the organization can propose a new concept. If proposers can get a peer review group to approve the idea, they get funds to develop the concept to the point where it can be formally evaluated. T.I. has developed a similar approach, but uses several different kinds of funding mechanisms. One is called the IDEA program. This is a small pool of funds under the direction of several senior technical managers, each of whom can approve an expenditure of funds for concept development.

At some point, however, the project's protective shielding must be removed, and it will have to undergo an objective review to decide whether the organization should invest in a commercial proposal. This review is best done by a group of line managers, chosen from different functional areas and possessing a broad range of perspectives. They are often tough reviewers, but they bring a level of expertise in the technology and markets that is essential.

The project's commercial attractiveness should be the subject of a later review. It should be conducted by senior managers with a mix of functional backgrounds; their task is to ensure that the development pipeline is primed with a continuous stream of attractive projects. Beyond this point the organization begins to commit substantial resources to the concept's development and commercialization.

Since the decision to approve a project usually involves a sizable investment, many of the same capital budgeting issues that were discussed in Chapter 3 surface here as well. Moreover, the framework developed there provides a useful way to structure its evaluation. In the case of development projects, that means approval must rest not on technical issues or financial considerations alone but also on the project's fit with the strategic thrust of the business.

This same framework also makes it possible to link functional maps to funnel management. Maps, and the mapping process, provide the kind of perspective senior managers need in order to evaluate and compare alternative projects, and select appropriately from them. Moreover, maps can also help establish clear expectations for the projects that start down the narrow neck. Thus, linking maps with the review process not only increases the likelihood that attractive projects get started but that they are launched with a solid foundation of organizational support.

The same kind of preproject concept investigation is essential to process development. Careful selection of a sequence of process projects is critical because such projects are the principal means by which advanced new technology is introduced into the factory. Despite this, we have found that process proposals receive even less preproject attention in most companies than do product proposals. A major reason for this is that frequently no one is given primary, ongoing responsibility for process development. Too many companies rely exclusively on vendors for new process ideas. The ones they see, as a result, have usually already been incorporated into equipment options. Thus, the preproject concept-investigation phase is implicit, submerged in the evaluation and selection of equipment, rather than being the kind of explicit projection of one's manufacturing requirements that leads to the generation of a broad range of options. The recent trend in U.S. companies to reconstitute advanced manufacturing groups—something quite common thirty years ago—suggests that this shortcoming may have been recognized. If an organization cannot afford such a dedicated group, it is important that it establish some other system for generating process development projects.

Matching Product Windows with Process Windows
Each development project is built around an established base of scientific knowledge, and one should be explicit about what that knowledge base consists of. A decision to allow a proposal for a next-generation project to pass into the narrow neck of the funnel should not be made in the expectation that some key scientific breakthrough will occur during a certain time period to keep the project on schedule. In fact, an organization should try to separate its forecasts of the development of basic knowledge (inventions) in various technologies from the application of that knowledge (innovations) to specific product and process development projects.

One way to characterize this separation is presented in Figure 10–16. The three parallel lines (I, II, and III) in the top portion represent research paths for different technologies. At certain points inventions or new knowledge can be transferred to specific new-product projects, indicated in Figure 10–16 by product windows A, B, and C. Notice that only fundamental technological knowledge that is available prior to the start of the formal development project is expected to be incorporated into a given product.[6]

Basic and applied research should also be separated for new process development, as depicted in the lower portion of Figure 10–16. Our experience suggests that it is almost impossible to work out the basic research involved in a new manufacturing process while a product development project is trying to meet a preset time schedule, performance specs, and resource-utilization goals. Failing to understand the idiosyncrasies of an invention that is likely to have been developed for a different purpose, and underestimating the problems that will be encountered in trying to apply it in a new setting, can be catastrophic. This is as true for developing software, such as a Materials Requirements Planning system, as it is for developing equipment hardware.

The diagram also embodies the notion that product and process innovation interact. Because of the competitive power that results from combining proprietary products with proprietary processes, an attempt should be made during preproject planning to align "product windows" with complementary "process windows." This helps

Figure 10-16   Preproject Technology Development (Invention) and Its
Application to Projects

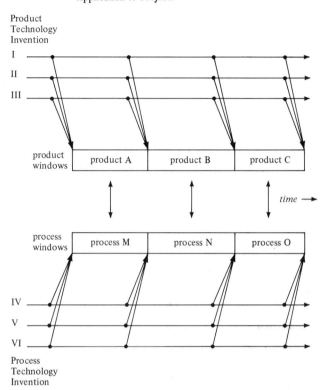

ensure both that future products take advantage of the best available processes, and that future processes provide the best possible capabilities for those products.

Developing the Human Resources

Superior development projects are rooted in the abilities of the people involved—designers, producers, marketers, and managers. No amount of planning and organizing will compensate for a lack of the necessary human resources. Improving one's new product and process capabilities must therefore begin with a program to improve the skill and capability of one's people.

Many different skills are required; they fall into two broad classes: *technical* and *managerial*. Technical skill encompasses knowledge of a particular functional discipline and the ability to apply that knowledge in solving technical problems. A person's technical skills can be measured in terms of both depth and breadth, where depth refers to the extent of knowledge within a particular discipline, and breadth to the range of knowledge across disciplines.

The importance of technical depth has long been recognized. Indeed, it underlay the notion of specialization that was enshrined in Taylor's system of scientific management. Specialization is not the same as depth, however. We have found many companies where specialized engineers have become expert only at looking up things in a handbook. Nor does technical depth consist simply of raw technical knowledge; it also involves the ability to use that knowledge to solve practical problems.

Knowledge breadth is just as important, for it facilitates the early identification of potential problems and the integration of the activities performed by various disciplines. Outside of one's principal discipline, only a working knowledge is necessary: a basic understanding of how the choices one makes affect other people's work. For example, both design and manufacturing engineers should be able to predict the impact of a design choice on other elements in the system.

As regards managerial skills, project managers are not the only people who need them, although they clearly ought to be able to communicate and manage people effectively. Companies should also try to nurture skills in supervision (selecting people, organizing their work, evaluating their performance, and providing feedback) and organization building throughout the development organization. The extent to which such skills are useful will vary with the role and position of the person, but our experience suggests that they are more important than is usually assumed. Take, for example, conflict resolution (which we expand upon in Chapter 11). Effective problem solving in a conflict situation depends only partly on technical skill and understanding. Skills in communication and negotiation are also required in order to identify what the underlying issues are and to work through to a solution. Furthermore, follow-through after an agreement has been reached requires the ability to work within the organization to acquire the necessary resources and support. Even engineers who are technically gifted will be far more effective if they have developed solid managerial skills.

Beyond the ability to supervise, communicate, and negotiate, effective product and process development also requires leadership— the ability to motivate others, to develop and articulate a vision of the fundamental concept embodied in the product or process, and to champion that vision throughout the organization. Given the ambiguity, uncertainty, and natural conflict that accompany any development project, a sense of direction and constancy of purpose are essential.

Increasing the capabilities of the people in a development organization requires systematic and comprehensive planning. On-the-job training through occasional project assignments is seldom sufficient by itself. Nor, given the technical, organizational, and competitive importance of this effort, is it something that should be delegated to a staff group. Skill development should take place at three different levels:

1. *Building-block level.* The skills required for specific development assignments—engineers, project leaders, technicians, product planners—need to be defined and a plan prepared for their acquisition so that when an individual is given a task, he or she has a good chance of carrying it out successfully.

2. *Overall-organization level.* Functional maps can guide an organization in developing a portfolio of competent people whose skills match the directions being pursued by the various functions and who can staff the range of product and process projects that are likely to be undertaken.

3. *Career planning.* This meshes individual abilities with organizational requirements in a dynamic environment. Its purpose is not only to provide a pool of the specific skills that will be needed in the future but to systematically cultivate those skills throughout the organization. Career planning not only enhances a person's personal value; it offers a choice of sensible paths for personal advancement, both within project management and (often of equal concern) beyond it.

Although a systematic plan for developing the required technical and managerial skills in one's people is a necessary foundation for development projects, establishing guidelines for allocating those people among various projects is equally important. Capacity planning is a subject that manufacturing managers have long wrestled with, but its application to development resources has received much less attention. Yet it is equally needed there and fortunately can be based on approaches that are analogous to those used in production environments. Capacity problems (e.g., missed schedules, expediting, overtime, and stretched resources) are common in development projects, and problems in one area invariably spill over into others as people are shuffled around to deal with them.

To illustrate, there is strong pressure in most firms to keep engineers fully utilized; thus these firms generally follow a policy of allocating 100 percent of available engineering capacity to planned projects. In fact, if the needs created by various projects are highly uncertain, many companies plan for utilization beyond 100 percent. But this is counterproductive. By focusing only on the cost of underutilized engineers, it ignores the far greater costs that arise when a development project takes longer than it should.

It is our view that the right starting point for product and process-development capacity planning is never to allocate 100 percent of engineering capacity to known project needs. Just as a manufacturing facility producing a high-margin product should not plan on utilizing 100 percent of its capacity for known production requirements at the start of any period, those managing product and process development should preserve some slack. The amount of slack required depends on the nature of the uncertainty—both within projects and across the portfolio of projects—associated with the possible demand for that capacity. In a highly stable environment it might be possible to allocate up to 95 percent of the available development resources at the start of a year; the remaining 5 percent can then be held in reserve to cover the few unanticipated needs that inevitably arise, whether because approved projects require more resources than originally planned or new projects arise that were not envisioned when initial allocations were made. In an environment with much greater uncertainty, it may make sense at the start of the year to allocate only 75 percent of the available development capacity.

The point is that if 100 percent of capacity is allocated at the start of a planning period, the organization will be disrupted when it has to shift resources. Not only do such unexpected reallocations disturb the projects that are required to give up resources; they add confusion to those receiving them. Worse, over time they stretch the people involved to the burn-out point. A careful analysis of the amount of slack required, based on estimates of the amount that should be held in reserve for the unanticipated needs of approved projects and late-surfacing projects, together with clear guidelines for allocating that slack, can greatly improve the likelihood that the right projects will be completed successfully.

If total development resources are not expanded, providing excess capacity implies that the firm must undertake fewer projects. And this is exactly what most firms need to do. The value of focus in product and process development is similar to that in manufacturing.

Instead of pursuing eight or nine projects simultaneously—which stretches resources, necessitates multiple assignments, creates confusion, and requires frequent reallocation of resources—a firm is much better off to focus attention on three or four really critical projects and ensure that they are done quickly and well. Although some reassignment of resources may be inevitable, the goal should be to keep it low, manage it according to guidelines that minimize its disruptive impact, and prevent it from affecting other projects' priorities. In situations that we have studied where projects got into trouble, it has often been due to shifting priorities and the continual churn in personnel assignments. Conversely, those projects whose priorities did not shift, and where there was continuity in resource commitment, almost invariably did better in meeting their targets. They also provided more rewarding growth experiences to the people involved.

Summary

A company's ability to make product and process development a source of competitive advantage is dependent on how it is managed. In this chapter we have emphasized the importance of laying a good foundation for such projects. The techniques themselves are much less important than the thought processes and planning that lie behind them. The best foundation for successful development is not a set of diagrams. Rather, it is a shared understanding of the strategies that drive the various functions and a clear strategic direction from senior management, complemented by programs that provide the talent, skills, and focus needed to pursue that direction.

A successful product or process development project is not the result of outstanding engineering, marketing, or manufacturing alone. It should be managed as a minibusiness, bringing together and meshing the skills and insights of all the important functional groups. Some of the necessary strategic integration should occur during the project itself, but much should take place well before the project is launched. In fact, it may be possible to undertake many critical activities in advance, so that the actual project can take on a more limited scope. Creating functional maps, managing the development funnel, aligning process windows with product windows, and preparing a pool of people with appropriate technical and managerial abilities all set the stage for superior project execution, the topic of Chapter 11.

11

Managing Product and Process Development Projects

Introduction

Over the past several years, we have studied a variety of development projects (both product and process) in many different industries around the world. In the course of our study we have been struck by two things: (1) the similarity in the problems that development projects encounter in all industrial settings and (2) the wide disparity in the effectiveness with which different managers meet these problems. Projects that face similar technical challenges and market requirements often result in very different costs, market (and organizational) satisfaction, and time to completion.

Building on the concepts developed in Chapter 10, we focus in this chapter on why some projects seem to be so much more effective than others. To create a common base of understanding, we begin with a description of a specific product development effort: the Super Food Processor at the Household Appliance Corporation. Although this situation is a composite drawn from a number of situations that we have observed, it provides a context that illuminates a variety of important issues.

In the third section of this chapter we explore four areas that lie at the heart of successful product and process development: problem solving, conflict resolution, project organization, and the role of manufacturing. Although these four areas will be examined initially in connection with product development efforts, in the fourth section we argue that they are equally applicable to process development.

In the fifth secton we contrast a new emerging paradigm for managing development projects with the traditional paradigm. We show that the full power of the new approach is rooted in the tight way it integrates the various functions and activities associated with a development project. Comparing the recent experience of two competitors—one following the old paradigm, the other the new—conveys an idea of the competitive impact created by moving to the new approach. This sets the stage for the final section, which describes how an organization can improve its performance steadily over a sequence of development projects.

The Managerial Challenge in Development Projects

Although every development project is different, they all confront the common problem of creating and implementing something new. The success of such a project in meeting its goals depends both on the quality of the work done within various functions and on how those efforts are integrated. To illustrate the approach to development that is widely followed, and (by contrast) to infer the basic changes in behavior ·patterns required to make dramatic improvements in development cycle times and other measures of project performance, we describe here the Household Appliance Corporation's (HAC) development of its Super Food Processor.

The Super Food Processor
Francis Riesmann, director of product planning for HAC, recalled the initial new product proposal: "I liked the concept the first time I saw it, but it was a big change in several ways. Most of our new products over the last few years have been lower-cost or 'defeatured' versions of established products. This product was different. It was smaller but much more powerful, with added features and modern styling. We called it the Super Food Processor."

Riesmann presented the idea to the product planning committee, composed of senior executives, arguing that HAC had the necessary technology and that the time was right. The committee had some reservations but agreed to take the first step: concept investigation. Like all products at HAC, the development of the Super Food Processor was expected to follow the five-phase process (and associated timetable) outlined in Figure 11–1.

During the concept investigation phase the preliminary ideas developed by Product Planning were refined. Riesmann's group developed more precise performance specifications, while engineering de-

Figure 11-1   HAC Timetable for the Super Food Processor Development Project

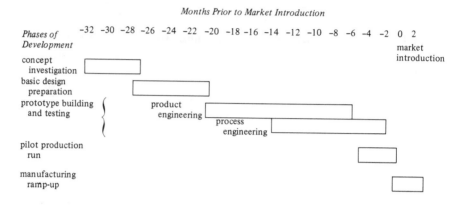

veloped a few preliminary designs and investigated their feasibility. Early on it became apparent that a new plastic material, which was being developed and tested in the engineering laboratory, might be applicable to the new product. In addition, early feasibility studies suggested that an automated assembly process, requiring new equipment and a new control system, would have to be developed if the Super Food Processor were to attain its anticipated performance and profitability goals.

At the beginning of the second phase of development (basic design preparation), the Super Food Processor continued to look promising. Nobody had yet uncovered any major flaws in the concept, and the initial studies generated considerable excitement. Jack Korbelinski, director of product engineering, commented: "There was a good atmosphere around that product; you could feel it. The detailed planning we did—manufacturing feasibility, market estimates, detailed engineering studies—really confirmed Product Planning's initial estimates. We did not have everything pinned down when we went to full-scale product engineering, but the concept looked very good."

The preparation of a detailed product plan included a schedule for product introduction, as well as estimates of the likely investment required, prices, potential market demand, production costs, and the overall financial return on the project. Although the product planning group coordinated the development of this plan, within a few weeks the engineering organization was effectively running the project. The engineers assigned to it investigated alternative component choices and built a few scale models of the product in order to conduct engineering feasibility studies. Although the need for manufacturing process development had been stressed in the initial proposal, very little process work was undertaken during this phase.

As the design of the Super Food Processor began to take shape, Korbelinski named Mark Thomas, a young design engineer, to be the project manager. His job was to coordinate the activities of each of the company's major engineering disciplines and functional groups: sales, marketing, manufacturing, and purchasing. Each of those functions designated a specific individual to represent it on the project team. Mark was also responsible for the preparation of the final product proposal, to be submitted to senior management for approval at the conclusion of the design preparation phase.

When this product proposal was approved, the project moved into prototype building and testing. During this phase various engineering groups engaged in detailed work based on the mock-ups that had been created during the design phase. All went well until official drawings began to be released. Korbelinski commented:

> Any project has its ups and downs, and the Super Food Processor hit a couple of downs at that point. Some of the problems came from the fact that we were working with a new plastic, but the really tough ones involved product performance trade-offs. Some of them didn't surface until fairly late in the project.

Mark Thomas was heavily involved in one of these "late problems":

> One afternoon I went down to the shop to see the first of the second-generation prototypes. Just by chance I saw one of the technicians working with a part that seemed a little odd. I found out that somewhere along the line someone in product engineering had designed in an old, bulky connector that was used in one of our current products. Even though it was a bit less expensive, it forced us to make some compromises in other places. The electrical department had been on a real cost reduction kick, and I guess the engineer who did this was just following orders. I did not realize what I was getting into at the time, but when I pursued that issue I opened up a can of worms. Several other parts were in the same boat. The issue got so hot, it went all the way to the top.

During what some people later called the "dark ages" of the project, various people confessed to some serious doubts. "I thought it was going to end up just like most of our other new products," recalled Francis Riesmann, but she and Jack Korbelinski pushed hard for the original concept. Senior management eventually approved the use of new connectors and other parts, even though they anticipated that this would delay the project's completion date by several months.

The resolution of the parts design issue did not end the project's problems, unfortunately; difficulties were also experienced in getting the manufacturing process on stream. Little work had been done on process development until the prototype building and testing phase of development. Although a group in Process Development had been working informally on advanced plastics processing and automated assembly for several years, it did not begin active development of the manufacturing process for the new food processor until after the first product prototypes had been tested. Only when the designs of the product and its key components were reasonably firm was manufacturing management willing to begin process development, even though senior managers were pushing them to move faster because they hoped thereby to recover some of the time lost when the parts were redesigned.

Process development required the design of the assembly sequence, the creation of specific tools and machines, and the development of associated control systems. Rick Larson, a process engineer, was selected to head up this phase of the project. He met often with Mark Thomas to discuss various issues that arose. Their close working relationship paid off when several problems developed as the date for the pilot production run drew near. For one thing, the advanced plastic material being used proved to be quite difficult to work with. The screws normally used in assembly had been eliminated by designing the new product so that all assembly connections were able to "snap-fit." However, the new plastic parts being produced by the new equipment were found to have tiny fissures and burrs. This prevented them from fitting together properly, and they often broke during automated assembly. Changes both in equipment and in the design of the product were eventually required.

At the height of the efforts to solve these problems, top management became increasingly concerned about schedule slippage. New products recently introduced by competitors required an immediate response, so the process development group was pressured to increase its pace. At about the same time, Product Engineering came up with a new version of the design that had an automatic speed-control mechanism; this required new tooling and several new assembly steps. With a heroic effort (working twelve-hour days and on weekends), the process engineering organization met the challenge; by the start of the pilot production run the project was almost back on schedule.

During the product's pilot-production run a batch of 100 Super Food Processors was to be produced very slowly at HAC's primary production facility, and each step of the production process was to be thoroughly checked out. All the tooling, equipment, and parts to be used in commercial production should have been available for testing and debugging before the pilot phase. Parts coming from outside suppliers, however, were not delivered on schedule; in fact, they trickled in rather slowly. This jeopardized the schedule for commercial ramp-up, but top management was unwilling to change the product's introduction date.

To speed things up, manufacturing began producing pilot units with prototype tools and handmade parts, and without some of the equipment that had been designed specifically for the process (it was still being installed and debugged). It was also decided to reduce the pilot production run to 50 units. A host of problems surfaced during pilot production, many of which necessitated engineering changes. The combination of product design changes and the arrival of new equipment and tooling made life hectic during this period.

According to the original schedule, product design was to have been completed before the start of pilot production, and process design (including debugging) before manufacturing ramp-up. It didn't quite work out that way, however. Mark Thomas commented:

> Ramp-up is a manufacturing responsibility. But with the Super Food Processor it was really part of the development process. A lot of engineering changes had to be made to get the product ready. Most were little things like changing the routing of a wire to make assembly easier. But there were a few big ones. For example, we had to redesign the molds used in injection molding; that took us three months and about five people. Rick Larson and his people were right in there with us, trying to break bottlenecks and get quality up.

All these changes had a significant impact. Although the product's production rate had increased to about 30 percent of the capacity of the new process by the time of market introduction, three more months passed before the ramp-up target of 70 percent of capacity was reached. Throughout that period the demand for the Super Food

Processor seemed insatiable; it remained in a "sold out" position for many months.

The Conventional Development Paradigm

The development of the Super Food Processor at HAC is representative of what we call the "conventional" approach or paradigm for product development. The sequence of activities, the organizational approach, and the pattern of behavior are familiar in a wide variety of industries, whether for product or process development. Under this conventional paradigm the project is driven by a set of objectives established early in the program. Management approval of the resources required to initiate a formal project is given only if the organization is willing to commit itself to achieving a prespecified set of objectives, or "stakes." These stakes typically relate to the project's schedule (particularly the date of market introduction), its cost (the resources consumed up to that point), and resulting product characteristics (its performance, features, and manufacturing costs). In the vast majority of projects we have studied these reference stakes are rarely changed once established, even though the project itself may be redefined several times.

Once underway, most projects encounter changes in technology, in strategic direction, and in concept definition. Effective preproject planning can soften the impact of the first two, but a change in the basic concept can lead to friction between various groups even if there has been good project preparation. At some point Murphy's Law usually begins to operate. The project leader is expected to deal with all such problems.

The project team (if there is one) is typically headed by a design engineer and, even though other functions are typically included, it is usually dominated by engineering. Although project leaders and functional representatives may have worked out procedures for dealing with unexpected problems, the schedule usually begins to slip as the responsibility for different aspects of the project shifts from one function to another, as bottlenecks appear, and as people are moved about because of changes in the priorities of their home departments.

Such schedule slippages generally cause project costs to rise. Many project teams react by denying that the schedule has slipped, by skipping steps that were in the original plan (arguing that for some reason they are no longer essential), and by beginning the next phase before the previous stage is completed—because the calendar says it is time to do so. Further schedule slippage occurs as a result, so that the project is finally completed long after the original target date.

As delays like those shown in Figure 11–2 (taken from an actual project) mount up, most project leaders find themselves with two options. The first is to ask senior management to change the reference stakes. This kind of request is usually turned down, as those stakes are considered sacrosanct; some may even have been announced publicly. The second option is to plow ahead and try not to miss the stakes by an amount that is considered ''unacceptable'' by the organization; different firms, depending in large part on their market position, the importance they place on being a product or process leader, and their prior experience, define this differently. This second option, the one usually adopted, simply postpones the day of reckoning and further compounds problems. The product's design continues to be modified, through a series of engineering changes, long after it has been introduced to the market. To illustrate, the pattern of engineering changes for one representative consumer product is shown in Figure 11–3. Many of the ECOs shown there reflected attempts to correct mistakes made when steps were skipped, rushed, or done out of sequence earlier in the project.

Figure 11-2   Schedule Slippage Observed in Representative Development Project

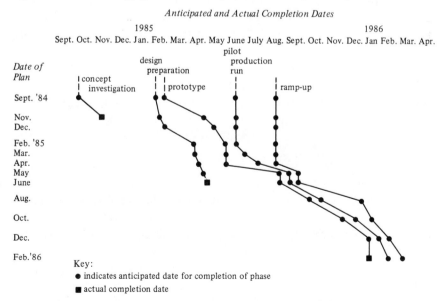

Anticipated and Actual Completion Dates

1985   1986

Sept. Oct. Nov. Dec. Jan. Feb. Mar. Apr. May June July Aug. Sept. Oct. Nov. Dec. Jan Feb. Mar. Apr.

Key:
● indicates anticipated date for completion of phase
■ actual completion date

Figure 11-3   Engineering Changes Required for a Representative New Consumer Product

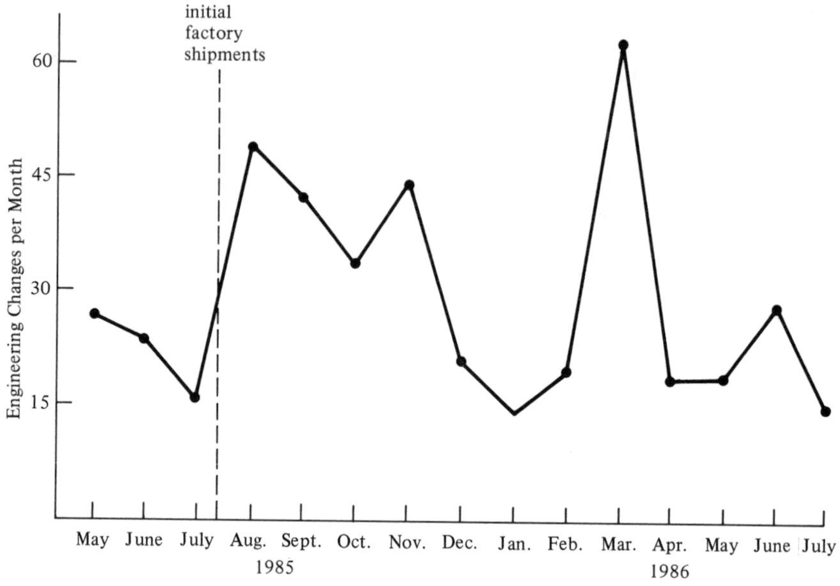

Inevitably this scenario weakens a firm's reputation with customers, raises costs, and prevents development people from moving on to their next scheduled assignment. Just as quick fixes and stopgap measures undermine a factory's competitiveness, they also undermine the effectiveness of product and process development. The fault does not usually lie in a lack of resources or commitment. The problems encountered by development projects like the Super Food Processor at HAC and those depicted in Figures 11-2 and 11-3 arose more from the way the various project phases were managed.

Four Determinants of High-Performance Development Projects

Both product and process development require a complex set of activities that must be performed while markets, competitors, and technologies are all in flux. Moreover, the people involved tend to be relatively specialized and are therefore difficult to coordinate. The process is complicated and politicized further by the important trade-offs that must be faced. The fragmented nature of the project team, composed of people whose primary allegiance is to a home department, specialty, or function, often leads to the perception that each trade-off decision results in a winner and a loser. Each group therefore tries to minimize its risk of losing, which tends to lead either to safe, noninnovative decisions or to bureaucratic gridlock.

These underlying characteristics call attention to four issues that seem to have great impact on project success:

1. The approach taken to problem solving, specifically the way the solutions to different problems are linked together;
2. The way conflicts are resolved, and who gets involved;
3. The structure of the project organization, and the nature of its leadership; and
4. The role of manufacturing throughout the development process.

Problem-solving

Problem-solving is a central activity in any development effort. A development team has to match its knowledge of technical options with its understanding of customer needs. How to make that match is usually far from obvious; existing technologies often fall short of what the market requires. That gap may represent a competitive opportunity, but it also leads to problems. Engineers then generate alternative solutions and test them against the requirements until they find an approach that works—or are able to negotiate a modified set of requirements. We call this a "problem-solving cycle."[1]

Because of the complexity of most new products and processes, companies normally delegate various portions of their development to different departments or groups. These specialized groups usually interact sequentially with one another, so that the solution to one group's problem establishes constraints within which another group must seek the solution to its problems. Eventually, however, the solutions that come out of these specialized groups all have to fit together. The way that firms link the problem-solving activities of such upstream and downstream groups strongly influences the effectiveness of the overall development effort.

Figure 11-4 depicts two basic approaches that we have seen for doing this.[2] (Although applicable to all phases of the development process, for illustrative purposes we can think of the upstream activity as product engineering and the downstream activity as process engineering.) The first is what we call the phased approach: problem solving proceeds in the upstream activity until most of its decisions have been made; then this information (in the form of drawings and models) is transmitted to the downstream group in one large chunk.

Figure 11-4   Linking Problem-Solving Cycles

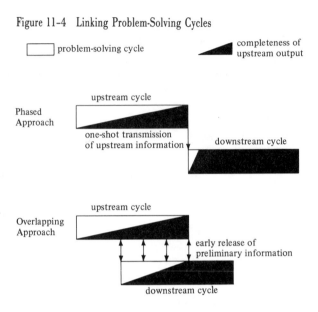

The downstream group then begins its work, having access to all the information provided by the upstream group. It might seem that this would simplify the downstream group's problem-solving activities, but it actually creates subtle difficulties. Although downstream personnel are informed about what the upstream group has decided to do, they may not fully understand the choices and trade-offs that underlie those decisions or how they are interrelated. In addition, the downstream group may face constraints that are not reflected in the upstream design.

Resolving these issues requires a feedback mechanism that usually does not exist, so companies that follow the phased approach have to find ad hoc ways to deal with them. The downstream group may initiate preliminary studies before the upstream information is received, or it may accelerate its normal development cycle by beginning pilot production without the specified parts or production equipment. Such actions tend to compound problems; therefore the phased approach usually results in longer development times, poorer use of resources, and lower quality designs.

The second approach, called overlapping problem-solving, is generally more effective. The downstream activity is encouraged to begin its work well before the upstream activity is complete. The two phases of development are linked together not by occasional memos or meetings but by a continuous stream of information that passes back and forth between the two groups.[3] In contrast to the phased approach, this information moves in both directions and is often tentative and fragmentary.

Moreover, this early, incomplete information moves between upstream and downstream activities in small doses instead of in one large chunk. For example, instead of waiting until the design of a particular part is complete and can be transmitted in an official drawing, the upstream group might provide downstream personnel with an early sketch, or discuss with them their design intent. This gives the downstream group insight into the problems being wrestled with upstream, the solutions that are likely to result, and how these solutions might influence its own work.

Not only must there be a dense flow of this kind of information, but both the upstream and downstream groups must know how to exploit it. In organizations that have made this approach work, we have found that downstream groups have become quite adept at forecasting what upstream groups are likely to do, based on the early clues they receive. This allows them to eliminate a number of alternatives and focus on the options that they are most likely to encounter. Not only can this enable a downstream group to get a head start on its own design, but once it develops a good idea of where an upstream group is headed, it may be able to negotiate changes in upstream decisions that would subsequently constrain its own work severely and imperil the overall project.

Significant benefits can arise if the downstream group begins its work early, even if with only fragmentary information. But the extent of those benefits depends on its ability to make subsequent changes relatively quickly and at low cost. It has to push ahead while leaving itself room to maneuver should the upstream groups deviate from their expected paths. In automotive design, for example, engineers working on dies for body panels learn to build in cutting margins to provide flexibility in case the design changes.

The ability to rapidly identify a problem, pull together the right people to work on it, and solve it is the key to overlapping problem-solving. In contrast, recall how HAC (which employed the phased approach) attempted to deal with the fissures and burrs discovered in the Super Food Processor's plastic parts in a sequential fashion. Each group worked within its own domain, the process-development group awaiting the completion of the product's redesign before beginning its own work. That example suggests why adopting the overlapping approach requires such fundamental changes in behavior on the part of both upstream and downstream organizations.

Product designers are usually reluctant to release preliminary information to a downstream group, fearing that it will treat such information as final and make decisions that would limit their ability to make necessary changes at a later date. If an organization has adopted overlapping problem-solving, on the other hand, people in the upstream group have to trust the downstream group's ability to cope with a certain amount of ambiguity and later changes. Moreover, a perfectionist mentality—one that is unwilling to show outside groups anything other than a finished design—or worse, a superiority mentality, can destroy the benefits of overlapping.

Similarly, the downstream group must be willing to take the risk of starting its own work before upstream work is complete. This makes its position less clearly defined than it is under the phased approach. A wait-and-see attitude, an unwillingness to live with ambiguity, will undercut overlapping. Mutual trust in the motives and competence of upstream and downstream colleagues must exist; otherwise the latter will be unwilling to start early, and the former will be unwilling to provide the information needed to do so.

It is the absence of these skills, attitudes, and trust in an organization that has long followed the conventional paradigm that makes breaking out of its traditional behavior pattern so difficult. In fact, when competitive pressure forces such an organization to try to compress its development cycle time or to make up slippage in a project's time schedule, things usually get worse. If it decides to adopt the overlapping approach without the prerequisite skills, attitudes, and trust, it soon finds ample justification for following the phased approach in the first place!

The joint responsibility placed on various groups for the outcome of their interlinked efforts requires a much deeper level of commitment than might be expected simply from asking them to coordinate their efforts better. An upstream group must not only make sure that its design is right but also that downstream groups can implement it properly. A downstream group must also feel responsible for the fit between product and process and not use "poor product design" as an excuse for whatever production problems develop. This shared responsibility, and the managerial incentives and information systems required to support it, are the foundation of superior problem-solving.

Resolving Conflicts

Disagreements over what course of action to pursue are an inherent part of product and process development. They reflect its complexity and uncertainty, as well as the important trade-offs, many of which are largely judgmental in nature, that must be made. Some types of conflict are healthy, of course. They signal the presence of an important issue, one whose resolution may teach the organization something useful. Conflicts that stem from poor communication, a lack of clear objectives, inappropriate incentives, or organizational politics, on the other hand, are dysfunctional, and companies should attempt to avoid them through the kind of preproject activities described in Chapter 10. But conflicts will still arise, even though the ground has been carefully prepared.[4]

The most effective development projects that we have studied were characterized by early conflict identification and low-level resolution. Resolving a conflict in a way that is satisfactory to all usually requires that both sides compromise. The later a conflict emerges in the development process, generally the greater the amount of change that each side must make—and the more difficult and expensive it is to resolve. Thus, our *first rule of thumb:* Surface the conflict as early as possible. Early discussion of such issues as customer needs, the segmentation of target markets, the degree of automation, vendor selection, and plant location can surface conflicts and encourage their resolution long before decisions have been made that become difficult and expensive to change. Many conflicts cannot be anticipated at the outset of a project, of course. They may arise out of internal knowledge or external pressures that develop unexpectedly. The greater the information-sharing between upstream and downstream activities, however, the earlier such conflicts are likely to surface.

Once identified, there are a variety of ways for dealing with conflict, ranging from unilateral action by someone in a position of power, to delaying action in the hope that it will go away, to suppressing discussion of it in the interests of organizational harmony. Many conflicts are only artificially resolved: even though a decision is made, there is little organizational support for it. Open disagreement is thereby pushed underground, where it evolves into guerrilla warfare.

We have found that a combination of bargaining and mutual adjustment is most effective. Hence, our *second rule of thumb:* Resolve conflicts through mutual accommodation. This requires that a good deal of information about the issue at hand be developed and exchanged. In fact, conflict resolution is a form of problem solving and can be dealt with using many of the same techniques. Since most conflicts reflect real trade-offs, both parties should understand the nature of those trade-offs and explore together possible mutual adjustments. This often results in a decision that is preferable to one that either party could arrive at acting independently.

Another important issue concerns where in the organization the conflict should be dealt with. In the most successful development efforts, conflicts are generally resolved at relatively low levels in the organization—where the most information resides. If there is a conflict over a component or the details of a design, for example, it is likely to be most effectively resolved in discussions between working-level engineers, or between the best-informed people in engineering and marketing. Thus our *third rule of thumb:* Resolve conflicts at the lowest competent level. This rule has a corollary: As part of its preproject activities the organization should make efforts to ensure that the lowest level of the organization *is* competent.

The implication is that top-management involvement in conflict resolution should be relatively rare. The intervention of top management usually grows out of a process in which successively higher levels of the organization get drawn into the conflict because lower levels are not able to resolve it. The resulting top-manager involvement generally has two consequences, neither desirable. First, since these managers are seldom adequately informed about the details of the issues involved, the higher in the organization a conflict is addressed, the more likely its resolution will rest on incomplete understanding. Worse, issues tend to become personalized and politicized, warped into decisions as to who should win and who should lose. Second, elevating the conflict to senior levels tends to slow down its resolution—and therefore the entire development effort. Not only must they be brought up to speed regarding the details of the problem, but as the conflict moves up through the organization its different sides often attract outside allies who form unpredictable coalitions. Thus, other issues besides the one that created the particular conflict tend to get dragged into the discussion, and more people get involved than are needed to resolve the core issue.

Of course, some conflicts can only be resolved by senior management. If a particular issue has significant long-term consequences, requires major investment, or has implications that rise above the particular issue at hand, then top management must get involved. But most of these considerations should surface in the preproject planning. In general we have found that early conflict identification followed by low-level resolution, based on mutual accommodation, is the best means for resolving most of the conflicts that arise in product and process development.

Once all parties have come to an agreement about how to proceed on a particular issue, it is essential that there be appropriate follow-through. In organizations where development projects proceed slowly and ineffectively, we have found a lack of this kind of follow-through. The situation is a familiar one: Groups of people from different parts of the organization leave a meeting where a particular conflict has been discussed, thinking that a decision has been made. A few weeks later, however, they begin to discover that the issue is still open. One party to the supposed agreement, it turns out, has not followed through, and the issue is back on the table. Or other parties have taken actions that undercut it, causing it to be brought back for further discussion. Even worse, unbeknown to others one group may have taken contrary actions that eventually surface and force unexpected changes later in the project.

The absence of appropriate follow-through causes an organization to bog down in repeated rounds of discussion and leads to a waste of resources. Moreover, it tends to cause higher and higher levels of management to get involved. Finally, it undermines the trust that must exist between upstream and downstream groups, making overlapping problem solving impossible. The management attention profile shown in Figure 10–2 arises out of this type of dysfunctional behavior.

Organizing Development Projects

Effective product and process development requires both that all of the organizational groups involved develop the appropriate specialized capabilities, and that the efforts of all these groups be integrated. How a firm chooses to organize a development project can have a significant bearing on its performance. In our studies we have observed four basic ways to organize such projects, each having its own distinctive strengths and weaknesses.[5] These are illustrated in Figure 11–5.

The upper left-hand corner depicts the traditional functional organization, commonly used where the conventional paradigm is followed. People are grouped together by discipline, each working un-

Figure 11-5 Types of Organizations for Development Projects

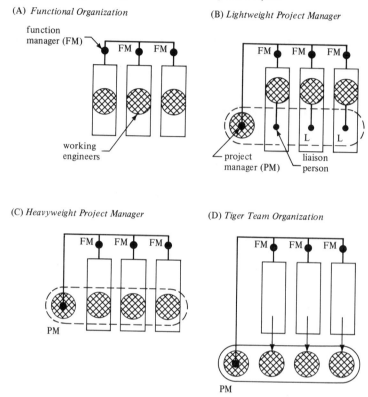

(A) *Functional Organization*

function
manager (FM)
FM   FM

working
engineers

(B) *Lightweight Project Manager*

FM   FM   FM

L   L

project
manager (PM)

liaison
person

(C) *Heavyweight Project Manager*

FM   FM   FM

PM

(D) *Tiger Team Organization*

FM   FM   FM

PM

der the direction of a senior functional manager. Within each engineering discipline, for example, specific engineers specialize in various aspects of the product or process under development. The work of the different functional areas is coordinated either through a set of detailed specifications, agreed to by all parties at the start of the project, or by occasional meetings where issues that cut across groups are discussed. Primary responsibility for the project passes sequentially—although often not smoothly—from one function to the next. The transfer of responsibility for the project from one function to the next is sometimes referred to as "throwing it over the wall."

The second approach, shown in panel B, is what we call the "lightweight" project manager system: people physically reside in the functions, but each functional organization chooses a person to represent it on the project team. These liaison representatives work with a lightweight project manager (usually a design engineer) who has responsibility for coordinating the activities of the different functions. This was how the development of HAC's Super Food Processor was organized.

The project manager in this setup is a "lightweight" in two respects. First, he or she is generally a middle- or junior-level person who, although having considerable expertise, usually has little status or influence in the organization. Second, although they are responsible for informing and coordinating the functional organizations, the key people (including engineers) remain under the control of their respective functional managers. The project manager does not have the power to reassign people or reallocate resources.

The third organizational model, the "heavyweight" project manager system, is shown in panel C. In contrast to the lightweight setup, the heavyweight project manager has direct access to, and direct responsibility for, the work of all the people involved in the project. They are "heavyweights" in two important respects. First, they are senior managers within the organization; in some organizations they are at the same level as, or even outrank, functional managers. As a result, not only do they have expertise and experience, they also wield significant organizational clout. Second, they have primary control over the people working on the development effort and supervise their work directly, rather than through liaison personnel. The longer-term career development of these people, however, rests with their functional managers rather than with the project manager because they are not assigned to any project team on a permanent basis.

The fourth form of project organization is the "tiger team," shown in panel D, where individuals from the different functional areas are formally assigned and dedicated to the project team. The project leader is usually a heavyweight in the organization and has full control over the resources contributed by different functional groups. When people become members of a tiger team, they often co-locate, physically moving out of their functional offices. Even though they may not be assigned to the team permanently, a core group usually stays on for the project's duration.

Although each of these organizational forms has strengths and weaknesses, our research suggests that the heavyweight project manager and the tiger team are the most effective. There are some situations, however, in which a functional organization works quite well. Its strength lies in its ability to focus a critical mass of technical resources on a project, but it tends to require long development cycle times and consume excess resources. Therefore, it is most appropriate for companies that compete on the basis of technical excellence and have such a strong market position that they can afford to engage in fairly long and resource-intensive development projects. For example, many European auto companies that compete on the basis of superior product performance tend to organize their development projects this way.

Although the functional project organization works fairly well in a stable environment, or one where a firm has considerable power in its target markets, the environment facing most firms today is increasingly unstable. Shifting customer needs, new competitors, and technological advances begin to expose the weaknesses in the traditional functional organization. Under such pressures companies using them often decide to adopt a lightweight project structure. Its effectiveness tends to be highly dependent on the abilities of its lightweight project managers, however. Moreover, problem solving and conflict resolution—which become increasingly important in an unstable situation—are dealt with in the same way as they were in the previous functional organization. The project manager is expected to "fill the gaps." Only an exceptional manager, one who has many of the characteristics of a heavyweight project manager, can pull this off.

Heavyweight project managers are usually more effective coordinators because they can see the project as a whole and bring a general management perspective to it. Because of their experience and position, they are familiar with each of the major functional groups. Perhaps more important, they can develop a vision of the project's ultimate output and anticipate the critical issues that have to be dealt with if that vision is to be achieved.

Their job is to persistently communicate that vision to the project team's members, to provide them with a sense of direction, and to motivate them to contribute all their skill and ingenuity to the common task. In this context, however, effective leadership requires more than just the ability to motivate. Real decisions have to be made on a daily basis for the project to succeed. Project managers cannot make all these choices by themselves; they must rely on the assistance of many different people. If their vision is clearly articulated and the development path well understood, the people who are making such choices are much more likely to do so in a consistent and complementary manner.

Both the heavyweight project manager and the tiger team approaches can provide the kind of leadership just described. However, the two approaches are not equivalent. A tiger team is more appropriate in those situations where the firm is seeking to develop a breakthrough product or process, or one that is expected to lay the foundation for subsequent work. The heavyweight setup, on the other hand, seems to work better when the team's output is not expected to be unique but must be coordinated with existing products or processes—such as when product compatibility or parts commonality is desired.

Manufacturing Capability
HAC's experience in the pilot production and ramp-up phases of the development of the Super Food Processor is not atypical. Pulling a new product and a new production process together into an effective commercial operation—which requires finding and eliminating all the bugs—imposes significant demands on an organization. But it is a critical step, in that no development project can be considered to be complete until the manufacturing organization is well on its way to achieving targeted levels of production, yields, cost, and reliability.

Many of the problems that arise in launching a new product or implementing a new manufacturing process are very similar to those that arise in normal production. Therefore, it is not surprising that the attributes required for effective introduction of new products and processes are strikingly similar to those that we uncovered in our study of high-performance manufacturing organizations (see Chapters 6 through 9): they have their processes under control, confusion is minimal, and everybody is continually learning. To implement a low work-in-process, short-cycle, high-quality production system, for example, a manufacturing organization must be able to identify and solve problems rapidly. Engineers, line operators, and supervisors must be able to diagnose problems as they occur and solve them quickly. Moreover, problem solving must continue beyond the immediate problem, in an effort to eliminate its causes and, in the process, add to the organization's store of knowledge. A high level of technical competence throughout the organization, particularly at low levels, allows problems to be recognized more rapidly and solutions to be implemented more effectively than if such competence is confined to a centralized staff group, or purchased from external organizations.

Given the close relationships between pilot production, ramp-up, and subsequent commercial production, and the fact that the manufacturing organization is intimately involved in all three, it is not surprising that manufacturing excellence is critical to the success of product and process development. But we have found that the principles of high-performance manufacturing can also have a powerful impact at earlier project stages as well. Engineering design and development, for example, involve many production-like activities. The way such activities are managed has an important influence on project performance.

Take, for example, the development of a prototype unit. Once designed, prototypes need to be constructed, tested, and their operating characteristics determined. Manufacturing excellence is absolutely essential in this effort. If the prototype shop is run like a traditional job shop, with high levels of work-in-process inventory and inadequate process control, prototype construction is likely to require excess resources and time. In contrast, prototype shops (and associated parts-manufacturing activities) that operate with short production cycles, low work-in-process inventory, precise tolerances, and under tight control, will require less time and resources. Moreover, the quality of the resulting prototype will generally be better.

The speed and quality of prototype construction can have a significant influence on the speed and quality of the overall development effort. We have observed companies that can produce high-quality prototypes in less than half the time it takes their competitors. If the prototype is available sooner, designers get faster feedback and their turnaround time is less. In addition, more prototypes can be produced. Other development activities—including the operation of analytical laboratories, the conduct of test procedures, and the design and development of components, tools, and dies—are enhanced by the ability to quickly diagnose problems, generate creative alternatives, conduct experiments, and implement solutions. Attempting to shorten the prototype development time is therefore a powerful way to improve overall project effectiveness.

In many cases, simply asking "Why does this set of operations take so long?" can lead to insights into how to eliminate unnecessary steps and reduce the time required to execute the critical ones. Consider design engineering. It is generally organized as a job-shop operation: different skills are grouped together to focus expertise on specific technical tasks (materials, components, processes, etc.), and individuals work on many different projects in sequence, maintaining a backlog of tasks in order to maximize their time utilization—just as in the typical job shop.[6]

A very different approach would result if just-in-time principles were applied. Queue times would be reduced by establishing a more stable flow of jobs and finding ways to reduce changeover times (perhaps through the use of CAD or other computer-assisted techniques). Efforts would be made to find out why certain tasks build up backlogs, and to eliminate those reasons.

For example, in most engineering facilities there is an analytical laboratory that provides testing as a support service to individual development projects. One of the reasons that analytical labs and other such specialized support groups exist is that they require very expensive equipment, and most companies prefer that it be fully utilized and operated only by specialists. When development engineers request some type of analysis, therefore, it is placed in the lab's queue of waiting projects. Eventually, often after two or three weeks, the test is performed and the results returned. (We know of one circuit-board layout group that takes four weeks to respond to an engineer's request for information.)

Some companies, however, have begun allowing their development engineers to conduct their own analytical tests. In this way the time for a test can usually be substantially reduced, sometimes from weeks to hours. Such a reduction provides not only quicker feedback to the engineer but also better information. Under the old approach a project engineer would not wait idly until the test was completed but would work on something else. When the test results were finally returned, the engineer would have to reconstruct his or her thought process, trying to remember all the reasons for requesting it before deciding what to do next. A recurring pattern of waiting, forgetting, and then starting up again prevails in such an environment.

Obviously, letting project engineers run their own tests in a lab requires significant changes for an organization. They must be trained to use the equipment, and increased maintenance may be required to keep it running properly (since it is now used by a variety of people). A technician might also have to be assigned to the equipment to work with those conducting tests. Finally, since the goal is now rapid feedback rather than maximum utilization of each piece of equipment, somewhat more equipment may be required. By focusing on key activities in this fashion, we have seen companies dramatically shorten their engineering cycle time while enhancing the quality of the work done and improving the project group's rate of learning.

Not only must improvements be pursued in the individual tasks called for by standard procedures, but basic changes in the procedures themselves need to be considered. Take, for example, the experience of one design engineer working for a major German automobile manufacturer. He was involved in the design of a critical component for a new drive train. Speed was essential, yet the existing procedure for getting the part designed, built, and tested was slow and cumbersome. It would take two or three months if he followed the usual procedure of going to the drafting department, then getting approvals from purchasing and quotes from at least two suppliers, and finally waiting for the part to be made.

Since he needed the part much more quickly than that, the engineer came up with a bold solution: arrange a lunch with Hans. A local parts-maker, Hans was highly knowledgeable about the manufacturing processes required for that component. Over lunch the two of them discussed a rough sketch of the part. Hans made suggestions about changes that would simplify processing and left with a handshake and a napkin with drawings on it. Three days later the engineer had his prototype.

The lesson is not that all procedures for procuring parts should be abandoned. Most procedures have been developed for specific reasons, and those reasons need to be understood. Usually their goal is either tighter control, reduced cost or risk, or increased utilization of people and equipment, but it is seldom reduced cycle time. In a competitive environment that rewards short development times, however, procedures that encourage low cost or low risk at the expense of speed may lead to a loss in market share and thus be very costly. Given a different objective, it is usually possible to redesign the development process so as to simplify and compress it.

Since product and process development involves all the functional organizations, and can only be as strong as its weakest link, a company can improve its development effectiveness only about as fast as it improves its manufacturing capabilities. As a result, building a competitive advantage through manufacturing takes on even greater significance and urgency for a company—or a country—that wishes to compete on the basis of innovative products and processes.

Moreover, both good design and good manufacturing are rooted in solid, old-fashioned engineering skill. Too many of the engineering groups we have studied are staffed with "handbook" engineers:

people whose instinctive reaction when faced with a problem is to reach for a handbook to see if the answer is there. So much of their work is routine, they have never been pushed to attain the level of expertise required to develop really creative solutions to the problems they face. They are neither good analytical scientists nor practical artisans, and they should be both. As essential as effective managerial processes are, there is no substitute for technical competence. Companies become good at development not through clever strategies, slogans, or luck. They simply try to make themselves ever better at the things that matter most: good engineering, good management, and effective supporting capabilities throughout the organization.

Process Development

As was stated previously, our experience suggests that the same principles and approaches that lead to superior product development also apply to process development. Let us examine why this might be so.

During the past few years hundreds of companies have made substantial investments in a variety of new manufacturing processes. The result has been thousands of "islands of automation," incorporating robotics, programmable flexibility, computer-aided engineering, group technology, and advanced materials handling. Unfortunately, the benefits expected from these projects have too often been slow to materialize. Even those that have been put into day-to-day operation have frequently failed to meet their expectations regarding cost, start-up dates, and subsequent performance.

A variety of explanations for such disappointing results have been proposed, including simple resistance to change. As Machiavelli pointed out almost 500 years ago in *The Prince:* "There is nothing more difficult to plan, more doubtful of success, nor more dangerous to manage than the creation of a new system. For the initiator has the enmity of all who would profit by the preservation of the old institutions and merely lukewarm defenders in those who would gain by the new."

At the other end of the spectrum is research suggesting that implementation failures are due largely to a lack of detailed planning and poor execution. In one study of advanced manufacturing projects, for example, the outcome was found to depend primarily on

1. the equipment supplier-customer relationship,
2. the fit between one's product(s) and production process,
3. the fit of the process with one's manufacturing strategy,

4. the education and training of one's personnel,
5. the integration with other support systems (materials, tooling, maintenance, etc.),
6. the commitment and support of top management, and
7. the pace of adoption.[7]

These factors appear to apply equally well to new products and so don't explain why the difficulties and disappointments encountered in process development by many firms are even greater than those encountered in product development. We suggest two additional reasons for this. First, major process development efforts—the type that require significant investment in people, equipment, and procedures—typically occur less frequently and are larger in magnitude than most product development projects. As a result, they are less natural to the organization. Second, more of the critical tasks in a process effort are generally subcontracted, usually to equipment suppliers, so that success depends on more than one organization. Not only does this make coordination more difficult; it requires close communication and trust between organizations and individuals who may not have worked together previously.

This added complexity heightens the need for careful preproject preparation: establishing a direction for process evolution (process maps), placing the project into the context of an overall manufacturing strategy, aligning process planning with marketing and design engineering efforts (through functional maps), and linking them all to the business unit's competitive strategy. The development funnel must also be managed so as to ensure that a variety of proposals are generated for consideration and a steady stream of appropriate projects move down it.

As in product development, process development consists of separable phases, and organizations expose themselves to similar dangers when attempting to skip one or more. Consider the conventional approach to these phases:

1. *Concept investigation:* typically quite narrow; only a few options are considered, both because the needs prompting the project—such as improved product cost or process tolerances—are defined narrowly, and because senior managers (or influential manufacturing specialists) express a preference for certain approaches early on.
2. *Basic design preparation:* Except for the factory's basic layout (and the resulting material flow paths), this step is assumed to

be primarily the responsibility of suppliers. Most manufacturers imagine they either are buying proven technology or that the equipment supplier is the "expert" and therefore should be delegated the basic design of the process.

3. *Prototype building and testing:* This is the equipment supplier's responsibility as well. However, suppliers tend to define this and the preceding phase rather narrowly, confining themselves to meeting the equipment's technical requirements.

4. *Pilot production:* Typically, a supplier's goal is to get the line up and running to the point where it meets technical specifications. The tendency is to do so with special help and under somewhat artificial conditions. As a result, this phase has more of the characteristics of a prototype test than a real pilot run under ongoing production circumstances. Little attention is generally given to training all those affected by the new process, except the direct operators.

5. *Manufacturing introduction and ramp-up:* This final phase tends to be an over-the-wall handoff from the supplier organization (and perhaps the company's own advanced manufacturing engineering group) to the factory. Because of its limited involvement and lack of broad training, the factory tends to exploit the capabilities of the new process somewhat gingerly (e.g., limited product variety, long runs, easy materials, etc.). As a result, its full potential is unlikely to be realized until considerable time has elapsed.

Following this approach usually causes the factory to experience a significant drop in productivity and performance when the new process is introduced, as we described in Chapter 6. It may take months, even years, for it to gain real control over the new process, and what could have become a significant competitive advantage turns out to be neutral at best. Avoiding such problems requires approaches similar to those discussed earlier in this chapter in connection with product development.

Overlapping problem-solving between upstream and downstream groups also facilitates process development projects. Since equipment and system suppliers play such a large role in most such efforts, their solutions to various problems must be aligned with the buyer's. The buyer must also ensure that all the important problems are being addressed by someone, and that it captures a good portion of the supplier's knowledge. Moreover, the extent to which equipment operation and maintenance, the information and materials handling systems, and all the other support groups affected by the new process mesh together largely depends on how well various specialists have coordinated their respective activities.

The three rules of thumb for conflict resolution that we discussed earlier in this chapter also apply to process projects. Much of the inability of a factory to realize the full potential of a new process can be traced to a violation of one or more of them: failing to recognize the impact of a change made in one part of the process on other parts until well into manufacturing ramp-up, letting internal staff specialists or external suppliers make choices and trade-offs without adequate input from those who will run and maintain the process, and forcing important decisions up to higher levels in the organization where decisions are made more on the basis of political judgments and financial calculations than on technical expertise.

The diversity of the specialist groups involved in process development projects implies that careful attention be paid to the project team's organization. A functional organization works well, we have found, only in firms where process development is constant and carried out in a fairly stable environment by an in-house advanced process development group. As outside suppliers take on a greater role, that form of organization becomes less reliable. Specifically, it tends to undermine the effectiveness of a lightweight project manager, since that person does not have real authority even within his or her own organization. As before, the heavyweight project manager organization is generally most effective, with the tiger team approach appropriate only when developing a new factory or replacing an entire production department.

The fourth determinant of superior product development efforts—manufacturing excellence—is obviously even more important in process development. If one wants superior processes that can provide a real competitive advantage, real manufacturing expertise is essential. Reactive and preventive control may be sufficient to keep a factory running, but they do not provide an adequate base for the quick implementation of new, advanced processes or the realization of their full potential. This requires the kind of capabilities and process knowledge associated with progressive and dynamic control. As was mentioned in Chapter 3, many companies tend to underinvest in the expensed items associated with capital investment, such as worker training and systems support. Neglecting to develop the underlying manufacturing capabilities needed to extract the full potential of a new process inevitably leads to additional expense later on. In factory after factory we have heard the same complaint: "Never enough money to do it right, but always enough to do it over."

A New Paradigm for Development Projects

Firms that excel in product and process development tend to exhibit a distinctive pattern in their approaches to each of the issues examined in this chapter, and this pattern represents an alternative paradigm for product and process development. Under this new paradigm, a development project is viewed as a business venture. It is therefore directed by a broad, experienced manager who is given substantial resources, is good at recruiting highly competent people, and can enlist the support of a variety of specialists and functional groups. Development is characterized by extensive overlap, with continual two-way interchange of information at low levels. Different phases of the project are integrated through a shared understanding of the primary purpose(s) of the product or process. Fast, effective problem solving and early conflict resolution are the rule.

The projects undertaken by organizations that adopt this new paradigm are highly focused, fitting into a well-planned sequence of related projects. Certain kinds of common problems are avoided by keeping the project team small and stable, sticking to preset priorities, and maintaining a steady pace throughout development. Major problems are confronted and resolved as they arise, with the full participation of functional specialists and floor-level personnel, rather than being tabled or "taken upstairs." The organization continually works to reduce the time required for design, prototype, and test cycles.

These characteristics stand in sharp contrast to those of the conventional paradigm, as can be seen from the summary contained in Table 11-1. Perhaps nowhere do the differences become more apparent than when considering the contrasting approaches taken to early manufacturing involvement and design for manufacturability.

For an organization that follows the conventional paradigm, early manufacturing involvement usually implies that the manufacturing function gets more time to carry out its part of the project, more complete information (and documentation) when engineering does make its handoff, and fewer subsequent ECOs. In addition, both manufacturing and design engineering perceive such involvement as

Table 11-1 Contrasting the Conventional and New Paradigms for Product and Process Development

Dimension	Conventional Paradigm	New Paradigm
Reference stakes		
project cost	nonnegotiable, set early	may require occasional revision
product/process performance specs	one seen as primary driver for the firm	all given significant attention
project schedule		
Project team	led by design engineering	led by broad, experienced business manager
Project focus	starts in marketing, shifts to engineering, ends in manufacturing	cross-functional team effort throughout
Project phases	sequential	extensive overlapping
Management obstacles	people transferred	managed through better plans, discipline, skills, and follow-through
	priorities changed	
	bottlenecks affect limited design resources	
	slow turnaround	
	vendor delays	
	excessive engineering changes	

Responses to schedule slippages	deny slippage has occurred skip steps announce completion, handoff to operating organization	much less frequent, but addressed realistically as they arise
Handling of key tasks		
problem solving	within functional group or discipline	overlapping and cross-functional
conflict resolution	suppressed, postponed, or sent upstairs	addressed early and at low levels
project organization	primarily functional with handoffs	heavyweight project managers maintain integration
Manufacturing control	only lower forms of control considered necessary	progressive or dynamic control necessary
Information transfers	large batches, transferred downstream only after completion of phase	many smaller two-way exchanges throughout development
Early manufacturing involvement	looked upon as (undesirable) constraint	based on trust and mutual respect; adds value
Design for manufacturability	gives manufacturing veto power over design engineering	provides improved products and processes

constraining the designers by forcing them to accept certain tolerances or to avoid designs that would cause significant changes in manufacturing requirements. This notion of placing constraints on design engineering is taken even further when a conventional organization attempts to design for manufacturability. This is often interpreted as requiring an explicit agreement from manufacturing *before* design engineering can incorporate any material, feature, or specification that requires a change in a manufacturing process, procedure, or system.

For both groups, the implication is that manufacturing will gain power at the expense of design engineering. Manufacturing typically views this as an appropriate "affirmative action," given the lack of respect it has long received from the "ivory tower types" in engineering (whose contribution, manufacturing people feel, has long been overrated within the firm). From the design engineers' viewpoint, this perceived veto power is regarded as undeserved, because manufacturing has done nothing to earn its increased importance (as they have). More important, they fear that such a change will limit their creativity, leading to inferior product designs.

An organization whose behavior pattern reflects the new paradigm attaches completely different meanings to these concepts. Early manufacturing involvement takes place naturally through a project organization that includes all functions from the beginning. The manufacturing group is willing to accept preliminary, fragmented information, which allows it to spot potential process problems. This information is not used to constrain designers but to suggest new options and ideas, often enhancing those already being pursued.

As manufacturing develops the skills and talents needed to fill this expanded role, design for manufacturability comes to mean designs that are superior to those developed under the conventional approach. This superiority arises because manufacturing can help designers become more creative: suggesting new options, indicating how existing manufacturing capabilities could be utilized more fully, and working jointly to identify process improvements that might make new products more distinctive and strengthen the foundation for subsequent development efforts. Neither function considers this relationship as increasing the power of one at the expense of the other. Both see mutual enhancement as the result, as occurred in the development of the Hardcard® by PLUS and JEMCO (described in Chapter 6).

A specific example, involving two direct competitors in the telecommunications industry, illustrates the nature of the advantage that can be gained through following the new paradigm. The conventional approach to development was followed by firm A, whereas the new paradigm had been adopted in firm B during the early 1980s. By the mid-1980s, their approaches to product development were quite different. So were their results, as shown in Figure 11-6. At that point firm B could bring to market in twenty months a product that required thirty months at firm A.

Operating procedures and overhead costs at the two firms were also very different. Firm A viewed new product development as a sequence of activities undertaken by separate organizational units; this diffused responsibility for the overall success of the project across several groups. To coordinate that diffused responsibility, firm A had put into place an extensive product development bureaucracy that required formal checkoffs before transferring responsibility from one function to another.

At firm B, new product development was viewed as a seamless web of activities that could be grouped into phases but were not assigned to functional groups. Design, advanced process development, and manufacturing buildup did not have clear organizational counterparts. At firm B all phases were conducted by a core team of people who had both functional and general management experience

Figure 11-6   Comparing New Product Development Approaches
in Two Telecommunications Firms

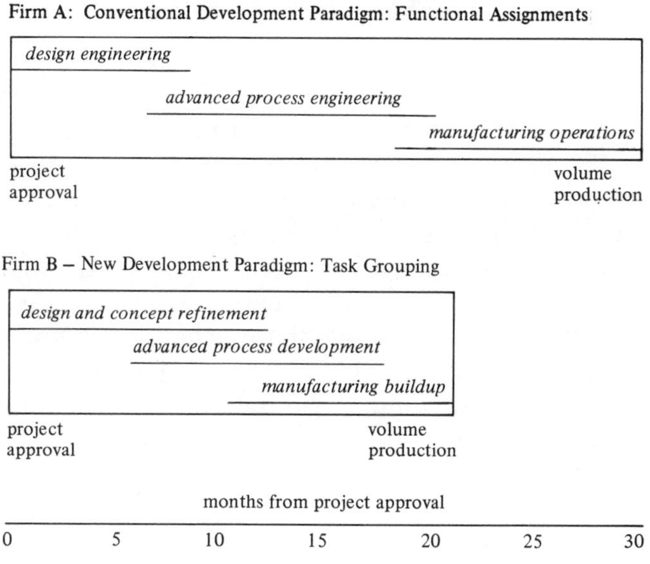

Firm A: Conventional Development Paradigm: Functional Assignments

Firm B – New Development Paradigm: Task Grouping

and who could call on others within the organization as the need arose.

Although firm B's overall development cycle time was much shorter than firm A's, the length of each phase was actually somewhat longer, implying much greater overlap between phases. Firm B spent much more time proving the concept in the design phase before moving on. Substantial parallelism of various activities was the rule, as was continuity in the people assigned to the team. Although the milestones used to measure progress at firm A represented calendar dates, in firm B they were tied to the completion of key tasks or decisions. Even though firm B continually sought to shorten its development cycle times, it refused to move ahead on a project until prerequisite tasks had been adequately addressed.

The impact of these different approaches, and the two companies' resulting product-development capabilities, rapidly became clear. Although firm A had historically been its industry's market leader, it recently has seen both its product leadership and its market share erode at the hands of firm B. It has sensed that its products are not quite as well integrated or defended by proprietary manufacturing processes as are firm B's; nor is it as effective at exploiting recent advances in technology. It therefore finds itself falling behind a competitor that possesses superior development capabilities.

Tomorrow's Challenge: Learning Across Development Projects

Although many firms can point to one or two particularly successful projects, few achieve superior performance on a consistent basis. Even fewer show steady improvement in their development efforts over time. Yet, getting better and better at product and process development is the key to an enduring competitive advantage.

Managers offer us many explanations for their failure to learn from project experience: the urgent need to reassign key resources to the next project (often before the current one is finished); the separation (physically, organizationally, and psychologically) of different functional groups, which inhibits cross-functional sharing; the natural resistance to change in any organization; and staff and system-support groups' preference for fine-tuning the status quo. One very successful CEO of a high-technology company even warned us against studying this subject. "You will never get anywhere," he said. "No two projects are the same. It's all personalities, and even when you get someone good you cannot be sure they will do well in the next project. There are just too many variables and too much random noise to make sense of anything.''

In spite of this complexity, improving product and process development is at or near the top of the managerial agenda today in a wide range of industries around the world. We have found very few companies where improving product and process development was not a central concern. Yet only a handful have been able to tap the potential for ongoing improvement that is inherent in the new paradigm.

One reason, in our view, has to do with the contrasting approaches that they take to learning and improvement. Under the conventional approach, illustrated in Figure 11–7, the improvement of the development process is conceived of as a staircase: a set of procedures is followed over the course of several projects, the lessons from this experience are collected, and the approach to project management revised. This leads to a measurable drop in the time required for the next ''showcase'' project. The organization then operates along the

Figure 11-7   Two Approaches to Development Improvement

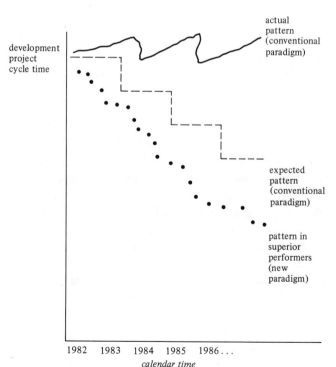

1982   1983   1984   1985   1986...
calendar time

new horizontal path until its cumulative knowledge allows it to further refine the approach and drop to a still lower path.

Unfortunately, the reality is usually quite different. Instead of staying on a horizontal path until management finds a way to improve project management, performance usually deteriorates (drifts upward). The reason is embedded in the way managers in these organizations respond to problems. As mistakes are made or unexpected difficulties encountered (for example, someone forgets to double-check something or does not get a necessary sign-off), managers add steps to the procedures to make sure that those problems do not recur. As a result, procedures become more and more cumbersome, and project performance deteriorates. Eventually the organization decides that its procedures have become too bureaucratic and need to be streamlined. A major effort to improve the process is made, but generally this only brings the organization back to where it was before the cycle started. The sawtooth horizontal pattern in Figure 11-7 generally fits reality better than does the expected staircase improvement pattern.

The new paradigm incorporates a very different approach: it seeks smaller but more frequent improvements, as indicated by the dotted line in Figure 11-7. Superior performers manage to learn from each project they undertake, continually streamlining and integrating the overall process. Even more important, they are constantly building and reinforcing the capabilities needed for further improvements.

The differences in the actual path of improvement under the two paradigms reflect a basic difference in managerial philosophy and practice. Managers following the new paradigm believe that continual improvement in project effectiveness is both possible and essential, and that the development process is amenable to systematic study and focused problem solving. Continual improvement is sought not through procedures and organizational approaches alone but also through mechanisms that facilitate both individual and organizational learning across projects.

The competitive prowess that characterized U.S. manufacturing fifty years ago was not due to the fact that companies (or individual factories) were smaller, product lines were narrower, or technological evolution was slower then. Product and process development was just as challenging then as it is today. What has changed are the principles and approaches that most organizations have adopted over the past few decades. Gradually a new philosophy has replaced the one that was described earlier in Table 2-2:

1. Technological development is evolutionary; progress occurs in small steps.
2. A close interaction between commercial needs and work in the laboratory is essential.
3. Product innovation and process innovation are intimately related; internal development of equipment is imperative for success.
4. Progress occurs through organized effort and teamwork; collaboration across functional boundaries is critical.

Adopting the new paradigm requires that these principles be reinstituted. Each development project then becomes more than just an opportunity to improve a product or process; it also becomes the means by which an organization (and its people) develops Stage IV capabilities.

Several of the tools that can be used to enhance a firm's ability to plan and execute development projects have been described in this and the preceding chapter: (1) functional maps to integrate previous experience, environmental trends, available resources, and strategic choices; (2) performance measures that track improvements in resource productivity, project cycle times, and project success; (3) procedures to improve both the idea generation and the implementation ends of the development funnel, so as to ensure a steady flow of good projects; and (4) building the technical and managerial abilities of an expanded group of people who are assigned according to a careful plan. If an organization develops skills in problem solving and conflict resolution, institutes new ways to organize projects, and develops broad-based manufacturing expertise, it can continually improve its development effectiveness.

| 12 |

Molding the New Manufacturing Company

Introduction

In each of the preceding chapters we have identified one or more key activities that can significantly enhance the contribution that a manufacturing organization makes to a company's competitive success. We have also described a number of approaches and principles that have helped companies in a variety of industries improve their manufacturing competitiveness. These principles are remarkably consistent in their impact, in that the behavior that results from following them in one activity usually is supportive of the behavior desired in others. From our vantage point, therefore, getting the bedrock principles right is the key. If the principles that drive a company's behavior are wrong, no amount of effort, additional resources, or wishful thinking will fill the gap.

Here we begin by identifying four unifying themes that weave these principles together. Then we turn to the challenge of becoming a world-class manufacturer, asking, in turn, Why does this transformation seem so difficult for most firms? How can a company or a factory diagnose its strengths and weaknesses and the current state of its manufacturing competitiveness? How can it initiate an improvement process? After describing the experience of one factory that is well along in this process, we return again to the role that management must play in the transition process. We conclude by summarizing our view of the challenge facing manufacturing companies today, and the opportunity that challenge presents their managers.

Getting the Basic Principles Right: Four Unifying Themes

Four underlying themes shape the behavior of the truly superior manufacturing company and weave together the principles that we have discussed up to now. The first is: *Management makes the difference.* The kind of impact that management has on manufacturing performance, in our experience, is not on the order of 5 or 10 percent but of 50 or 100 percent. This is the magnitude of the productivity differences observed, for example, in the factories we have studied— many of which (see Chapter 6) produced similar products for the same markets, using similar manufacturing processes and operating under the same corporate infrastructure—as well as among different companies within the same industry. These are also the kinds of improvements that have resulted, time and again, in turnaround situations like those described in Chapter 1.

Most of the manufacturing managers within a given country and industry have access to the same books and articles, subscribe to the same journals, belong to the same professional organizations, go to the same conferences, and look to the same flagship companies for instruction. Moreover, they have roughly equal access to most of the resources that are required to build an outstanding manufacturing organization: people, equipment, suppliers, software systems, and outside consultants. How they exploit that information, select among, combine, and develop these resources, and wield them in building a competitive advantage is what makes the difference between success and mediocrity. By this we do not mean to imply that people, technology, and capital are not important, but simply that the ability of an organization to extract the full potential from them is primarily dependent on how well its managers do their job.

The second unifying theme is: *the importance of adopting a holistic perspective.* We have repeatedly emphasized how different kinds of manufacturing decisions interrelate and reinforce one another: equipment technology decisions must dovetail with facilities size, focus, and location decisions; these, in turn, must mesh with make-versus-buy decisions and supplier relationships; process design, facilities location, and supplier decisions must integrate with inventory control, production scheduling, and quality management decisions; and all must fit with human resource policies, performance measurement systems, and organizational design.

But manufacturing is only part of the whole business. One must also understand the pressures and opportunities created by markets and individual customers, the implications of design choices on both, and the signals emanating from stockholders and financial markets. As if that weren't enough, one must combine the artisan point of view with that of the scientist and the systems analyst, understand tactical details in the context of broad strategy, long-run objectives in the light of short-term pressures, and the needs of the individual within the panorama of those of the organization as a whole.

The third unifying theme is: *The whole organization must relentlessly pursue customer value and competitive advantage.* The job of manufacturing is not to run machines, keep people busy, or make products; it is to satisfy customers' needs. Its goal is not to be good but to be better. No resource, whether it be direct workers, equipment, floor space, staff personnel, or current assets, should be wasted on any activity that does not either create value directly or build the capabilities that will create more value in the future. Efforts should not be wasted on patching over the symptoms of problems; the problems themselves should be identified and resolved.

Once this idea is implanted firmly in an organization, nothing can be taken for granted again. A rejected part, a pile of half-finished items lying on the shop floor or waiting in front of a machine, or a new product that is not developed on time all become red flags; time and money are being wasted and competitive opportunities missed. Developing elaborate systems to deal with complexity and uncertainty becomes suspect; why not simplify and stabilize the process instead? Coordinators, expediters, and consultants look out of place; why not have the line organization do its own coordinating, compress production cycle times so that there is less need for expediting, and train one's own people to be experts?

The final unifying theme underlying manufacturing competitiveness is: *the centrality of continual learning and improving.* A firm's competitive position at the point in time a snapshot is taken of it is less important than its rate of improvement over time as compared with its competitors'. An important corollary is that if manufacturing competitiveness is a dynamic, rather than a static, process, the company's infrastructure must be dynamic as well. If its systems and policies become static, over time they will fail to reflect competitive needs. Production control systems, performance evaluation procedures, capital budgeting processes, and project management structures must all be developed with flexibility and improvement in mind.

This kind of ongoing improvement requires ever-increasing knowledge, of a scientific as well as a practical nature. As was discussed in Chapter 8, acquiring that knowledge through effective experimentation, problem-solving, and information transfer is a prerequisite for progressive and dynamic control. Learning about one's manufacturing process goes hand in hand with learning how to improve the effectiveness of one's product and process development projects. As we saw in Chapters 10 and 11, moreover, group learning is as important as individual learning. The cornerstone of such group learning is establishing honest interaction among functional peers at low levels in the organization.

Incorporating these four themes—

- management makes the difference
- a holistic perspective is essential
- customer value and competitive advantage should be relentlessly pursued
- continual learning and improvement is the objective—

and the principles embedded in them, into the very fiber of an organization's behavior leads to a pattern of structural and infrastructural decisions that is characteristic of what in Chapter 1 we described as a Stage IV organization. Over time they nurture the growth of superior organizational capabilities, ones that complement and extend, rather than constrain, one another. These capabilities form the basis for a truly sustainable competitive advantage.

Why Do Companies Find This So Difficult?

If the long-term consequences of failing to adopt these basic principles, of neglecting to rebuild one's manufacturing competitiveness, are so obvious, and so ominous (as described in Chapter 1), the methods for improving one's manufacturing and product development capabilities (Chapters 6 through 9, along with 10 and 11, respectively) so straightforward, and the benefits so substantial, why don't more companies begin to move in the directions we have been advocating? It is not that these approaches are untried or that their efficacy is unproven. On the contrary, literally hundreds of companies have followed some combination or variation of the ideas we have described here. Most of the elite Japanese companies that are proving so formidable in international competition have embraced them and transplanted them successfully to foreign subsidiaries. Many of the examples of enlightened practice that were provided in previous chapters involve American and European firms. These approaches, when applied with constancy of purpose, adequate resources, and full commitment from top management on down, have proven remarkably successful in company after company.

Nor is this paralysis due to a lack of understanding of the basic concepts and principles we have presented, or to an absence of experts who could help one understand and implement those principles. Literally dozens of authors have been advocating some combination of these ideas, often on the basis of successful firsthand experience. Their names are liberally sprinkled throughout the Notes and References for each chapter at the end of this book.

After observing literally hundreds of manufacturing organizations over the past two decades, we have concluded that this reluctance to change is due simply to the fundamental, wrenching, far-reaching transformations that are required throughout the enterprise. These transformations affect, most immediately and profoundly, the manufacturing function, but they go far beyond it. Changes must also take place within other functions, and in their relationships with manufacturing. Finally, even more difficult changes must be made in the way the corporation as a whole is managed. Its fundamental assumptions and organizing principles must be realigned. This demands a much greater magnitude of change than most organizations, and most individuals, have the stamina, commitment, and dedication to undertake. A number of obstacles must be overcome.

Obstacles Within Manufacturing

Within manufacturing itself there are three common obstacles. The first is the natural assumption that the changes being embarked upon are simply "another program" for manufacturing improvement. Over the past decade, every major company we have visited has adopted one or more programs aimed at improving its competitiveness (quality improvement, inventory reduction, productivity improvement, quality of work life, and so on). Unfortunately, these have tended to dull the senses of people at all levels, especially those in the factories. Senior managers act as if all that is required to implement a program, once defined, is to put somebody in charge of it and measure its results. Down at the factory level, however, both managers and workers usually respond with the attitude that "just like the other programs, this will pass and a different one will take its place next year. So we'll just wait it out." Operating under the assumption that nothing fundamental is going to change, since it never has in the past, they withhold support for everything except the most obvious immediate improvements.

The second obstacle arises out of the fact that, because of its size, complexity, and physical nature, fundamental changes in manufacturing take longer than those in any other part of a business. Yet, paradoxically, it is also under the greatest short-term pressure to meet daily delivery schedules and resolve operating crises. Manufacturing managers are typically so busy responding to these pressures and coping with problems that they have neither the time nor the resources to eliminate the causes of those problems and so prevent their recurrence. Thus, even if they wanted to support this new effort and had the skills and knowledge required to do so, they would still feel constrained by the all-consuming day-to-day deadlines and pressures of their jobs.

The third obstacle is the typical manufacturing organization's lack of experience in dealing with anything other than tactical operating issues. Most manufacturing managers who have come up through the ranks have learned that "getting the product out the door" is what counts. Thus, even if they had the time and the inclination to pursue the kinds of changes we have described in earlier chapters, they usually don't have the basic skills and knowledge required to do so.

Obstacles Within Other Functional Areas
Adding to the obstacles within manufacturing are those created by the other functions and organizational units with which manufacturing must work. Perhaps foremost is the second-class image of manufacturing that has built up in many companies over the years. The rest of the organization sees manufacturing as a constraint, not an asset. The repeated failure of a traditional manufacturing organization like factory A to keep its promises continually reinforces this negative image, undercutting manufacturing's efforts to improve itself.

Other obstacles are created by the advocates of easy answers. Increasingly impatient as the competitive pressure they are under (arising partly out of manufacturing's limited ability to support their efforts) intensifies, people outside of manufacturing tend to look for actions that promise quick relief. Thus, at the very point when external pressures might provide the energy needed to catalyze the organization's commitment to dramatic change, that energy gets deflected toward short-term palliatives. Instead of undertaking a long-term program for improving manufacturing, some will argue for reducing its impact by contracting out more activities, or moving them offshore.

Finally, the kinds of changes that we have been proposing profoundly change the nature of the power balance within a company. In most companies, moving to greater equality between functions implies a relative increase in the power of manufacturing. But in actuality, as we have pointed out, no organizational group loses power; they all gain through combining their power more effectively. The initial perception of other functional groups, however, is that because they are no longer as free to make decisions, unconstrained by consultation with or agreement from another group, they have lost a certain degree of freedom.

This perception is reinforced by the removal of status symbols within the company, as discussed in Chapter 9. People who have been given status—through perks, autonomy, or other means—are usually able to convince themselves that these are rightly deserved; their loss, therefore, becomes a sort of perceived punishment. Finally, as a different breed of manufacturing manager appears on the scene—more broadly qualified people who generally have much different expectations regarding compensation and authority—even these artifacts of relative importance are removed. Few groups take kindly to such a reordering of relationships.

Obstacles At the Corporate Level

At the corporate level, these changes face a whole host of additional obstacles: the infrastructure elements that we have been probing throughout this book. The internal restructuring that is required is likely to call for profound changes in the company's capital budgeting and resource allocation systems, the subject of Chapter 3; in its organizational structure, and the resulting roles of line and staff (Chapter 4); and in its performance measurement and accounting systems (Chapter 5).

Finally, and probably most important, there are the ingrained attitudes and behavior patterns that were discussed in Chapter 2. Today it is not uncommon to find companies that live or die on the basis of their manufacturing prowess being run by people at the top who have little direct experience with manufacturing itself. Many do not even have technical training. Growing up in an era when manufacturing lacked credibility, respect, and perceived opportunity, they chose advancement through other paths. Many of them, in fact, go so far as to attribute their personal success to their ability to minimize their company's dependence on manufacturing. Faced with a set of competitive challenges that are largely manufacturing-related, with which they are neither familiar nor comfortable, they are unwilling to change the approaches that have worked so well for them for so many years—and got them to where they are. They find themselves unable to comprehend fully the nature of the revolution that is occurring, or the necessity of their personally leading the change process. They behave like rabbits on the road, transfixed by the glare of the onrushing headlights.

Reinforcing the obstacles represented by senior managers who don't understand the true nature of the changes required to achieve manufacturing competitiveness are those created by the people they usually turn to for advice: their corporate staffs. The systems, procedures, and approaches that these groups have created seldom reflect the needs of an organization that wishes to develop a distinctive competence in manufacturing. In fact, as we pointed out in Chapter 4, even the corporate manufacturing staff, which is supposed to support and serve the line organization, typically responds primarily to the pressures and expectations of senior managers. Therefore it often comes to be viewed by the plant floor as disruptive and interfering, a source of problems and constraints rather than of solutions and support.

This description of the obstacles encountered by companies that choose to embark upon a dramatic and pervasive change in their manufacturing competitiveness may sound overly pessimistic, but it is very real. Time and again we have watched manufacturing managers who had decided to move in the direction we have outlined here get worn down, outflanked, and used up in the process. As a result they eventually begin looking around for other, less far-reaching changes that appear to be easier to implement. They are encouraged in this by others in the organization who feel threatened by more fundamental changes.

For example, if the organization is not facing an imminent crisis, sticking with the previous business-as-usual approach and simply "trying harder" can look more attractive than pursuing a disruptive change. Or, if a company decides to search around, it can almost always find some other company that is willing to be its supplier, taking on some portion of its manufacturing needs at lower cost and perhaps even better quality than it has been able to achieve itself. If a company's manufacturing problems are severe and deep-seated, turning them over to somebody else almost always provides a temporary feeling of relief.

Those firms that still feel some gut-level commitment to manufacturing, and are unwilling to subcontract it all, have the option of paring back and cutting fat—as well as, perhaps, a few ancillary appendages. Many managers have discovered in the last few years that once their manufacturing arm gets into enough trouble, this kind of cost cutting and organizational restructuring often produces dramatic and relatively quick results. Unfortunately, however, although the resulting manufacturing organization may end up leaner and more clearly focused, it usually continues to operate under the same principles and systems as before.

Thus, even though a comparison of before-and-after "snapshots" of the manufacturing position of a company that has adopted one of these easier-to-implement options may show dramatic improvement, seldom is any strategy put in place for building the capabilities that will prevent a recurrence of the same problems once the new snapshot begins to age. If the natural obstacles within the organization are not enough to block a firm's flirtation with the idea of becoming excellent at manufacturing, these alternatives, with their apparently quick payoffs, are usually able to do so.

Diagnosing One's Manufacturing Capabilities

A starting point for any serious long-term effort to improve the competitive contribution of a company's manufacturing organization is a realistic diagnosis of its current status, role, and capabilities. In this section we will describe several approaches, falling into two broad categories, to this kind of self-diagnosis. The first category is primarily introspective (internal) in nature, in that it attempts to link the observed patterns of behavior within manufacturing to the basic organizational and managerial principles that drive that behavior. The second consists of diagnostic tools that are externally oriented; their use provides an objective evaluation of the manufacturing organization's impact on the firm's overall competitive performance, and a comparison of its policies with those of its competitors. In the process a company may be able to assess the extent to which its future success is likely to depend on its manufacturing ability.

Internal Diagnostic Tools

At many points in preceding chapters, we have used dichotomies to describe the range of behavior that is observed in various aspects of manufacturing management. In some cases we argued that superior performance came from combining or balancing extreme positions. For instance, in Chapter 2 we contrasted the strengths and limitations of the analytical or scientific approach with those of the artisan approach and then emphasized the power of combining their strengths. In Chapter 3 we described several of the biases and blind spots in the traditional theory and practice of capital budgeting and suggested how strategic considerations might be incorporated to compensate for those weaknesses.

In other chapters, however, our recommendation was not to pursue a balance between extreme positions but rather to adopt one that represented what we referred to as the new paradigm. Thus, in Chapters 7, 8, and 9, the dichotomy between two different approaches to manufacturing architecture, control, and human resources was illustrated by describing a conventional factory (factory A) and a more effective one (factory B). In Chapters 10 and 11, we contrasted the conventional paradigm for managing new product and process development efforts with a new one that is based on a very different and, we argued, far superior set of principles.

We can combine the concept of the four stages of manufacturing, as described in Chapter 1, with these dichotomies by viewing them as defining a spectrum, one end of which is typical of Stage II manufacturing and the other of Stage IV. (We omit consideration of Stage I because few organizations rate themselves below the industry norm.) Recall that a Stage II manufacturing company seeks *external neutrality* by following the decision patterns in widespread use in its industry, so as to reduce the chances of being surprised and outdistanced by competitors. This typical industry practice is often closely akin to the behavior patterns exhibited by factory A, as well as to the conventional approach to product and process development projects.

At the other end of the spectrum, a Stage IV manufacturing organization plays an *externally supportive* role: it is more proactive, attempting to anticipate the potential of new manufacturing approaches and developing its capabilities prior to the appearance of opportunities for using them. Close, partnership-like integration with other functional groups and with customers is also indicative of Stage IV manufacturing. Factory B, whose architecture was designed to reduce complexity and eliminate waste, which was continually building its knowledge base and achieving ever-higher levels of control, and which was constantly enhancing the technical competence and problem-solving abilities of its people, is an archetypal Stage IV organization. The new paradigm for product and process development projects, with its emphasis on preproject planning, its team-based approach to project management, and its emphasis on ongoing improvement, is also very representative of Stage IV.

An organization can locate itself on this continuum by examining the policies it has adopted for each of the decision categories that define a manufacturing strategy (see Chapter 1). These categories are arrayed down the vertical axis of Figure 12–1, whereas the horizontal axis represents the continuum from Stage II through Stage IV. For each decision category, we indicate the decision patterns that typify Stage II and Stage IV behaviors.

Stage I and II companies tend to build general-purpose facilities, attempting to minimize costs and provide maximum flexibility, whereas Stage IV companies build facilities that are designed to give them a specific competitive advantage in a particular market. Early-stage companies favor general-purpose equipment purchased from outside equipment suppliers, often switching suppliers to take advantage of temporary price opportunities; Stage IV companies try to design a significant proportion of their own equipment, and tailor the equipment they do buy to fit the specific needs of their own process. They want better equipment, not "safe" equipment. Early-stage companies view direct workers as constraints and problems; their goal is to automate them out of their processes. Stage IV companies look upon workers as resources and problem solvers; they seek to develop their capabilities. The former use the term *hourly workers,* implying expendability, the latter use *associates,* implying partnership. The former are preoccupied with head count; the latter, with head content. Early-stage companies consider suppliers interchangeable and somewhat untrustworthy; Stage IV companies consider them valued long-term partners whose destinies are inextricably linked to theirs.

We have found Figure 12–1 to be an extremely powerful tool for

Figure 12-1   Assessing a Manufacturing Organization's Existing
Pattern of Decisions

Decision Category	Stage II	Stage IV
Capacity	lags demand; capital-request driven	matches or leads demand; capability driven
Facilities	general-purpose; static design	focused; evolving design
Process technologies	cost cutting; external sources	capability enhancing; internal sources
Vertical integration/ vendors	cost minimization; seek leverage over	provide capabilities; shared responsibility
Human resources	reduce skills; source of energy	develop competence; source of improvements
Quality	acceptance levels; police role	performance improvement; eliminate sources of errors
Production planning/ materials control	centralized; detailed shop control; uncertainty accommodating	decentralized; closely linked; uncertainty reducing
New product development	sequential; over-the-wall handoffs	parallel activities; interactive team
performance measurement and reward	detailed measurement of individual contribution	focus on total organization's performance
Organization/ systems	fragmented; staff coordinates	integrated; line responsibility; staff supports

assessing a company's existing decision patterns and identifying the underlying principles that drive its behavior. Although individual firms may want to modify the descriptors attached to each end of the various continua, most find them quite representative. Experienced manufacturing managers tend to be surprisingly consistent in assessing where their organization falls on the continuum for each decision category. They have a good sense of what is really going on in manufacturing, both in their industry and within their own organization, and they tend to be coldly objective in describing how key manufacturing decisions are made in their company.

In contrast, managers outside of manufacturing (including upper-level general managers) tend to display much less consistency when asked to assess their company's manufacturing capabilities and policies. Many have trouble even identifying the decision patterns followed by their manufacturing organization, since they are involved in them only sporadically, and know even less about how their competitors address those same issues. Furthermore, they tend to overrate their organization in areas that have been the target of recent improvement efforts, whereas manufacturing managers appear to be more realistic in recognizing the difference between what is and what one would like there to be.

Two other diagnostic tools are useful in seeking to understand a firm's current position and the magnitude of the changes that it faces if it wants to become a Stage IV manufacturer. One of these is an assessment of how individual managers within manufacturing allocate their time. In a Stage II organization, as shown in Figure 12–2, the bulk of that time is typically spent dealing with day-to-day operating challenges—essentially coping with the tactical aspects of manufacturing. This tends to be true for both lower- and upper-levels of factory management. In a Stage IV manufacturing environment, on the other hand, a significant portion of the time of those at the superintendent level and above is spent on strategic concerns; even department managers and supervisors spend some time on such issues.

It should be kept in mind, when contemplating Figure 12–2, that what a Stage IV manufacturing organization's managers consider strategic is often quite different from what is considered strategic in a Stage II organization. A Stage II firm tends to regard only decisions that have a major financial impact as being strategic: constructing a new facility, making versus buying a certain component, and so forth. For a Stage IV organization, on the other hand, any long-term effort—even of a tactical nature—that is directed at enhancing its capabilities and providing value to its customers is viewed as strategic.

A third way to assess manufacturing's role is to ascertain whether it actively contributes to the development of a company's competitive strategy or simply reacts to the plans developed by other functional groups. Although the ends of the spectra shown in Figure 12–3 may require some modification to reflect the situation at any

Figure 12-2 Assessing Manufacturing Managers' Use of Their Time

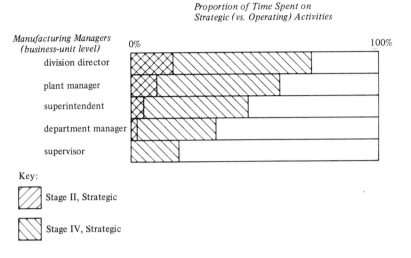

*Proportion of Time Spent on
Strategic (vs. Operating) Activities*

Manufacturing Managers
(business-unit level)

division director

plant manager

superintendent

department manager

supervisor

Key:

Stage II, Strategic

Stage IV, Strategic

particular firm, this approach can provide further insight to complement the other diagnostic tools described above.[1]

A company can also reveal its stage of manufacturing competitiveness by the way it reacts to declining profitability and tougher competition. Earlier in this chapter we alluded to an implicit, and ultimately self-defeating, course of action that many manufacturing
companies in high-wage countries have been following in recent
years. Let us now examine how such a policy often plays its way out
over time, eventually forcing the company to exit a business:

1. It becomes increasingly unwilling or unable to meet the ever-
   more-demanding requirements of its customers.
2. It subcontracts out those things (usually the more difficult or
   the more capital-intensive things) that it can no longer do prof-
   itably.
3. Such subcontractors, often using lower-cost labor, are required
   (and often trained) to meet the organization's quality and dependability standards.
4. They are also encouraged to expand their capacity in anticipa-
   tion of future business; this additional capacity subsequently
   allows the buyer firm to contract out further work.
5. If the company's own capacity utilization drops below a certain
   level or the output of one or more items falls below the point
   where its own manufacturing operations become uneconomic,
   it pulls business away from its subcontractors.

Figure 12-3   Assessing Manufacturing's Role in the Business

Stage II Role	Stage IV Role
1. Functional Involvement in Business-Unit Strategy	
Business unit strategy is based on information and issues provided by one dominant function.	Business-unit strategy is based on information and issues provided by all functions.
2. Functional Knowledge and Use of Business-Unit Strategy	
Centralized knowledge of business-unit strategy is maintained in dominant function and at high levels. Lack of integration of functional strategies with business unit strategy.	Broad, clear communication of business-unit strategy across functions and organizational levels. Deliberate integration of functional strategies with business unit strategy.
3. Source of Competitive Advantage	
Competitive advantage determined by competence in one dominant function. Investment in capabilities is primarily in the dominant function.	Excellence is pursued in all functions by conscious development of capabilities in each. Source of competitive advantage changes over time.
4. Functional Communication and Decision Making	
No cross-functional communication on strategic or operating issues. All functional decisions dictated by requirements of the dominant function.	Numerous cross-functional project teams. Constant formal and informal interaction to resolve strategic and operating issues.
5. Level of Benefits	
Benefits are unequal and highest in the dominant function.	Benefits are relatively equal across all functions.
6. Cross Functional Movement and Training	
Talent concentrated in the dominant function. Little lateral movement or training across functions.	Talent is developed and located in all functions. Frequent lateral movement and cross-functional training.
7. Composition of General Management	
General managers come from the dominant function. Source is constant over time.	General managers come from several functions; composition changes over time.

6. To protect its declining profitability, it holds up a price umbrella that makes it attractive for its former subcontractors (which have been left with unused capacity) to become competitors.

7. The buyer firm begins to emphasize higher-priced, higher-margin products, either leaving the volume segments to its new competitors or purchasing these high-volume products from subcontractors and selling them under its own label.

8. Finally, realizing that it no longer has any special manufacturing expertise, it is forced to begin subcontracting the higher-priced products as well.

This scenario is distressingly familiar; in fact, it is the natural one for a Stage II manufacturing firm to follow. It is totally unnatural, however, to a company whose manufacturing organization has achieved Stage IV. Thus, the nature of the strategy that a company follows, implicitly or explicitly, often reflects its underlying assessment of its manufacturing capabilities and opportunities.

External Diagnostic Tools
We have found two external diagnostic tools to be useful complements to the internal ones just described. These external diagnostics attempt to establish the link between a business unit's manufacturing capabilities and its overall competitive performance. They also reflect the extent to which it has been able to translate its manufacturing capabilities into a competitive advantage.

The first is linked directly to the competitive priorities that a company has set for itself. As outlined in Chapter 1, the most important dimensions of competitive differentiation are low-cost, high-quality (performance), dependability, flexibility, and innovativeness. An assessment of a manufacturing organization's capabilities along each of these dimensions can provide an understanding of the nature of the contribution it is making to the company's overall success in the marketplace. In Chapter 5 we described ways to calibrate an industry's position on each of these dimensions, and how a company's performance compares with that calibration. Figure 12–4 depicts three of the competitive patterns that this kind of assessment often reveals. The top panel depicts an organization whose manufacturing function is in a catch-up mode: It is failing to meet customer expectations across a broad front and finds that its performance along all five dimensions is inferior to its primary competitors'. Such a manufacturing organization will come under pressure to make major improvements simultaneously on all five dimensions.

The middle panel of Figure 12–4, by contrast, is a snapshot of a company whose manufacturing organization is both strong and "in sync" with its business strategy. Having chosen to emphasize flexibility and innovativeness in its competitive strategy, for example, this company's manufacturing group has developed superior capabilities in these areas and is better than most of its competitors. In the three areas of cost, product performance, and dependability, it is not only within the acceptable range as defined by industry standards but near the high end of that range. This company is in an "attack" mode, looking to strengthen its current advantage and build new ones.

Figure 12-4 Assessing a Company's Manufacturing Position on Competitive Priorities

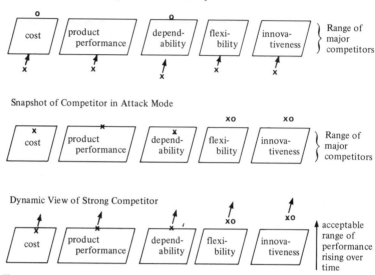

Key:
   x in-house manufacturing capability
   o business strategy emphasis

The bottom panel of Figure 12–4 reflects the dynamics at work in most industries today: the acceptable range of performance for all five criteria, as defined by industry competitors and customer expectations, is continually rising over time. Thus, an organization that simply maintains its current capabilities will eventually find them to be below the acceptable range. The companies that can prevail in such an environment will have to work continually to strengthen their capabilities and performance along all five dimensions. The old adage, "Even if you're on the right track, if you slow down you're liable to get run over," is applicable to this situation.

If a business unit starts by defining the acceptable range for each of these criteria in its industry, focusing particularly on the one or two criteria that are emphasized in its competitive strategy, it becomes relatively easy to compare the performance of its own manufacturing organization both against the requirements of its competitive strategy and against its major competitors. Such an assessment can also indicate how rapidly each criterion's acceptable range, as well as one's manufacturing capabilities, have been shifting over time.

The second external diagnostic tool is based on an evaluation of a company's overall business performance over an extended time horizon. Short-term performance measures tend to reflect the vagaries of business cycles and other transient phenomena, but long-term performance is generally the result of an organization's basic underlying capabilities and capacity for improvement. The best performers in many industries achieve performance far beyond that of the average firm in their industries, just as the best factories in the study described in Chapter 6 outperformed by 50 to 100 percent some of their sister factories within the same company. In fact, the best firms in industries that are generally considered unattractive often outperform the average firms in so-called attractive industries.[2] Not only do they achieve significantly better performance over the long term, but the fluctuations in their year-to-year performance tend to be less. The breadth and depth of their capabilities imbue their overall performance with a robustness that is the envy of their weaker competitors.

Using a variety of diagnostic tools to assess a manufacturing organization's role within its company, and the overall contribution it is making to competitive success, has several benefits. First, it establishes an agreed-upon base from which to launch a major program of change, making it possible to track progress and compare it against the goals set. It also helps top managers understand the depth and pervasiveness of the changes required to move from a lower stage to a higher one. In addition, it spotlights the areas needing the most dramatic improvements and provides information about the approaches that other companies have followed. Finally, it begins to focus the organization's attention on the potential value of converting a manufacturing organization that is at best neutral in its contribution to corporate success to one that can provide a strong competitive advantage.

Getting Started

A management team can follow a variety of paths in launching an effort to enhance the competitive contribution of its manufacturing organization. Virtually all those we have observed fall into one of three categories; in this section, we explore each of these categories, describing their strengths and limitations and how each relates to the diagnostic tools discussed earlier. Then we identify some of the common elements that characterize the more successful efforts that we have observed. Finally, we describe one such program, focusing particularly on the changes made in the organization's infrastructure.

Separable Manufacturing Projects

By far the most common approach that companies have taken in attempting to improve their manufacturing competitiveness is to focus on a subarea of manufacturing activity that offers significant opportunity for improvement. One might address an area of major weakness that can be worked on at a local level, such as high work-in-process inventory, excessive factory overhead, or even an under-performing plant. Or one might pursue a major untapped opportunity. For example, returning to Figure 12-1, if an organization felt that it was significantly deficient in one particular decision category, it might select that category as its starting point. Building the problem-solving capabilities of one's personnel or improving vendor coordination and cooperation are examples of this type of project.

Another place to start is with an issue that is targeted for corporatewide attention, across all factories and business units. We have seen several major companies designate quality or productivity improvement as a way to start focusing more attention on manufacturing. Each factory then is asked to develop its own projects for improving that designated area. Finally, one might use a major pending decision, such as the purchase of an expensive new piece of equipment or the implementation of a new production scheduling system, as a way of getting started.

Such separable manufacturing projects are relatively easy to implement because they are wholly contained within manufacturing, are limited in scope (they are usually aimed at improving the performance of an individual factory unit), and can be carried out by local teams. Not only can they lead to improvements at the grass roots in individual manufacturing units, but the people involved are encouraged to develop new skills. These projects often become an organization's initial tests of some of the ideas presented in this book.

On the other hand, there are also several disadvantages associated with employing such limited projects as a starting point. One is that they tend to be viewed as "manufacturing only" projects. Thus, they fail to have much impact on the behavior of others in the organization, and their diffusion throughout the company tends to be slow.

Because of their limited nature, moreover, they do not force the company to reassess its underlying manufacturing assumptions and their impact on the bottom line is often hard to detect. Worse, although such projects are sufficiently challenging that they usually succeed in holding the interest of the people at the operating-unit level for many months, without significant bottom-line impact they tend to lose the attention of more senior managers. Therefore, unless upper-level managers become really committed to them as a matter of principle, they tend to lose visibility in the organization.

Developing a Strategic Plan for Manufacturing
As defined in Chapter 1, a manufacturing strategy consists of a pattern of decisions relating to the different elements of a manufacturing organization's structure and infrastructure (see Figure 12–1). Developing a comprehensive strategic plan of action for manufacturing requires that a company identify its previous decision patterns, compare those patterns with the demands of the competitive strategy it has chosen, and target those areas that are most in need of change. Then it must initiate activities that will eliminate the inconsistencies between the current patterns of decisions and the desired ones. This process provides another approach to kicking off a major effort to improve manufacturing competitiveness.

This approach has particular appeal where one or more senior manufacturing managers want to be involved personally in improving the competitive contribution of their manufacturing organization. Since few managers have much experience with formulating a manufacturing strategy, it is often necessary to preface this effort with a management development program whose objective is to implant the necessary concepts and principles firmly in the minds of those who will be involved in preparing the plan. Although typically dominated by senior manufacturing managers, the development of a long-term manufacturing plan often benefits from the involvement of managers from other functions that interact closely with manufacturing. Such people can provide a useful perspective when assessing the manufacturing organization's status and role in the company, and how well its capabilities match the business unit's competitive priorities.

The real weakness of this approach is that the plan is generally prepared without broad involvement of those who must implement it. In most of the cases we have observed, the senior managers who developed the manufacturing plan were not heavily involved in executing it; they simply turned over a set of recommendations to their subordinates. Although such a top-down sequence fits many managers' image of how manufacturing ought to be managed, it is unlikely either to implant the desired principles or make the fundamental changes required throughout the organization.

Businesswide Demonstration Projects

A third approach is to tackle a major project, high on the business unit's agenda, that requires cooperation from all the functions. A good example of such a project would be the development and introduction of a new product or the design and construction of a new factory. The goal of this approach is to demonstrate to everybody how the different functions can work together in Stage IV fashion, with the hope that this kind of experience will encourage changes in operating procedures and strategic direction so that the entire organization moves toward Stage IV. This approach works particularly well in situations where a senior manager wants to achieve dramatic results and can put together an interfunctional team that has the skills and resources required to carry out the project.

All too often, unfortunately, the rest of the organization tends to regard such demonstration projects as "exceptions," discounting their results and failing to learn from them. Since the project team is usually freed from many of the organization's conventional systems (such as those used for capital budgeting, performance measurement, and bonus awards) while the project is under way, the benefits of such projects will be ongoing only if permanent changes are subsequently made in those systems. Once a demonstration project has been declared successful, however, the people involved in it tend to get promoted and move on quickly; the last thing they want to do is stick around and work on improving systems and procedures. As a consequence, within a relatively short time the company tends to forget what it learned and regresses back to where it was before the project was initiated. Thus, even if the project is successful at achieving Stage IV behavior for a short period of time, the business unit generally finds it difficult to transfer that behavior to its day-to-day activities.

Putting Together a Comprehensive Effort

Whichever type of approach is used as a starting point for improving manufacturing competitiveness, our experience suggests the necessity of linking those initial efforts to an ongoing and expanded program that incorporates a set of common elements. First, one should identify a set of *tools and techniques* to assist those involved in the effort, such as the diagnostics outlined in Figures 12–1 through 12–4. Other examples include the framework for analysis built around the four levels of control discussed in Chapter 8 and the functional maps of Chapter 10. These tools and techniques help capture the experience of other organizations and facilitate new modes of communication within the company.

Second, one should initiate an *education and development* program. Whether it simply provides instruction on using the aforementioned tools or is a more ambitious effort to develop the strategic skills of those in manufacturing, a systematic educational effort can provide significant dividends. We know of companies that have established three- to five-year training programs for providing various organizational levels with the skills needed to improve their manufacturing competitiveness. These programs include attendance at university courses, in-house training programs, regular off-site working sessions, and preplanned job rotations.

Third, one must ensure *corporate-level support*. Although such support is no substitute for line-management initiative, it can supplement the line organization in important ways. For example, it can articulate and communicate basic principles and a sense of their importance throughout the entire business.[3] Getting the corporate staff to adopt a common set of tools can provide the advantages of standardization and facilitate the sharing of information across organizational units. In addition, corporate staff personnel can help educate senior managers about the manufacturing improvement programs that have been put into place, and encourage their support.

Fourth, one must establish *an extended time horizon*. No organization can reach its full strategic potential in manufacturing until its manufacturing managers understand their strategic role, have gained experience in that role, and have learned to work closely with the rest of the organization in developing it. A substantial improvement in a manufacturing organization's competitive contribution usually requires a minimum of three years.

Fifth, one or more key line managers must be encouraged to serve as *program champions*. Although the support of top management is critical, we have yet to see a substantial improvement in a manufacturing organization where at least one champion did not step forward to spearhead the effort. These people should have "fire in their bellies"; they must believe in the potential payoff that can result and be willing to tie their personal careers to their organization's success in achieving that payoff. A good champion will attract and develop others, until a cadre of such people are leading the charge.

The important thing is to get started. Choose an approach—or, better, some combination of all three of the approaches we outlined earlier (separable manufacturing projects, comprehensive manufacturing planning efforts, and businesswide demonstration projects)—and push forward. Don't spend a lot of time trying to figure out where to begin; just do something. Unfortunately, this is not as simple as it ought to be, because there is a roadblock in every company that almost invariably rises to impede progress. That roadblock is the organization's infrastructure: its systems, practices, and policies.

These infrastructural elements drive individual decisions in a certain direction, for good or ill. In Chapters 7 through 9, for example, we saw the tremendous impact that reducing complexity, eliminating waste, and developing problem-solving skills and self-discipline could have on the flows of information and materials through a factory. If the infrastructure that drives the factory's behavior fails to support or reward such policies, however, it is unlikely that individual actions and decisions at the floor level will reflect them. As another example, in Chapter 5 and earlier in this chapter we argued that the measures used to evaluate a business unit's performance should both reflect the competitive advantage it is pursuing and allow it to compare itself with competitors. If a company's measurement system does not reflect this principle, neither will the decisions and actions that are based on information provided by it.

Old habits are as tough to break for organizations as for people. The whole purpose of a factory's infrastructure should therefore be to make "doing the right thing" the easiest thing to do. Changing the infrastructure is essential if, in the words of one manager, a manufacturing organization is to "overcome the tyranny of the status quo."

As systems become more and more complex and inflexible, changing them becomes increasingly difficult. Therefore, when attempting to overcome the obstacles created by hostile systems, one should make sure that the new systems created to replace them are as simple, streamlined, and flexible as possible. Line managers and line operators must be able to understand and adapt them as the need arises. Just as systems provide a means of institutionalizing the continual improvement of operations, so must they also be continually renewed and improved.

H-P's plant in Vancouver, Washington (see Chapter 7), provides a useful case history of an organization that has been following this kind of change process. That facility, which employs over 500 people, makes six different models of printers for computer work stations. These fall into two product families, each with its own technology. The manufacturing process used to make both families is quite similar, however: components are first installed onto printed circuit boards, and these are then assembled with other components to form the final product. H-P Vancouver chose to begin the improvement of its manufacturing competitiveness by working on a series of small incremental manufacturing projects, as summarized in Figure 12-5. Over a twelve- to eighteen-month period, these projects expanded to include worker involvement, production scheduling, and information and material flow patterns.

Once they had achieved considerable progress in these areas, Vancouver's manufacturing managers turned their attention to some of

Figure 12-5 H-P Vancouver: Pursuing Stage IV Manufacturing

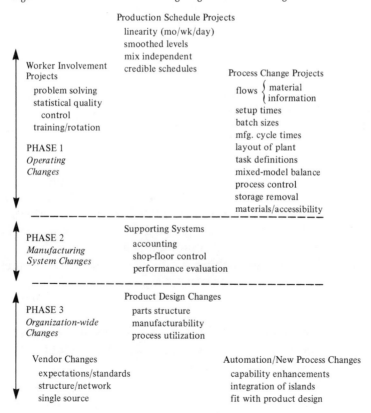

the infrastructure elements that were hindering further progress, particularly its cost accounting system (which tracked costs as items moved into and out of inventory), shop floor control (which focused on detailed reporting of the exact work that had been done), and performance evaluation (which emphasized individual contributions). They wanted an accounting system that tracked material movements into and out of the entire factory, not just into and out of inventory. They moved from reactive control of their manufacturing process to preventive and progressive control. Finally, they wanted a performance evaluation system that was group oriented. Most of the manufacturing managers involved in this effort found that changing these systems was much more difficult, both behaviorally and conceptually, than making the earlier improvements in the factory. This was partly because such systems were the responsibility of groups other than manufacturing, and partly because these line managers lacked experience at making such changes.

Once those new systems were in place, however, it became possible for H.-P. Vancouver to move to a third phase: implementing the type of improvements described in Chapters 10 and 11. Today, the plant operates under a demand-pull production schedule—which extends back to several major nearby suppliers. No centralized stocks are held; the only inventory in the plant is on the production line. As a result, the plant's inventory-to-sales ratio has improved by a factor of almost four, and the floor space required has been cut in half. Labor productivity has improved by 50 percent, and there has also been a substantial improvement in the reject rate (the production line is immediately stopped whenever a quality problem is detected).

Less tangible, but just as important in the eyes of plant management, is the development of a "new" methodology that encourages continual improvement in cost and quality. This methodology enables the manufacturing group to integrate its activities better, so that new products get up and running much faster than before, and with fewer bugs. As one senior plant manager put it, "As you eliminate the number of questions that have to be asked every time a problem arises, you find you can get to a good solution much sooner than you did before."

This increased competence, in turn, has led to improved relationships and interactions with other functions. This is where the real payoff from manufacturing competitiveness comes. Rather than devoting all its energy to fighting fires and shoring up weaknesses, a company can focus on strengthening its competitive advantage. Unfortunately, too few firms make it to this third phase, tending to stall out when confronting the need to change the corporate infrastructure.

The Role of Management in Manufacturing Competitiveness

Throughout this book we have stressed again and again the critical role that management plays in fostering manufacturing competitiveness. Although at times we have addressed ourselves primarily to manufacturing managers, our intended audience is much broader; manufacturing organizations, and manufacturing managers, simply can't make the transition required all by themselves.

Perhaps the role that top management has to play in transforming an average manufacturing company into one that is world-class will be clearer if we consider reversing the process. Suppose that you, the reader, have just been made CEO of a highly successful manufacturing company: profits and sales are growing, facilities and equipment are modern and well-maintained, the capabilities and commitment of workers and managers throughout the organization and their ability to work together harmoniously are the envy of your competitors. Productivity, quality, production throughput times and new product and process development cycle times are continually improving. Your mission, as stated by the board of directors that selected you, is to drive that organization back to Stage I or II status within ten years, to cause its productivity growth to stagnate, its inventories to mount up, its quality to deteriorate, and its new product and process development to slow to a crawl. A huge bonus (not, fortunately, in the form of company stock!) and pension await you if you are successful. How would you proceed, given such a charter?

You might consider beginning by altering the systems for measuring the performance of people and operating units so that they focus only on short-term financial results. Ignore any consideration of human-resource training and development efforts, quality and work-in-process inventory levels, experimentation that leads to new capabilities, or other soft measures of performance. Then you might divide up the organization into many small, highly independent organizational units and encourage competition among them based on the aforementioned performance measurement systems. Require that the same measuring stick be used when evaluating the performance of all your plants, whether they be old or new, whether they produce lots of new products (or small volumes of replacements parts) using manual production processes, or highly automated ones for making large volumes of proven products: the same profit-to-sales ratio or return on investment, say. Give large bonuses and recognition to the units that come out on top, according to those measurements, over short time periods (a calendar quarter, say, or at most a year).

To further reduce the natural communication and attempts at coordination that go on in any organization, encourage the development of strong boundaries between organizational units, particularly functional groups. If somebody is a manufacturing person, make sure that he or she stays in manufacturing; once an engineer, always an engineer. Reinforce this policy by prohibiting any sort of training program that would equip anybody to move into another function or into general management. Insulate lower-level managers from strategy considerations as much as possible by making these the responsibility of staff groups and senior managers. Then drive your point home periodically by taking a person who has been carefully sheltered from such broadening experiences and give him or her a significant managerial responsibility. When they fail, note in passing (in some forum where it will be heard and passed on quickly) that "engineers don't make good managers." Instead, turn your attention to training your accountants and financial analysts to be managers.

Then, as part of your promotion and hiring decisions, favor people who do not have technical backgrounds or direct manufacturing experience. Encourage your general managers to delegate key manufacturing decisions to specialists, either within manufacturing or, preferably, in outside consulting firms. Similarly, reduce expenditures on R & D, instead purchasing "proven" technology from outside organizations. Now that your manufacturing organization has been relieved of much of its responsibilities and need for expertise, you can safely reduce salaries and head count and staff it with less competent people. To ensure that they do not chafe in this restricted role, choose those with limited career aspirations. Since such people tend to be narrowly interested in such tactical issues as inventory management, production scheduling, quality control, and so on, you can safely turn your attention to more strategic issues that require the long-term perspective that only high-level managers can now provide.

Split up your clusters of technological expertise and assign the resulting fragments to market-oriented divisions that are under continual pressure to increase their sales and profits. Change the top managers in these divisions frequently, so that they will tend to avoid committing themselves to long-term R & D projects that are unlikely to produce attractive returns in less than five to ten years. Encourage your technical people to work, instead, on narrow extensions of the current product line and short-term productivity improvements.

Spend less on new equipment and facilities than you did in the past. Require that any such investment be carefully scrutinized by your financial staff and meet strict financial criteria. Favor locations in low-wage areas, particularly those several thousand miles away. To reduce the risk that any such investment entails, favor proven general-purpose equipment whose primary purpose is to reduce the number of skilled people in your organization. Even though it may not be at the leading edge of technology, it is safe and can be shifted to other purposes if its original use disappears. Eliminate immediately any group that is dedicated to building your own production equipment, as this is better left to the equipment supplier firms that service a broad range of customers (including most of your competitors).

Discourage long-term relationships with parts and equipment suppliers. Always ask, What have you done for me lately? To keep them on their toes, offer them short-term contracts for small pieces of your business, and change them frequently. Do not give them any confidential information, as they are likely to pass it on to your competitors.

Any time some part of the system that you have set up misfunctions or shows signs of a lack of proper coordination, set up a new staff group whose job it is to coordinate, expedite, or police the work of other line and staff groups. Since these are critical jobs, promote the best people out of your line organization into them.

Finally, since the organization is running so well without your continual involvement, turn your attention outside, to major, highly visible ventures such as acquisitions or mergers. Or sell off one or more of your divisions. This will be both personally exciting and will prevent you from getting entangled in day-to-day operating details. It will also provide a challenge for the small army of financial experts that you have assembled to run your financially dominated control systems and then promoted into higher positions because of their broad understanding of the company.

If the foregoing sounds like a plausible set of recommendations, given the stated objective, look around you and compare them with what many companies have actually been doing over the past three decades. Then consider that moving in the opposite direction—from Stage II to Stage IV—is likely to require even more time and even more top management involvement if it is to be similarly effective. Destroying capabilities is always easier than creating them. Moreover, moving toward Stage IV will not require just a change in approach or a simple adjustment of managerial priorities. In many companies it is likely to require a whole new generation of managers.

A few years ago we used to hear a common complaint from manufacturing managers: "Top management doesn't understand me. They don't understand the pressures I operate under, the constraints I have to deal with, or the limited resources that I can wield. If only they would give me the authority and resources I need, I could achieve the goals they set for me." Today we hear a very different complaint from many top managers: "My manufacturing managers don't understand me. They don't understand the seriousness of the competitive situation we're facing, or the magnitude of the improvements we have to make if we're going to be able to survive in the years ahead. I tell them, 'Let me know what your ideas are, and what additional resources you need.' But all they come back with is more of the same approaches. They don't seem to realize that a new situation requires new approaches."

What has happened is that over the past thirty years or so, as we described in Chapter 2, companies have tended to choose a certain kind of person to manage their manufacturing organizations. They acted on the assumption that if the manufacturing process had been carefully set up, staffed, and equipped, all that was needed was a group of caretakers to keep everything running smoothly and in good condition. Worse, they favored a high level of specialization, to the point where many factories today resemble the overly specialized academic institutions that Emerson railed against 150 years ago, staffed with people who "strut about like so many walking monsters—a good finger, a good neck, a stomach, an elbow, but never a man." Today, however, these companies are beginning to realize that they need something more than caretakers and specialists. They need architects and generalists: people who can pull out a fresh sheet of paper and design a totally new system.

The problem is that it is not easy to convert caretakers into architects. It takes a long period of training, and a whole new set of expectations and rewards. It probably will also require some new people, people who are more like the giants who established, in the first half of this century, most of the manufacturing systems now in common use. Where are companies to find people like that today? Probably in a variety of places—but not necessarily within their manufacturing organizations or in the places where they have been accustomed to looking for manufacturing managers in the past few decades.

One way to measure the extent of the change, and therefore the kind of manager, that is required is in terms of *breadth*. Within manufacturing, changes are required in performance measurement, production control, plant layout, information and material flows, human-resource management, and technology management. Comparable changes are required in those areas that interact closely with manufacturing, such as vendors and suppliers, design engineers, marketing and sales, and customer service. These changes reach into every corner of the organization, touching all its activities.

Although the breadth of the changes required is extensive, the *depth* of the change is perhaps even more challenging. It is not enough simply to change the actions and decisions made in these diverse areas of the firm's activities. The systems that determine and drive those actions must also be changed, and that means that the principles underlying those systems must be reformulated. A cultural revolution is necessary, one that requires many organizations to unlearn much of what they long considered core values and replace them with a new set of values.

A third way to measure the amount of change required is the *time span* required to achieve it. Pursuing manufacturing advantage is a long-term process that takes persistent incremental effort—a neverending journey. Lots of base hits are more effective than a few home runs; it is a game that tortoises are better at than hares. In many manufacturing organizations, short-term issues are those that must be addressed before lunch, those that can be dealt with "sometime this week" are medium-term, and those that can be delayed for a few months are regarded as long-term. To accomplish the kind of changes that we have been describing requires that one adopt at least a three- to five-year perspective. Making such a shift in time horizon, while continuing to operate in an environment that almost daily presents one with new competitors, new technologies, new legal constraints, and new customer demands, requires tremendous commitment.

As if the breadth, depth, and time span of this change were not enough, the logic and concepts embodied by it are radically different as well. Building a competitive advantage is not based on defending an existing product or market position but on learning and building distinctive capabilities throughout the organization. Products, markets, facilities, and other aspects of an organization's position at any given point in time must be viewed as simply a static snapshot that reflects these underlying capabilities. Management's attention must shift from conventional measures of competitive advantage to others that are even more difficult to define, measure, and pursue: the ability to learn, improve incrementally, and work together across functions at low levels.

Finally, the driving force that most organizations have come to rely on for direction and motivation—that from external customers, competitors, and suppliers—is usually inadequate to push the organization to accomplish these changes. In fact, total reliance on external sources of pressure will often cause an organization to compromise its pursuit of real manufacturing excellence. Instead, the organization must develop and come to depend on internal forces, provided by managers and workers within the organization, as much as on external pressures. Everybody in the organization has to internalize the principles we have described, work to make them successful, and link their own individual success to the success of the change process.

Making this happen requires leaders, not just administrators and controllers: people who can (1) provide a long-term vision of manufacturing's potential contribution; (2) become a source of energy that moves the organization toward that long-term vision; (3) provide focus and direction so that the vision remains clear and energy is not sidetracked by short-term problems; (4) set clear expectations for results that are to be obtained and use those results to further focus and energize the organization; and (5) act as the protector and the champion of Stage IV principles.

Unless an organization understands these principles thoroughly and is committed to them, it is likely to begin compromising them under the press of events. Our experience suggests that companies seldom maintain their commitment unless a critical mass of top managers act as "defenders of the faith." In every case where we have seen a company build a manufacturing organization that was clearly superior to those of its competitors, one or more key managers have been credited with establishing the bedrock principles underlying that superiority and with leading their implementation throughout the organization.

Conclusion

Many companies seem to believe that the solution to their competitive problems lies in better strategic planning. But there is little evidence that strategic planning has been very helpful to American industry, despite the resources that have been poured into it over the past twenty years. Today, most large American firms engage in some form of (usually annual) strategic planning process; many have set up their own internal strategic planning departments staffed with high-caliber, highly paid experts. A whole new industry—the strategy consultant—has emerged to service those companies that have not; its annual revenues today exceed half a billion dollars. Some firms, in an attempt to cover all bases, use both internal and external experts.

Keeping in mind the fact that the whole purpose of strategic planning is to help a firm get from where it is to where it wants to be, and in the process develop a *sustainable* advantage over its competitors, it is therefore somewhat puzzling to observe that a growing number of U.S. industries and companies (among them many that have devoted the most thought and resources to strategic planning) find themselves today more vulnerable competitively than when they started. Not only have they fallen short of the goals they set for themselves; they find themselves falling behind competitors, largely of foreign origin, who place much less emphasis on strategic planning. How can companies that impose upon themselves the discipline of modern strategic planning and employ its sophisticated techniques end up worse off than when they started?

The answer, we propose, is that the strategy that many American and European manufacturing companies have actually been following is quite different from those they claim to have adopted. That strategy, stripped to its essentials, is the following:

1. Make essentially the same products as your best competitors, and introduce new products at about the same rate;
2. Use essentially the same manufacturing equipment and approaches as they do;
3. Employ workers and managers who have equivalent skills and motivation as theirs; and
4. Pay your workers and managers substantially more than they pay theirs.

That, in starkest terms, is a losing strategy. A company doesn't usually lose everything right away, of course; it may be able to stave off the inevitable for a while by cutting costs, adopting creative accounting practices, siphoning off money from other, more profitable activities, or soliciting government protection or subsidization in various ways. But over the long run all the water will get squeezed out of the stone, the company's accountants will run out of ways of counting something that doesn't exist, its other bills will come due, and the government will decide that it is a hopeless indigent and cut it off the dole.

The irony is that the fathers and grandfathers of these companies' managers—even though they didn't talk as much about strategic planning—understood the futility of that "high-wage imitator" strategy very well. America and northern Europe have had high wages, relative to the rest of the world, for over fifty years. Their industrial leaders long knew that the only way for a high-wage country to win against low-wage opponents was either to

1. Make different, and better, products than one's competitors', and be able to develop them in less time;
2. Utilize more sophisticated manufacturing equipment and techniques than one's competitors, or
3. Increase the capabilities and motivation of one's workers and managers to the point where they can coax more or better output from their equipment than one's competitors can.

(Actually, it's more "and" than "or" because, as we have discussed in earlier chapters, designing and producing better products or using more advanced equipment almost inevitably requires better-skilled personnel.) The alternative is to reduce salaries until one becomes a low-wage country oneself—which is what has been happening, in effect, in the United States for over fifteen years.

The severe competitive problems that America's steel industry has faced in recent years did not arise out of the fact that it pays higher wages than do steel companies in other countries. U.S. steelworkers have been the highest paid for over fifty years. Instead, that industry is having problems today because it started losing its technological edge in steelmaking over the rest of the world in the late 1960s, and its work force thereupon lost its skill (and resulting productivity) advantage.

Similarly, America's semiconductor industry is not in crisis today because Japan suddenly erected import barriers. Until fairly recently, in fact, Japanese companies were among the biggest customers of American-made ICs. But over the last ten years the United States fell behind Japanese companies on all three fronts—products, processes, and human resources—in certain product sectors, even though it literally invented the industry. How can American producers expect to sell 256K DRAMs in Japan when they have largely dropped out of that market? How can they overcome the Japanese cost advantage when they are buying manufacturing equipment that is produced by the same Japanese companies that are their fiercest competitors?

Since the winning strategy is so obvious, one would expect that most American manufacturing companies would be following it. If they were, the evidence would be clear:

1. If the United States were again taking the lead in product innovation, its companies would be spending more on industrial (nonmilitary) R & D than anybody else, and managers from around the world would be coming to study the approaches American companies use to compress product development cycles and increase the rate of product innovation. Instead, both Japan and Germany spend more on industrial R & D, as a percentage of sales or GNP, than does the United States. And American managers visit Japanese companies to learn how, in the same industry, they are able to bring out new products so much faster and cheaper, following the approaches described in Chapters 10 and 11.

2. If American companies were again the leaders in manufacturing technology, managers from around the world would be visiting them to tour the world's most automated factories, to study the latest manufacturing management approaches, and to see the world's most advanced FMS, CIM, and robotics systems. American products would be the highlights of the annual manufacturing equipment trade fairs. Instead, American managers now go to Germany and Japan to see the latest equipment—both at their trade shows and in their factories. They marvel there at totally automated facilities, whirring untended in the semidarkness. And they bring back such Japanese imports as just-in-time production control, parts-per-million defect levels, and single-digit setup times—the kinds of approaches we described in Chapters 6 through 8.

3. If American companies were again taking the lead in human resource and management development, managers from around the world would be coming to study their approaches to employee motivation, their selection and training practices, and their innovative worker-manager relationships (see Chapter 9). Instead, American

managers go to Europe and Japan to study their approaches—and come back shaking their heads and muttering that "it won't work here." Then they watch Japanese companies establish subsidiaries, employing many of these same approaches, on American soil.

Why, if Japanese companies enjoy the advantage of lower labor costs, are they moving ahead so rapidly in product and process innovation and management approaches? Because they understand the nature of a winning strategy in international competition, just as American companies once did. The low-cost countries that they worry about, however, are Korea, Taiwan, and Singapore, who are trying to do to them what they did to the United States. If the managers of U.S. companies want to regain their position in world markets, at some point they will have to redirect their energies from complaining about high labor costs and unfair trade practices (which are probably both better, in comparative terms, than they were thirty years ago) to addressing the real problems. When they do, their counterparts in other countries will soon let them know if they've succeeded: they will start visiting American factories again.

And even if they do succeed, even if companies make the kind of changes we have proposed, it will not mean that they have won the competitive battle. They will simply be back in the game. Long-term success is not the same as simple survival—increasingly difficult though that may be. It requires developing an organization that can build and continually renew its competitiveness in all functions, not just in manufacturing. It means creating and sustaining the learning organization.

Appendix A

Analyzing Manufacturing's Financial Impact on the Profitability of the Firm

The approach we outline here has its roots in the well-known Du Pont Formula, which allows one to decompose the return on investment achieved by a given business unit into its component revenues, costs, and assets.[1] The traditional Du Pont Formula (described in Figure A-1) implicitly downplays the impact of fixed costs on profitability. Since the interaction between a manufacturing unit's fixed costs and its production volume is critical to its profitability, however, we have modified the formula somewhat to incorporate fixed costs more directly. The key variables used in this analysis are shown in Figure A-1, and defined as follows:

1. *profit contribution:* the average selling price of the product(s) produced, less the costs that vary with production over the time period being considered:

    Profit contribution = selling price − purchased materials
    − variable conversion costs

2. *fixed costs:* the costs that will not (or cannot) be changed during the same time period, regardless of the production volume achieved; these include both the interest charges incurred on the capital invested in the facility and an amount reflecting the change in the facility's economic value over the time period (which is not always the same as the depreciation that is calculated for tax purposes)

3. *capacity:* the sales level that could be achieved if the facility were operating at the limit of the resources available to it during the same time period

Figure A-1   Interrelationships of Common Ratios

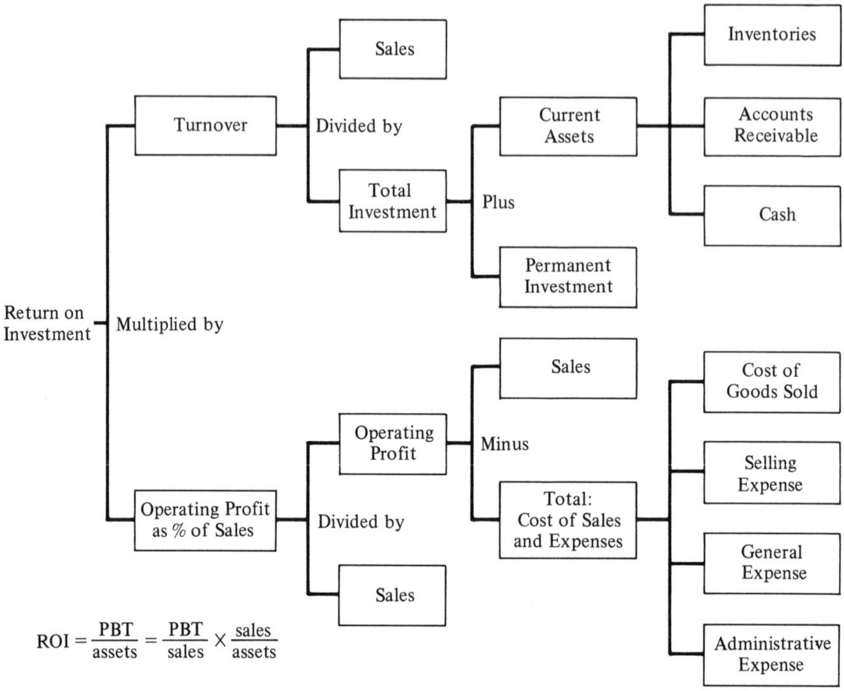

$$ROI = \frac{PBT}{assets} = \frac{PBT}{sales} \times \frac{sales}{assets}$$

SOURCE: From Erich A. Helfert, *Note on Financial Analysis,* 9-206-047 (Boston: Harvard Business School, 1960). Reprinted by permission.

4. *assets:* the amount of investment required to support this capacity

From these basic values we can construct five derived measures:

1. *percent contribution* (% contr.): the total profit contribution before tax (for all products produced by the business) divided by the total sales revenue from those products

2. *profit before tax* (PBT):

   PBT = (sales)(% contr.) − fixed costs

3. *break-even level* of sales (B-E sales); the level of sales revenue at which the business would just cover its fixed cost of operation:

   B-E sales = (fixed costs)/(% contr.)

4. *capacity utilization* (cap.util.):

   Cap.util. = sales/capacity

5. *sales-to-assets* ratio (sales/assets)

The business's return on investment before taxes can now be expressed in terms of these component and derived measures. We begin with the basic relation between asset intensity and the profit margin on sales:

$$\text{ROI} = \left(\frac{\text{PBT}}{\text{assets}}\right) = \left(\frac{\text{PBT}}{\text{sales}}\right)\left(\frac{\text{sales}}{\text{assets}}\right).$$

We can break this down further by expressing the profit margin on sales in terms of contribution, break-even sales, and utilization.* The expression for ROI thus becomes

$$\text{ROI} = \frac{\text{PBT}}{\text{assets}} = \%\ \text{contr.}\left[1 - \left(\frac{\text{B-E sales}}{\text{capacity}}\right)\left(\frac{1}{\text{cap.util.}}\right)\right]\left(\frac{\text{sales}}{\text{assets}}\right)$$

In a sense, the percent contribution measures the raw profitability of each sales dollar; the ratio of break-even sales to capacity measures the inherent profit potential of the facility (a low value indicates a high profit potential), the capacity utilization measures the degree to which this profit potential is being tapped, and the sales-to-assets ratio reflects the effectiveness with which investment is converted into capacity and sales.

*Since

$$\text{PBT} = (\%\ \text{contr.} \times \text{sales}) - \text{fixed costs}$$

then

$$\frac{\text{PBT}}{\text{sales}} = (\%\ \text{contr.})\left[1 - \left(\frac{\text{fixed cost}}{\%\ \text{contr.}}\right)\left(\frac{1}{\text{sales}}\right)\right]$$

$$= (\%\ \text{contr.})\left[1 - \left(\frac{\text{B-E sales}}{\text{capacity}}\right)\left(\frac{\text{capacity}}{\text{sales}}\right)\right]$$

Appendix B

The Measurement

of Total Factor Productivity

The concept of total factor productivity, introduced in Chapter 5, provides a means of measuring the overall performance of a factory (or department or other productive unit) in transforming a variety of inputs into products. In this appendix we describe an approach for calculating TFP and illustrate its application.

To begin, suppose that we wish to determine whether the overall productivity of the process that transforms labor, material, capital, and energy into a single product (call it product A) has increased or decreased. To do this, we begin by calculating the product's total factor productivity:

$$\text{TFP}_A = \frac{\text{output of product A}}{\text{sum of the resource inputs}}$$

As was pointed out in Chapter 5, to calculate the sum of the resource inputs, we have to combine inputs measured in different units: labor-hours, pounds, machine-hours, or BTUs. One obvious approach is to use the monetary values of each resource or output. In fact, replacing physical units with monetary values solves (at least partially) a number of perplexing measurement problems that plague the simple definition of productivity that is based on physical quantities. For example, how can we measure the *real* output of a product whose characteristics are changing over time?

Consider the automobile. Over the past fifty years, its size, weight, horsepower, safety, and efficiency have all fluctuated widely. Many items that used to be options are now standard. Therefore, measuring output simply in terms of the number of units produced is clearly not appropriate. The same is true of medical care: the quality of care provided today is generally acknowledged to be far superior to that available fifty years ago. Again, measuring output simply in terms of "patient days" ignores these qualitative differences.

One solution is to utilize either the sales price or the manufacturing cost (in real terms—that is, adjusted for inflation) of the product as an implicit measure of its capabilities and quality. The product's "output," therefore, would either be equal to its sales revenue or its total cost. Unfortunately, a product's price is affected by a number of other factors besides quality differentials, so it is not a perfect surrogate. Nor is manufacturing cost. Although cost reflects the usage of resources, it only captures quality changes if the new version of the product consumes more resources. So neither approach is without flaws, but either is usually better than using unit data without correcting for changes in product characteristics.

The use of monetary values also makes it possible to estimate changes in the quality of the different resources consumed in production. The labor-hours utilized in producing a given product, for example, are contributed by people possessing a variety of skills, ranging from the relatively unskilled workers at the loading dock to highly skilled tool-and-die makers and process engineers. As companies make changes in their production processes, the mix of these skills usually changes. Therefore, the raw number of labor-hours used does not adequately reflect the level and mix of the skills contained in those labor-hours. An obvious way to reflect those skills is to weight them by the wage rates of the various persons who contribute them.

Calculating Total Factor Productivity

An example may help to illustrate the kind of calculations required when monetary values are used to measure productivity. To keep matters as simple as possible, we will consider one product, and only three of the inputs utilized in making it: raw materials, energy, and labor (later we will include the effect of capital resources). We assume that we have data on physical units and prices of output and the inputs. Our first set of calculations, shown in Table B–1, expresses values of output and inputs in base-period prices. Here we use the most recent period (period 2) as our base period.

This calculation provides measures of output and input that are not affected by price changes. This allows us to examine how the

Table B-1 Calculation of Unit Values in Base-Period Prices: Product A (thousands)

	(A) Units		(B) Base (period 2) Prices	(C) = (A) × (B) Inputs and Outputs in Base-Period Prices	
	Period 1	Period 2		Period 1	Period 2
Output	58.17	61.95	$2.00	$116.34	$123.90
Inputs:					
materials (lb)	4.478	4.650	$10.00	44.78	46.50
energy (kwh)	240.53	246.70	$0.03	7.22	7.40
labor (hrs)	6.51	7.02	$5.00	32.55	35.10
Total input	—	—		$84.55	$89.00

performance of the factory changed in real terms between periods 1 and 2. In Table B–2 (p. 382) we calculate the productivity of each input, as well as the productivity of all inputs taken together (TFP).

In Table B–2 the productivity of each input in a period is calculated by dividing that period's output by the value of the inputs used, all in base period prices. The total factor productivity is similarly calculated: output divided by the sum of all input values. These data show that the productivity of materials and energy increased from period 1 to period 2, but the productivity of labor declined. Had our measurement system only focused on direct labor, we might have concluded that the factory's efficiency in producing A had deteriorated. However, the net effect was an increase in TFP of 1.16 percent.

We can also calculate the impact of productivity changes on *profitability* changes, as shown in Table B–3 (p. 383).[1] Columns A and B (which give actual values) indicate that profits increased by $4.0 million between period 1 and period 2. To estimate how much of that change was due to price changes, how much to changes in volume, and how much to productivity growth, we first calculate two additional columns. Column C contains period 1 values in period 2 prices, taken from Table B–1. This tells us what profits would have been if period 1's outputs and inputs had been experienced at period 2 prices. The difference between actual profit in period 1 ($30.8 million) and the estimated profit (column C: $31.79 million) indicates that profit increased by $0.99 million simply because of changes in prices.

The next step is to determine the impact of volume changes. Column D suggests that real volume (at period 2 prices) increased by 6.5 percent between period 1 and period 2. If productivity had not changed between those periods, all inputs would have increased by that same percentage. In column E we apply that output growth ratio (column D) to period 1 values expressed in period 2 prices. The result, in column E, tells us what output and inputs would have been if both prices and volume had changed but productivity had remained constant: profits would have been $33.85 million. The difference between columns C and E—$2.06 million—therefore is the impact that the increase in output volume alone had on profit. The impact that better productivity had on profit is therefore the difference between the total change in profits and the sum of the price and volume effects ($4.0 − $0.99 − $2.06 = $0.95). The results are summarized in Table B–4.

Table B-2 Calculation of Total Factor Productivity: Product A

	Unit Values in Base Period Prices		Productivity Ratios (output/input)		Productivity Growth Rate (%)
	Period 1 (A)	Period 2 (B)	Period 1 (C)	Period 2 (D)	[(D/C)−1]×100 (E)
Output	$116.34	$123.90	1.00	1.00	—
Inputs					
materials	44.78	46.50	2.598	2.665	2.58
energy	7.22	7.40	16.114	16.743	3.90
labor	32.55	35.10	3.574	3.530	−1.23
Total input	$ 84.55	$ 89.00	1.376	1.392	1.16

Table B-3 Calculating the Impact of Productivity on Profits: Product A

| | Actual Values | | Period 1 Values in Base Period Prices | Real Growth in Output (123.90 ÷ 116.34) | Implied Equivalent Physical Usage in Period 2, at Period 1 Productivity |
	Period 1 (A)	Period 2 (B)	(C)	(D)	(E) = (C) × (D)
Output	$110.70	$123.90	$116.34	1.065	$123.90
Inputs					
materials	$ 43.40	$ 46.50	$ 44.78	1.065	$ 47.69
energy	6.40	7.40	7.22	1.065	7.69
labor	30.10	35.10	32.55	1.065	34.67
Total input	$ 79.90	$ 89.00	$ 84.55	1.065	$ 90.05
Profit	$ 30.80	$ 34.80	$ 31.79		$ 33.85

Table B-4   Change in Profitability: Product A (millions)

From price changes	$0.99
From volume changes	$2.06
From productivity changes	0.95
Total change	$4.00

Issues in Implementing the TFP Approach

The calculations we have presented in this appendix are based on a simple example. Although similar approaches have been applied to real (and more complex) situations, there are a number of issues that often need to be addressed before that is possible. We present a brief summary here; for a more detailed discussion see the references in footnote 8 to Chapter 5.

Confusion with Traditional Accounting Concepts

Attempts to implement productivity accounting in many companies often lead to confusion. Much of this confusion is due to the apparent similarity between the productivity measures that we have defined and the variety of related measures that are part of traditional accounting systems. For example, many companies routinely compare the amount of the resources actually used in producing a given volume of a certain product to what should have been consumed had preestablished standards been achieved. The resulting efficiency ratios, as they are commonly called, are different from the productivity ratios that we have defined.

To illustrate, suppose that ninety-three hours were required to produce a certain product during a given week, and ninety-six hours would have been required if the "standard" labor-hours per unit had been achieved. The efficiency ratio for labor during this period would therefore be 96/93 = 1.032, or 3.2 percent better than standard. This would be equal to our single factor (labor) productivity growth rate only if the standard-hours figure was based on the actual hours during the preceding week.

Similarly, many companies maintain accurate records of the usage of various key pieces of equipment and calculate the percentage of the time that they are being utilized. Such utilization ratios are often incorporated into performance measurement systems and considered measures of "efficiency" because they relate, in a rough sense, to the efficiency of the managers and the systems that scheduled them. This source of confusion would disappear if the concept of utilization were clearly differentiated from that of productivity.

Choice of Base Period

The approach that we have followed uses prices in a base period (in our case, period 2) to weight output and input. Another approach, called the Laspeyres method, uses a beginning period as the base. If the base period is several years in the past, substantial changes may have occurred in the quality of products or in technology; the use of the Laspeyres method might therefore introduce distortion into the calculations. As a result, most companies prefer to use the approach (called the Paasche method) used in this Appendix, where the most recent period is used as the base. The calculations performed in either approach are essentially the same, but the Paasche method uses data that are likely to be more accurate and credible to managers, particularly if major changes have occurred between the beginning and ending periods.

Use of the Paasche method does not do away with the need to take quality changes into account, however. When the price of a product changes, we still need some way to estimate what part of that change is due to a change in the product and what part to a change in the general inflation rate. Only the latter part should be factored out: otherwise, an increase in product quality would not show up as an increase in "real" output.

Measuring Capital Inputs

The cost of the capital tied up in a production system is an important component of total cost, but estimating its contribution to total factor productivity raises complicated problems. Most of them have to do with the fact that, unlike labor-hours or materials (which disappear, once consumed), capital represents a *stock* of assets. This stock is used over and over again as goods flow through the system and are replaced by other goods. To make capital costs comparable with labor and material costs, we must measure the value (in real terms) of the *flow* of capital services in each period of time. A variety of different approaches to this problem have been proposed (see footnote 8 to Chapter 5 for references); we will only illustrate the one we used in the study described in Chapter 6, which we found worked reasonably well.

The first step is to calculate the gross (book) value of capital in base-period prices. (Experts disagree as to whether gross value or net value should be used; we prefer the latter, as do most managers.) Table B–5 presents an example, using data on the actual value of machinery purchased in different years, and a machinery price index that reflects changes in machine capacity and performance. The plant in question was opened in 1985, and depreciates its equipment over 20 years on a straight line basis.

To simplify this calculation we have assumed that all investment takes place at the beginning of the year and is depreciated over the course of the year. The net value of the capital equipment in place in 1988 was $120,460, expressed in 1988 dollars. To transform this into an estimated flow of capital services we multiply it by the plant's cost of capital (adjusted for the rate of inflation). This reflects the implicit annual cost to the plant of a dollar of capital stock. Using a cost of capital of 12.5 percent, we can apply these estimates of capital costs each year to our earlier example (see Table B–2). Table B–6 (p. 388) restates the TFP calculation with 1988 as period 2. Notice that taking capital into account has led to an increase in the previous estimate of the rate of productivity growth.

Product Mix

By focusing our attention on the production of a single product, we have been able to avoid the impact of changes in the sales mix of several products. A monetary measure of the firm's total output that does not correct for changes in the product mix may lead to distorted productivity values because shifts to higher-priced (or higher–value-added) products can easily lead to the conclusion that productivity has increased. Fortunately, the approach we use here (in which units of output are weighted by a base-period price) will take mix changes into account when applied to a factory with multiple outputs. However, when a new product enters the mix, one must exercise care when choosing what price to assign to the new product. For example, if the cost of the product is expected to decrease substantially as production experience is gained, the initial cost of a new product may not reflect its true value. One may instead want to use an estimate of the long-run expected price that will exist when the product's cost begins to bottom out.

Scale Effects and Technological Change

Our calculations have assumed that the ratio of output to variable inputs, such as direct labor and material, is the same no matter what

Table B-5 Calculating the Value of the Stock of Invested Capital

	Value of Machinery Purchased (thousands)	Price Index (1988 = 1.00)	Value of Purchases in 1988 Dollars (thousands)	Total Gross Machinery Value in 1988 Dollars (thousands)	Cumulative Depreciation in 1988 Dollars (thousands)	Total Net Machinery Value in 1988 Dollars (thousands)
	(A)	(B)	(C) = (A) ÷ (B)	(D)	(E)	(F) = (D) − (E)
1985	$100.00	0.847	$118.06	$118.06	$ 5.90	$112.16
1986	12.00	0.888	13.51	131.57	12.48	119.09
1987	10.00	0.938	10.66	142.43	19.60	122.83
1988	5.00	1.00	5.00	147.43	26.97	120.46

Table B-6 Total Factor Productivity with Capital Input Included

| | Unit Values in Base Period Prices | | Productivity Ratios (Output ÷ Input) | | Productivity Growth Rate (in percent) |
	1	2	1	2	
Output	$116.34	$123.90	1.00	1.00	—
Inputs					
materials	44.78	46.50	2.598	2.665	2.58
energy	7.22	7.40	16.114	16.743	3.90
labor	32.55	35.10	3.574	3.530	−1.23
capital	15.35	15.06	7.579	8.227	8.55
Total input	$ 99.90	$104.06	1.165	1.191	2.23

the production level. However, many processes use proportionally less of certain inputs as output expands, a phenomenon referred to as economies of scale. Yet most productivity calculations, for want of a better approach, ignore this critical aspect of production. Building it into our calculation would require that we estimate a curve specifying the ratio of inputs to output at each production level of each product in the firm's product line. Otherwise, the effect of changes in production levels (or changes in the product mix) would be confounded with productivity changes.

Technological change presents additional problems of interpretation. Although it is helpful to know the changes that have occurred in TFP, it is difficult to disentangle the changes that are due to more efficient utilization of existing technologies from those that are due to the introduction of new technologies. Yet the expectation of long-term productivity improvement is based largely on the assumption that more effective product designs and process technologies will gradually supplant existing products and processes. Hence, even though companies will be able to learn important things about the amount and causes of productivity change by following the approaches described in this appendix, they may be misled by the apparent precision of the resulting numbers unless they flesh out their understanding with a considerable amount of informed judgment.

Notes

CHAPTER 1. Rebuilding a Manufacturing Advantage

1. Karen Pennar, "The Good News We're Waiting for May Never Come," *Business Week,* August 18, 1986, p. 85.
2. "The Anderson Bombshell," *The Rosen Electronics Letter,* March 31, 1980, pp. 3–5.
3. David Garvin, "Quality on the Line," *Harvard Business Review,* September-October 1983, pp. 64–75.
4. Kasra Ferdows, Jeffrey G. Miller, Jinichiro Nakane, and Thomas E. Vollmann, "Evolving Global Manufacturing Strategies: Projections into the 1990s," *International Journal of Operations and Production Management* 6(4) (1986), 6–16.
5. J. D. Powers and Associates, "1986 Customer Satisfaction Survey," Los Angeles, 1987.
6. "The Bad News Behind the Capital Investment Surge," *Business Week,* March 4, 1985, p. 20.
7. *Advanced Processing of Electronic Materials in the United States and Japan: A State-of-the-Art Review Conducted by the Panel on Materials Science of the National Research Council* (Washington, DC: National Academy Press, 1986).
8. *Report on International Industrial Competitiveness* (Geneva: The European Management Foundation, November 1986).
9. See, for example, Robert H. Hayes and William J. Abernathy, "Managing Our Way to Economic Decline," *Harvard Business Review,* July-August 1980, pp. 67–77.
10. Remarks by Roger B. Smith at the Annual Dinner of the Advertising Council, New York, November 20, 1986.
11. See, for example, Steven Prokesch's report, "Flak After Darman's Speech," *The New York Times,* November 11, 1986, pp. D1 and D4.
12. Robert D. Buzzell and Mark J. Chussil, "Managing for Tomorrow," *Sloan Management Review,* Summer 1985, pp. 3–14.
13. Robert H. Hayes and Steven C. Wheelwright, *Restoring Our Competitive Edge: Competing Through Manufacturing* (New York: John Wiley, 1984).

14. John Maynard Keynes, *The General Theory of Employment* (New York: Harcourt, Brace, 1936), pp. 161–62.

CHAPTER 2. The Lessons of History

1. According to testimony before the British Parliament in 1868, the American worker "readily produces a new article; he understands everything you say to him as well as a man from a college in England would; he helps the employer by his own acuteness and intelligence; and, in consequence, he readily attains to any new knowledge, greatly assisting his employer by thoroughly understanding what is the change that is needed, and helping him on the road towards it." See "Report from the Select Committee on Scientific Instruction, Parliamentary Papers," citied in Nathan Rosenberg, ed., *The American System of Manufacturers: The Report of the Committee on the Machinery of the United States, 1855* and *Special Report of George Wallis and Joseph Whitworth, 1854* (Edinburgh: Edinburgh University Press, 1969), p. 15.

2. This account is drawn primarily from two articles in the *Wall Street Journal:* "Turnabout in Fortunes of Mesta Machine Is History. With a Moral," January 3, 1984; and "Foreign Competition, Labor Costs Helped Sink Mesta Machine," January 4, 1984.

3. This quote and other material in these pages were taken primarily from Frederick Taylor's testimony before Congress in 1912. See U.S. Congress, House of Representatives, "Hearings Before Special Committee to Investigate the Taylor and Other Systems of Shop Management." Reprinted from Harper & Row edition, 1947 (Westport, CT: Greenwood Press, 1972). Also available (Washington, DC: Government Printing Office), vol. 3, p. 1394ff.

4. See "George Eastman and the Coming of Industrial Research in America" by Reese V. Jenkins, quoted in *Technology in America: A History of Individuals and Ideas,* ed. Carroll W. Pursell, Jr. (Cambridge: MIT Press, 1981), p. 136.

5. For additional insight into this issue, see Robert H. Hayes and Steven C. Wheelwright, *Restoring Our Competitive Edge: Competing Through Manufacturing* (New York: John Wiley, 1984), Chap. 13; and Robert H. Hayes, "Strategic Planning—Forward in Reverse?" *Harvard Business Review,* November-December 1985, pp. 111–19.

6. For background on Edison and his laboratory, see Thomas P. Hughes, "Thomas Alva Edison and the Rise of Electricity," in C. W. Pursell, Jr., ed. *Technology in America* (Cambridge: MIT Press, 1981), pp. 117–28.

7. See Chap. 10, "The Meaning of Time," in *Today and Tomorrow* by Henry Ford in collaboration with Samuel Crowther (New York: Doubleday, Page, 1926).

8. Shigeo Shingo, *Study of Toyota Production System* (Tokyo: Japanese Management Association, 1981), pp. 138–45.

9. The vignettes in this section are taken from Donald Nelson, *Arsenal of Democracy: The Story of American War Production* (New York: Harcourt, Brace, 1946), pp. 225–26, 260–68; and Christy Borth, *Masters of Mass Production* (New York: Bobbs-Merrill, 1945), pp. 170–205.

10. See William Green, *Famous Fighters of the Second World War* (New York:

Hanover House, 1957), and Frank Taylor and Lawton Wright, *Democracy's Air Arsenal* (New York: Duell, Sloan and Pearce, 1947).

11. Green, *Famous Fighters,* p. 98.

12. See "Creating Japan's New Industrial Management: The Americans as Teachers" by Kenneth Hopper, in *Human Resource Management,* Summer 1982, pp. 13–34; and Ghary Gappelberg, "'CCS' and Modern Japanese Management: The Influence of American Management Concepts on the Japanese Communications Industry, 1945–1950" (Unpublished senior thesis, Harvard University, March 1986).

13. Hopper, *Human Resource Management,* p. 23.

14. George G. Hyde, *Fundamentals of Successful Manufacturing* (New York: McGraw-Hill, 1946); see pp. 18–20, 31, 42, 44, 72, and 85.

15. Hopper, *Human Resource Management,* p. 23.

16. See "Chief Executive Background and Firm Performance" by Philip Jarymiszyn, Kim B. Clark, and Lawrence H. Summers, in *The Uneasy Alliance,* eds. Kim B. Clark, Robert H. Hayes, and Christopher Lorenz (Boston: Harvard Business School Press, 1985), pp. 115–36.

17. Margaret B. W. Graham, "Industrial Research in the Age of Big Science," *Research on Technological Innovation, Management and Policy,* vol. 2 (Greenwich, CT: JAI Press, 1985), pp. 47–79.

18. See Michael J. Gent, "Theory X in Antiquity, or the Bureaucratization of the Roman Army," *Business Horizons,* January-February 1984, pp. 52–56.

CHAPTER 3. Thinking Long Term: The Capital Investment Process

1. See, for example, J. Fred Weston and Eugene F. Brigham, *Essentials of Managerial Finance* (Hinsdale, IL: Dryden Press, 1977).

2. For a perspective on how this system worked at one large, diversified U.S. company, see Joseph L. Bower, *Managing the Resource Allocation Process* (Boston: Division of Research, Harvard Business School, 1970).

3. For additional information see "The Super Project" (Boston: HBS Case Services, Harvard Business School), 9-122-034.

4. For additional information see "Carborundum, Inc." (Boston: HBS Case Services, Harvard Business School), 9-672-131.

5. For an analysis of irreversibility in economic terms, see Claude Henry, "Investment Decisions Under Uncertainty: The 'Irreversibility Effect,'" *American Economic Review* 64 (December 1974), pp. 1006–12, which uses the example of demolishing the cathedral of Notre Dame and replacing it with a parking lot. Another perspective is provided by Colin W. Clark, in "The Economics of Overexploitation," *Science* 181 (1981), 630–34, which examines the possibility of irreversible overexploitation of a renewable resource.

6. As related in Bela Gold, "The Shaky Foundations of Capital Budgeting," *California Management Review* 19(2) (Winter 1976), pp. 51–60.

7. See, for comparison, the use of these terms in a somewhat different context by T. Burns and G. M. Stalker, *The Management of Innovation* (London: Tavistock Press, 1961); also T. Kagano, I. Nonaka, K. Sakakibara, and A. Oku-

mura, "Mechanistic vs. Organic Management Systems: A Comparative Study of U.S. and Japanese Firms," Discussion Paper 116, Hitotsubashi University, Tokyo (September 1983).

8. See Robert S. Kaplan, "Must CIM Be Justified by Faith Alone?" *Harvard Business Review,* March-April 1986, pp. 87–97.

9. See Marc Ross, "Capital Budgeting Practices of Twelve Large Manufacturers," *Financial Management,* Winter 1986, pp. 15–22. An arithmetic example of the problems this creates is contained in Harold Bierman, Jr., and Jerome E. Haas, "Are High Cut-offs a Fallacy?" *Financial Executive,* June 1973, pp. 90–91.

10. Kaplan, "Must CIM Be Justified by Faith Alone?" p. 94.

11. There is growing evidence that this gap is not as large as commonly supposed, if all the pertinent factors have been included. See William Osterberg, "The Japanese Edge in Investment: The Financial Side," *Economic Commentary of the Federal Reserve Bank of Cleveland,* March 1, 1987.

12. Additional discussion of this point is contained in Robert H. Hayes and David A. Garvin, "Managing as if Tomorrow Mattered," *Harvard Business Review,* May-June, 1982, pp. 71–79.

13. For additional information see "Great Lakes Diversified Corporation: The Detroit Plant" (Boston: HBS Case Services, Harvard Business School), 9-679-121.

14. For further discussion of this important issue, see Stewart C. Myers, "Finance Theory and Financial Strategy," *Interfaces,* January-February 1984, pp. 177–88; and W. Carl Kester, "Today's Options for Tomorrow's Growth," *Harvard Business Review,* March-April 1984, pp. 153–60.

15. For another discussion of vineyard economics in a different context, see Reiul Shinnar and Meir Shinnar, "Which Bottom Line?" *Chemtech,* July 1978, pp. 418–23.

CHAPTER 4. Organizing the Manufacturing Function

1. For further information on the issues raised in this section, see Paul R. Lawrence and Jay W. Lorsch, *Organization and Environment: Managing Differentiation and Integration* (Boston: Harvard Business School Press, 1986), which uses the term "differentiation" in place of "specialization"; James Thompson, *Organizations in Action* (New York: McGraw-Hill, 1967); Gene Dalton and Paul Lawrence, *Organizational Change and Development* (Homewood, IL: Irwin, 1970); and Allan Cox, *The Cox Report on the American Corporation* (New York: Delacorte Press, 1982).

2. See Alfred D. Chandler, Jr., *The Visible Hand* (Cambridge: Harvard University Press, 1977).

3. Arthur Schlesinger, Jr., "Bureaucracy and the Republicans' Businessmen," *Wall Street Journal,* January 7, 1981.

4. Much of the material in this section has been adapted from Robert H. Hayes and Roger W. Schmenner, "How Should You Organize Manufacturing?" *Harvard Business Review,* January-February 1978, pp. 105–18.

5. See Wickham Skinner, "The Focused Factory," *Harvard Business Review,* May-June 1974, pp. 113–21.

CHAPTER 5. Measuring Manufacturing Performance

1. See Thomas H. Johnson and Robert S. Kaplan, *Relevance Lost: The Rise and Fall of Management Accounting* (Boston: Harvard Business School Press, 1987).

2. More complete descriptions of the development of the modern cost accounting system are contained in Johnson and Kaplan, *Relevance Lost;* Robert H. Parker, *Management Accounting: An Historical Perspective* (New York: Macmillan, 1969); and Alfred D. Chandler, Jr., *The Visible Hand* (Cambridge: Harvard University Press, 1977).

3. For example, see Charles Horngren, *Cost Accounting: A Managerial Emphasis* (Englewood Cliffs, NJ: Prentice-Hall, 1977); Robert N. Anthony and James S. Reece, *Management Accounting Principles* (Homewood, IL: Irwin, 1975); and Robert S. Kaplan, "Accounting Lag: The Obsolescence of Cost Accounting Systems," in *The Uneasy Alliance: Managing the Productivity-Technology Dilemma,* eds. Kim B. Clark, Robert H. Hayes, and Christopher Lorenz (Boston: Harvard Business School Press, 1985).

4. A concise example of this approach is contained in Neil C. Churchill and John K. Shank, "Managing Against Expectations (A): A Note on Profit Variance Analysis" (Boston: HBS Case Services, Harvard Business School), 9-176-182.

5. More detail is provided by Robert H. Hayes and Kim B. Clark, "Exploring the Sources of Productivity Differences at the Factory Level," in *The Uneasy Alliance: Managing the Productivity-Technology Dilemma,* eds. Kim B. Clark, Robert H. Hayes, and Christopher Lorenz (Boston: Harvard Business School Press, 1985).

6. For a more complete exploration of this issue, see Robin Cooper and Robert S. Kaplan, "How Cost Accounting Systematically Distorts Product Costs," in *Field Studies in Management Accounting and Control,* eds. William J. Bruns, Jr., and Robert S. Kaplan (Boston: Harvard Business School Press, 1987).

7. See Robert S. Kaplan, "Measuring Manufacturing Performance: A New Challenge for Managerial Accounting Research," *The Accounting Review* 63(4) (October 1983), pp. 686–705; and Kenneth A. Merchant and William J. Bruns, Jr., "Measurements to Cure Management Myopia," *Business Horizons,* May-June 1986, pp. 56–64.

8. There is a large and rapidly growing literature on various approaches to measuring productivity. For a representative sampling, see John W. Kendrick and Daniel Creamer, "Measuring Company Productivity," *The Conference Board Studies in Business Economics,* no. 89 (1965 ed.); *New Developments in Productivity Measurement and Analysis: Studies in Income and Wealth,* vol. 44, eds. John W. Kendrick and Beatrice N. Vacarra (Chicago: University of Chicago Press, 1975); C. E. Craig and C. R. Harris, "Total Productivity Measurement at the Firm Level," *Sloan Management Review* 14(3) (1973), pp. 13–29; and James Mammone, "Productivity Measurement: A Conceptual Overview," *Management Accounting,* June 1980, pp. 36–42.

9. We have left out the productivity of working capital because it must be treated differently, as described in Appendix B. There it is also shown how one can extend this analysis to determine how much of the change in profits between

period 1 and period 2 is due to price changes, how much is due to volume changes, and how much is due to productivity changes.

10. This point is provocatively made by Wickham Skinner in "The Productivity Paradox," *Harvard Business Review,* July-August 1986, pp. 55–59.

11. The information for this comparison was drawn from public sources and from interviews with managers and engineers in the industry conducted by a team of M.B.A. students—Gary King, Mary Ng, and Tom Saxe—under the direction of one of the authors.

12. See Frances Tucker, Seymour Zivan, and Robert Camp, "How to Measure Yourself Against the Best," *Harvard Business Review,* January-February 1987, p. 8.

CHAPTER 6. The High-Performance Factory

1. For additional information about this study, see Robert H. Hayes and Kim B. Clark, "Exploring the Sources of Productivity Differences at the Factory Level," in *The Uneasy Alliance: Managing the Productivity-Technology Dilemma,* eds. Kim B. Clark, Robert H. Hayes, and Christopher Lorenz (Boston: Harvard Business School Press, 1985), pp. 151–88.

2. See, for example, Robert H. Hayes and Steven C. Wheelwright, *Restoring Our Competitive Edge: Competing Through Manufacturing* (New York: John Wiley, 1984), particularly Chap. 7.

3. For additional insight into these issues, see Bruce Chew, "Short-term Effects of Investments on Factory Level Productivity" (Unpublished Ph.D. dissertation, Harvard University, 1986); and Russell Radford, "The Impact of Management on the Introduction of Process Technology" (Unpublished D.B.A. dissertation, Harvard Business School, 1986).

4. For further information, see Gordon Shirley, "Management of Manufacturing Flexibility: Studies in the Design/Manufacturing Interface" (Unpublished D.B.A. dissertation, Harvard Business School, 1987).

5. This discussion of the PLUS experience is based on the case "PLUS Development Corp." (Boston: HBS Case Services, Harvard Business School), 9-687-001.

CHAPTER 7. The Architecture of Manufacturing: Material and Information Flows

1. See "Toyo Kogyo Corporation Ltd. (A)" and "(B)" (Boston: HBS Case Services, Harvard Business School), 9-682-092 and 9-682-093 for additional information. Toyo Kogyo, the maker of the Mazda line of cars and trucks, changed its corporate name to Mazda in 1985.

2. Kiyoshi Suzaki, "Japanese Approaches to Managing Manufacturing Operations," Speech Notes, Los Angeles, January 30, 1985.

3. Adapted from Richard C. Walleigh, "What's Your Excuse for Not Using JIT?" *Harvard Business Review,* March-April 1986, pp. 38–54.

CHAPTER 8. Controlling and Improving the Manufacturing Process

1. Throughout this chapter we discuss a number of ideas whose roots can be found in the writings of various experts on quality. For an introductory comparison

of those, see David A. Garvin, "A Note on Quality: The Views of Deming, Juran, and Crosby" (Boston: HBS Case Services, Harvard Business School), 1-687-011, 1986. For a discussion of the development and application of some of these ideas within Japanese management practice, see Masaaki Imai, *Kaizen* (New York: Random House, 1987). For additional discussion on quality, see W. Edwards Deming, *Quality, Productivity and Competitive Position* (Cambridge: MIT Center for Advanced Engineering Study, 1982); Joseph M. Juran and Frank M. Gryna, Jr., *Quality Planning and Analysis* (New York: McGraw-Hill, 1980); Philip B. Crosby, *Quality Is Free* (New York: McGraw-Hill, 1979); and David A. Garvin, *Managing Quality* (New York: Free Press, 1987).

2. This classification of various kinds of process knowledge is loosely adapted from Roger Bohn, "An Informal Note on Knowledge and How to Manage It," Harvard Business School Working Paper, 1986.
3. For example, see E. L. Grant and R. S. Leavenworth, *Statistical Quality Control,* 5th ed. (New York: McGraw-Hill, 1980).
4. See Ramchandran Jaikumar, "Postindustrial Manufacturing," *Harvard Business Review,* November-December 1986, pp. 69–76.
5. For further information see "Signetics Corporation: Implementing a Quality Improvement Program (A)," "(B)," and "(C)" (Stanford, Calif.: Stanford University Graduate School of Business, Case Development Service), S-MM-3A, 3B, and 3C.
6. Charles C. Harwood, "The View from the Top," *Quality Progress,* October 1984

CHAPTER 9. People Make It Happen

1. See Ramchandran Jaikumar and Roger Bohn, "Production Management: A Dynamic Approach" (Boston: HBS Case Services, Harvard Business School), 9-784-066.
2. For additional insight on these issues, and further references, see Richard Walton, "From Control to Commitment: Transforming Workforce Management in the U.S.," Chap. 6 in *The Uneasy Alliance,* eds. K. Clark, R. Hayes, and C. Lorenz (Boston: Harvard Business School Press, 1985).
3. See Janice Klein, "Why Supervisors Resist Employee Involvement," *Harvard Business Review,* September-October 1984, pp. 87–95; and Janice Klein and Pamela Posey, "Good Supervisors Are Good Supervisors—Anywhere," *Harvard Business Review,* November-December 1986, pp. 125–28.
4. See "The Lincoln Electric Company" (Boston: HBS Case Services, Harvard Business School), 9-376-028.
5. An excellent description of how such small groups might operate, some of the tools and techniques that are useful to them, and the procedures that they might follow in problem-solving are included in the *Quality Circle Member Manual,* Rolm Corporation, 1982. See also *QC Circles: Applications, Tools and Theory,* eds. Davida and Robert Amsden (Milwaukee: American Society for Quality Control, 1986).
6. Robert Cole, University of Michigan (personal communication), 1982.
7. See Paul Adler, "New Technologies, New Skills," *California Management Review,* Fall 1986, pp. 9–28.

8. Arndt Sorge, Gert Hartmann, Malcome Warner, and Ian Nichols, *Microelectronics and Manpower* (Berlin: Gower, 1983).
9. See Ramchandran Jaikumar, "Postindustrial Manufacturing," *Harvard Business Review,* November-December 1986, pp. 69–76.
10. See, for example, J. Anderson, R. Schroederm, S. Tupy, and E. White, "MRP—A Study of Implementation and Practice," American Production and Inventory Control Society (APICS), 1981.

CHAPTER 10. Laying the Foundation for Product and Process Development

1. Written communication from the Japanese Productivity Center, Washington, DC, August 1984.
2. As quoted in "Japan's Robot King Wins Again" by Gene Bylinsky, *Fortune,* May 25, 1987, pp. 53–58.
3. This example is drawn from "Apple Computer: The First Ten Years" (Stanford, Calif.: Stanford University Graduate School of Business), PS-BP-245; "Apple Computer, Inc.—Macintosh Abridged" (Stanford, Calif.: Stanford University Graduate School of Business), S-BP-235, 1986; and John Sculley, *Odyssey* (New York: Harper & Row, 1987).
4. See "Strategic Mapping: The Start of the Product Renewal Process" (Eindhoven, The Netherlands: N. V. Philips, 1986).
5. For additional discussion of preproject activities, see Robert R. Rothberg (ed.), *Corporate Strategy and Product Innovation,* 2nd ed. (New York: Free Press, 1981); Richard Foster, *Innovation* (New York: Summit Books, 1986); Steven C. Wheelwright and Spyros Makridakis, "Qualitative and Technological Approaches to Forecasting," Chap. 13 in *Forecasting Methods for Management,* 4th ed. (New York: John Wiley, 1985).
6. For additional discussion on the separation of invention and innovation (commercialization), see Nathan Rosenberg, *Perspectives on Technology* (Cambridge, Eng.: Cambridge University Press, 1976); Nathan Rosenberg, *Inside the Black Box* (Cambridge, Eng.: Cambridge University Press, 1982).

CHAPTER 11. Managing Product and Process Development Projects

1. For additional discussion on problem-solving involving multiple functional groups, see J. D. Weinauch and R. Anderson, "Conflicts Between Engineering and Marketing Units," *Industrial Marketing Management,* 11 (1982), pp. 291–301; Frederick P. Brooks, Jr., *The Mythical Man-Month* (Reading, MA: Addison-Wesley, 1982).
2. These two approaches are more fully described in Kim B. Clark and Takahiro Fujimoto, "Overlapping Problem Solving in Product Development," Harvard Business School Working Paper, 1987.
3. See, for example, Hirotaka Takeuchi and Ikujiro Nonaka, "The New New-Product Development Game," *Harvard Business Review,* January-February 1986, pp. 137–46; and Ken-ichi Imai, Ikujiro Nonaka, and Hirotaka Takeuchi, "Managing the New Product Development Process: How Japanese Companies Learn and Unlearn," in *The Uneasy Alliance: Managing the Productivity-Technology Dilemma,* eds. Kim B. Clark, Robert H. Hayes, and Christopher Lorenz (Boston: Harvard Business School Press, 1985).

4. An extensive literature exists on conflict resolution. See, for example, Paul R. Lawrence and Jay W. Lorsch, *Organization and Environment: Managing Differentiation and Integration* (Boston: Harvard Business School Press, 1967); David T. Hickson, C. R. Hinings, C. A. Lee, R. E. Schneck, and J. M. Tennings, "A Strategic Contingencies Theory of Intraorganizational Power," *Administrative Science Quarterly,* 16 (1971), 216–29; C. R. Hinings, D. J. Hickson, J. M. Tennings, and R. E. Schneck, "Structural Conditions of Intraorganizational Power," *Administrative Science Quarterly,* 19 (1974), pp. 22–44; G. R. Falaneik and J. Pfeffer, "Who Gets Power—and How They Hold onto It," *Organizational Dynamics,* 5 (1977), pp. 3–21.
5. Alternative approaches for organizing project teams are described in Erik W. Larson and David H. Gobeli, "Matrix Management: Contradictions and Insights," *California Management Review,* 29(4) (1987), pp. 126–38; and Gary Jacobson and John Hillkirk, *Xerox: American Samurai* (New York: Macmillan, 1986).
6. In following such a path, an organization must choose between project effectiveness (measured by cycle time) and apparent resource utilization (measured by engineering time spent on design). For a discussion of the latter, see Jeffrey K. Liker and Walton M. Hancock, "Organization Systems Barriers to Engineering Effectiveness," *IEEE Transactions on Engineering Management,* EM-33(2) (1986), pp. 82–91.
7. John E. Ettlie, "The Implementation of Programmable Manufacturing Innovations" (Ann Arbor, MI: Industrial Technology Institute, March 1985).

CHAPTER 12. Molding the New Manufacturing Company

1. We are indebted to three Stanford M.B.A. students—Sally Atkinson, Rick Beckett, and José Cofiño—who developed and tested this approach on a group of managers who were familiar with the four-stage framework.
2. See William Hall, "Survival Strategies in a Hostile Environment," *Harvard Business Review,* September-October 1980, pp. 75–85.
3. Examples of this are provided in Chap. 14 of Robert H. Hayes and Steven C. Wheelwright, *Restoring Our Competitive Edge: Competing Through Manufacturing* (New York: John Wiley, 1984).

APPENDIX A: Analyzing Manufacturing's Financial Impact on the Profitability of the Firm

1. For a more detailed explanation of this system, see C. A. Kline, Jr., and Howard C. Hessler, "The duPont Chart System for Appraising Operating Performance," *Readings in Cost Accounting, Budgeting, and Control,* ed. William E. Thomas (Cincinnati: South-Western, 1955), pp. 753–75.

APPENDIX B: The Measurement of Total Factor Productivity

1. For a more detailed discussion of the relationship between TFP and profitability, see R. Banker, S. Datar, and R. Kaplan, "Productivity Measurement and Management Accounting," Harvard Business School Working Paper, May 1987.

References

Abernathy, William J.; Clark, Kim B.; and Kantrow, Alan M. *Industrial Renaissance*. New York: Basic Books, 1983.

Adler, Paul. "New Technologies, New Skills." *California Management Review,* Fall 1986, pp. 9–28.

Advanced Processing of Electronic Materials in the United States and Japan: A State-of-the-Art Review Conducted by the Panel on Materials Science of the National Research Council. Washington, DC: National Academy Press, 1986.

Amsden, Davida, and Amsden, Robert, eds. *QC Circles: Applications, Tools and Theory*. Milwaukee: American Society for Quality Control, 1986.

Anderson, J.; Schroeder, R.; Tupy, S.; and White, E. "MRP—A Study of Implementation and Practice." American Production and Inventory Control Society (APICS), 1981.

"The Anderson Bombshell." *The Rosen Electronics Letter,* March 31, 1980, pp. 3–5.

Anthony, Robert N., and Reece, James S. *Management Accounting Principles*. Homewood, IL: Irwin, 1975.

"Apple Computer: The First Ten Years." Stanford, Calif.: Stanford University Graduate School of Business, Case Development Service (S-BP-245), 1985.

"Apple Computer, Inc.—Macintosh" (Abridged). Stanford University Graduate School of Business, Case Development Service (S-BP-235), 1986.

Automotive Action Group. *The Japanese Approach to Productivity*. Videotaped Presentation, Detroit, 1983.

"The Bad News Behind the Capital Investment Surge." *Business Week,* March 4, 1985, p. 20.

Banker, R.; Datar, S.; and Kaplan, R. "Productivity Measurement and Management Accounting." Harvard Business School Working Paper, May 1987.

Beer, Michael; Spector, Bert; Lawrence, Paul R.; Mills, D. Quinn; and Walton, Richard E. *Managing Human Assets*. New York: Free Press, 1984.

Bierman, Harold, Jr., and Haas, Jerome E. "Are High Cut-offs a Fallacy?" *Financial Executive,* June 1973, pp. 90–91.

Bohn, Roger. "An Informal Note on Knowledge and How to Manage It." Harvard Business School Working Paper, 1986.

Borth, Christy. *Masters of Mass Production.* New York: Bobbs-Merrill, 1945, pp. 170–205.

Bower, Joseph L. *Managing the Resource Allocation Process.* Boston: Division of Research, Harvard Business School, 1970.

Brooks, Frederick P., Jr. *The Mythical Man-Month.* Reading, MA: Addison-Wesley, 1982.

Burns, T., and Stalker, G. M. *The Management of Innovation.* London: Tavistock Press, 1961.

Buzzell, Robert D., and Chussil, Mark J. "Managing for Tomorrow." *Sloan Management Review,* Summer 1985, pp. 3–14.

Bylinsky, Gene. "Japan's Robot King Wins Again." *Fortune,* May 25, 1987, pp. 53–58.

"Carborundum, Inc." Boston: HBS Case Services, Harvard Business School (9-672-131).

Chandler, Alfred D., Jr. *The Visible Hand.* Cambridge: Harvard University Press, 1977.

———. "Commentary." In *The Uneasy Alliance: Managing the Productivity-Technology Dilemma.* Edited by Kim B. Clark, Robert H. Hayes, and Christopher Lorenz. Boston: Harvard Business School Press, 1985.

Chew, Bruce. "Short-term Effects of Investments on Factory Level Productivity." Unpublished Ph.D. Dissertation, Harvard University, 1986.

Churchill, Neil C., and Shank, John K. "Managing Against Expectations (A): A Note on Profit Variance Analysis." Harvard Business School Technical Note (9-176-182).

Clark, Colin W. "The Economics of Overexploitation." *Science* 181 (1981): 630–34.

Clark, Kim B., and Fujimoto, Takahiro. "Overlapping Problem Solving in Product Development." Harvard Business School Working Paper, 1987.

Cohen, Stephen S., and Zysman, John. *Manufacturing Matters.* New York: Basic Books, 1987.

Cooper, Robin, and Kaplan, Robert S. "How Cost Accounting Systematically Distorts Product Costs." In *Field Studies in Management Accounting and Control.* Edited by William J. Bruns, Jr., and Robert S. Kaplan. Boston: Harvard Business School Press, 1987.

Cox, Allan. *The Cox Report on the American Corporation.* New York: Delacorte Press, 1982.

Craig, C. E., and Harris, C. R. "Total Productivity Measurement at the Firm Level." *Sloan Management Review* 14(3) (1973): 13–29.

Crosby, Philip B. *Quality Is Free.* New York: McGraw-Hill, 1979.

Dalton, Gene, and Lawrence, Paul. *Organizational Change and Development.* Homewood, IL: Irwin, 1970.

Day, Charles R., Jr. "Solving the Mystery of Productivity Measurement." *Industry Week,* January 26, 1981, pp. 61–66.

Deming, W. Edwards. *Quality, Productivity and Competitive Position.* Cambridge: MIT Center for Advanced Engineering Study, 1982.

Ettlie, John E. "The Implementation of Programmable Manufacturing Innovations." Ann Arbor, MI: Industrial Technology Institute, March 1985.

Falaneik, G. R., and Pfeffer, J. "Who Gets Power—and How They Hold onto It." *Organizational Dynamics* 5 (1977): 3–21.

Feigenbaum, Armand V. *Total Quality Control,* 3rd ed. New York: McGraw-Hill, 1983.

Ferdows, Kasra; Miller, Jeffrey G.; Nakane, Jinichiro; and Vollmann, Thomas E. "Evolving Global Manufacturing Strategies: Projections into the 1990s," *International Journal of Operations and Production Management* 6(4) (1986): 6–16.

Ford, Henry, in collaboration with Crowther, Samuel. *Today and Tomorrow.* New York: Doubleday, Page, 1926.

"Foreign Competition, Labor Costs Helped Sink Mesta Machine." *Wall Street Journal,* January 4, 1984.

Foster, Richard. *Innovation.* New York: Summit Books, 1986.

Fox, Robert E. "MRP, KANBAN, or OPT—What's Best?" *Inventories and Production* 2(4) (July-August 1982).

Gappelberg, Ghary. "'CCS' and Modern Japanese Management: The Influence of American Management Concepts on the Japanese Communications Industry, 1945–1950." Unpublished Senior Thesis, Harvard University, March 1986.

Garvin, David A. "Quality on the Line." *Harvard Business Review,* September-October 1983, pp. 64–75.

———. "A Note on Quality: The Views of Deming, Juran, and Crosby." Boston: HBS Case Services, Harvard Business School (1-687-011).

———. *Managing Quality.* New York: Free Press, 1987.

Gent, Michael J. "Theory X in Antiquity, or the Bureaucratization of the Roman Army." *Business Horizons,* January-February 1984, pp. 52–56.

Global Competition: The New Reality. The Report of the President's Commission on Industrial Competitiveness. Washington, DC: U.S. Government Printing Office, 1985.

Gold, Bela. "The Shaky Foundations of Capital Budgeting." *California Management Review* 19(2) (Winter 1976): 51–60.

Graham, Margaret B. W. "Industrial Research in the Age of Big Science." *Research on Technological Innovation, Management and Policy,* vol. 2. Greenwich, CT: JAI Press, 1985, pp. 47–49.

Grant, E. L., and Leavenworth, R. S. *Statistical Quality Control,* 5th ed. New York: McGraw-Hill, 1980.

"Great Lakes Diversified Corporation: The Detroit Plant." Boston: HBS Case Services, Harvard Business School (9-679-121).

Green, William. *Famous Fighters of the Second World War.* New York: Hanover House, 1957.

Gunn, Thomas G. *Manufacturing for Competitive Advantage: Becoming a World Class Manufacturer.* Boston: Ballinger, 1987.

Hall, Robert W. *Driving the Japanese Productivity Machine.* MacLean, VA: American Production and Inventory Control Society, 1980.

———. *Zero Inventories.* Homewood, IL: Dow-Jones Irwin, 1986.

Hall, William. "Survival Strategies in a Hostile Environment." *Harvard Business Review,* September-October 1980, pp. 75–85.

Harwood, Charles C. "The View from the Top." *Quality Process,* October 1984.

Hayes, Robert H. "Strategic Planning—Forward in Reverse?" *Harvard Business Review,* November-December 1985, pp. 111–19.

Hayes, Robert H., and Abernathy, William. "Managing Our Way to Economic Decline." *Harvard Business Review,* July-August 1980, pp. 67–77.

Hayes, Robert H., and Clark, Kim B. "Exploring the Sources of Productivity Differences at the Factory Level." In *The Uneasy Alliance: Managing the Productivity-Technology Dilemma.* Edited by Kim B. Clark, Robert H. Hayes, and Christopher Lorenz. Boston: Harvard Business School Press, 1985, pp. 151–88.

———. "Why Some Factories Are More Productive Than Others." *Harvard Business Review,* September-October 1986, pp. 66–73.

Hayes, Robert H., and Garvin, David A. "Managing as if Tomorrow Mattered." *Harvard Business Review,* May-June 1982, pp. 71–79.

Hayes, Robert H., and Schmenner, Roger W. "How Should You Organize Manufacturing?" *Harvard Business Review,* January-February 1978, pp. 105–18.

Hayes, Robert H., and Wheelwright, Steven C. *Restoring Our Competitive Edge: Competing Through Manufacturing.* New York: John Wiley, 1984.

"Hearings Before Special Committee to Investigate the Taylor and Other Systems of Shop Management," vol. 3. U.S. Congress, House of Representatives. Washington, DC: Government Printing Office, 1912, pp. 1394+.

Henry, Claude. "Investment Decisions Under Uncertainty: The 'Irreversibility Effect.'" *American Economic Review* (64) (December 1974), pp. 1006–12.

Hickson, David T.; Hinings, C. R.; Lee, C. A.; Schneck, R. E., and Tennings, J. M. "A Strategic Contingencies Theory of Intraorganizational Power." *Administrative Science Quarterly* (16) (1974), pp. 216–29.

Hinings, C. R.; Hickson, D. J.; Tennings, J. M.; and Schneck, R. E. "Structural Conditions of Intraorganizational Power." *Administrative Science Quarterly* 19 (1974), pp. 22–44.

Hodder, J. E., and Riggs, H. E. "Pitfalls in Evaluating Risky Projects." *Harvard Business Review,* January-February 1985, pp. 128–35.

Hopper, Kenneth. "Creating Japan's New Industrial Management: The Americans as Teachers." *Human Resource Management,* Summer 1982, pp. 13–34.

Horngren, Charles. *Cost Accounting: A Managerial Emphasis.* Englewood Cliffs, NJ: Prentice-Hall, 1977.

Hounshell, David A. *From the American System to Mass Production, 1800–1932.* Baltimore: Johns Hopkins University Press, 1984.

"How Xerox Speeds Up the Birth of New Products." *Business Week,* March 19, 1984, pp. 58–59.

Hughes, Thomas P. "Thomas Alva Edison and the Rise of Electricity," in *Technology in America.* Edited by C. W. Pursell, Cambridge: MIT Press, 1981, pp. 117–28.

Hyde, George G. *Fundamentals of Successful Manufacturing.* New York: McGraw-Hill, 1946, pp. 18–20, 31, 42, 44, 72, and 85.

Imai, Ken-ichi; Nonaka, Ikujiro; and Takeuchi, Hirotaka. "Managing the New Product Development Process: How Japanese Companies Learn and Unlearn." In *The Uneasy Alliance: Managing the Productivity-Technology Di-*

lemma. Edited by Kim B. Clark, Robert H. Hayes, and Christopher Lorenz. Boston: Harvard Business School Press, 1985.

Imai, Masaaki. *Kaizen.* New York: Random House, 1987.

Jacobson, Gary, and Hillkirk, John. *Xerox: American Samurai.* New York: Macmillan, 1986.

Jaikumar, Ramchandran. "Postindustrial Manufacturing." *Harvard Business Review,* November-December 1986, pp. 69–76.

Jaikumar, Ramchandran, and Bohn, Roger. "Production Management: A Dynamic Approach." Harvard Business School Working Paper (9-784-066), 1984.

Jarymiszyn, Philip; Clark, Kim B.; and Summers, Lawrence H. "Chief Executive Background and Firm Performance." In *The Uneasy Alliance: Managing the Productivity-Technology Dilemma.* Edited by Kim B. Clark, Robert H. Hayes, and Christopher Lorenz. Boston: Harvard Business School Press, 1985, pp. 115–36.

Jenkins, Reese V. "George Eastman and the Coming of Industrial Research in America." In *Technology in America: A History of Individuals and Ideas.* Edited by Carroll W. Pursell, Jr. Cambridge: MIT Press, 1981, p. 136.

Johnson, Thomas H., and Kaplan, Robert S. *Relevance Lost: The Rise and Fall of Management Accounting.* Boston: Harvard Business School Press, 1987.

Juran, Joseph M., and Gryna, Frank M., Jr. *Quality Planning and Analysis.* New York: McGraw-Hill, 1980.

Kagano, T.; Nonaka, I.; Sakakibara, K.; and Okumura, A. "Mechanistic vs. Organic Management Systems: A Comparative Study of U.S. and Japanese Firms." Discussion Paper 116, Hitotsubashi University, Tokyo, September 1983.

Kantrow, Alan M., ed. *Survival Strategies for American Industry.* New York: John Wiley, 1983.

———. "Wide-Open Management at Chaparral Steel: An Interview with Gordon E. Forward." *Harvard Business Review,* May-June 1986, pp. 96–102.

Kaplan, Robert S. "Measuring Manufacturing Performance: A New Challenge for Managerial Accounting Research." *The Accounting Review* 63(4) (October 1983), pp. 686–705.

———. "Yesterday's Accounting Undermines Production." *Harvard Business Review,* July-August 1984, p. 95.

———. "Accounting Lag: The Obsolescence of Cost Accounting Systems." In *The Uneasy Alliance: Managing the Productivity-Technology Dilemma.* Edited by Kim B. Clark, Robert H. Hayes, and Christopher Lorenz. Boston: Harvard Business School Press, 1985.

———. "Must CIM Be Justified by Faith Alone?" *Harvard Business Review,* March-April 1986, pp. 87–97.

Kendrick, John W. "The Productivity Factor in Phase 2." *The Conference Board Record,* March 1972, pp. 28–35.

Kendrick, John W., and Creamer, Daniel. "Measuring Company Productivity." *The Conference Board Studies in Business Economics,* No. 89, 1965 edition.

Kendrick, John W., and Vacarra, Beatrice N., eds. *New Developments in Productivity Measurement and Analysis: Studies in Income and Wealth,* vol. 44. Chicago: University of Chicago Press, 1975.

Kester, W. Carl. "Today's Options for Tomorrow's Growth." *Harvard Business Review,* March-April 1984, pp. 153-60.

Keynes, John Maynard. *The General Theory of Employment.* New York: Harcourt, Brace, 1936.

Klein, Janice. "Why Supervisors Resist Employee Involvement." *Harvard Business Review,* September-October 1984, pp. 87-95.

Klein, Janice, and Posey, Pamela. "Good Supervisors Are Good Supervisors—Anywhere." *Harvard Business Review,* November-December 1986, pp. 125-28.

Kline, C. A., Jr., and Hessler, Howard C. "The duPont Chart System for Appraising Operating Performance." In *Readings in Cost Accounting, Budgeting and Control.* Edited by William S. Thomas. Cincinnati: South Western, 1955, pp. 733-75.

Kraus, Jerome. "Productivity and Profit Models of the Firm." *Business Economics,* September 1978, pp. 10-14.

Larson, Erik W., and Gobeli, David H. "Matrix Management: Contradictions and Insights." *California Management Review* 29(4) (1987), pp. 126-38.

Lawrence, Paul R., and Lorsch, Jay W. *Organization and Environment: Managing Differentiation and Integration.* Boston: Harvard Business School Press, 1967.

Liker, Jeffrey K., and Hancock, Walton M. "Organization Systems Barriers to Engineering Effectiveness." *IEEE Transactions on Engineering Management* EM-33 (2) (1986): 82-91.

"The Lincoln Electric Company." Boston: HBS Case Services, Harvard Business School (9-376-028).

Lubben, Richard T. *Just-in-Time Manufacturing.* New York: McGraw-Hill, 1988.

Malpas, Robert. "The Plant After Next." *Harvard Business Review,* July-August 1983, pp. 122-30.

Mammone, James. "Productivity Measurement: A Conceptual Overview." *Management Accounting,* June 1980, pp. 36-42.

———. "A Practical Approach to Productivity Measurement." *Management Accounting,* July 1980, pp. 40-44.

Mayer, Otto, and Post, Robert C., eds. *Yankee Enterprise—The Rise of the American System of Manufacturers.* Washington, DC: Smithsonian Institution, 1981.

Merchant, Kenneth A., and Bruns, William J., Jr. "Measurements to Cure Management Myopia." *Business Horizons,* May-June 1986, pp. 56-64.

Miller, Jeffrey G. "Fit Productions Systems to the Task." *Harvard Business Review,* January-February 1981, pp. 145-54.

Miller, Jeffrey G., and Sprague, Linda. "Materials Managers—Who Needs Them?" *Harvard Business Review,* January-February 1981, pp. 145-54.

Miller, J. G., and Vollmann, T. E. "The Hidden Factory." *Harvard Business Review,* September-October 1985, pp. 142-50.

Montgomery, Douglas C. *Introduction to Statistical Quality Control.* New York: John Wiley, 1985.

Mowery, David. "The Emergence and Growth of Industrial Research in American Manufacturing, 1899-1945." Unpublished Ph.D. Dissertation, Stanford University, 1981.

Myers, Stewart C. "Finance Theory and Financial Strategy." *Interfaces,* January-February 1984, pp. 177-88.

Nakane, Jinichiro, and Hall, Robert W. "Management Specs for Stockless Production." *Harvard Business Review,* May-June 1983, pp. 84–91.

Nelson, Donald. *Arsenal of Democracy: The Story of American War Production.* New York: Harcourt, Brace, 1946, pp. 225–26, 260–68.

"A Note on KANBAN and Just-in-Time Inventory Systems." Boston: HBS Case Services, Harvard Business School (9-682-094).

"A Note on Quality: The Views of Deming, Juran, and Crosby." Boston: HBS Case Services, Harvard Business School (1-687-011).

Osterberg, William. "The Japanese Edge in Investment: The Financial Side." *Economic Commentary of the Federal Reserve Bank of Cleveland,* March 1, 1987.

Parker, Robert H. *Management Accounting: An Historical Perspective.* New York: Macmillan, 1969.

Parsons, Talcott. "Professional Training and the Role of Professors in American Society." In *Scientific Research: Its Administration and Organization.* Washington, DC: Government Printing Office, 1950.

Pennar, Karen. "The Good News We're Waiting for May Never Come," *Business Week,* August 18, 1986, p. 85.

Peters, Thomas J., and Waterman, Robert H., Jr. *In Search of Excellence: Lessons from America's Best-run Companies.* New York: Harper & Row, 1982.

"PLUS Development Corp." Boston: HBS Case Services, Harvard Business School (9-687-001).

Porter, Michael E. *Competitive Strategy.* New York: Free Press, 1980.

———. *Competitive Advantage.* New York: Free Press, 1985.

———., ed. *Competition in Global Industries.* Boston: Harvard Business School Press, 1986.

Powers, J. D., and Associates. "1986 Customer Satisfaction Survey." Los Angeles, 1987.

Prokesch, Steven. "Flak After Darman's Speech." *The New York Times,* November 11, 1986, pp. D1 and D4.

Quality Circle Member Manual. Santa Clara, Calif.: Rolm Corporation, 1982.

Radford, Russell. "The Impact of Management on the Introduction of Process Technology." Unpublished D.B.A. Dissertation, Harvard Business School, 1987.

Rees, Albert. "Improving Productivity Measurement." *American Economic Review,* May 1980, pp. 340–42.

Report on International Industrial Competitiveness. Geneva: The European Management Foundation, November 1986.

"Report from the Select Committee on Scientific Instruction, Parliamentary Papers." In *The American System of Manufacturers: The Report of the Committee on the Machinery of the United States, 1855.* Edited by Nathan Rosenberg. Edinburgh: Edinburgh University Press, 1969.

Rosenberg, Nathan. *Perspectives on Technology.* Cambridge, Eng.: Cambridge University Press, 1976.

———. *Inside the Black Box.* Cambridge, Eng.: Cambridge University Press, 1982.

———. "The Commercial Exploitation of Science by American Industry." In *The Uneasy Alliance: Managing the Technology-Productivity Dilemma.* Edited by Kim B. Clark, Robert H. Hayes, and Christopher Lorenz. Boston: Harvard Business School Press, 1985.

Rosenberg, Nathan, and Birdzell, L. E., Jr. *How the West Grew Rich.* New York: Basic Books, 1986.

Ross, Marc. "Capital Budgeting Practices of Twelve Large Manufacturers." *Financial Management,* Winter 1986, pp. 15–22.

Rothberg, Robert R., ed. *Corporate Strategy and Product Innovation,* 2nd edition. New York: Free Press, 1981.

Ruwe, Dean M., and Skinner, Wickham. "Reviving a Rust Belt Factory." *Harvard Business Review,* May-June 1987, pp. 70–76.

Sandras, William A. *About Face to JIT.* Johnstown, CO: Productivity Centers International, 1984.

Schlesinger, Arthur, Jr. "Bureaucracy and the Republicans' Businessmen." *Wall Street Journal,* January 6, 1981.

Schmenner, Roger W. *Making Business Location Decisions.* Englewood Cliffs, NJ: Prentice-Hall, 1982.

Schonberger, Richard J. *Japanese Manufacturing Practices.* New York: Free Press, 1982.

———. *Japanese Manufacturing Techniques: Nine Hidden Lessons in Simplicity.* New York: Free Press, 1982.

———. *World Class Manufacturing: The Lessons of Simplicity Applied.* New York: Free Press, 1986.

———. *World Class Manufacturing Casebook: Implementing JIT and TQC.* New York: Free Press, 1987.

Scott, Bruce R., and Lodge, George C., eds. *U.S. Competitiveness in the World Economy.* Boston: Harvard Business School Press, 1985.

Sculley, John. *Odyssey.* New York: Harper & Row, 1987.

Shingo, Shigeo. *Study of Toyota Production System.* Tokyo: Japanese Management Association, 1981.

Shinnar, Reiul, and Shinnar, Meir. "Which Bottom Line?" *Chemtech,* July 1978, pp. 418–23.

Shirley, Gordon. "Management of Manufacturing Flexibility: Studies in the Design/Manufacturing Interface." Unpublished D.B.A. Dissertation, Harvard Business School, 1987.

"Signetics Corporation: Implementing a Quality Improvement Program (A)," "(B)," and "(C)." Stanford University Graduate School of Business, Case Development Service (S-MM-3A, 3B, and 3C).

Skinner, Wickham. "The Focused Factory." *Harvard Business Review,* May-June 1974, pp. 113–21.

———. *Manufacturing in the Corporate Strategy.* New York: John Wiley, 1978.

———. *Manufacturing: The Formidable Competitive Weapon.* New York: John Wiley, 1985.

———. "The Productivity Paradox." *Harvard Business Review,* July-August 1986, pp. 55–59.

Smith, Roger B. Remarks at the Annual Dinner of the Advertising Council. New York: November 20, 1986.

Sorge, Arndt; Hartmann, Gert; Warner, Malcome; and Nichols, Ian. *Microelectronics and Manpower.* Berlin: Gower, 1983.

"Strategic Mapping: The Start of the Product Renewal Process." Eindhoven, The Netherlands: N. V. Philips, 1986.

Sumanth, David J. "Productivity Indicators Used by Major U.S. Manufacturing Companies: Results of a Survey." *Industrial Engineering,* May 1981, pp. 70–73.

"The Super Project." Boston: HBS Case Services, Harvard Business School (9-122-034).

Suzaki, Kiyoshi. "Japanese Approaches to Managing Manufacturing Operations." Speech Notes, Los Angeles, January 30, 1985.

———. *The New Manufacturing Challenge.* New York: Free Press, 1987.

Takeuchi, Hirotaka, and Nonaka, Ikujiro. "The New New-Product Development Game." *Harvard Business Review,* January-February 1986, pp. 137–46.

Taylor, Frank, and Wright, Lawton. *Democracy's Air Arsenal.* New York: Duell, Sloan and Pearce, 1947.

Taylor, Frederick. "Scientific Management." Taken from "Hearings Before Special Committee to Investigate the Taylor and Other Systems of Shop Management." U.S. Congress, House of Representatives, 1912. Washington, DC: Government Printing Office, vol. 3, p. 1394ff. Reprinted from Harper & Row edition, 1947 (Westport, CT: Greenwood Press, 1972).

Teece, David J., ed. *The Competitive Challenge: Strategies for Industrial Innovation and Renewal.* Boston: Ballinger, 1987.

Thompson, James D. *Organizations in Action.* New York: McGraw-Hill, 1967.

Toward a New Era in U.S. Manufacturing: The Need for a National Vision. Manufacturing Studies Board. Washington, DC: National Academy Press, 1986.

"Toyo Kogyo Corporation Ltd. (A)" and "(B)." Boston: HBS Case Services, Harvard Business School (9-682-092, 9-682-093).

Tucker, Frances; Zivan, Seymour; and Camp, Robert. "How to Measure Yourself Against the Best." *Harvard Business Review,* January-February 1987, pp. 8–10.

"Turnabout in Fortunes of Mesta Machine Is History. With a Moral." *Wall Street Journal,* January 3, 1984.

Uttal, Bro. "Speeding New Ideas to Market." *Fortune,* March 2, 1987, pp. 62–66.

Walleigh, Richard C. "What's Your Excuse for Not Using JIT?" *Harvard Business Review,* March-April 1986, pp. 38–54.

Walton, Richard. "From Control to Commitment: Transforming Workforce Management in the U.S." In *The Uneasy Alliance: Managing the Productivity-Technology Dilemma.* Edited by Kim B. Clark, Robert H. Hayes, and Christopher Lorenz. Boston: Harvard Business School Press, 1985.

———. "From Control to Commitment in the Workplace." *Harvard Business Review,* March-April 1985, p. 76.

Weinauch, J. D., and Anderson, R. "Conflicts Between Engineering and Marketing Units." *Industrial Marketing Management,* vol. 11, 1982, pp. 291–301.

Weston, J. Fred, and Brigham, Eugene F. *Essentials of Managerial Finance.* Hinsdale, IL: Dryden Press, 1977.

Wheelwright, Steven C., and Hayes, Robert H. "Competing Through Manufacturing." *Harvard Business Review,* January-February 1985, pp. 99–109.

Wheelwright, Steven C., and Makridakis, Spyros. "Qualitative and Technological Approaches to Forecasting." In *Forecasting Methods for Management,* 4th edition. New York: John Wiley, 1985.

Index